AF361617

The Intelligence Intellectuals

The Intelligence Intellectuals

Social Scientists and the Making of the CIA

PETER C. GRACE

Georgetown University Press / Washington, DC

The publisher is not responsible for third-party websites or their content. URL links were active at time of publication.

Cataloging-in-Publication Data is on file with the Library of Congress.

978-1-64712-643-8 (hardcover)
978-1-64712-644-5 (paperback)
978-1-64712-645-2 (ebook)

∞ This paper meets the requirements of ANSI/NISO Z39.48-1992 (Permanence of Paper).

EU GPSR Authorised Representative
LOGOS EUROPE, 9 rue Nicolas Poussin, 17000, LA ROCHELLE, France
E-mail: Contact@logoseurope.eu

27 26   9 8 7 6 5 4 3 2   First printing
Printed in the United States of America

Cover design by Nathan Putens
Interior design by BookComp, Inc.

The world and life are too fragmentary!
A German professor will give me the solution.
Magisterially he puts life back together,
Makes an intelligible system out of it;
With scraps from his nightgown and dressing gown
He stops up the holes in the universe.

—Heine, *Buch der Lieder LVIII*

Contents

Illustrations

Note on Archival Documentation

Declassifying secret documents must be a thankless task. Archiving them afterward even more so. When I first started researching this book, the Cold War national intelligence estimates (NIE) were scattered to the four corners of the internet. Many were on the CIA's website, but others were located at the Internet Archive, National Security Archive, the State Department's history.state.gov, and university special-interest websites. There are at least twelve million files on the CIA Records Search Tool (CREST) database in the Electronic Reading Room. I would not like to be given the job of tidying it up.

The CIA recently redesigned its website and, in doing so, lost the links to most of the previous files. I have therefore deleted most of the URL links I was going to provide and have instead given the file numbers (usually prefixed CIA-RDP or DOC with sometimes as many as twenty digits following). You will find them fastest by using Google (or other search engine) and putting either the name or "CIA" and then the file number. Other documents, like the Director's Diaries, are often simply named with a date. The search engine on the CIA's online Reading Room is very hit and miss; you need to be prepared to spend many hours clicking on every link, hoping you will find what you are looking for. It is literally a treasure hunt.

Because there are over 150 separate CIA files cited in this book, you will only find them listed in the endnotes and not the bibliography. Some files have multiple (and random) documents on them, some of which have the pages numbered, and others are numbered twice or more. I have done my best to number them correctly. There are often multiple versions of the same document, so I have avoided giving the PDF page numbers: you may not be working with the same PDF as I did. Finally, as many of the documents start without a title page or, because the CIA's archivists may have quickly noted down the basics of the title page (there is more than one titled "Sanitized"), I have in some cases retitled them with a better description than the one provided. This will not necessarily help you find the document.

Acknowledgments

I would like to thank Stephen Walt for his early encouragement and suggestions for leads. Richard Aldrich was always available (I wondered if he ever slept). I am very much in debt to him for his advice on so many things. Inderjeet Parmar pointed me to useful sources. A two-month visit to King's College War Studies in 2019 as a visiting researcher was made memorable through the kindness of Joe Maiolo, Christopher Kinsey, and Lawrence Freedman. Michael Goodman saw an earlier version of the book and made some excellent recommendations. The trip was made possible through a Shirtcliffe Fellowship.

A Beinecke Fellowship at Yale in 2024 allowed me to do a thorough read of the Sherman Kent Papers, for which I thank the Beinecke/Sterling librarians as well as Meghan Freeman, Jae Rossman, Sarah Martone, and Josh Cochran. I was lucky to make the acquaintance of the Yale History Department while there, including David Engerman, John Gaddis, Jay Gitlin, Paul Kennedy, and Avril Winks (widow of Robin Winks). Thanks, too, to Peter Rutland of Wesleyan University for some fascinating conversations.

Thanks to Sherman T. Kent, Vladimir Kontorovich, Daniel Kuehn, Stephen Aftergood, Vic Currier, Daniel Lomas, and the late John Prados for their comments and help with sources. Thanks also to A. Ross Johnson, James J. Wirtz, David E. Hoffman, Daniel Bessner, Gregg Herken, and Michael Warner.

At the University of Otago, I would like to express my deep appreciation to Robert Patman, Nicholas Khoo, and Philip Nel. Also to the late Bill Harris and Jim Flynn, who both taught me so much. And to the always enthusiastic Otago librarians, who chased around the world endlessly for my interlibrary loan requests. Sincere thanks to Paul Winter, who read most of the drafts and gave great feedback.

Mark Stout has been an enthusiastic and kind supporter. He brought the book to Georgetown University Press, and Acquisitions Editor Don Jacobs took it over. Don and his team were a pleasure to work with. I would also like to thank Mark's series coeditors, Mark Phythian and Christopher Moran, and the two blind peer reviewers, who both read it twice and gave valuable recommendations. Any errors, of course, are mine.

Finally, I would like to thank my family: Eloise for helping me get the final manuscript to Georgetown University Press, and Madeleine, Sam, Oliver, James and Ari for their constant support. Kirsty Cameron has been a valued supporter. My partner—Beth—was part cheerleader and part realist. She rescued me from doing the same old thing in my former career, bankrolled my new vocation, and enthusiastically kicked my butt out the door, forcing me to take on new challenges. I dedicate this book to her.

Abbreviations

A-2	Air Force Intelligence
AFTC	Adjusted Factor Theory Cost
BNE	Board of National Estimates
CIG	Central Intelligence Group
COI	Coordinator of Intelligence / Office of Coordination
CREST	CIA Records Search Tools
DCI	director of central intelligence
EIC	Economic Intelligence Committee
G-2	Army intelligence
GNP	gross national product
HASC	House Armed Services Committee
HUMINT	human intelligence
IAC	Intelligence Advisory Committee
JANIS	Joint Army–Navy Intelligence Studies
JCS	Joint Chiefs of Staff
NIE	national intelligence estimate
NSC	National Security Council
OIR	Office of Intelligence Research
OIT	Office of International Trade
ONE, O/NE	Office of National Estimates
ONI	Office of Naval Intelligence
OPC	Office of Policy Coordination
ORE	Office of Research and Evaluation / Office of Reports and Estimates
ORR	Office of Research and Reports
OSS	Office of Strategic Services
OWI	Office of War Information
R&A	Research and Analysis
RDB	Research Development Board
SASC	Senate Armed Services Committee

SE   special estimate
TR/TOR   terms of reference
WSA   War Shipping Administration
X-2   Counterintelligence (OSS)

Introduction

Clear and Prescient Danger

In May 1949 William Harding Jackson, a lawyer and former intelligence officer, penned a book review for *The New York Times*. The book he was reviewing, titled *Strategic Intelligence for American World Policy*, was written by the Yale history professor Sherman Kent. Jackson had read the book with skepticism, having a low opinion of professors and even lower view of anyone who had served in the maverick Office of Strategic Services (OSS). He was instead surprised at what he read.[1] Despite his initial doubts, Jackson believed Sherman Kent had successfully crossed the tenuous bridge between academia and the secret world of national security. "This book," said Jackson, "should be read by all high officials charged with responsibility for the security of the country and all those who work in the field of intelligence."[2]

In August of the following year, Jackson joined the Central Intelligence Agency (CIA) as deputy director of central intelligence.[3] If Jackson had been initially wary of Kent, he was outright dismissive of William Langer, the Coolidge Professor of History at Harvard who joined CIA alongside Kent in late 1950.[4] Langer, who, like Kent, had served in the OSS's Research and Analysis unit in World War II, was a scholar of European history and an expert on alliances and diplomacy. He was about to become Kent's immediate superior at CIA's Board of National Estimates and Office of National Estimates. Jackson, who was engaged in a major overhaul of the Agency, was distressed at the choice of Langer as chair of the group. He was even more "disgusted" when he realized that Langer was filling the positions on the board with *professors*.[5] Jackson believed academics were more out of touch with reality than were the bureaucrats at CIA who he was trying to shake up. His boss, however, the new director of central intelligence, Gen. Walter Bedell Smith, had no such qualms. Recognizing the success Langer and Kent had brought to the OSS, Smith hired Langer and "ordered" Kent to an interview.[6]

2430 E Street NW, Washington, DC, was the first home of CIA, before the move out to Langley in the early sixties. Prior to that, the E Street property was the HQ of the OSS. During World War I a number of temporary buildings went up around the National Mall, made of wood and wallboard and rather pragmatically given letters to find them by. These were added to during World War II: the Office of the Coordinator of Intelligence was housed in "Q" Building. Chief of the Office of National Estimates, William Langer's office, was in "M" Building. Spy hunter James Angleton was assigned to the "L" Building. It was an Alphabet City of War. The Research and Analysis branch, originally set up at the Library of Congress a quarter of an hour away by cab, was later housed in an old red-brick apartment on 23rd and E Street in what was then, and is now, the sprawling compound of the US Department of State at Foggy Bottom. A popular haunt like the Metropolitan Club was five minutes by car from 2430 E Street.[7] William Jackson ate at the Metropolitan Club at least twice a week, rubbing shoulders with the Washington elite: Dean Acheson, James Forrestal, George C. Marshall, Allen Dulles, and the influential newspaper columnist Walter Lippmann.

By all accounts Jackson was a hard drinker: this was a time when martinis broke the ice of business meetings. A few stiff drinks may have been wholly justified. This was a defining time for American intelligence and particularly CIA. The United States had exited the war with a vague understanding of its new position in the world and an even vaguer conception of its need for intelligence in a cold war. As a result of this uncertainty, the initial attempts at creating a national security institution of strategic intelligence frequently faltered. Experts were now being called in first to identify what was needed, then to pinpoint what was going wrong, and finally to fix it. A frustrated president, an anxious or angry Congress, and a skeptical national security community all watched as CIA struggled with its mission, to determine its ways and means as a new type of intelligence service, and to assert itself among the warring tribes of the US armed services. Jackson knew that turning CIA around was not going to be easy.

Today we are familiar with the role of the academic as a commentator on international events. We see them interviewed on television and read their op-ed columns in *The New York Times* and *The Washington Post*. We know, too, of their occasional role as government advisers and of more famous professors, like Henry Kissinger, who became national security policymakers. Less well known is that scholars are frequently asked to share their views on trends and outcomes with intelligence agencies, particularly those "area specialists" who are experts on certain states or regions of the world. What took place in 1950, however, was something quite different—professors were seconded from their universities to help *fix* CIA. They were brought in to make major changes to the way the organization developed its most important "product," the far-seeing and far-ranging national intelligence estimate (NIE). How did they approach the problems that they faced? Did they think their social science skills would seamlessly dovetail into strategic intelligence analysis? What was the promise of social science for America's intelligence sector that made General Smith so convinced that the practitioners of history, political science, economics, geography, sociology, anthropology, and psychology provided an answer to CIA's problems?

By 1950 the Agency was reeling from accusations that it had failed to predict the Soviet Union's development of the atom bomb (August 1949), China falling to the Communists (October 1949), and the outbreak of the Korean War (June 1950). Given the United States' emergence as a superpower and the existential conflict that it faced with the Soviet Union (and now Communist China), these intelligence failures were unacceptable to President Harry S. Truman, Congress, and ultimately the American public. The director of central intelligence (DCI) was quickly replaced and the new director, General Smith, began the challenging task of remaking the CIA into an organization that would be structured to avoid making such critical mistakes again.

General Smith was responding to the now urgent calls for CIA to put America's leading minds to work at producing strategic intelligence: coordinating the best available knowledge of the world in a way that met the needs of the president and his foreign policymakers, and safeguarding US interests abroad. Professors like Langer of Harvard, Kent of Yale and Max Millikan of MIT were given permission to take leaves of absence from their universities. They brought with them their social science–trained associates from OSS and hired new PhD graduates with the intention of fashioning them into a new generation of civilian peacetime intelligence analysts.

This book is a snapshot in time: the period building up to and including the reform of CIA under General Smith's tenure as DCI between October 1950 and February 1953. "It was General Smith who finally established the Central Intelligence Agency in the role that had been intended for it by the President in 1946 and Congress in 1947," writes CIA historian Ludwell Lee Montague. "Thus, the [early] history of US intelligence is clearly divisible into two distinct areas: before Smith and after Smith."[8]

The Element of Surprise

At 6 a.m. on December 7, 1941, 181 fighters and dive and torpedo bombers took off from the six aircraft carriers of the Japanese 1st Air Fleet, or Kidō Butai, to attack the US base at Pearl Harbor, Hawaii. An hour and half later, another 170 Japanese planes attacked a second time. The surprise attack was devastating. Nineteen US warships and 300 planes were destroyed or damaged. Almost 2,500 lives were lost and a further 1,100 wounded.[9]

"It is not true we were caught napping at the time of Pearl Harbor," believed Thomas Schelling. "Rarely has a government been more expectant. We just expected wrong. And it was not our warning that was most at fault, but our strategic analysis."[10]

In a book that surgically reviewed every step and miscalculation before that attack, Roberta Wohlstetter argued that it was the failure to distinguish between "noise" and "signals" that proved the United States' undoing. She described the information coming in regarding Japan's intentions as "buzzing and blooming confusion" set against larger questions as to whether Japan would invade the French, Dutch, and English territories in Southeast Asia or the Russians to the north. Intelligence came in from embassies and consulates, from Chinese sources like Chiang Kai-shek, from naval observations of Japanese shipping movements, and from the cryptography of their naval and diplomatic cables, including communications to and from Nazi Germany. "The amount of material that has to be weighed and discarded must always be remembered," wrote Wohlstetter in her review of the evidence, "and the discarded items (with a few exceptions) do not appear in the record."[11]

Regardless of whether the attack on Pearl Harbor could have been avoided, America vowed never to be caught by surprise again. The Office of the Coordinator of Intelligence, set up six months earlier, was part of a strategy to share information among the intelligence wings of government. It was replaced by the OSS a year later (in June 1942), and in January 1946 by the Central Intelligence Group. In 1947 it changed again to the Central Intelligence Agency. The lesson to be better prepared from surprise attacks was firmly understood and entrenched in US national security thinking. What was not decided was what sort of organization was needed to deliver it.

By the close of World War II there were few parts of the globe in which American interests were not deeply involved. The atomic bomb made decision time frames shorter and more prone to miscalculation.[12] This trend would be accelerated with the development of missiles in the 1950s. A dangerous and unknown competitor, the Soviet Union, was now joined by Communist China. These challengers to the "free world" thought differently and had long-term goals. They measured power in a more holistic way than the West did: the Marxist–Leninist "correlation of forces" concept, which saw the United States as a class enemy. As a result, future war would be waged not just with military means but with ideological weapons as well.[13] The Communist states were closed societies, making them difficult to get information out of and difficult to assess what policy actions to take against them. What was clear was that if the new leader of the free world was to defend itself and promote its interests in the future, it needed to think and act as one national security unit.

The national security state was brought to life in July of 1947 with the National Security Act, which brought together the three intensely competitive military services—Army, Navy, and Air Force—under the umbrella of a new Department of Defense. It also created the Central Intelligence Agency, headed by a director of central intelligence. CIA was charged with the coordination and evaluation of intelligence relating to national security, told to report to the new National Security Council, and was responsible for the dissemination of such intelligence using, where appropriate, existing agencies and facilities. It was to be a true centralized intelligence agency, working with the military, diplomatic, scientific, and domestic intelligence wings of government. This imperative to coordinate and deliver intelligence that could warn of imminent threats quickly spiraled into an existential crisis for the fledgling organization.

With the onset of the Cold War after 1947, the intelligence requirements had fundamentally changed, particularly for a United States that had little history of sustained international engagement. The United States looked to social science as an instrument of securing its leadership in global affairs. Social science had proven itself during World War II with economists calculating the best way to get men and supplies to the front; historians and geographers digging out old maps of German ports and railway networks; and, together with political scientists, sociologists and psychologists working on campaigns to influence enemy morale and policies for occupying governments when the war ended. In peacetime—even a peace that might become a tense Cold War balancing on the knife edge of nuclear annihilation—the behavioral sciences promised even greater insights. Foremost among them was the possibility of employing rigorous social science methods to discover the intentions and capabilities of a new global adversary. For an organization like CIA, struggling with one too many failures of their analytical expertise, the co-opting of social science would give the Agency's methods immediate legitimacy and effectiveness.

Helping to Make History

The sociologists Talcott Parsons and Gerald Platt wrote in 1968 that the modern world was built on a foundation of "cognitive rationality." This had its roots in the Protestant Reformation and the Renaissance and "entails an appreciation of the importance of systematic knowledge of empirical reality as a constituent of and instrumental means to the realization of an ideal order."[14] The American Puritanical order had made a virtue of achieving mastery over both human and environmental resources: knowledge was put to use to create power and profit. (Parson's PhD supervisor was none other than Max Weber, the author of *The Protestant Work Ethic*.) The US university system had become one of the servants of this order. Taking its cue from the German university system, American academia had turned itself into a profession, with the degree training of the PhD providing a workforce of people who had, through systematic training, developed critical and discriminating approaches to every aspect of their work.[15] "The effective mastery of the environment through cognitive rationality," wrote Parsons and Platt, "depends on the unremitting application of the criterion of rationality, includes valid observation, clarity in conceptualization and logical coherence in relating facts with each other and with concepts. Every intellectual discipline is directly legitimated by the evaluation of cognitive rationality."[16]

The sociologist and father of the modern focus group, Robert K. Merton, believed that the intellectual (and the social scientist was one he singled out in particular) had a vital role to play in public bureaucracy. Writing almost twenty years earlier than Parsons and Platt, in 1949, Merton claimed that "bureaucratization involves an accent on rationality of procedure . . . which requires intellectually specialized personnel."[17] This rationality of procedure involved the use of methodology, defined as "the logic of scientific procedure."[18] The intellectuals of the mid-twentieth century were turning to the civil service as a way of "helping to make history"—by moving to professions closer to where decisions were being made.[19] The professors who stood outside the bureaucracy offered policymakers a way of solving problems that de-emphasized prior assumptions and could consider alternatives they had ignored or rejected.[20] This concept of the rationality of procedure was brought to CIA with the intention of enhancing the performance of the Agency's analytical processes. These social scientists— the intelligence intellectuals (or intel intellectuals)—imposed the logic of scientific procedure on CIA's far-seeing estimates with the intention of creating a truly "strategic" intelligence.

Change Agents

Organizational scholars think about the founding of new institutions like CIA as exercises in creating "reasons for existence." Without certain critical elements in place, says Lynn Zucker, the new body "will be highly unstable in its structures, public theories (how others perceive it and its value) and programs."[21] We can think about this very fragile condition by imagining the creation of a new concept: a hospital. Someone comes up with the idea of creating an institution for the treatment of illnesses that will be called a hospital. Perhaps there are already institutions that exist for the treatment of ill people: the local witch doctor is one, the faith healer another, the herbalist a third. These are accepted institutions, but the idea of a hospital is something new. Zucker says the first thing a hospital needs to gain legitimacy (to be accepted as having a right to exist) is doctors. At this early point in the life of the hospital institution you can't advertise for doctors: they don't exist. You need to create a workforce that can staff these hospitals, so you need to create a career pathway for people to become doctors. The second thing Zucker says is needed is expertise. Mary Douglas says that this expertise needs to be built around a cognitive formula based on "reason and nature"; in hospitals, this formula is medical science.[22] You need to train the new doctors to be experts in using medical science to treat ill people. This establishes the third factor Zucker says is necessary: a product that the competitors don't offer. The witch doctors and faith healers continue to use their traditional folk medicines, but the new hospital offers medical science–based outcomes. The last thing that Zucker identifies is a need by society for this new institution. It would be a need that recognized hospitals as an institution that had earned a right to exist based on the expertise of doctors, the product of healing using medical science, and the fact you couldn't get that type of treatment by going to the competitors. We can think about CIA in a similar way. For a new organization creating an institution and profession of civilian peacetime strategic intelligence, the organization needed to create a workforce of civilian intelligence analysts, develop expertise and a product that competitors couldn't offer, and fulfill a need demanded by the national security stakeholders.

This book is built around three main themes: the importance of social science as a foundation for CIA's analytical processes; the social science processes that transformed the Agency's NIE into a critical instrument for informing US national security policy; and the strategy of reform that made CIA into a world-class intelligence organization with a new profession of civilian peacetime intelligence analysts. It is also an account of how the intel intellectuals who were seconded to CIA dealt with the problem, what succeeded for them, and what failed.

Chapter 1 considers the development of social science in the United States and traces the growing promise of it for national security applications. The chapter also explains what the professors arriving at CIA knew about their craft, what conventions were important to them, and where they might be applied to their new intelligence discipline.

Chapter 2 is an analysis of what was going wrong with the early CIA and why the pressures to reform became greater and greater. Focusing on the years 1946–50, the chapter traces the increasing frustration with CIA's performance, leading to calls from Congress and other high-level commissions for reform, culminating in the hiring of General Smith as the new director.

In chapter 3 we look at the organizational and intellectual failure of CIA's Office of Reports and Estimates. It was that office that should have provided the essential reports—estimates—that would inform US security policy. Instead, the chapter gives the account of poor leadership, a lack of focus, and a willingness to overcome outside criticism through short-term solutions and sophistry. It also illustrates a long-standing tension in intelligence between detailed local and regional knowledge versus "big picture" generalization of the international environment.

Chapters 4 and 5 tell the story of the four-step strategy implemented during General Smith's leadership period by William Langer, Sherman Kent, and Max Millikan. Management ought to play a key role in identifying a course of action in any organizational change. In chapter 4 we look at General Smith's brief to reform CIA, which centered around its prior failure to produce "the most authoritative [estimates] available to policy makers."[23] We then review Langer's management style, recruitment philosophy, and the rigor he brought to the processes of the new strategic intelligence discipline. We look at how Langer sought to give CIA a "reason for existing" by creating a specialized career-based workforce, providing a unique product, creating a unique expertise, and meeting stakeholder demand. These are key to an understanding of how the intel intellectual contributed to the making of the Central Intelligence Agency.

Processes also needed to be developed, often from scratch, to bring together vast and varied amounts of data and compile them into actionable and forward-thinking reports that national security policymakers would value. In chapter 5 we investigate the processes institutionalized by Yale historian Sherman Kent at the Office of National Estimates. Did these analytical processes help CIA fulfill its operational goals and earn respect as a reputable service to policymakers? Were they the foundations of a new craft of strategic intelligence? We also look at how Kent embedded the new analytical processes into CIA's institutional memory.

In chapter 6 we survey the NIEs from 1950 to 1953 to determine what role social science methods played in developing them into the product the policymakers demanded. Here we see the impact of Kent's thinking about how the estimates process would benefit from better definitions, more precise language, inductive and deductive reasoning, source selection and evaluation, and hypothesis testing. We also see that the political and security environment politicized their research and did not make it value-free. This shows that while social science provided many of the answers for intelligence analysis, it was not, as Kent had declared, the same as executing social science research in the university.

We return to reviewing the four-part strategy in chapter 7, this time to investigate how CIA's economic intelligence unit was set up. Max Millikan was seconded from MIT for one year to determine what processes could be used to expose the secrets of the Soviet Union's economy and defense expenditure.

Millikan recruited economists, designed the research program, and wrote the organizational strategy that CIA presented to its superiors for approval. Economic methodology is also an integral part of the story here: it would have been impossible for Millikan and his team to have made any progress without it.

The ultimate goal was to create a CIA proprietary analytical methodology that could grow on its own account without the guidance of university professors. In chapter 8 we review the work of a special committee, the Princeton Consultants, formed as an external sounding board to the Office of National Estimates' estimates. Formed originally by William Jackson, the committee quickly became a scholarly rubber stamp for CIA. As analytical methods matured within CIA, the professors themselves became mere adjuncts, and over time the pupils became the teachers.

In chapter 9 we look at Kent's relationship with uncertainty, expressed in his rough, locker-room language. The Yale historian's humility is perhaps his greatest legacy, and his struggle to articulate his ideas and to shape them teaches us a great deal about how we should deal with the present violence in the world.

The conclusion asks what really changed when social science was employed in American intelligence. We find that the intel intellectuals played an important part in developing strategic intelligence analysis and consolidating CIA's role as a major instrument in US Cold War strategy. Yet Kent and Millikan were circumspect about what they had achieved and what their new profession might achieve. The lessons they learned about the delicate balancing act of intelligence for policymaking, the contingency of their predictions, and the politicization of their findings are problems that still confront us today. So, too, is the question of the role the academic plays in society, although in this story the role was urgent, critical, and on an international scale.

This book analyzes the role of the intelligence intellectuals in the making of CIA. It adds to the existing histories of the involvement of scholars in wartime activities, particularly Robin Winks's *Cloak and Gown: Scholars in America's Secret War* (1987) and Barry M. Katz's *Foreign Intelligence: Research and Analysis in the Office of Strategic Services* (1989), which, as the titles suggest, concentrate mainly on the World War II period. It draws on CIA's own histories (see below), particularly organizational ones, and analyzes the reform period, which Amy Zegart and Brent Durbin have both done for CIA and the national security sector over a longer time frame (Zegart's *Flawed by Design* [1999] and Durbin's *The CIA and the Politics of Intelligence Reform* [2011]). It is, however, the first history to combine these themes: to look at the promise of social science, the processes social science brought by scholars to intelligence analysis as a discipline, and the impact of their work on CIA's reform in 1950–53. The reform years are instructive: it was a period of great uncertainty, the mission of CIA was critical to the establishment of a *Pax Americana*, and social science was needed to explain what was happening in the world and to provide the necessary informational power.

There is a good amount of overlap between the dramatis personae and the sources themselves. Key individuals in the story also wrote CIA histories: notably, Ludwell Lee Montague, Sherman Kent, and Ray Cline. Their biases are also part of the story. Montague, for example, was frustrated with his boss, Roscoe Hillenkoetter, and after a glowing hagiography of Hillenkoetter from historian Arthur Darling, Montague wrote his own narrative to correct the record. This is the color a story like this cannot be without: with US security at stake, tempers often ran hot.

Finally, a note about sources. The intention is to demonstrate that the intel intellectuals were working with social science tools that they understood, knew how to apply, and could, if necessary, modify to meet the needs of the new strategic intelligence discipline. For that reason, this book focuses particularly on primary sources in chapter 1 and puts more emphasis on primary sources that describe the way the intel intellectuals thought about the problem, employing secondary sources to underscore how their legacy was perceived for the remaining chapters.

The Intelligence Intellectual

In his book on the German emigre sociologist Hans Speier, Daniel Bessner defines a defense intellectual as someone who "researched, analyzed, and advised decision makers on national security issues while moving between a newly created network of think tanks, government institutions, and academic centers that historians have termed the 'military-intellectual complex.'" Defense intellectuals, says Bessner, "based their authority on training in the social or natural sciences or their deep engagement with scholarly texts" and "developed and implemented some of the most important US foreign and national security policies, from nuclear strategy to counterinsurgency doctrine."[24] As Fred Kaplan explained in *Wizards of Armageddon* (1991), the defense intellectuals "invented a new language and vocabulary" and taught politicians and military generals how to think about war and peace, using the scientific method as a lens.[25]

It is appropriate to give a definition of the intel intellectual. Like Bessner, I focus on intel intellectuals as social scientists: political scientists, historians, economists, psychologists, geographers, sociologists, and anthropologists. I define their role as engaging with the intelligence services to develop methodology and produce and critically examine intelligence analysis, sometimes under conditions of secrecy and urgency, with the aim of assisting or improving national security decision-making. Bessner focuses his book on think tanks, government institutions, and academic centers—the organizations that defense intellectuals founded or joined that attracted funding for their work on operations research, psychological warfare, decision-making theory, and modernization theory—to name just four examples. I focus on intel intellectuals as individuals who were either recruited to the intelligence services or stood outside of it as occasional contributors. Often there is an overlap, but the emphasis here is on the individual thinking that they brought to their assignments.

Defense intellectuals may have advised decision-makers on national security issues, but the intel intellectuals interacted more at the level of gathering and analyzing intelligence. They helped shape the intellectual framework of intelligence analysis, provided the basic country-by-country research as US interests spread to parts of the globe it knew very little about, and formulated the theoretical foundations from which to assess national security strategies.

The story of the intel intellectual begins (as it does for the defense intellectual) during World War II, but it is tied to the growth of the civilian intelligence community in the early Cold War. This was when academics were brought into the nascent CIA—particularly during the reform years of 1950 to 1953—and later were engaged as freelance consultants. By definition, then, the intel intellectual had little to do with the armed forces, whereas the operations researchers, economists, political scientists, and natural scientists at RAND were defense intellectuals primarily because their contributions were often to (although not limited to) military strategy, warfare methods, weapon systems development, and deployment.[26]

The best-known defense intellectuals are those economists working on nuclear strategy, such as Bernard Brodie (Yale), Thomas Schelling (Harvard), and Albert Wohlstetter (Columbia and Chicago). Other scholars who tried to divine Soviet thinking and strategy, like the anthropologist Margaret Mead (American Museum of Natural History and Columbia), the sociologist and political scientist Nathan Leites (Chicago), and political scientist and communications scholar Harold Lasswell (Yale), did so under the well-funded auspices of those institutions.[27]

By contrast, the intel intellectuals included those who worked specifically within CIA, such as Langer, Kent, and Millikan, and those who were consultants to CIA, including Arnold Wolfers (Yale); Harold Hinton (George Washington University); Chalmers Johnson (University of California–Berkeley); Ernest May, Richard Pipes, and Samuel Huntington (all Harvard); and Robert Jervis (Columbia).[28] Many of the consultants, like Hinton, Pipes, and Johnson, were area studies specialists.[29] Johnson says his consultative duties included intelligence analysis: "submitting these findings to fierce scrutiny and debate, and then instructing senior policy makers about the true state of the world." He says that a panel of fifteen—mostly academics from universities—met three or four times a year to review the national intelligence estimates that "strategy and policy are based on."[30]

Social Science and Soviet Intelligence

A relevant question to consider when reviewing the history of US social science in intelligence is whether there was similar use of social science methods in the Soviet Union. Paul Maddrell has demonstrated that, at least in East Germany's Main Directorate for Reconnaissance (the HVA), the role of the analyst was not to antagonize the party by stating uncomfortable truths or by predicting outcomes that might go against Marxist–Leninist doctrine:

> The department's reports avoided prediction and concentrated on stating what was taking place or being planned at the time. In American terminology, they represented "current intelligence." Predictions were dangerous because they might contradict the wishful thinking of the leadership. It was safer to report on what was happening, being planned, or had happened. The reporters did not recommend any course of action. Consequently, the HVA had no view of the Federal Republic that was independent of that of the SED leadership. That view was generated by Marxism-Leninism.[31]

The logic of this holds for the USSR generally. Raymond Garthoff believes Soviet "intelligence fared poorly in competition with other influences and sources of information," and George Kennan said, "I for one am reluctant to believe that Stalin himself receives anything like an objective picture of the outside world."[32] It was not until 1968, with the creation of an American institute within the Academy of Sciences, that the Soviet regime received any kind of independent scholarly analysis—in this case, Soviet reports on the US economy, which unsurprisingly concluded that America was in trouble.[33]

Social Science and other US Intelligence Agencies

While the focus of this book is on the agency designed to coordinate the work of the other intelligence agencies, CIA, it is worth exploring briefly whether the other US intelligence agencies also sought out social scientists for analysis work. As Mark Stout has argued, US intelligence history tends to be CIA-centric, and a narrative prevails that intelligence collection and analysis began with the OSS, despite both the Office of Naval Intelligence (ONI) and the Army's Military Intelligence Division services being founded more than fifty years earlier. During World War I, the Army's G-2 intelligence unit recognized the need to collect such data as the amount of France's coal reserves, knowing that if France ran out of coal, this might precipitate an early surrender. Before the Great War, military intelligence agencies restricted their intelligence collection to the size and capabilities of their potential enemies' forces. The Bureau of Secret Intelligence was founded in 1916 by the State Department, and its successor, U-1, was a highly influential forerunner of centralized intelligence but was disbanded in 1927.[34] State would not get another such intelligence wing again until after World War II, when the Office of Intelligence Research was formed out of the ashes of the OSS.[35] Yet the State Department did not do much analytical intelligence during the war. In 1941 Dean Acheson, then an assistant secretary of state, claimed that the State Department as a whole was unequipped to assess foreign capabilities and intentions and did not possess a system for the correlation of the intelligence gathered overseas.[36]

The intelligence needed for espionage during the war broadened the work of the researchers for the ONI and the Military Intelligence Division. Sending spies into enemy territory required in-depth knowledge of transport routes, dissenters who could lend a sympathetic hand, and what sort of business and diplomatic channels could be used to smuggle information out. It also required trained people who could determine what political, economic, or cultural information was important before it was appropriated. The Bureau of Secret Intelligence had as many as fifteen agents in Egypt, Switzerland, the Netherlands, Russia, and Mexico.[37]

ONI employed the businessman Whitney Hart Shepardson on a nine-month trip through England, France, South Africa, Australia, and New Zealand. During Franklin D. Roosevelt's presidency the executive made use of business moguls like Vincent Astor, whose private yacht traveled on fact-finding trips to Europe. William Donovan, the future head of the Office of the Coordinator of Information and OSS, was sent by President Roosevelt to London to determine Britain's chances of winning the war against Nazi Germany.[38]

As signals intelligence began to establish itself during World War I, it became obvious that the new data was not something a military intelligence analyst had been trained to read or understand. As a result, artists were often recruited to study aerial photographs, having the "quick intelligence, the temperament and knowledge of the effect of light and shadow" necessary to read bird's-eye views of the battlefield. In cryptology, classicists, medievalists, Egyptologists, and philologists were seen as trained codebreakers. And as the scope for intelligence broadened, the head of Army's G-2 called for "military men trained in historical research, newspaper men of long training who can spot propaganda, and generally the skeptically minded group, [who] have good preliminary training for this work."[39]

Yet military intelligence remained an instrument of warfare. Stout says that during the Great War, the ONI never appreciated the value it could bring to war planning and was the weakest at foreign intelligence collection.[40] From the end of World War I, Navy intelligence embarked on a number of surveys, including "monographs" on Britain and the colonies, Japan, China, Mexico, Nicaragua, and Cuba. In 1933 the ONI defined intelligence as "the product of a scientific and systematic collection and evaluation of information on the Political, Economic, Social and Psychologic [*sic*], Military and Naval Services, and the Geographic Situation of a specified nation, for the purposes of arriving at a definite conception of its naval strength and effort, and an estimate of its probable initial intentions of its naval forces in case of war."[41] Evaluation was determined as "the critical and systematic analysis of enemy information for the purpose of determining its probable accuracy, significance and importance."[42] By 1940 naval intelligence was categorized as geographic region, state or foreign trade, special intelligence, statistical, or strategic. Each of these topical "desks" focused on intelligence that met the definition above—that is, serving a naval warfare purpose. Equally, Army leadership did not value foreign intelligence: At the beginning of World War II, the Army had thirty military attachés abroad but got little out of them. They were not fighting a modern war.[43]

Nor was military intelligence seen as being a good career move. Even as late as 1949, the Eberstadt Report criticized the military intelligence wings as lacking in professionalism.[44] Gen. Omar Bradley put it this way:

> Instead of grooming qualified officers for intelligence assignments, we rotated them through conventional duty tours, making correspondingly little use of their special talents. Misfits frequently found themselves assigned to intelligence duties. And in some stations G-2 became a dumping ground for officers ill-suited to line command. I remember how scrupulously I avoided the branding that came with an intelligence assignment in my own career. Had it not been for the reservists who so capably filled our intelligence jobs throughout the war, the Army would have found itself badly pressed for capable intelligence personnel.[45]

Similarly, Carl Norcross discussed his role in the Strategic Bombing Survey during 1945: "A basic weakness in the air force was that the top people wanted to get out and do things—bomb or shoot down enemy planes—rather than sit and think about targets. I know several Air Force generals who were put into intelligence work and always apologized for what they were doing. There was no real appreciation of the importance of intelligence."[46]

Charles Kindleberger, who served with the OSS, claimed it was Donovan's assumption that academics could prove useful that was a defining moment in intelligence analysis: "In the case of intellectuals he was entirely right, and it was found that the intelligence services of the Army, Navy, and Air Force were extremely limited, bureaucratized, and ineffective."[47] A CIA history argued that the War and Navy Departments of 1946–47 in no way produced the kind of intelligence that OSS's analysts had been capable of. "Though respecting the scholarship evident in the armed services, one must concede that it was present in neither the amount nor the steady application to research and analysis that were essential to the production of national estimates."[48] Speaking of the lead-up to the Pearl Harbor attack, Wohlstetter believed the newspapers were better informed than Army intelligence, saying, "the only conclusion possible is that G-2 [Washington] was less informed and less equipped to estimate the situation than a good news agency, and even more cautious."[49]

It appears, then, that while there was a growing need for information outside of (or at least complementary to) traditional military intelligence, there was little organizational recognition of a need for social science to enhance the methods of analysis. Nor were social science methods seen to add weight to the accuracy or predictive strength of reporting. It wasn't until much broader studies began to be needed during World War II—concerning the logistics of getting supplies to the front lines; propaganda and supporting resistance movements behind enemy lines; and the question of how to deal with Germany, Italy, and Japan after the war—that social scientists came to be seen as integral to this work. Even then, a good amount of their work was research rather than estimative (predictive) analysis. This was to change markedly when in 1950 CIA moved from delivering mostly current intelligence and began to focus on the NIE. It was the beginning of an experiment in applied social science.

Notes

1. Montague, *General Walter Bedell Smith*, 131–32.
2. William H. Jackson, Review of "Military Intelligence: Strategic Intelligence for American World Policy, by Sherman Kent," *New York Times*, May 1, 1949.
3. CIA insiders often refer to the organization as "the Agency" and "CIA," less so "the CIA." This book will mostly follow that convention.
4. Montague, *General Walter Bedell Smith*, 131–32.
5. Montague, 135.
6. Davis, *Sherman Kent and the Profession of Intelligence Analysis*.
7. See Kirkpatrick, *The Real CIA*, 9; and Cline, *Secrets, Spies and Scholars*, 41.
8. Montague, *General Walter Bedell Smith*, xxv.
9. US Naval History and Heritage Command, "Overview of The Pearl Harbor Attack." See also the National WWII Museum website: Rob Citino, *Pearl Harbor Attack, December 7, 1941*, accessed November 8, 2024, https://www.nationalww2museum .org/war/topics/pearl-harbor-december-7-1941#overview.
10. From Thomas Schelling's foreword to *Pearl Harbor*, by Roberta Wohlstetter, vi.
11. Wohlstetter, *Pearl Harbor*, 39, 55.
12. See Houghton, *The Nuclear Spies*.
13. Patman, *The Soviet Union in the Horn of Africa*, 63.

14. Parsons and Platt, "Considerations on the American Academic System," 500.
15. Parsons and Platt, 500.
16. Parsons and Platt, 500.
17. Merton, *Social Theory and Social Structure*, 151. For more about Merton and the history of the focus group, see Morrison, *The Search for a Method*.
18. Merton, *Social Theory and Social Structure*, 280.
19. Merton, 274.
20. Merton, 279.
21. Zucker, *Institutional Patterns and Organizations*, 14–15.
22. Douglas, *How Institutions Think*, 45.
23. Warner, *The CIA Under Harry Truman*, 304.
24. Bessner, *Democracy in Exile*, 3.
25. Kaplan, *The Wizards of Armageddon*, 4.
26. For the story of RAND Corporation, see Kaplan; and Kuklick, *Blind Oracles*.
27. Brodie, "Learning Secrecy in the Early Cold War," 656.
28. On Hinton, see Shambaugh, "Obituary: Harold Hinton," 215. For Chalmers Johnson, see his article "The CIA and Me." For Huntington, see CIA, CREST Archive, Doc. VII-52, Soviet Concepts for Employment of Nuclear Weapons in a Conflict with NATO—Evidence from Warsaw Pact Military Exercises, CIA/DI/OSR Blind Memorandum for Col. William Odom and Dr. Samuel Huntington, NSC, March 24, 1978. On Ernest May, see Rober Wampler, *Ernest May, 1928–2009: An Appreciation*, ed. Robert A. Wampler (National Security Archive, 2009), https://nsarchive2.gwu.edu/NSAEBB/NSAEBB277/index.htm.
29. McGeorge Bundy, former dean of Harvard and later national security adviser to President Kennedy, said the first great center of area studies was the OSS. See Diamond, *Compromised Campus*, 10.
30. Johnson, "The CIA and Me," 34–36. The Princeton Consultants group operated, he says, until 1972, when Kissinger closed it down because it did not support his policies.
31. Maddrell, "The Stasi's Reporting," 75.
32. Garthoff, *Soviet Leaders, Soviet Intelligence*, 29.
33. Garthoff, 28–29.
34. Stout, "World War I and the Birth of American Intelligence Culture," 381. For a fuller story on US intelligence in World War I and the interwar years, see Stout, *World War I and the Foundations of American Intelligence*.
35. John Prados, "The Mouse That Roared: State Department Intelligence in the Vietnam War" (National Security Archive, 2004), 5, accessed October 5, 2024, https://nsarchive2.gwu.edu/NSAEBB/NSAEBB121/prados.htm. See also Stout, "World War I and the Birth of American Intelligence Culture," 380.
36. Cline, *Secrets, Spies and Scholars*, 13.
37. Stout, "World War I and the Birth of American Intelligence Culture," 380.
38. Stout, 383–84.
39. Stout, 383–87.
40. Stout, *World War I and the Foundations of American Intelligence*, 95.
41. Packard, *A Century of U.S Naval Intelligence*, 143–45.
42. Packard, 143–45.
43. Stout, *World War I and the Foundations of American Intelligence*, 99–100.
44. Best and Boerstling, *Staff Study Permanent Select Committee on Intelligence*.

45. Quoted in Telford Taylor, "To Improve Our Intelligence System," *New York Times*, May 27, 1951.
46. Letter Carl Norcross to Kent, November 13, 1978, MS 854, Box 13, Series 1, Correspondence, 1920–1980, Folder 279: N (Ng-No), Sherman Kent Papers, Manuscripts and Archives, Yale University Library.
47. Richard D. McKinzie, Oral History Interview with Charles P. Kindleberger (1973), https://www.trumanlibrary.gov/library/oral-histories/kindbrgr, Harry S. Truman Library and Museum.
48. The DCI Historical Series, *The Central Intelligence Agency: An Instrument of Government, to 1950*, chapter 4, "The Central Intelligence Group Vandenberg's Regime" (1953), 70, DOC_0005772735, CIA, CREST Archive.
49. Wohlstetter, *Pearl Harbor*, 125.

The Promise of Social Science Before 1945

In all of the intelligence that enters into waging war soundly and waging peace soundly it is the social scientists who make a huge contribution. The government of the United States would be well advised to do all in its power to promote the development of knowledge in the field of the social sciences. . . . Were we to develop a dearth of social scientists, all national intelligence agencies servicing policy makers in peace or war would be directly handicapped. . . . [The] research of social scientists [is] indispensable to the sound development of national intelligence in peace and war.

—Brig. Gen. John Magruder (1945)

October 1950. William Langer, a diplomatic historian, sat alone in his office at the Central Intelligence Agency. Four hundred miles away in Cambridge it was cold: 34 degrees. His office at Harvard University would have a fire in the grate and a cozy tapestry of books on its shelves. In Washington, DC, it was cold too, but this was a cold that had spread over the entire world: only a fear of firing the first bullet kept it from turning hot. Langer was familiar with wartime intelligence, but mostly the kind of research his library at Harvard could supply him with: maps showing railroads and ports, foreign news reports, and the tattletale of political tussles in far-off states. He was not prepared for the new project at hand, to look into the future of international politics and to divine what might come next. That would test his skills more than his old job at OSS had done.

Langer must have wondered if he was up to the task. Social science was beginning to change every level of government. It promised an understanding of how humankind behaved and a link to how governments planned and committed resources to their advantage. Langer was a historian, but he knew the power that social science offered the intelligence sector and the promise it held of a new profession run not by military men but by civilians with good minds and proven skills.

This chapter provides a window into Langer's thinking that day, what he believed he was bringing to the Central Intelligence Agency and what his peers thought social science was in theory and practice. We begin by looking at the earliest manifestations of social science in the United States and how it was, at least in part, founded with the intention of bringing authority to intellectual and moral matters. We then progress to ideas about the historical method and about causality and rationality in theory making, as at least some social scientists understood these concepts in the pre–World War II years. We consider what social science promised for the furthering of US national interests and security, contrasting an example of how it failed to deliver on this promise during World War II with the optimism that existed for its future employment once the war ended. Indeed, social science was widely accepted as having a very valuable application for national security, and the methods of social science would have been well understood when the intel intellectuals began to apply it to CIA's national intelligence estimates in the reform years of 1950–53.

Establishing Authority

The roots of a legitimate social science in the United States, writes Thomas Haskell in *The Emergence of Professional Social Science* (1977), started in the late nineteenth century as an attempt to "institutionalize sound opinion."[1] It was, he argues, part of a larger desire to "establish or reestablish authority in intellectual and moral matters."[2] What was mostly an amateur concern was driven by professionals (in law, medicine, and divinity) who sought to create specialized academic disciplines in the areas of political science, sociology, economics, and history.

Any definition of social science as a whole must take into account the characteristics of its separate parts. History, as a much older discipline, often considers itself distinct from social science, and yet it shares many of its aims and methods.[3] Psychology considers itself much closer to the natural sciences. For quite some time during its early inception, sociology thought of itself as being the central and governing discipline in the social sciences. Dorothy Ross claims a better description of the field should be the "social and behavioral sciences," reflecting focuses on culture, personality and social structure, and behavioral and quantitative analysis.[4]

It is completely fair to raise the question whether the social sciences can be grouped together at all. In 1945, when social science practitioners were debating whether to join (and whether they would be included in) the new National Science Foundation, the issue of homogeneity came up. The political scientists were those who were the least interested in joining, and it spoke to an unwillingness of the disciplines to be "packaged" as one lot.[5]

History, of course, has always been a field with its own distinct traditions and methodologies. Yet the Social Science Research Council, created in 1923 as part of a drive to professionalize the disciplines, included history along with statistics and psychology. And history began to align itself with the empirical sciences from the 1920s on.[6]

One of the things that brought social scientists together was the inclusion of their programs into universities and being grouped together, if in somewhat arbitrary arrangements.[7] Coming under the umbrella of university structures also created pressure for social scientists to prove themselves as proper scientists. It pushed them to give more thought to their methodology and how well it might stand up against those of the natural sciences.[8]

The drive to professionalize the social sciences was to free them from their religious origins and ground them in a science based more on biology and psychology. After World War I this intensified: "Social scientists began to call for a more objective version of empiricism and social intervention. The new program was more quantitative and behavioristic and urged that social science eschew ethical judgements altogether in favor of more explicit methodology and objective examination of the facts. While the call for objectivity sometimes expressed itself as a renewed commitment to empiricism, it was also apparent in efforts to revise general theory."[9]

The Historical Method

The historians were by nature a more conservative group. In a 1946 book, *Guide to the Historical Method*, Father Gilbert J. Garraghan attempted to update Ernst Bernheim's 1889 treatise, *Lehrbuch der historischen Methode*, for a more contemporary academic audience.[10] Garraghan was a Jesuit, and his reworked historical method book was as much a catechism as a review of practices. Bernheim had defined the historical method as "a systematic body of principles and rules, designed to aid effectively in gathering the source-materials of history, appraising them critically, and presenting a synthesis (generally in written form) of the results achieved." Garraghan broke the method down into three steps, not necessarily chronological. The first was the search for sources of information, called "heuristic." The second, an appraisal of the value of the sources, was called "criticism." This he felt to be the most important step. The third was assembling the sources into a formal statement, including a discussion of their objective truth and significance. This was called "synthesis," or exposition. A trained historian could often do all these things simultaneously, pulling together a number of documents and quickly determining their value and where they might take his thesis.[11]

Garraghan believed the historical method was appropriate to any number of uses. In one paragraph he makes a judgment that most intelligence analysts would agree with: "A person without proper criteria for evaluating the information that reaches him from the outside, runs the risk of a thousand deceptions and errors." For Garraghan, history was one of the inexact sciences, like the other social sciences. It was a body of systemized knowledge with an effective method. It dealt with a very defined subject matter, and it worked toward the formation of general truths. The Jesuit scholar was accepting that, while history concentrated on unique events, it also looked to the general and even the universal. A historian would be equally at home with a conclusion like "the Athenians were an art-loving people" as he would with a general law or truth like "a strongly centralized government is the best in war time."[12]

In this respect, the historian's use of a hypothesis was in accordance with the discipline being considered one of the sciences. A hypothesis was "a supposition made with evidence recognized as insufficient, in order to account for some fact or law known to be real." There were two types of hypotheses: explanatory, which looked at the reasons why things were happening; and descriptive, which helped bring together scattered facts into a unifying framework. A hypothesis must also consider probability, which might increase over time and with further research. A hypothesis should not be treated as a truth until proved, and could be falsified with only a single fact, at which point it should be abandoned.[13]

Finally, the historian should understand causality. Here Garraghan quoted the British historian John Bagnall Bury, who, in his customarily brusque way, stated the law of causality: "a hypothesis which we are obliged to assume if the world is not to become a chaos and science to commit suicide. For as the function of science is to explain phenomena and explanation means the assignment of causes, it is clear that if a phenomenon containing lawless elements may occur, science is impossible."[14]

Causality and Social Science Theory

Ten years earlier Talcott Parsons had attempted to use theory to account for some of the vagaries of human behavior.[15] His book *The Structure of Social Action* (1937) gives us further understanding of what constituted a "social science method" in the prewar period. While *The Structure of Social Action* met with initial criticism from traditional practitioners for its emphasis on the subjective rather than the objective scientific method, by the early 1950s Parsons had carved out a niche for sociology as a discipline distinct from economics and politics. This was a marked departure from the sociology of the 1920s, where sociologists had broad conceptions about how their discipline worked but "had no established subject matter and few clues about how to analyze what they addressed."[16]

The Structure of Social Action would become "mandatory" reading in universities and an important source of sociological theory.[17] His biographer, Uta Gerhardt, says the book became "a milestone of sociology's development as an academic discipline."[18] In his book, Parsons sought more than an objective,

FIGURE 1.1. Harvard sociologist Talcott Parsons, 1949.
Schlesinger Library/Harvard Radcliffe Institute

Comtean positivist explanation for social action: he saw it as deeply rooted in the subjective.[19] Yet, in order to explicate that, Parsons needed to describe how the scientific method asserted itself in social science. For Parsons, "true scientific theory is not the product of idle 'speculation,' of spinning out the logical implications of assumptions, but of observation, reasoning and verification, starting with the facts and continually returning to the facts."[20] By this he meant that a theory "must fit the facts but not follow the facts themselves," otherwise it would be, rather than a theory, a generalization about the facts observed.[21]

Instead, a theory must be able to tell us what empirical facts we might expect to see in any given set of circumstances.[22] Other scientists, said Parsons, must be able to investigate phenomena with the expectations derived from the theory in mind and see whether the facts actually found agreed with these expectations.[23] "All theories have to explain facts, otherwise they are entirely useless. The theory is valuable just in so far as it explains facts which are comprehensive and significant. If new facts turn up which do not fit the theory, the theory must be modified, not the facts."[24] If the facts did agree, then (allowing for possible errors of observation) the theory was seen to be "verified"; if not, then the facts disproved the theory or were a series of facts that did not have a place in the theory.

Theory would then become a force of its own. It might spark similar theories because of its success, perhaps in other fields. It would direct scientific eyes to certain facts worth studying. "Theory not only formulates what we know," said Parsons, "but also tells us what we want to know, that is, the questions to which an answer is needed."[25]

Theories were also closed systems. A system was made up of a series of propositions (that could be expressed algebraically) that all related to each other and to the observable facts. The combination of propositions built up the logical framework of the theory. When a system was not closed, there would be a proposition that was only supported by an assumption but not by observation. It meant that the logic of the whole argument hinged on what we might call "the elephant in the room"—an unstated and worrying assumption. Criticism of the theory required finding the gaps and unmasking unsupported assumptions. As new facts came to light that tested the theory, or perhaps new knowledge in other disciplines that also impacted on the theory, it would evolve—either by amendment or being replaced by a new theory.[26]

However, it was at this point that Parsons departed from the conventional view. The study of human behavior could not be solely limited to the scientific method, he believed. Acknowledging the part that epistemology, in particular, plays in any systematic observation of the world, Parsons sought a more active role for philosophy in a theory that would encompass problems like human motivation. In all human action there was a subjective aspect that any theory must take in. Writing was subjective, with alphabets and punctuation being symbols. Different languages had similar words for things that could be subtly different in meaning. Man expresses ideas that may be nonscientific, even philosophical, but can motivate an individual, a nation, or even all of humanity to action. Without a theory that broadened the objective scientific method to include subjective considerations, a study of human behavior was not possible.[27]

Parsons then broke down the components of theory, what he called "concepts," into three categories: First, the spatiotemporal framework, where the subject under study exists in time and space; second, the analytical elements or a description of the subject itself—its parts and whole—and what sets it belongs to (also known as variables); and, third, analytical laws or the relation each subject has to another variable that is both uniform and can be compared with or measured against the subject. Any theoretical system would include all three types of concepts, each of them interdependent. However, each of these concepts presented a problem for a theory of human behavior, not least the analytical laws where the measuring of variables or ranking them in any order was often more complex than in the physical sciences. Yet it must be done. "It is a methodological requirement," stated Parsons, "that the facts which enter into a scientific theory should be capable of determination with a degree of precision adequate for the theoretical purposes of the system."[28]

Parsons was clear that even subjects studied by social science could perform to some degree according to analytical law. For instance, an action could be said to be rational in that it conformed to a law of maximizing utility, although it might be difficult to determine the (numerical) value or degree of its rationality. Statistics appeared to be the one area of social science where analytical laws were most prevalent, but even statistics had been found wanting when it came to dovetailing into a general social science theory, usually because of the number of variables involved.[29]

Of most interest to Parsons was the analytical element concept of theory.[30] Here the social scientist concentrated on the definition of the subject under study, its classification, and its relation to other units in the theoretical system. This would lead to what he called a structural view of systems in action. The most basic unit of a subject under study in social science he called a "unit act." Just as any unit in the physical sciences can be observed for its mass, velocity, location in time and space, or the direction it is moving in, the properties of a social science unit must be similarly able to be broken up into parts of an "act," which Parsons said would be (1) an agent or actor is involved; (2) the act must have an end or future state of affairs it is moving toward; and (3) the act must be initiated by a situation that in turn could be (3a) beyond the control of the agent or (3b) something the agent can control, alter, or prevent. Finally, (4) there must be a relationship between the elements, either a set of alternatives to the end or what Parsons called a normative end for which the agent ought to aim. The act would be a process in time where the agent did not choose an end state of affairs randomly or was only constrained by the situation but chose through an independent, selective, and determinate factor that moved the agent toward a future state that could be described as attainment, realization, or achievement. While the agent might be faced with a choice of means and ends toward this goal, the agent is also capable of making errors in their choice or a failure to reach the goal.[31] The external world is an important source of information and influence on the agent; however, how the agent sees the world when they analyze and consider what to do is subjective.

As a student of Max Weber, Parsons was attuned to the idea of value neutrality in science. In social science, however, subjectivity complicated matters not only for the agent but the scientist too.

> It may be said that all empirical science is concerned with the understanding of the phenomena of the external world. Then the facts of action are, to the scientist who studies them, facts of the external world—in this sense, objective facts. That is, the symbolic propositions the scientist calls facts is to phenomena [epistemologically] "external" to the scientist, not to the content of his own mind. But in this particular case, unlike that of the physical sciences, the phenomena being studied have a scientifically relevant subjective aspect. That is, while the social scientist is not concerned with studying the

content of his own mind, he is very much concerned with that of the minds of those people whose actions he studies. This necessitates the distinction of the objective and subjective points of view. . . . By "objective" in this context will always be meant "from the point of view of the scientific observer of action," and by "subjective," "from the point of view of the actor."[32]

Similarly, the relationship between agent and situation was more complicated in social science theory. For the physical sciences, the human being is an organism, separate from its environment in a concrete way. For the social scientist, the human being is both a self, or ego, and the subject's body (his physical ability to move, or not move, based on a decision made in his mind)—making it difficult to observe a separation of the two. There are also two levels of analysis: the concrete and the analytical. An agent will have a concrete goal in view even though he can only visualize it for the time being. He will also have concrete means of getting there, for instance, the tools he needs to build a house or the plane he needs a ticket for so he can travel to a distant country. There are also concrete conditions that he has no control over, for example, the snowstorm that is stopping him from building or that is grounding all the planes at the airport. These concrete matters can be described as facts, can be placed in some sort of order, and can be categorized into ends, means, and conditions. What is lacking, though, is an analysis, an explanation of what is happening and why.

Parsons followed up on his thinking about theory in a further article, *Social Science: A Basic National Resource*, published in 1948.[33] This was a report commissioned by the Social Science Research Council three years earlier as part of its promotion to be included in the government-funded National Science Foundation. Here Parsons was more specific about the value of each discipline and the practical contribution of its methods to the national interest. Political science had not lived up to its potential, Parsons thought, having dealt too much with the details of the government process and focused too little on theory making. Economics had made more progress, thanks to more finely tuned theories, greater technical sophistication, and the increased availability of statistical data. History's turn toward the collection of empirically validated facts had been, like political science, made at the expense of analytical generalization. Psychology had benefited from both the scientific methods of biology and the influences of sociology. Of all the social sciences, it had been most willing to incorporate laboratory experiments (on behavior), test schema (on human traits like intelligence), and perform clinical studies (of personality). Psychology also held out the most promise for a more rigorous understanding of phenomena such as goals, values, wishes, means and ends, sentiments, and emotions. Anthropology had made a significant contribution to the comparative method. While it focused mainly on smaller, nonliterate societies, this narrow study had helped in two ways: by raising the problem of cultural relativity and by bringing anthropology and psychology closer together. Yet it had not achieved much in larger-scale societies, which might have been of considerable value to political science and economics. Finally, sociology, which Parsons thought had the ability to integrate all the social sciences, could provide well-articulated and well-conceptualized schemes for the institutionalized patterns of the structure of social systems and their relation to behavior.[34]

While *Social Science: A Basic National Resource* was not at all what the Social Science Research Foundation had expected, or even wanted, of Parsons, this discussion would have profound implications for the grafting of social science onto a new strategic intelligence discipline.[35] Unlike the physical science approach, with the "science" of intelligence analysis, epistemological concerns are never far from the surface, the problem being not only "how do we know this to be true?" but also "how much does the truth bring to bear on cases where disinformation, or untruth, still has consequences?" Definitions and classification play important roles in intelligence analysis, particularly when faced with a new world order where traditional categories may no longer seem to fit. Facts that are crucial to strategic understanding and that don't fall into conventional classifications may be overlooked. Behavior—that is, action, goals, and alternatives—all require theories that the analyst must contrive to determine enemy intentions.

Prediction, particularly after the crisis of Pearl Harbor, became an expectation of those investing in the creation of a new intelligence capability. An appreciation of the workings of theoretical frameworks and a more general understanding of what social science could and could not do would become a critical factor in the relationship between analyst and policymaker. Parsons took on what would become a cause for concern for CIA analysts twenty years later. Citing the economist Alfred Marshall, Parsons argued that "the most reckless and treacherous of theorists is he who professes to let facts and figures speak for themselves."[36] Theory and facts were in a symbiotic relationship, and conclusions on empirical evidence could not be drawn without being frank about the theoretical process that uncovered them. At CIA, it would become a growing concern that intelligence analysts would end up becoming mere providers of facts to policymakers and not providers of logically (or theoretically) derived conclusions.

Rationality and Irrationality in Social Behavior

Parsons had been one of a clique of Harvard scholars influenced by the work of the economist Vilfredo Pareto (1812–82). Best known for his Pareto principle (the 80/20 rule), he also contributed one of the central ideas of game theory,

Pareto optimality, to economics and political science. It was his foray into sociology, however, that excited the Cambridge, Massachusetts, professors and was crucial to the development of the discipline in the United States.[37] His 1917 magnum opus *Trattato di sociologia generale* was published in English in 1935 as *Mind and Theory*. The following year a review of the four-volume set by a young and promising Yale economist, Max Millikan, appeared in *Econometrica*.[38]

To say Millikan had found Pareto's work hard to read is an understatement. The reviewer had high hopes for the Italian scholar's theory, but those hopes had proved false. Recalling that Pareto had been hailed as "the founder of true social science and a profound student of the scientific method," Millikan had been surprised to find very little of worth in what he saw.[39] Instead, Millikan chose to write a review that praised some of Pareto's ideas but was damning about his methodology. This is important not because it represents the precocious arrogance of a young scholar (which it may) but because Millikan would go on to be the first director of CIA's economic intelligence unit.

Pareto had been puzzled that the mathematical models of classical economics did not seem to bear any resemblance to the reality of people making choices. He saw a good deal of irrationality in the way people behaved, what he called nonlogical social action. In classical theory, people made choices based on cost–benefit analyses, armed with the best information and in the pursuit of their economic ends. In the real world, they did not. Rather, decisions could not be made without bringing along what we today call "baggage" (Pareto called it "residues"). Pareto identified six categories of residues: (1) ideas about abstract things, of which superstition was one manifestation; (2) values about people, customs, and institutions; (3) or the pressure to act upon emotions, as we do when we celebrate an important holiday. Next there was (4) an obligation to act according to certain norms, like the rules of living in society. This was followed by (5) ideas about individuality, honor, and integrity. Finally, there were (6) attitudes about sex, which could be about morality or about the desire to destroy those mores. Millikan thought these residues were not simply instincts or drives to motivation; instead, they were "manifestations of social behavior."[40] People also gave reasons for their "residual" behavior or beliefs, which Pareto called "derivations." Some beliefs were justified simply because they were "facts" (even wrong-headed beliefs). There were also beliefs justified as being moral or in the public good and those justified on indefinite proofs, either badly rationalized or supported through metaphor, allegory, or analogy. As Millikan saw it, Pareto was concerned with how people talked about and justified their actions within social groups. There were many examples of this in civil society—for example, the political speech, which often drew on common beliefs and was full of "proofs" that were presented as facts, that appealed to the public good, or that were demonstrated through shaky analogies. Millikan felt Pareto was saying something very valuable and expressing this in an original way. Derivations could not be simply destroyed unless the underlying residue was changed first. If you wanted to get people to stop believing political conspiracy theories, for example, you needed to take down not the demagogue but the fundamental beliefs that drove people to listen to the demagogue.

Millikan didn't believe Pareto's intellectual musings had amounted yet to a science. "These then are the building blocks of Pareto's theory," he claimed. "They are a little more than tools of analysis, but they are by no means a science of sociology."[41] Millikan was deeply skeptical that Pareto had used the scientific method to prove his theory, despite Pareto's constant assurances that he was indeed doing so. There was, thought Millikan, a difference between a scientific attitude and the use of a method:

> We must distinguish here between what is loosely termed the scientific attitude and what we may designate precisely as the scientific method. The former is an attitude of mind; the latter is a fairly clearly delimited methodology. The scientific attitude includes most of the obvious characteristics of the good scientist: a completely objective mind, a willingness to abandon any theory in the face of one better able to explain the facts, a healthy skepticism toward any statement not adequately demonstrated, a stern insistence on rigorous definition but an understanding of the purely arbitrary character of definition, and so on.[42]

Pareto, to Millikan's mind, had not followed through on his fine talk. His definitions were imprecise and often contradictory; his arguments were inconsistent, and he frequently let his own subjective opinions flavor his logic. Moreover, his logic was entirely inductive, argued Millikan: "Science, as conceived by the proponents of this view, is at least in its early stages completely divorced from hypothetical assumption. The scientist proceeds by examining systematically as vast a collection of facts as he can gather together. When he has all these facts before him he will perceive without speculation certain uniformities. He classifies them on the basis of these uniformities, generalizing the classification into laws."[43]

Pareto had broken the very rules Parsons and Marshall insisted upon. At one point in the text, Pareto says, "We start with facts to work out theories, and we try at all times to stray from the facts as little as possible. We are looking for the uniformities presented by the facts, and those uniformities we may even call laws."[44] But Millikan saw this as induction divorced from deduction, a reliance on the Baconian method rather than the Newtonian. Pareto's view that uniformities could be discerned within facts could be guilty of selection bias: it required an assumption on behalf of the scientist that the facts observed were alike enough to be uniform. There is a danger the scientist imposes uniformity through arbitrary rules of selection. Instead, the scientist needs to move from an inductive collection that needs to be researched to hypotheses about what might happen; a theory (as Parsons had elucidated) must be able to tell us what empirical facts we might expect to see in any given set of circumstances. This was an unforgivable flaw in Pareto's *Mind and Theory*, Millikan believed. Pareto had given an instance of residues in a parable about the ancient Greeks and the rites they performed in trying to control storms. He had concluded that, as a result of his research, a belief must exist that storms can be controlled. But that was a conclusion that had been there from the start, Millikan complained, it was tautology. "He looks at all the facts that contain element *a*. After an exhaustive study he concludes that all these facts contain a constant element *a* while the other elements vary from fact to fact. Therefore, *a* is constant."[45]

Millikan's diagnosis of Pareto's errors is insightful for any study of the history of intelligence analysis as a discipline. The logic of a long-range national intelligence estimate relies on finding patterns and building an argument based on what are deemed relevant facts. Which facts—whether they are historical justifications of enemy behavior, ideological assessments of intentions, or observable actions of military maneuvers—are for the analyst to reckon with and would become key to CIA's claim that its methodology was robust.

Millikan also distinguishes between what he calls "tools of analysis" and scientific theory. As we shall see, his economic intelligence unit at CIA used a "building block" method as a tool of analysis when trying to ascertain the Soviet defense expenditure. The deployment of scientific theories—particularly those that observe behavior in order to make predictions—would remain elusive.

The Promise of Social Science for Strategic Intelligence

Shortly after Parsons published *The Structure of Social Action*, the president of Williams College gave an induction speech to the class of 1937. James Phinney Baxter III, the future head of the Office of Strategic Services' Research and Analysis unit, argued that "to prepare himself to keep his feet in a world of change and to attack its problems . . . the American student . . . must familiarize himself to some degree with both the content and methods of the whole range of social sciences."[46] Baxter saw an insecure world ahead, one where peace was precarious and the concept of collective security was rapidly disintegrating. The inability of politicians to understand or foresee change, whether it be technological or ideational, was at the root of this insecurity. For Baxter, the preparation of young men and women to manage change was the solution, and he saw their application of the social sciences as part of that. "He must understand the contemporary world in light of its past, and to bring to its study the techniques of the economist and of the political scientist."[47]

Baxter was one of an academic elite that had enormous influence selling social science to the intelligence services. Beginning his intelligence career as head of research at the office of the Coordinator of Intelligence, the forerunner of OSS, he was instrumental in co-opting Yale's Institute of Human Relations. As the war heated up, he asked its director, Mark A. May, to submit an anthropological study on the Japanese mandated islands as part of research on how to go to war with Tokyo.[48] The Institute of Human Relations had been created in 1929 as part of a grander scheme to marry medicine, social science, and law at Yale and was funded by the Rockefeller Foundation with a $4.5 million grant.[49] The aim was to practice "an integrated, synthetic science, cooperatively managed and oriented to eventual practical applications."[50] May wrote back to the Coordinator of Intelligence promising Yale's cooperation in developing skills in the collection and analysis of intelligence.[51] The universities were beginning their long period of direct collaboration with the strategic intelligence people.

Writing in October 1942, Yale political scientist Harold Lasswell began to knit together the functions of social science and policymaking and the role of intelligence.[52] Lasswell highlighted the great strides made by social science in methods of observing, analyzing, and reporting data. This had taken place at the same time as the structure of society, state, and government went through enormous changes, with resulting demands on policy responses. "Greater clarity may reduce the amount of fumbling that is invariably associated with new efforts to adapt old functions to different conditions," he believed.[53]

Lasswell's focus was mostly internal: to discern what the aims of a democratic society were and to use intelligence to inform domestic policymaking. But the problems he saw were associated with the growing pains of a functioning democracy and were very much a part of a larger picture: the present challenge from the Nazis, who saw democracy as "decadent and contemptible," and the Marxists' rejection of capitalism embedded in democracy as hypocritical.[54] Set against this global backdrop, Lasswell saw the imperatives of intelligence as discovering the facts about the thoughts, feelings, and conduct of human beings to support ideological objectives to strengthen the fighting spirit of the American people, to win allies, and to weaken the morale of the Axis powers.

The intelligence function could contribute to these aims in three ways: to clarify goals, clarify alternatives, and provide the necessary knowledge. Because policymaking would center on an understanding of human behavior, this would require three types of knowledge: the distribution of attitudes; the trend of attitudes; and comparisons of available alternatives with past situations, comparing these against scientific findings.

FIGURE 1.2. Harold D. Lasswell, professor of political science. *University of Chicago Library, Special Collections Research Center*

Lasswell's essay demonstrated how academics were thinking, even as the Navy base at Pearl Harbor was going up in flames: that social science would contribute to the larger ideological war of democracy against authoritarianism. At its foundation was a commitment to a deep understanding of how society works, but Lasswell also saw other functions of social science playing a part. For diplomatic purposes, he saw psychology predicting when the optimum time to strike a trade deal might be. For the military, he envisaged operations research solving problems of which strategy would inflict the most damage on the enemy while saving the most Allied lives. Economics could determine the best allocation of steel for tanks and shipbuilding. And the fields of political science, sociology, psychology, and anthropology might suggest whether civilians respond to propaganda detailing their soldiers' parts in horrible atrocities—a tool that might be brought to bear on the Japanese enemy.

By 1947 Parsons was championing the social sciences as worthy of investment by the postwar national security state. In an article featured in the January edition of the *Bulletin of Atomic Scientists* he advocated for what he called a rational understanding of man and society:

Most scientists, as well as other intelligent citizens, would agree that the great problems of our time are not those of the control of nature but of the stability and adequacy of the social order. It is not the urgency of social problems; it is the question of whether the scientific method is capable of making a significant contribution to their solution which needs discussion.[55]

Parsons believed that there was a fundamental unity between the natural and social sciences; that, despite the many failures to extend the methods of natural science into the new fields, man was essentially an organism; and that biology, psychology, and sociology were interdependent. Furthermore, he saw that the functioning of society depended on trained specialists and applied social science. "Technically trained personnel," he stated, "are playing a larger and larger part—for instance, in the administrative process, in the adjustment of industrial relations, in the field of communications, in the control functions of the economy as through the central banking system, in the control of foreign trade, and various such fields."[56]

Sherman Kent on the Historical Method

In a book review in the *Journal of American History* in mid-1947, the Yale historian and soon-to-be CIA analyst Sherman Kent commented on Garraghan's *A Guide to Historical the Method.*[57] Kent found little wrong with Garraghan's method but was deeply critical of his audacity in speaking for all historians, particularly contemporary ones (Garraghan was, rather unsurprisingly, a medieval religious scholar). For Kent, the guide's bare mention of economics and politics as near cousins of history was a serious oversight, one that failed to put history in the company to which it belonged. The man soon charged to be an overseer of CIA's national intelligence estimate also made a telling point. Speaking of the magnitude of documents being filed away in an attempt to fully record the machinations of the contemporary period, Kent was reluctant to ascribe quality to quantity. "People who work in twentieth century history," Kent warned, "are by no means convinced that the voluminous record of the times is necessarily a full record."[58] The plethora of material available for scholarly consideration presented a problem, the Yale historian believed, to which Garraghan had not given enough thought.

Some Doubts Set In: Leonard Doob's Wartime Experience

Again in 1947 Yale's Leonard Doob, a psychologist and associate of Yale's Institute of Human Relations, published an autobiographical account of his work at the Office of War Information (OWI) on what he hoped might be the opening discourse of a guide to the social scientist working in government.[59] Doob's experience was in managing the Overseas Office of the OWI, responsible for "white" (clearly labeled US) propaganda against the Axis powers as well as "information" to the allies and neutral states outside the Western Hemisphere. The office worked closely with the armed services, with directives coming from the War, Navy, or State Departments and the execution of propaganda (theoretically) supervised by them. Before such an operation was undertaken, the Overseas Office would help identify a likely target or task, determine which "buttons to push" in any propaganda campaign, and supply any background information that would provide other insights for the policymakers and propaganda operators.

The Overseas Office appears to have followed a similar trajectory that CIA did later. Despite the best efforts of the staff, the organization struggled to prove itself. Doob was careful to say that the work carried out fit the category of social science very loosely and belonged to no particular social science discipline. This was not for want of trying: the application of social science methods was somewhat hampered by the lack of data available. Pursuing questions like "what is happening inside a particular country," "what are the people doing and thinking," and "what are the leaders plotting and planning," the Overseas Office often found the information they needed was classified or was low-quality research performed by another branch of government or another state altogether. With no charge or budget available to source its own data, Doob's office was hamstrung, and this was reflected in the hit-and-miss results of their psychological operations. His social scientists were jealous of OSS's Research and Analysis division and of the intelligence units of the Army, Navy, and State Department, which appeared better resourced and with greater access to information.

Reports were produced, some with great detail. An anthropologist might study public morale in Germany or Japan. Researchers frequently drew on interviews with prisoners of war or with nationals living in the United States, or they read or listened to foreign broadcasts or newspapers:

> Sometimes, the analysis was too refined and represented a deductive leap into the unknown, motivated by the social scientist's desire to use his social science or by his impulse to compete with journalists on their own terms. Far too many risky and dogmatic inferences concerning the state of morale in enemy countries, for example, were made on the basis of radio transcripts and newspapers simply because these data were at hand by the trainload. What was seldom done was to pool the available data and information of all experts in order to determine systematically—in terms of social-science principles—how people might respond to propaganda. Instead, the easier and quicker solution was simply to consult one of the self-styled or recognized experts concerning the desirability of the propaganda innovation. This was a hit-and-miss approach in a situation in which no one except an omniscient deity will ever know in detail what hit and what missed.[60]

Despite social scientists making up the top 5–10 percent of the Overseas Office, and journalists, advertising and public relations specialists, and foreign nationals largely making up the rest, the social science method was relegated to the role of critic in the process. Too frequently the journalists arrived at solutions faster, although less systematically. Otherwise, foreign nationals, primarily employed as linguists, usurped their positions to become the founts of knowledge on their home countries. Without strong data to back him up, the social scientist, Doob, says he was "intellectually paralyzed" and capable only of applying cautionary standards of verification against the shrewd and wild guesses of the less formally trained. "The social scientist could not protest, inasmuch as his own position was too vulnerable; if he talked in terms of principles or theories, he ran the risk of being called a 'professor' and of delaying fast-moving operations."[61]

The question mark over both the role of the social scientist and his inability to effectively use his research and methodological skills had an impact on the morale of those working at OWI. Many wanted to jump ship to agencies where opportunities lay to use their science more rigorously. Others longed to return to the university. For the most part, their skills were in hibernation, and there were few examples of their research having any impact. Occasionally their work would be acknowledged in a propaganda policy document, and sometimes news would come of opposition soldiers surrendering waving leaflets dropped behind enemy lines. As the putative leader of the Overseas Office, Doob believed research had played a limited role in propaganda operations, mostly in confirming or substantiating decisions already made. Important strategic decisions like the demand for the unconditional surrender of Germany and Japan, where research by psychologists, anthropologists, or sociologists may have provided genuine insights, were made without their help. Instead, the policy was guided by "a few elementary facts" about the enemy soldiers on the ground, supplied by the Army's G-2 intelligence unit.[62]

The policymakers did not want in-depth social science research from OWI. Doob wanted to prove the worth of his discipline—for instance, by gauging public opinion on policy issues—but his seniors would have none of it. The background reports that his office did produce were often done under enormous pressure: "The word 'research' seemed to suggest to some that a miracle could be quickly wrought and that the innermost secrets of any enemy or occupied country ought to be immediately discovered and made available for operations. Or sometimes a round-up report for background purposes was requested which would have terrified a team of scholars with ten years, and not ten days, at their disposal to complete the job."[63] Doob himself gave up in the last months of the war and moved to a policy coordination role. The only successes he could lay claim to, he asserts, came from policymakers whom he befriended or made their lives easy, and not through any intrinsic belief in the power of social science. Even then, he says it was common knowledge that "the facts were limited and the analyses unavoidably tentative and inconclusive."[64]

As the head of the Overseas Office, Doob was invited to policy meetings:

> Whether or not in this role he was functioning as a research worker, a social scientist, or just a more or less intelligent human being, is a purely academic question. Research and social science, in short, were the excuse which enabled him to get into the policy discussions in the first place. This point must be clearly understood. Expressed differently, it suggests that in some situations, where social science data are inadequate or where social science itself can provide only principles or a way of approach to a problem, the social scientist must hurl himself into the debate, participate on an equal or unequal footing with men and women who are not social scientists, toss some of his scientific scruples to the winds, and fight for what seems to him to be valid or even good. A strict adherence to the scientific credo in such circumstances leaves the social scientist impotent and sterile as far as policy is concerned. He is faced with these alternatives: to keep quiet, stay within the confines of his research, and leave the decision to others; or to speak up, go beyond his research and social science, and thus share in the decision. Certainly, this writer asserts, the judgment of a social scientist ought to be no worse than the judgment of someone outside the fold when the problem concerns other human beings; and maybe it can be better in some instances.[65]

The example of the Overseas Office illustrates some of the problems CIA was to have between 1947 and William Langer's arrival in 1950. First, despite the pedigree of being a professor from Yale with a book on propaganda to his name (*Propaganda: Their Psychology and Techniques*, 1935), Doob and his social science team found it difficult to establish a new field as legitimate propagandists. They competed with journalists, advertising men, public relations specialists and other mass communications people, all of whom brought their own disciplines and methods to their work. With information either inaccessible (classified) or empirically poor, Doob struggled to infer strong conclusions in his studies, which made them no more persuasive than the "wild guesses" of his competitors or the biased assurances of the foreign nationals on his staff. Policymakers understood little of social science methodology or how to engage with its caveats. Relationships with policymakers were built on popularity and meeting deadlines. Without a strong social science base from which to build, Doob was less able to sell unpopular conclusions or buy time for more research. CIA had the same problem prior to Smith's and Langer's arrival: With no mandate to create in-depth national intelligence estimates, only daily briefs, the research staff made few inroads with policymakers. With no intelligence-gathering resources of its own, CIA depended on what the military and diplomatic agencies would share with it. Yet the wartime experience of Leonard Doob at OWI was not the experience of Langer at OSS's Research and Analysis.

No Doubts Now: A Military Man Champions Social Science

In his deposition to the Senate's 1945 hearing to determine the role of the physical sciences in national security, Brig. Gen. John Magruder stressed the need for equal investment in the social sciences.[66] Magruder was an artilleryman by training, an Army intelligence officer in practice, and did not have a university education. During the war he moved to OSS and from 1943 was deputy director of intelligence, responsible for the Research and Analysis (R&A) section, the SI (Secret Intelligence, the collection wing of OSS), FNB (Foreign Nationals Branch), X-2 (Counterintelligence) and IDC (Interdepartmental Committee for the Acquisition of Foreign Periodicals) sections.[67] He assumed responsibility for the covert operations Strategic Services Unit after OSS was disbanded in 1945 and moved to the US Army.

Magruder told the assembled subcommittee that he had come into contact with a number of social scientists during his two years at OSS, having had no previous experience of them in military intelligence. Soldiers like him, he said, were laymen in the field of social sciences, and social scientists in turn were laymen in the military field. "But in all of the intelligence that enters into waging war soundly and waging peace soundly it is the social scientists who make a huge contribution in the field in which they are professionals and the soldiers are the laymen."[68] Wars, he believed, were not fought by brute force alone. Citing Carl von Clausewitz, he argued that war was not only a matter of politics but also economics and psychology. Estimates of an enemy's strength would include "knowledge of its population . . . and manpower resources, of the economy's ability to support itself and at the same time maintain costly military operations in the field, of the Polity's ability to hold the Nation together in the face of the sacrifices of war."[69] Magruder then presented a diagram (figure 1.3, below) that detailed how each social science could bring greater understanding to policy and operational needs during war and could manipulate and enhance economies and government during peacetime. For the former Army intelligence officer, his experiences with R&A in World War II had been an eye-opener to a new way of executing intelligence analysis. In short, Magruder saw the potential for social science and intelligence activities in the postwar period:

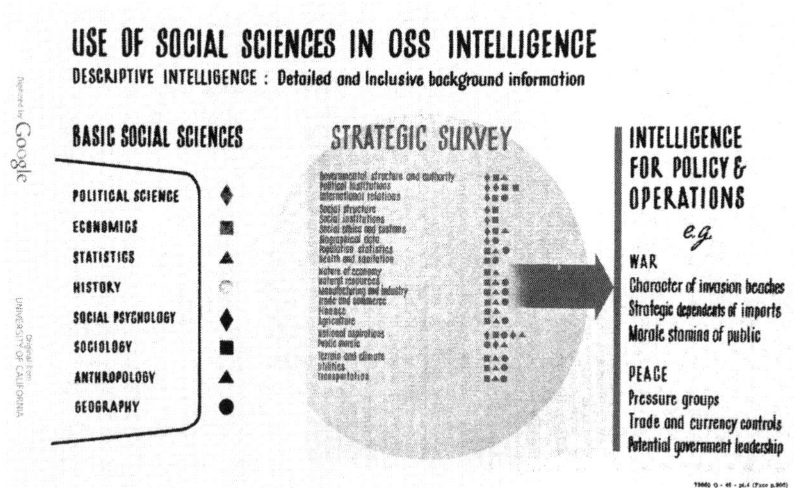

FIGURE 1.3. Brig. Gen. John Magruder's presentation to the Senate Committee for Military Affairs about the use of the social sciences in intelligence during World War II. *US Congress, "Hearings on Science Legislation,"* 901

The government of the United States would be well advised to do all in its power to promote the development of knowledge in the field of the social sciences. Without Federal encouragement we may find our best minds diverted from the study of politics, history, economics, geography, psychology and the other branches of social science, into fields of less value to the future national good. Were we to develop a dearth of social scientists, all national intelligence agencies servicing policy makers in peace or war would be directly handicapped. . . . As the research of physical science is essential to the nation's industrial strength, so is the research of social scientists indispensable to the sound development of national intelligence in peace and war.[70]

Conclusion

The founders of the social sciences in the United States had been intent on institutionalizing "sound opinion" and claiming a place for themselves as the legitimate analysts of man's behavior in modern society. This came to be applied not only to human actions in peacetime but also to the manifestations of such behavior in war.

Legitimacy for social science meant emulating the physical sciences with supportable propositions derivable from the observable world. Historians lent a tradition of the historical method, one that focused on good sources, evaluating their value, and synthesizing the information available to try to uncover truths. When information was incomplete, historians made hypotheses, which helped explain the matters before them or connected data into sets or frameworks. Occasionally historians offered generalizations or universal laws, rather than treating every event as unique. This might allow for some degree of prediction or at least reveal patterns that might anticipate future events.

Other social scientists, such as sociologists, took the scientific method and reshaped it to allow for the vagaries of human experience, constructing theories about behavior that entailed classification in time and space, definitions of units, and discoverable laws of action. But human behavior encompassed too many variables to be treated the same way as the laws of physics or biology; an element of the subjective had to be acknowledged for both the subject and the scientist. Yet even this could be allowed in the study of man's motivations, which promised greater clarity for where society was heading and how to deal with the enormous changes and conflicts of the modern world.

As the sociologists began to think about motivations, the economists tried to impose more abstract, mathematical ideas not only about rational behavior but regarding irrationality where information was not perfect and man-made decisions were influenced by beliefs and values. There might someday be theories that could be used to predict human behavior, but there were many useful tools of analysis that would help bring clarity to the seeming chaos in the meantime. Inductive methods could help sift through the huge repositories of unordered information now available, and deductive methods could lead the social scientist to conclusions free of selective bias in sorting that information.

As a result, there was a great deal of optimism about the promise of these new methodologies for strategic intelligence analysis. Social scientists saw their discipline as pivotal not only in peacetime policymaking but also in times of war. The experience of historians, economists, psychologists, sociologists, and political scientists and their decision-making superiors during wartime had at least partially proved the value of social science in defense matters. In the depositions that followed the war, the national security community demonstrated its desire to incorporate social scientists into the fabric of the intelligence infrastructure.

Still, there would be problems establishing a primary position for social science in wartime strategy making. When facts were disputed, information was unavailable, or secrets were not shared, then the whole edifice of empirical calculation came crashing down, leaving the unshakable stuff of opinion and sentiment still standing. Social scientists depended on the resources of good data; when they had these tools, they won the confidence of their policymaking superiors. The warning signs were evident in the testimony of academics like

Leonard Doob. Without access to valid and comprehensive information, the social scientist was powerless to demonstrate that his argument was any better than the opinions and anecdotal evidence of competitors.

A new kind of strategic intelligence analysis predicated on social science could therefore rebuild respect in the analytical product of CIA. As we have seen, social science had not only been fostered in the United States with the aim of delivering authority, it had also reached the point by the end of World War II where it was being championed by hardened military men as being right for policy and operations. Building trust and confidence in the intellectual and informational power the United States needed to adopt to fight the Cold War meant employing methods currently practiced in the social science departments of America's universities.

Notes

Epigraph: US Congress, Senate, Committee on Military Affairs, "Hearings on Science Legislation (5:1297), 79th Cong., 1 Sess., October–November 1945, part 4, 1945, 899–902," quoted in Simpson, "US Mass Communication Research," 325.

1. Haskell, *The Emergence of Professional Social Science*, vi.
2. Haskell, vi.
3. See Hughes, "The Historian and the Social Scientist."
4. Ross, "The Development of the Social Sciences," 124–25.
5. Klausner and Lidz, *The Nationalization of the Social Sciences*, 11.
6. Ross, "The Development of the Social Sciences," 107–8.
7. Ross, 124–25.
8. Ross, 125.
9. Ross, 107–8.
10. Garraghan, *A Guide to the Historical Method*, v.
11. Garraghan, 33–35.
12. Garraghan, 35, 39, 146.
13. Garraghan, 153, 155–57.
14. Garraghan, 351.
15. The choice of Parsons might seem like selective bias to some readers, particularly those acquainted with C. Wright Mills's criticisms of Parsons on the relation between theory and fact. For a closer reading and refutation of Mills, see Bernard Baber, "Theory and Fact in the Work of Talcott Parsons."
16. Ross, "The Development of the Social Sciences," 112.
17. Gerhardt, *Talcott Parsons*, 2–3.
18. Gerhardt, 2–3.
19. Augustus Comte (1798–1857) is considered the founder of positivism as well as a forerunner of the philosophy of science and sociology. His *Course on Positive Philosophy* (1830–42) is considered the major work on positivism, which included the differentiation of the sciences: the "positive method" (which, depending on the science, could be observation, experimentation, and comparison) and classification, with the view that the natural order could be modified by man as he replaces it with a man-made one. See the Stanford Encyclopedia of Philosophy, "August

Comte," October 1, 2008; rev. January 27, 2022, https://plato.stanford.edu/entries
/comte/.

20. Parsons, *The Structure of Social Action*, 1:xxii.
21. Parsons, 1:8.
22. For a definition of "facts," Parsons cited L. J. Henderson's an "empirically verifiable
    statement about phenomena in terms of a conceptual scheme." Parsons takes issue
    with the word "statement," instead saying it is a proposition about one or more
    phenomena. Parsons, 1:41.
23. Parsons, 1:8.
24. Gerhardt, *Talcott Parsons*, xii.
25. Parsons, *The Structure of Social Action*, 1:9.
26. Parsons, 1:8–10.
27. Parsons, 1:20–27.
28. Parsons, 1:27–41.
29. Parsons, 1:36.
30. Parsons, 1:38–39.
31. Parsons, 1:43–45.
32. Parsons, 1:46.
33. See Parsons, "Social Science," in Klausner and Lidz, *The Nationalization of the
    Social Sciences*, 41–112.
34. Parsons, 51–60.
35. Klausner and Lidz, xi.
36. Parsons, *The Structure of Social Action*, 10.
37. See Stegner, *The Uneasy Chair*, 138–39.
38. Millikan, "Pareto's Sociology," 324–37.
39. Millikan, 328, 324.
40. Millikan, 328.
41. Millikan, 328.
42. Millikan, 328.
43. Millikan, 328.
44. Millikan, 332.
45. Millikan, 328.
46. James Phinney Baxter, *Induction Address of President James Phinney Baxter III*
    (1937). Williams College Archives, http://unbound.williams.edu/williamsarchives
    /islandora/object/presidentialinduction:2, p. 17.
47. Baxter, 17.
48. Winks, *Cloak and Gown*, 44.
49. Schlegel, "American Legal Realism," 482–88.
50. Morawski, "Organizing Knowledge and Behavior."
51. Winks, *Cloak and Gown*, 44.
52. Lasswell, "Policy and the Intelligence Function."
53. Lasswell, 55.
54. Lasswell, 55.
55. Parsons, "National Science Legislation," 3.
56. Parsons, 3.
57. Kent, Review of *A Guide to the Historical Method*.
58. Kent, 113.
59. Doob, "The Utilization of Social Scientists," 650–52.

60. Doob, 652–53.
61. Doob, 652–53.
62. Doob, 658.
63. Doob, 660.
64. Doob, 660.
65. Doob, 662–63.
66. US Congress, "Hearings on Science Legislation," 899.
67. Smith, *The Shadow Warriors*, 174, 206.
68. Simpson, "US Mass Communication Research," 325.
69. US Congress, "Hearings on Science Legislation," 900.
70. Simpson, "US Mass Communication Research," 325.

CHAPTER 2

A Struggle for Existence, 1946–1950

For any agency in the guessing business, right and wrong guesses are the drops of water and grains of sand that enter into reputation and prestige.

—George S. Pettee (1946)

Any new institution goes through a process of proving itself, under the watchful eyes of those who have the most to gain—and lose—if it fails. Money is spent, time is invested in determining its scope, leaders are appointed, organizational structures and work processes established, and expectations are high. What the institution needs in its first months are some successes to reassure its stakeholders that the founding idea is a good one and that it fills a necessary gap, one that other institutions cannot fill. Institutional theorists speak of providing reasons for existence. Without them, plugs are quickly pulled. Between 1946 and 1950 the central intelligence agency (there were two iterations) was under continued pressure to lift its game. News by 1949 that the Soviets had the bomb and China had turned Communist, and in 1950 that North Korea had invaded the South, prompted an attempt to reform CIA to meet the urgency of the redoubled threat. Concerns about the new institution were voiced by the president and Congress as well as the State Department and armed services, who all had diminishing confidence in the leadership and a poor understanding of the deliverables of strategic intelligence analysis, and who therefore came to see the product as critically flawed.

This was not happy news for those within the Agency. The United States had entered the Cold War aware of the need for a good intelligence product. In his memoirs, President Harry Truman seems flabbergasted that intelligence had not been taken seriously until World War II. "Apparently," he said "the United States saw no need for a comprehensive system of foreign intelligence. . . . The war taught us a lesson—that we had to collect intelligence in a manner that would make the information available where it was needed and when it was wanted, in an intelligent and understandable form. If it is not intelligent and understandable, it is useless."[1]

Thirty years later the Church Committee agreed: "[The Agency] should gather information that is otherwise unobtainable; it should have the institutional independence that allows it to interpret information objectively and in a way that assists policymakers to make decisions; it should have the access that insures maximum use of its analysis; with appropriate direction from the Executive branch and oversight from the Legislative branch it might undertake clandestine operations in support of United States foreign policy."[2]

From the beginning, CIA did not have easy access to information otherwise unobtainable, it did not have institutional independence and struggled to get the respect of the executive in a way that would facilitate access. Each of these factors were symptomatic of a greater sickness: CIA was a new organization struggling to deliver a distinctive intelligence product and was failing to deliver what the executive, Congress, and other national security stakeholders expected of it.

The judgment in 1976 was that, as far as intelligence reporting was concerned, the early CIA had underperformed. The Church Committee stated, "As the CIA evolved between 1947 and 1950, it never fulfilled its estimates function, but [instead] continued to expand its independent intelligence function."[3] As a 1949 study found, CIA itself had been sidetracked by concentrating mainly on current intelligence, political reporting, and background studies on countries and their economies.[4] The upshot of this was that when it came to the original mission of a central intelligence agency—avoiding another Pearl Harbor—CIA had been found wanting.

The histories of CIA tend to paint a rosier picture of this period, particularly those that focus on the small, closed congressional committees that oversaw CIA's budget and tended to protect the Agency. As a result, Loch Johnson calls it part of an "era of trust."[5] L. Britt Snider is more equivocal, saying

> as the number of the Agency's actual or perceived failures began to mount—
> for example, the failure to predict the Soviet atomic bomb test in 1949 and
> the failure to predict the invasion of South Korea by the North in 1950—
> and members [of Congress] became increasingly aware of just how large the
> Agency had grown in a short period of time . . . doubts about the efficacy of
> the existing oversight arrangements began to appear with greater frequency.[6]

These failures rested with the analytical function of CIA and represented an existential crisis that even those who wanted to protect CIA had to acknowledge.[7]

A lack of understanding of CIA's mission and the value it could provide (but also the limitations of predicting the future) meant that the Agency's foundations were always unstable. The need for a centralized intelligence agency was understood by stakeholders, but CIA was by no means considered the only option: the Central Intelligence Group (CIG) had lasted only a year before being replaced, and prior to that both the Coordinator of Information and Office of Strategic Services (OSS) were quickly replaced when no longer needed.

President Truman's requirement for current intelligence prioritized the use of resources over national (strategic) intelligence and took the Agency's eye off meeting its original mission to create long-range assessments, including the enemy's future intentions and capabilities. Fraught relationships with the other intelligence agencies, who saw CIG/CIA as a threat to their own interests, resulted in the other intelligence agencies withholding their cooperation in contributing to intelligence reports. As a result, the stakeholders began to realize that CIG/CIA was not delivering what they wanted in a centralized intelligence agency and not listening to their demands for change.

CIG/CIA also struggled with the perception that its organizational structure and processes were poor. High-level commissions including the Eberstadt and Dulles-Jackson-Correa reports found fault with the organizational structure and processes of CIG/CIA.

This chapter begins by covering some important definitions: what a national intelligence estimate is and what the differences are between certain types of intelligence. The chapter then proceeds by telling the story of the central intelligence organization's formation and mission. It then reviews its patchy and often troubled experiences with its early directors: Sidney Souers, Hoyt Vandenberg, and Roscoe Hillenkoetter. It was under Hillenkoetter that CIA suffered its first major intelligence failures, and this drew attention to its organizational and procedural deficits. It is worth investigating a claim made by some historians that the upper echelons of Congress protected CIA and that, as a result, it was somewhat shielded from criticism. We shall see that the claim is not supportable. Finally, the chapter looks at how stakeholders tried to shape the Agency through formal commissions that outlined specific instructions on reform. These were largely glossed over by Hillenkoetter until the demands on the Agency reached such a level that he decided to quit and make a graceful exit back to the Navy. This series of events left the Agency in an existential crisis: with stakeholders dissatisfied with the Agency's performance, a poor understanding of its mission and practices, doubts hanging over the quality of its intelligence assessments, and the Agency being far from accepted as an efficient and valuable provider of strategic intelligence.

Strategic Intelligence

The most important example of the kind of classified reports that US social scientists contributed to is CIA's national intelligence estimate (NIE). The NIE is "the most authoritative written judgment concerning a national security issue," which is even today disseminated "to the highest level of policymakers—up to and including the President."[8] An estimate is produced after a request by the executive branch, Congress, or a military commander and "assesses the probability of a future course of action for an issue of importance to US national security policy."[9] The final NIE is sent to the requester as well as the president, senior policymakers, and relevant members of Congress. Senator Dianne Feinstein claimed she "deeply believe[d] that such an estimate is vital to congressional decision-making, and most specifically, [to] any resolution which may come before the Senate." It has been estimated that some 1,500 NIEs were produced in between 1947 and 1975.[10]

Strategic intelligence, of which the NIE is perhaps the most illustrative example, is differentiated from tactical intelligence, which is short-ranged or time limited and is information that contributes directly to the achievement of an immediate goal; and from operational intelligence, which supports an operation that is being planned or executed with specific information and provides insight into a specific target or activity. Strategic intelligence is more sophisticated: It comments on future possibilities or identifies potential issues, deals with threats, risks, and vulnerabilities; informs policymakers; helps determine the allocation of resources and requires in-depth knowledge about a target or activity. There are no definite walls between these three categories: sometimes something tactical or operational feeds into the strategic, and vice versa. Another category that is specific to the military is combat intelligence, which relates directly to information on the battlefield and information concerning targeting and battle damage reports.[11]

CIA was expected to deliver both strategic intelligence and current intelligence, the latter of which "focuses on issues that are at the forefront of the policy-maker's agenda and [receives] their immediate attention."[12] There is a natural split in terms of the administrative delivery of the two product types. The requirement for current intelligence was an inhibiting factor in CIA's perceived performance in its early days. Truman had requested only intelligence that was current; he wanted no long-term forecasts. Determined to answer the president's brief, CIA failed to invest any real resources into in-depth analysis of enemy intentions and capabilities. These resources would require a new approach to peacetime intelligence methods, and the recruitment of a specific kind of intelligence worker.

A Poor Understanding of the Mission

The need for a centralized intelligence agency was driven initially by the complexity of intelligence gathering and analysis and by the desire for more efficient methods of determining enemy intentions and capabilities. Wartime intelligence gathering had been served by three main agencies: the Army's G-2 unit, the Navy's Office of Naval Intelligence and the OSS.[13] In peacetime, the emphasis would shift from the collection of war operations intelligence to more strategic information about potential adversaries, including the strength of their economies as well as military power.

This complexity now manifested itself in two ways: competition for resources and influence between the armed forces, and the problem of coordinating the information their intelligence wings had collected, along with that of the State Department. This meant a good deal of duplication of effort and skewed intelligence because of the vested interests, poor channels of communication between each force, constant bickering between the groups, and ultimately—and most frustrating for Truman—no clear strategy for how to deal with the threat of future conflict.[14] This dysfunction had been a critical cause of the intelligence failure of Pearl Harbor, which one commentator said was "more like inter-governmental relations between friendly powers than like any effective inter-departmental operation."[15] This environment was both a catalyst for the formation of a centralized intelligence agency and a constraint on its growth and efficacy.

In September of 1945 Truman pulled the plug on the OSS with a medal ceremony for its founder, William "Wild Bill" Donovan, which the president rather tellingly did not attend. Presidential adviser Clark Clifford said Truman's decision to disband OSS was premature, abrupt, and unwise and was based on an Army intelligence critique that "was inspired by jealousy."[16] The president thought Donovan was a self-promotor, said Clifford, and did not like him. Yet OSS in many ways was exactly what CIA came to resemble most—both the good and the bad—and it housed the highly respected Research and Analysis branch, the intellectual forerunner of what came to be CIA's Office of National Estimates.

The president's poor view of the intelligence agencies had been shaped by the confusion of reports he received when he first took office and had worsened by the end of the war. Truman had been sufficiently annoyed about it to cite it in his memoirs.[17] As he told Secretary of State James Byrnes, it would be "a different kind of intelligence service from what this country had in the past."[18]

Donovan had pitched his idea of a centralized intelligence agency to Truman in August of 1944. While it was commonly agreed that this was a good idea, Donovan's mana was not sufficient for the role to fall to him. Instead, the idea was batted around from desk to desk as each of the service wings tried to shape it to their liking.

On September 19, 1945, a memorandum from Adm. William Leahy, submitted on behalf of the Joint Chiefs of Staff (JCS), recommended that a centralized intelligence agency could be set up even with the larger decision over the armed services merger still up in the air. The new agency ought to coordinate intelligence from the military, diplomatic, and other departments charged with national security matters; it ought to somehow control these activities in one agency; and it ought to synthesize the information in a way that answered the needs at national and strategic levels. The new director of central intelligence would be directed by an intelligence advisory board that would in turn be funded by the separate departments.[19] As CIA historian Ludwell Lee Montague argued, this was an example of power games in order to keep control of the new agency firmly in the hands of the JCS. Byrnes, at the Department of State, on the other hand, wanted the new agency to be in their control, including (rather tentatively) any role in covert operations.

By 1946, Clifford says, Truman was so tied up with the battles between the armed forces that Clifford was handed the project of shaping the new central intelligence agency.[20] Clifford says it was he who turned to Admiral Souers for help. Souers, a successful businessman prior to the war, had risen through the ranks to the post of assistant director and deputy chief of naval intelligence. He was considered an able administrator with a sharp mind.[21] Souers' opinion differed from Byrnes' at the State Department. He had contributed to the memo written by the JCS a year earlier, which centered the new agency within the military.[22]

Souers felt that covert work was not in safe hands at State. He also thought the president should appoint the head of the agency, not a branch of government like State. Clifford says he took Souers's views to Truman, who opted for neither the military nor State's proposals. Truman didn't want to formalize a central intelligence agency just yet. Clifford was told to direct an executive order establishing the National Intelligence Authority and a director of central intelligence (DCI) who would coordinate the CIG. He did so on January 22, 1946.[23] Truman signed it without consulting Congress or getting its approval.[24]

The directive of the president's memorandum of January 22 was—as would be the National Security Act of 1947—vague as to how the new central intelligence organization would work. It created a DCI charged with "distributing within government national security intelligence resulting from the correlation and evaluation of intelligence relating to the national security, to plan for the coordination of national intelligence activities and to perform services of common concern where indicated."[25] The last phrase, "services of common concern," was a euphemism for covert operations.

The job of DCI, who oversaw the early days of the CIG, was given to Souers. He lasted only a few months, resigning in June 1946. Souers's short stay at CIG was intentional. As the chief architect of the National Intelligence Authority and CIG structure, he had been christened "Director of Centralized Snooping" by the president, who had celebrated by throwing a party at the White House complete with black cloaks, black hats, and wooden daggers as costumes. Truman may have lampooned the department of his new head of intelligence, but he had enormous confidence in him personally. Souers, however, made it a condition of his taking on the job that he would only do it for a few months. His remit, directed by Truman in NIA-2 (February 8, 1946), was to provide a "digest every day, a summary of dispatches flowing from the various departments, either from State to our ambassadors or from the Navy and War departments to their forces abroad, wherever such messages might have some influence on our foreign policy."[26] These very early daily briefs did not make estimates or forecasts, keeping instead to current intelligence gleaned from important cables and telegrams.[27]

Unchecked Growth: Vandenberg as DCI

Souers stepped down, recommending Hoyt Vandenberg, a tall, unsmiling man with movie-star-good-looks take his place. A war hero (he was wounded at Pearl Harbor and had worked with anti-Vichy resistance groups), Vandenberg was also someone Marilyn Monroe had publicly chosen as being one of the three men she would have happily shared a desert island with.[28] He was a perfect public relations face for the new CIG.

Yet Truman may have been somewhat wary of Vandenberg, or of the connections Vandenberg had with Congress through his senator uncle. In his memoirs Truman says the new DCI was unanimously recommended to him: "I was glad, however, that Admiral Souers agreed to stay on as consultant to Vandenberg." Truman never let go of Souers, who went on to chair the National Security Council and, after William Leahy's retirement, joined the White House as special assistant to the president for intelligence, where he watched over meetings with CIA.[29]

Moreover, the decorated (as well as decorative) Vandenberg was ambitious and proved determined to move back to the Air Force as soon as he could. Clifford says Vandenberg was "clearly marked as a star of the next generation." It was taken for granted that this was a stepping-stone for the new role coming up, chief of staff for the Air Force.[30]

If Truman had few ideas about how his new intelligence agency should work, that was not the feeling of his senior staff. Commenting on some favorable press attention Vandenberg had managed to orchestrate, George Elsey—a one-time member of the White House map room—took issue with a newspaper columnist saying the daily summaries were "evaluated." "The morning summary is not an 'evaluated' summary at all," Elsey commented, "it is just a summary of Army, Navy and State dispatches."[31]

It didn't take long for Vandenberg himself to recognize the shortcomings of CIG. A month into his new job, in July 1946, he went to Truman asking for legislation to let CIG shake off the constraints the military wings put upon it and make it truly independent. Elsey and Clifford supported this and Truman, says Clifford, agreed.[32]

Yet Truman was reluctant to let the issue of a more independent CIG cloud the central debate over a civilian-led department of defense. Vandenberg pushed on and established the Office of Special Operations, a foreign intelligence collection unit, within CIG. He also took on Clifford in a fiery argument over Truman's decision not to announce the establishment of an independent intelligence agency in his State of the Union speech in January 1947.[33]

The vague understanding of CIG's mission was acknowledged by the DCI. At a February meeting of the National Intelligence Authority, CIG's governing body, Vandenberg spoke directly to the problem. He said the product of strategic and national policy intelligence "had been hindered further by an uncertainty among the agencies as to its definition."[34]

Vandenberg's performance at CIG was mixed. The Church Committee appraised his tenure as having improved the administrative authority and scope of the CIG's intelligence mission. As a career soldier and a previous head of the Army's G-2 intelligence unit, Vandenberg knew everyone and was not afraid to go into bat for his ideas. He was an aggressive, assertive personality: just what the CIG needed. He battled with the secretaries of War and State over getting funding for CIG to hire staff and resources.[35] He won, and this allowed CIG to conduct its own research as well as mount its own covert operations.[36] In doing so, Vandenberg grew the analytical staff to the point that there were more people than needed: his analytical team, the Office of Research and Estimates (ORE), reached 280 staff members, from an original 17.[37] This in turn created a cycle of writing reports simply to keep the machine going. On January 13, 1947, Vandenberg's deputy, Col. Edwin Wright, sent out a memorandum where he claimed he was continually being asked, "When is CIG going to produce intelligence?" The Agency was under constant pressure to "produce," and this led to an obsessive desire to create reports, even those that were not needed.[38]

CIA historian Montague says Vandenberg's rush to attain independence for CIG came at the cost of even greater interdepartmental friction, a fight that Vandenberg did not stick around long enough to deal with.[39] Eventually the call of the Air Force promotion was too great, and he left CIG in May 1947, becoming the youngest full general in US history just four months later.[40] He had been at CIG just short of a year. His successor was to inherit the bad blood Vandenberg had generated with the other agencies.[41]

Downward Spiral: Hillenkoetter as DCI

In the meantime, Truman continued to battle the heads of the Army and Navy to rationalize the defense structure. The National Security Act (P.L. 80-253), was formally signed on July 26, 1947. It at least partially resolved the infighting by bringing them under a Department of Defense led by a secretary of Defense, and the National Security Council (NSC), which undertook to coordinate defense efforts "with respect to the integration of domestic, foreign, and military policies relating to the national security." It also created the Central Intelligence Agency under the DCI.[42] But it said very little else about the new CIA that had not been expressed in Truman's letter of January 22, 1946.[43] What it did say was comparatively brief and vague: Section 102 of the Act noted:

d) for the purpose of coordinating the intelligence activities of the several Government departments and agencies in the interest of national security, it shall be the duty of the Agency, under the direction of the National Security Council—

1) to advise the National Security Council in matters concerning such intelligence activities of the Government departments and agencies as relate to national security;

2) to make recommendations to the National Security Council for the coordination of such intelligence activities of the departments and agencies of Government as relate to national security;

3) to correlate and evaluate intelligence relating to the national security, and provide for the appropriate dissemination of such intelligence within the Government using where appropriate existing agencies and facilities: Provided that the Agency shall have no police, subpoena, law-enforcement powers, or internal-security functions: Provided further—That the departments and agencies of Government shall continue to collect, evaluate, correlate and disseminate departmental intelligence: And provided further, That the Director of Central Intelligence shall be responsible for protecting intelligence sources and methods from unauthorized disclosure;

4) to perform, for the benefit of the existing intelligence agencies, such additional services of common concern as the National Security Council determines can be more efficiently accomplished centrally;

5) to perform such other functions and duties relating to intelligence affecting the national security as the National Security Council may from time to time direct.

e) To the extent recommended by the National Security Council and approved by the President, such intelligence of the departments and agencies of the Government, except as hereinafter provided, relating to the national security shall be open to the inspection of the Director of Central Intelligence, and such intelligence as relates to the national security and is possessed by such departments and other agencies of the Government, except as hereinafter provided, shall be made available to the Director of Central Intelligence for correlation, evaluation and dissemination: Provided, however, That upon the written request of the Director of Central Intelligence, the Director of the Federal Bureau of Investigation shall make available such information for correlation, evaluation and dissemination as may be essential to the national security.[44]

The role of CIA would wait six more months to be defined by its governing body, the National Security Council. It did so in two NSC intelligence directives, specifying that

The Intelligence Advisory Committee (IAC, the replacement for the Intelligence Advisory Board) was a key element in the DCI's coordination function.

The DCI was to coordinate national intelligence but avoid duplication of tasks the other agencies were already doing.

National intelligence reports must be agreed to by the IAC or dissents lodged.

There must be "free interchange of information" between the intelligence agencies under the IAC.

The director had control over hiring his own staff.

There were new directions given regarding the kinds of intelligence to be produced:

> "Basic intelligence," published by CIA but created by the other agencies;
>
> "Current intelligence," produced by all agencies (and it was not specified if CIA's current intelligence would also be national);
>
> "Staff and/or departmental intelligence," required by an agency for its own use but available for all; and
>
> "National intelligence," pertaining to national policy or security, which the director was tasked with coordinating and producing.[45]

The first DCI under the new Central Intelligence Agency was Rear Adm. Roscoe H. Hillenkoetter, who is considered the weakest of the DCIs during the formative years.[46] Montague says that Hillenkoetter "never wanted to be DCI and probably never should have been. He was unable to cope with the situation in which he found himself and gladly relinquished it to go to sea."[47] Hillenkoetter, Willard Matthias says, "had no political clout and no experience at policy level. It would take another three years before estimates received high-level recognition or exercised significant influence on foreign and military policy."[48] Russell Jack Smith agrees, saying:

To say it succinctly, CIA lacked clout. The military and diplomatic people ignored our statutory authority in these matters, and the CIA lacked the power to compel compliance. Our director was Rear Admiral Roscoe Hillenkoetter, a thoroughly decent, unpretentious man, but a rear admiral. In the hierarchical maze of official Washington his authority scarcely extended beyond the front door. Hillenkoetter's low rank precisely indicated the level of enthusiasm the rank-conscious armed services had for a centralized intelligence system.[49]

George Kennan at the Policy Planning Staff had few good things to say about Hillenkoetter, still wanting the covert operations side to be managed by State. Congress, too, had its doubts about the new leader. "I can get no comfort out of anything the Admiral has said to us!" said one senator after a secret committee meeting with the DCI over the agency's inability to predict the USSR's first atom bomb test. Hillenkoetter was sent on his way after only ninety minutes, the senator telling him he hadn't "the remotest idea" what Moscow was up to.[50]

Neither was he an influential DCI at the executive level. When, for instance, on June 25, 1950, the news broke that North Korea had invaded the south, Truman quickly assembled his closest advisers in a council of war. Despite his nominal role as the head of the intelligence community, Hillenkoetter was not invited. "CIA was still regarded in Washington as a fledgling agency in the foreign affairs business," says Matthias, "and its director looked down upon as a *locum tenens* until some more distinguished and active figure could be chosen for that position."[51]

A telling example of how CIA was struggling to define itself is shown in a paper prepared in 1949 for the Bureau of the Budget.[52] On September 19, 1949, Hillenkoetter tendered this in a self-criticism titled "Management Improvement Activities."[53] The report detailed three priorities: the difficulty of getting coordination between the intelligence community; the problem of fitting management processes around the covert departments; and the problems of producing estimates efficiently. The schedule for the year ahead was filled with the sort of promises any CEO might make to an impatient board of directors. This included the aim to reorganize the covert departments in accordance with the instructions of the NSC, and a further promise to integrate the intelligence production program, including establishing priorities better and allocating work between the intelligence agencies to avoid duplication. In what appears to be an earlier draft, however, the writer has compiled more of a list of frustrations, each annotated by hand.[54] In the entry for the integrated intelligence program, the writer has asked for a "better definition of the term 'National Intelligence.'" This has been deftly crossed out.[55]

Historian John Prados believed the early covert operations brought Hillenkoetter and CIA some degree of kudos. The Agency's attempt to steal the 1948 Italian election from the Communists was a success. Truman had been very happy with the outcome.[56] This prompted NSC-10/2, approved by Truman in June 1948. The new directive gave CIA autonomy to execute "any covert activities related to propaganda; preventative direct action, including sabotage, anti-sabotage, demolition and evacuation measures; subversion against hostile states, including assistance to underground resistance movements, guerrillas and refugee liberation groups, and support of indigenous anti-communist elements in threatened countries of the free world."[57]

Despite this green light to proceed on covert operations, Hillenkoetter was not an enthusiast.[58] He was bitter about Kennan's repeated attempts to bring them back under the control of State but at one point told a Truman aide that the State Department was welcome to it.[59] Regardless of this, the demands of covert activities on the Agency's time and resources continued. In 1948, during the passage of the Central Intelligence Act, Hillenkoetter told a House Armed Services Committee that "it was thought, when we started this back in 1946, that at least we would have the time to develop this mature service over a period of years. . . . Unfortunately the international situation has not allowed us the breathing space we might have liked, and so, as we present this bill, we find ourselves in operations up to our necks."[60]

Intelligence Failures

CIA's first high-profile intelligence failure came in 1948 in the middle of the Italian elections, which the Agency was busy trying to manipulate (providing political assistance to support the Marshall Plan), and just prior to the Berlin Blockade, which was arguably the first action by the Soviets to test American resolve and its new containment policy.[61]

As David Barrett describes in his book *The CIA and Congress*, George Gaitan, a popular liberal leader from Bogotá, was assassinated on April 9, 1948. This sparked a three-day riot, which risked the safety of Secretary of State George Marshall, then visiting Colombia at the Ninth International Conference of American States. A congressional investigation was mounted to find out whether CIA had known of the potential uprising and had warned State of the possible risk. Hillenkoetter acquitted the Agency well, pointing out that State's ambassador in Colombia had been informed but had decided not to pass it up the channels and scare the delegation to the conference. This, however, did not let CIA completely off the hook: critics had called it a "South American Pearl Harbor," and a Republican congressman railed against the Agency, saying, "the most neglected and incompetent of our national security efforts is in the field of intelligence" shown by "the fiasco in Bogotá." The representative pushed for a joint congressional intelligence committee to open an inquiry into the Central Intelligence Agency, whose shortcomings were "manifest."[62]

The lambasting continued. In an article in *The New York Times* in July 1948, columnist Hanson Baldwin claimed that not only had CIA shown its inadequacy in Bogotá but had also bungled covert operations in Finland, Romania, and Hungary. CIA was "one of the weakest links in national security" partly because the Agency was staffed by "empire builders" (e.g., Vandenberg) and "chair warmers" (Hillenkoetter).[63]

The Agency's second intelligence failure, while more important, came with less disapprobation. On September 24, 1949, *The New York Times* ran the headline "Soviet Achievement Ahead of Predictions by 3 Years." Truman had learned of the Soviet testing of the A-bomb several weeks earlier, not through CIA but through the US Air Force, who had flown over the testing site at Semipalatinsk in Kazakhstan with monitoring equipment. On July 6, 1949, CIA had estimated the "earliest date by which it is remotely possible that the USSR may have completed its first atomic bomb is mid-1950, but the most probable date is believed to be mid-1953."[64] The Soviets exploded their first bomb, RDS-1 "First Lightning," seven weeks later, on August 29, 1949.[65] Truman told his cabinet of the test on September 22, and announced it to the press the next day.[66] He wrote to his wife, Bess, and told her "Russia has at last shown her hand and it contains the cards Marshall and I thought it would."[67] This raised the question whether CIA really ever had its finger on the pulse. Willard Machle, head of CIA's scientific intelligence unit, complained the Agency had "failed completely to discharge its responsibility for covert collection of scientific and technical intelligence."[68] Months before the CIA estimate, the Atomic Energy Commission's David E. Lilienthal had complained to J. Edgar Hoover of the FBI that "foreign intelligence on atomic energy was dreadful," and that a major overhaul was required.[69] Now it seemed this criticism had hit the mark. Eugene Millikin, a firebrand senator on the Joint Nuclear Intelligence Committee, attacked the Agency saying they had been

> misled by previous assurances of the CIA Director Admiral Hillenkoetter . . . that the United States actually had agents in Russia; that it had gotten some of its agents out of Russia with information; that it was screening people leaving and escaping Russia; and the implication that it possessed much factual data upon which the previously estimated date of completion of the first weapon by Russia had been arrived at.[70]

Hillenkoetter's response to the Joint Committee was illuminating. Yes, he admitted, the Agency had probably given some of their espionage cases more credit than they deserved. The Soviets had worked hard to pry atomic secrets out of the West, and instead of beginning work in 1945 as CIA had believed, they may have begun as early as 1943. The analysts had assumed it would take five years for Moscow to produce a bomb, and the Agency "had not been far off." Yet Hillenkoetter argued he had frequently been accused of seeing "ghosts around every corner" when it came to him warning about keeping security tight.[71]

The DCI's answer might have been deemed sufficient had the committee not asked the next question: Were the Soviets now working on the thermonuclear bomb? "They must be in that," responded Hillenkoetter, "but we have come across nothing to indicate that at all so far, sir."[72] Did the Soviets only have two bombs? Yes, said Hillenkoetter, they were sure of that. Did Moscow know how the United States had learned about the testing? No, they did not know, Hillenkoetter assured them. "I would like to believe that," said Brien McMahon, who was perhaps the most technically adept member of the committee. But he clearly had doubts.[73]

In what was to prove somewhat ironic, the committee then drew attention to a speech Gen. Walter Bedell Smith had made the previous June, in which he claimed the Soviet test was imminent. The committee had written to Hillenkoetter seeking a response to this, to which he had simply said the general's claim was vague.[74]

Hillenkoetter then went on to field a number of questions on the likelihood of a Soviet attack on Europe, and whether an invasion of the maverick Communist leader Tito's Yugoslavia was about to take place. The DCI answered each question confidently and kept his temper until the inquiry circled around again to the Soviet bomb intelligence failure. Once again it was Millikin who fired the shots. "How did we muff it, and what is wrong with our system?" he demanded. "I think we made a mistake," Hillenkoetter confessed. "I want to know why we didn't get the information [as] to what is going on?" Millikin pursued. Hillenkoetter's answer was damning:

I can't answer that "why." We didn't get enough to do it. . . . We knew that they were working on it, and we started here, and this organization [CIA] was set up after the war and we started in the middle and we didn't know when they started and it had to be picked up from what we could get along there. That is what I say: this thing of getting a fact that you definitely have on the exploding of this bomb has helped us in going back and looking over what we had before, and it will help us in what we get in the future. But you picked up in mid-air on the thing, and we didn't know when they started, sir.[75]

Millikin's reply was curt: "That is not quite a victory for intelligence."[76]

The meeting was about to end on assurances from Hillenkoetter when Millikin threw in one last jab: "I just get no comfort from what the Admiral [Hillenkoetter] has said to us. We have not had an organization adequate to know what is going on in the past and he gives me no assurance that we are going to have one in the future."[77]

DCI Hillenkoetter must have thought he had sidestepped any criticism of "another Pearl Harbor" when North Korea invaded the south on June 25, 1950. Although only two days previously he had given no indication of an impending attack to the House Foreign Affairs Committee, he defended himself well in front of Congress to the Appropriations Committee on the twenty-sixth. Despite the usual sword-rattling from opportunistic Republicans, Hillenkoetter had convincingly showed that CIA had supplied considerable detail on troop movements, the clearing away of civilians near the thirty-eighth parallel, and the preparation of roads and bridges for heavy equipment movement. Sen. Styles Bridges, who had angrily asked Dean Acheson and Secretary of Defense Louis Johnson "why wasn't the Central Intelligence Agency on the job?," had calmed down after hearing Hillenkoetter's explanation, and *The New York Times* reported that the DCI's testimony had changed both his view and that of committee member Richard Russell Jr.[78]

Yet a rumor was circulating that the DCI would soon be replaced. Within a few days Appropriations Committee member William Knowland cited a newspaper article that said morale was low at the Agency, other departments were not cooperating with it, and Hillenkoetter might soon be replaced by General Smith. *The Record*, at the instigation of another legislator, claimed there had been a blackout of information from behind the Iron Curtain and that "there is no public clamor for scalps in connection with the Korean surprise, although there is word in Washington that will come, too." Neither was Bridges done with Hillenkoetter. On July 11 he came out attacking CIA again: "Our ability to detect in advance the antagonistic movements of a potential enemy is no better today than it was on December 7, 1941 [the date of the Pearl Harbor attack]," he argued. The Agency needed "far-reaching" reform. A follow-up came two days later from Sen. James Fulton, who asked why Hillenkoetter had said nothing of the invasion when in front of the Foreign Affairs Committee two days before the attack.[79]

Hillenkoetter continued to defend CIA's forecasts. The Agency was not able to predict that the invasion would happen precisely "at 5 o'clock in the morning" but it had given ample warning. There were between one hundred and two hundred tanks involved, and the estimates were consistent with that. Would China get involved, the DCI was asked. CIA knew of 200,000 Chinese troops positioned close to the border in Manchuria. The besieged DCI was challenged to revisit old intelligence failures and show that CIA had not been sleeping when Czechoslovakia was suppressed in 1948, when the Chinese Communist Party won China in 1949, or when it had missed crises looming in Columbia, Palestine, and Yugoslavia.[80]

Hillenkoetter was not a lone voice when it came to supporting CIA analysts. Senators Dewey Short and Kenneth S. Wherry both spoke out, saying neither Hillenkoetter himself nor the Agency was to blame. Yet the narrative now held full sway. "With our present system of intelligence, no proper evaluation of information is possible," Rep. James Patterson told the Senate Armed Services Committee (SASC).[81]

A recent CIA history says Hillenkoetter was blamed for CIA's perceived failure to warn of the outbreak of the Korean War.[82] CIA historian L. Britt Snider believes Hillenkoetter's "dour low-key style" worked against him in congressional hearings, and his tendency to take offense at probing questions at times when he needed to be his most persuasive undermined his testimony. His willingness to clear CIA of accusations of intelligence failures, particularly over Korea, deflected some of the blame onto the Truman administration, and this led to the choice to look for a new DCI.[83]

CIA's Congressional "Protectors"

A word now on an anomaly: the evidence that CIA may have been protected by an echelon at the very top of Congress. John Ranelagh argues that "for the first thirty years of its existence, the Agency's relationship with Congress was very informal indeed. In essence, the DCI and his close colleagues dealt personally with the chairmen of the important Senate and House committees. . . . The Agency was trusted, its directors were respected, and it was seen as being America's principal defense against the subterranean machinations of world communism."[84] Even though Ranelagh covers a much wider time frame of thirty years, is he correct in this claim?

In the period 1949 to 1955 CIA's operating budget is thought to have grown from around $50 million (1949) per year to $335 million (1955).[85] Most of that growth, however, is thought to be a result of the investment being poured into covert operations. As CIA house historian Michael Warner argues, "Agency-wide budgets serve another purpose—that of giving the researcher a benchmark of the quality of and challenges facing the organization's leadership."[86] In fact, the early CIA was protected from punishing budget cuts by a close cabal of senators who believed in the mission and kept their critical counterparts away. Right from the very beginning CIA budgets were considered secret and the decisions squirreled away into small subcommittees linked to the SASC and House Armed Services Committee.[87] Responsible for oversight of the military, the committees were run by senators who were internationalists and supported the president.[88] They met irregularly and informally, with members being given just a few hours' notice of a meeting, the intention being to shut other senators out of the conversation. In Snider's words, it created "the informal, highly personal nature of the relationship during that period. Information was routinely communicated by DCIs to members of Congress without anyone else being present."[89]

Representatives like John Taber (R-NY), Carl Vinson (D-GA), and Clarence Cannon (D-MO), and senators like Styles Bridges (R-NH), Leverett Saltonstall (R-MA), and Richard B. Russell Jr. (D-GA) ran these powerful subcommittees over a period of years. Russell had a good working relationship with his Republican counterpart, Saltonstall, who was a member of both the Appropriations and Armed Services committees from 1946 to 1947.[90] He chaired the Armed Services Committee from 1953 to 1955, with Russell chairing it the previous two years (1951–53) and for the two years after Saltonstall (1953–55).

The protectors were not as one when it came to letting CIG and, later, CIA have carte blanche. When, in 1947, DCI Vandenberg appeared in front of the House and Senate Appropriation Committees, both chairs (Taber and Bridges, respectively) initially objected to the Agency's budget. Yet they relented, and Vandenberg won not only the economic battle but also the bureaucratic one; from then on, CIG presented only to the small committees, not to Congress at large.[91]

David Barrett believes no legislator was more powerful than Russell when it came to dealing with CIA. Russell's power was strongest in the final two years of Truman's presidency, when Russell chaired the SASC. He was considered a fair dealer, and Truman trusted him. When Truman fired Gen. Douglas MacArthur, it was Russell who was seen as the peacemaker in the ensuing congressional hearings.[92] Yet he knew little detail of CIA's budget, with only the chair of the Appropriations Committee and his clerk knowing the real figures.

It wasn't until the period between the final year of Smith's tenure at CIA and the first year of Dulles's leadership that Saltonstall felt he understood how the Agency worked. However, the CIA subcommittee was largely kept in the dark on its activities. Saltonstall thought, in retrospect (in 1976), that he could have been more inquisitive. Yet the senator believed that CIA needed to work undercover, even if it meant the congressional watchdog took the Agency's work largely on faith. The same applied to the budget:

> Senator [Richard] Russell created a hush-hush committee from members of the Armed Services and Appropriations committees. I believe there were five in all. The House had a similar hush-hush group, and we met informally. The annual appropriation for the CIA was then running at about $500–600 million and was completely hidden in the Defense Department

budget. Only a couple of times did we go to the CIA administration to have this analyzed for us. . . . Bob Amory, an old friend of mine in Massachusetts, was Allen Dulles' budget-control officer. He and his deputy would attend our hush-hush meetings to explain how the appropriations they needed came from various parts of the Army and Air budgets. With a few members of the Senate this concealment did not sit well. Eugene McCarthy, Mike Mansfield, and others offered resolutions to bring CIA into the open, but they were defeated by Russell and [Sen. Alben] Barkley, then the majority leader, and I tried to help on the Republican side. It was clear to me that if the activities and budget of the CIA were made public, it would cease to be of value, and other countries would have the full knowledge of what we were doing.[93]

Saltonstall had enlisted in the Army during the last months of World War I and served briefly in France with the 301st Artillery Regiment. Yet he was strongly tied to the academic world and a consistent supporter of social science. He had finished his law degree at Harvard in 1917 and received an honorary degree from Harvard in 1943, to be elected president of the Board of Overseers the following year. His first two appointments in the Senate were to the Committee on Naval Affairs and the Committee of the District of Columbia in 1945.[94] It was there that he challenged the notoriously prickly (and racist) Sen. Theodore Bilbo. Having just listened to a Cambridge man testifying to the DC committee, Bilbo grunted, "He doesn't know what he is talking about. You can't believe those Harvard professors." Saltonstall quickly objected. "Mr. Chairman, you know I can't let that pass," he told Bilbo. "Oh, hell," replied the older man, "you know I didn't mean you."[95]

Saltonstall was also supportive of the establishment of the National Foundation of Sciences in 1947. As a member of the Appropriations Committee, he was instrumental in building a coalition that would fund the foundation, which required scrutiny of its aims and structure. Saltonstall's view was the foundation would play a constructive part in the advancement of the universities, and doctors and scientists, in particular. Together with two other senators, he pored over the proposed bill line by line: "how to set up the foundation, what type of scientist or professor should be the chairman, how the funds should be distributed—how much to the universities, to the government laboratories, to the hospitals . . . whether it should be an independent agency or put under an existing department."[96]

Saltonstall was made deputy chair of the Armed Services Committee in 1946, under chairman Chan Gurney. He supported James Forrestal's view that the services should be brought under a civilian-led defense agency. (Saltonstall was a supporter of Hillenkoetter during the hearings on the outbreak of the

Korean War and blamed General MacArthur for ignoring CIA's warnings[97].)
A letter dated June 2, 1947, shows how Saltonstall was involved in the setting
up of CIA. In the letter, Charles S. Cheston, who had been assistant director
to William Donovan in OSS, wrote to Gurney outlining his ideas on the new
agency. Cheston believed CIA should be run by a civilian; have its own independent budget; and the DCI should report directly to an individual, like the
new secretary of Defense, and not a committee. To find support for these,
Cheston had approached Saltonstall, Gurney's deputy.[98] In a further letter,
dated the next day, Hillenkoetter wrote to Gurney, citing a letter from William Donovan to Gurney dated a year earlier, and Cheston's missive. Hillenkoetter told Gurney about his conversation with Cheston and agreed with the
three points, including his view that if he became director of CIA, he would
be willing to retire from the Navy and make the Agency his new career. This
indicates how much senators like Gurney and Saltonstall were involved in the
early planning of the Agency.[99]

The CIA's protectors were mostly nonpartisan about foreign affairs and,
being busy on the major committees, tended to leave the untidy minutiae
unraked. "They did not want to be surprised," comments Snider, "but they had
no interest in the nuts and bolts of the Agency's work either. They had no
interest in micromanaging."[100] For the protectors, the organization's existence
was already taken for granted. "Despite the fact that the act which created the
CIA in 1947 appears to some people to be a blank check for the CIA to do
anything it wants to do, I have always felt it was a good piece of legislation,"
said Senator Saltonstall in 1976. "We were putting our confidence in CIA to
give us intelligence that might not have come through ordinary channels."[101]
He felt that too much congressional oversight over CIA was a mistake, that
there was a need for CIA to operate secretly if only so it could be trusted by
allied intelligence agencies like those of the United Kingdom and France. Having been on the hush-hush committee, Saltonstall did not claim to be privy to
all of CIA's goings-on, but whenever he traveled in the world, he always called
on CIA stations and believed he was getting access and pertinent responses
to his requests.

Yet the downside of having a group of senior senators and congressmen
with a very light touch on oversight was that when the public discussion on CIA
was negative, their support was not obvious. John Warner, who was deputy general counsel for CIA from 1946, becoming general counsel in 1973, lamented
that "they never did learn enough about us to know how we really functioned.
So they could not be active defenders."[102]

CIA's relationship with Truman prior to Smith's arrival tended to mirror
its relationship with Congress. Melvyn Leffler says the president was not very
invested in the national security machine. He rarely attended NSC meetings

until the Korean War made it necessary "and almost never gave any guidance on specific issues. Nor did he show much concern for the problems besetting the intelligence community. . . . His aloofness and support made him much beloved by many of his cabinet officers, but this management style complicated the task of policy coordination."[103] In other words, Truman was loosely supportive of CIA, but it was superficial support. He didn't know enough about what was going on to be wholeheartedly committed.

CIA's Walter L. Pforzheimer, who liaised with Capitol Hill for many years, says the Agency recognized it had an obligation to provide intelligence analyses to the congressional decision-makers.[104] In a review article written in 1981, the veteran intelligence analyst and national security adviser Roger Hilsman argued that command of information was also a source of power:

> Quite apart from the issue of whether or not information is bent to support a particular policy, in Washington the first to have a tidbit of information is the first to interpret its significance and to be on the scene when the discussion starts on what the policy implications might be. Where information is an asset, command over information is the power to withhold or grant that asset—to the congressman or the press, for example.[105]

In late 1951, when the Agency was beginning to recover from its reputation for intelligence failures, Pforzheimer saw an opportunity to "foster and engender considerable goodwill with an extremely powerful group [of senators]" by providing the Senate Foreign Relations Committee with a number of unclassified maps. DCI Smith had considerable success with his "'round the world" briefings during the Korean War, impressing Truman so much that the president asked Smith to brief two foreign affairs committees.[106] Many years later one of Smith's successors, Richard Helms, was invited to brief the Senate Foreign Relations Committee. He was approached by Richard Russell, who clearly thought it a bad idea. "He looked me right in the eye, and his eye got a bit glinty. He said, 'If you feel any necessity to go around and talk to other Senators about the Agency's business, I certainly can't stop you. But, I'll tell you this, I will withdraw my hand and my support from your affairs.'"[107]

Hilsman also thought the Agency basked in the glory of being a clandestine intelligence organization, and its mission accorded with the values of the hush-hush congressmen. This may explain why nonpartisanship was the order of the day. "The CIA derived power from the fact that the function it performs, like that of the FBI, is by nature politically appealing," argued Hilsman. "The CIA was at the forefront of the cold war. Its job was to smite our enemies—not negotiate with them, or compromise with them, or to make agreements with them. It had the appeal of patriotism."[108] During this time CIA's briefings usually fell into three categories: the Soviet threat, developments around the world, and updates on military theaters.[109]

Lyman Kirkpatrick says that however good the relationship between CIA and the congressional subcommittees was, it could also cause problems for the Agency. He recounts going with General Smith to a meeting of the House Appropriations Subcommittee in 1951. Smith staged a tour de force presentation on what was happening at CIA, and one that impressed the committee considerably. When he finished, Representative Cannon spoke. "Thank you, Mr. Director. Now it is understood that everything that has been said here today is secret, even the fact this meeting was held." Kirkpatrick says this was not helpful at all, and he wished that at the very least the committee could have reported they were satisfied with their review of CIA. "The fact that such meetings were held year after year," he says, "and were never announced, was to plague the Agency with repeated requests for investigations or for a Joint Congressional Committee by many who assumed that there was no established system for congressional review of CIA activities."[110]

While the evidence here is that CIA was to some extent protected by the senior members of Congress, it seems to be a very fragile support. As the complaints grew, there is no evidence that these "protectors" did very much about stemming the increasing and widespread perception that CIA was underperforming.

Pressure to Reform: The Dulles-Jackson-Correa Survey Report

Of all the pressures put on CIA to meet its mission, perhaps the most consistent came through Senate hearings. Congress is not only a system of checks and balances, it's also a marketplace of ideas. The hearings procedures allowed for a number of criticisms of CIA to be expressed, particularly at two meetings pivotal to the national security program, the National Defense Establishment hearings on the unification of the Armed Forces (which led to the National Security Act of 1947) and the Hoover report of 1949. Both hearings prominently featured the testimony of ex-OSS spy chief Allen Dulles (who would become head of CIA in 1953).

Although he didn't have the political sway of his brother John Foster Dulles, Allen Dulles did garner a good deal of respect as an intelligence expert. Perhaps the most important figure in CIA history other than OSS founder William Donovan, Dulles had led the clandestine operations of OSS in Switzerland and been central to its work in postwar Italy. Dulles understood the front-line work of intelligence collection and espionage probably better than anyone.

In 1947 Dulles was on the outside of the national security community looking in. Both he and his brother were Republicans, but Truman had made John

Foster a senior at the State Department as a concession to a bipartisan approach to postwar policymaking. The invitation had not extended to Allen Dulles, who had returned to his law firm, Sullivan & Cromwell, on his return from Switzerland but still retained his German contacts and a keen interest in what was going on at the fledgling civilian intelligence agency.[111]

Dulles became a constant in discussions about the nature of a new intelligence agency, telling a SASC hearing in April 1947:

> Much of our thinking relating to an intelligence agency is colored by our recent dramatic war experiences. Intelligence work in time of peace will require other techniques, other personnel, and will have rather different objectives. The prime objectives today are not solely strategic or military. They are scientific—in the field of atomic energy, guided missiles, supersonic aircraft and the like. They are political and social. We must deal with the problem of conflicting ideologies as democracy faces communism, not only in the relations between Soviet Russia and the countries of the West, but in the internal political conflicts within the countries of Europe, Asia and South America. For example, it may well be more important to know the trend of Russian communism and the views of individual members of the Politburo than it would be to have information as to the locations of particular Russian divisions.[112]

In Dulles's opinion, intelligence during peacetime was a very different animal from wartime analysis. During times of conflict the whole apparatus of the military was available, while in peacetime the main channels would be through civilian means. Dulles estimated a good 80 percent would be sourced through "open-source" collection, including newspapers and radio, or through business and professional contacts with Americans living overseas.[113]

In peacetime, Dulles argued, the State Department was likely to not only supply much of the intelligence but also be the main customer for CIA's product. The emphasis placed on the military's desires and needs was unwarranted. What the State Department needed was an impartial producer of intelligence that kept well clear of policy recommendations. "For the proper judging of the situation in any foreign country," said Dulles, "it is important that information should be processed by an agency whose duty it is to weigh facts, and to draw conclusions from those facts, without having either the facts or conclusions warped by the inevitable and even proper prejudices of the men whose duty it is to determine policy, and who, once having determined a policy are too likely to be blind to any facts which might tend to prove the policy faulty."[114]

For Dulles this meant keeping evaluation of intelligence out of the hands of State. The diplomats should continue to run their geographic "desks," with expertise in the various capitals and regions around the world where they had representation, but the analytical work must be divorced from this, in an agency staffed with "the most competent men which this country can produce to evaluate and correlate the intelligence obtained, and to present it, in its proper form, to the interested Government departments."[115]

Dulles also addressed the problem of hiring military men to run the central intelligence function. It was his view that a soldier ought to give up his military career on entering CIA and not be tempted to see it as a stepping-stone in his military career. He had seen the effect of temporary secondment to the military intelligence wings, and this had "crippled their efficiency and lessened their prestige." CIA had also suffered from the turnover of three DCIs in one year. This could only destroy morale within the Agency and prevent long-range planning, "which must be the task of a properly functioning intelligence agency."[116] He was clearly thinking of Vandenberg, whose short stay at CIG had been no more than a stepping-stone to a promotion in the Air Force.

Dulles had put his finger on some of the biggest issues facing the new organization: First, that strategic intelligence would be a combination of information: some military, some political or economic, much of it of a social and historical nature. Second, that a good deal of the information sourced would be from good, old-fashioned research; although the percentage that was human intelligence might be the very best, it would make up a very small component. Third, the ability to synthesize such a wide range of intelligence would require the very best minds. Finally, Dulles saw civilian intelligence as a career and the gathering of an understanding of enemy intentions and capabilities as a long-term investment in knowledge building.

Dulles's criticisms of 1947 would be mirrored in the Eberstadt Report, an offshoot of the Commission on Organization of the Executive Branch of the Government, also known as the First Hoover Report.[117] The Eberstadt Report, which was unclassified and 121 pages long, was handed over to Congress on January 13, 1949. It found that the intelligence community was "soundly constructed, but not working well" and that the tensions between CIA and other departments were counterproductive. The findings laid most of the blame not with CIA but the military and State agencies, yet the report complained that departmental intelligence estimates "have often been subjective and biased." To amend this, the Eberstadt Report recommended the creation "at the top echelon [of] an evaluation board or section composed of competent and experienced personnel who would have no administrative responsibilities and whose duties would be confined solely to intelligence evaluation."[118] As far as CIA specifically was concerned, the report found the Agency's structure was not properly organized. Clearer lines of departmental responsibilities and better recruitment and personnel training systems were needed. It also advised, as Dulles had mooted, that future DCIs should be civilians and permanent appointments.

John Bross, a New York lawyer and OSS veteran, visited CIA as part of the investigations of the Eberstadt Report. Bross found fault with the fact that the DCI and his assistants were spending too much time on administration to concentrate on analysis and evaluation. "Many of the greatest failures in intelligence have not been failures in collection," he believed, "but failures in analyzing and evaluating correctly the information given."[119]

At the same time that the Eberstadt Report was being written, Dulles had been commissioned to create his own critique of the Agency, this time with an important political backer. As secretary of the Navy, James Forrestal had been a prime mover in the decision to unify the armed forces under a civilian defense ministry a year earlier.[120] The debate over how to coordinate the military had involved everyone from the president down and had diverted attention away from the scoping out of the central intelligence function. Now, as secretary of Defense, Forrestal turned his focus on CIA. Forrestal had read Hanson Baldwin's columns and been impressed with some comments Baldwin had ascribed to Dulles's thinking on CIA. He arranged a meeting with Dulles at the Pentagon in February of 1948 and told him the agency was overstocked with "dead wood."[121] With an election looming, Forrestal sensed that the next president would be Republican candidate Thomas E. Dewey, not Truman, and as Allen Dulles had become Dewey's foreign policy adviser, he would be able to influence the future of the national security community. Forrestal wanted changes in the Agency and saw Dulles as the professional who would be able to determine what was needed. With an election in November of that year, Forrestal wanted a comprehensive assessment written in time for the new administration in January 1949. He suggested two friends to help Dulles write it: William Harding Jackson and Mathias F. Correa—with the implicit understanding it would be Dulles's show to run.

The Dulles-Jackson-Correa Survey Report was handed over to the National Security Council January 1, 1949, with the full title *The Central Intelligence Agency and National Organization for Intelligence.* Dulles himself had taken such an active part in it that it was often called the Dulles Report. The brief (from Sidney Souers, now executive secretary of the NSC) had been to survey "a) the adequacy and effectiveness of CIA, b) the value and efficiency of existing CIA activities, c) the relationship of these activities to other departments and agencies[, and] d) the utilization and qualifications of CIA personnel."[122]

The report began by highlighting some of the difficulties CIA was experiencing because of the lack of cooperation with other intelligence agencies. It singled out the turf wars between the FBI (responsible for domestic intelligence) and CIA, which Dulles and his cowriters felt needed access to espionage investigations and intelligence on "fifth column" movements. It also stressed the need for coordination on scientific and technological intelligence. For these problems the authors were critical of the Intelligence Advisory Committee, which oversaw the coordination of the competing departments. CIA, too, needed to do more internally to support the DCI, with a veiled criticism that all this could be solved with "the right measure of leadership"—that is, probably not Hillenkoetter.[123]

Dulles was more direct about the quality of work coming out of CIA. The Office of Reports and Estimates (ORE), which had been set up by Vandenberg, had failed to produce the kind of intelligence needed, instead focusing on "miscellaneous reports and summaries which by no stretch of the imagination could be considered national estimates."[124] When ORE did produce an estimate, it based its research on its own intelligence rather than coordinate the best available information from the combined intelligence wings. ORE's practice of then circulating its own estimate to the other agencies only caused them to further distance themselves from the work. Dulles felt the present office could be downsized to a much smaller ORE called the Estimates Division, which would meet the original mandate to coordinate work under the auspices of the IAC. A national intelligence estimate would therefore be an authoritative statement of what was known by the intelligence community. A second Research and Reports Division would keep "at least part of the personnel" as its nucleus and take up the remaining work of miscellaneous reports and summaries. This would also take in the Foreign Documents branch and the library. Dulles also wanted the Research and Reports office to handle economic, scientific, and technological intelligence.[125]

Dulles for the most part fell in with conventional thinking in staffing both the Estimates and the Research and Reports offices with representatives of the departments of Navy, Army, Air Force, and State. If the information wasn't available through the normal channels—and Dulles was talking specifically of the case of scientific intelligence—then it was appropriate to go outside of the community and find the best experts available from the Atomic Energy Commission and the Research Development Board.[126]

The Dulles-Jackson-Correa Survey Report made a few rather pointed criticisms directly at the staff of CIA's ORE, including that they were not well enough briefed about either operational matters or policy questions to be able to deliver useful intelligence estimates.[127] This was something that could not be fixed overnight but over years of patient work. All the organizational charts in the world would not make up for "competent and highly trained men and women." This went for both covert operations and intelligence analysis. The closing of the war had meant that many experienced people were no longer available, and new recruits were hard to find.[128]

When it came to the primary role of ORE to coordinate and prepare national estimates, the report baldly stated that "this responsibility has not been adequately discharged, and remedial measures are necessary."[129] Dulles was careful to define the type of "national intelligence" requested under the National Security Act: "intelligence relating to national security," distinct from departmental intelligence and "the coordination of *intelligence opinion* in the form of reports or estimates affecting generally the national security as a whole."[130]

Dulles then explained what an intelligence opinion in the shape of an estimate was:

> A national intelligence report or estimate as assembled and produced by the Central Intelligence Agency should reflect the coordination of the best intelligence opinion, based on all available information. It should deal with topics of wide scope relevant to the determination of basic policy, such as the assessment of a country's war potential, its preparedness for war, its strategic capabilities and intentions, [and] its vulnerability to various forms of direct attack or indirect pressures.[131]

The outcome of an estimate ought to be "an authoritative interpretation and appraisal that will serve as a firm guide to policy makers."[132] Yet the work of CIA to date had fallen short of such a goal. Partly that was because the other departments had not accepted CIA's coordinating role and continued to make their own assessments to inform their policies. Both the JCS and the State Department looked to their own intelligence people for guidance. Even the NSC was accepting contributions from the other agencies as well as the intended source of CIA.[133]

CIA itself had been sidetracked by concentrating mainly on current intelligence, political reporting, and background studies on countries and their economies. ORE staff largely worked in the dark, with poor briefs on what was important and what was not. When an estimate was attempted, the result was "not impressive," Dulles stated. The quality was variable, and the influence of the estimates questionable. The work was hardly ever relevant to policy, partly because there was no relationship with the policymakers. There was the added risk that policymakers might read the estimate thinking it a coordinated report when it was not.[134]

Current intelligence took the shape of a top-secret Daily Summary and a secret Weekly Summary. The first was composed almost entirely of State Department cables, and the contribution made by CIA was "gratuitous" and "added little weight to the material itself."[135] The Weekly Summary failed largely because it competed with those of other agencies, particularly from the State Department. The president, who was the ultimate customer of the Daily

Summary, could be easily misled as there was so much important intelligence being left out. A third summary was a monthly Review of the World Situation. All lacked a sense of historical context and policy relevance. The daily and weekly summaries, which were received by customers with views ranging from moderate interest to strong criticism, needed a rethink.[136]

The more formal reports the Agency produced fared no better, in Dulles's opinion. While they were "intended" to be surveys of current world problems, with titles like *Possible Developments in China* or *Opposition to the ECA*, they were circulated to a largely indifferent audience for whom the work matched little with their own departmental or national concerns and—in the case of the other agencies—a contribution or review was an unwelcome task.[137]

Sometimes work of a specific nature was commissioned, such as *Soviet Financing of the French Coal Strike* and *Tungsten and South Korea*. These reports Dulles dismissed as a necessary evil. He considered CIA's work in this area to be academic, a duplication of other agencies' work, and not national intelligence. Those longer reports that focused on whole countries (the national intelligence surveys) were criticized too, with CIA having farmed out whole chapters to the other agencies to write themselves. This solved the problem of duplication, but Dulles felt the "temporary editorial coordination" made for an inferior product.[138]

The long list of complaints against ORE continued. Although charged with producing intelligence on scientific, technological, and economic matters, once again CIA had seldom produced anything authoritative. This was despite having six dedicated geographical branches, a scientific branch, and special consultant panels. Despite the large size of the ORE staff, Dulles could see little value in their output. For economic intelligence, Dulles saw his idea of a research and reports office feeding its findings directly into the more important strategic work of the estimates office. This economic work would be staffed by the best economists and the science branch, by the best scientists.[139]

Dulles therefore called for "a revision of the present arrangements."[140] There needed to be a split between the production of estimates for policymakers and the kind of intelligence that would inform covert operations. ORE needed to be broken up into an estimates office and a research and reports office. The commissioning of estimates would be the job of the IAC, and the analysts would be well briefed on the policy context. Policymakers needed to be aware of biases creeping into both briefs and estimates and be prepared to constantly reevaluate assumptions that underscored both the intelligence requirements and the assessments.

It was up to the DCI to determine the most efficient way for the organization to be structured and to hire and fire as he saw fit. While the director had direct responsibility for ORE, the covert operations side was less clear, with two offices under his control and another predominantly under the control of State. This was a point that would not be lost on General Smith when he arrived a few months later: the operations structure was a result of historical grafting from other agencies (the Office of Policy Coordination having evolved from OSS, to the Army, State, and finally the Agency). CIA had been so busy taking orders from outsiders on its organizational structure that it had wound up with competing divisions within itself.[141]

Dulles himself believed the next DCI needed to take a strong hand in reforming CIA. He saw little in the way of congressional scrutiny and believed the NSC should be more involved in the supervision of the Agency. He may well have been thinking of himself when he criticized Hillenkoetter, telling the NSC's readers that, "with the right measure of leadership," some of the more pressing problems could be fixed. He continued, saying that the DCI's duties could only be performed with "leadership, imagination, initiative and a realization that only a joining of efforts can achieve the desired result."[142]

Overall, the Dulles-Jackson-Correa Survey Report damned CIA for not living up to its mission. The Agency had failed to carve out a position for itself that offered anything different from what the other intelligence agencies were already producing: "The principal defect of the Central Intelligence Agency is that its direction, administrative organization and performance do not show sufficient appreciation of the Agency's assigned functions, particularly in the fields of intelligence coordination and the production of intelligence estimates. The result has been that the Central Intelligence Agency has tended to become just one more intelligence agency producing intelligence in competition with older established agencies."[143]

According to Dulles's biographer Peter Grose, Dulles personally delivered the final report to Forrestal over lunch in January 1949. Forrestal was pleased with the work, saying it was a "guidebook" and a lasting "example of how a report should be prepared."[144] When Dulles went to submit the report to Truman, his brother John Foster told him to withdraw it until after the elections: Truman was not likely to give the job of DCI to Allen, and he would be better to wait until Dewey won the election. The report was successfully withdrawn.[145]

The Calls for Reform Continue

The Dulles Report was eventually referred to the IAC for comment. Reactions from the different agencies represented were varied. Mostly they were concerned about the report's call for the IAC to take more responsibility for estimates and what that implied, which was that the CIA's governing body needed an overhaul too. Hillenkoetter was conciliatory and praised the report but said its recommendations were either unfeasible or had already been implemented.[146]

Ludwell Lee Montague characterized it as "devastating." It found, Montague later reported, "that the CIA had failed in its responsibilities with regard to both the coordination of intelligence activities and the production of national intelligence estimates, and it attributed these failures primarily to a lack of understanding and leadership on the part of the Director of Central Intelligence."[147] Hillenkoetter was clearly dispirited by the damning critique of his leadership, but this appeared to slow him down rather than give him the impetus for real change. George Jackson and Martin Claussen say Hillenkoetter attempted a reorganization in seeming compliance with the report, but it amounted to an "uncertain retention of the status quo."[148]

The National Security Council asked the secretaries of State and Defense to distill the report into a more workable format, which resulted in NSC-50 in July 1949. The directive toned down some of the criticisms of Hillenkoetter and CIA but otherwise agreed with the report's recommendations. Hillenkoetter was given ninety days to comply.[149] Montague says the ensuing reorganization merely "pretended" to comply with NSC-50.[150]

This "evasion" (as Montague calls it) catalyzed Gen. John Magruder into action. Magruder had been an outspoken champion of social scientists in the intelligence services in 1946, having seen from close quarters what could be achieved at OSS. Now he was in the Defense Department and was of the view that cooperation between the IAC agencies could work, with a much stronger IAC taking control—and taking responsibility for the quality of the NIEs— rather than the DCI. In July of 1950 Magruder's report went to the undersecretary of State, James Webb, where it became known as the Webb Staff Study. CIA's response to this only added fuel to the fire. Lawrence Houston, the general counsel for the Agency, sent a proposal back to Webb reclaiming the authority for national intelligence estimates for the DCI, something DCI Hillenkoetter had expressly tried to distance himself from since 1947. Magruder was less than impressed, and tensions between CIA, Department of Defense, and the State Department continued unabated.[151]

Montague says this sad state of affairs was still the case when Gen. Walter Bedell Smith arrived in late 1950. By that time there were up to five different proposals on the reform of ORE: Bross's from the Eberstadt Commission in 1948, the Dulles-Jackson-Correa report in 1948–49, Magruder's from the Webb Staff Study in 1950, and two historical proposals—Montague's own and William Donovan's, both dating back to 1946. The output of ORE was often work for work's sake: reports commissioned by ORE staff and not by the NSC, duplications of reports done elsewhere and more likely done by junior staff simply as training exercises, or for morale's sake—the pleasure of having something published with the analyst's name written on the cover. For example, in 1949 the Agency produced a report titled *The Caribbean Legion.* According to Jackson, "there was little reason to think a national estimate on the subject was essential at the moment."[152] As a result, those reports that ORE called national intelligence estimates "were actually a melange of current and descriptive reporting with little, if any, analytical or estimative content."[153]

Conclusion

As we have seen, a number of stakeholders in the executive branch, in Congress, and in the national security community had found CIA's work in intelligence analysis underwhelming at best and deeply negligent at worst. They were often influential people: George Elsey in the White House, James Forrestal in the Navy and later Department of Defense, and key politicians attached to the Armed Services and Appropriations Committees in both houses. The criticisms of CIG and CIA had also played out in the national press, giving voice to people like Allen Dulles, an outsider looking for a way back into the intelligence world. Dulles in particular had been chosen for his political value as someone who could help Forrestal get the outcomes he wanted at CIA. Hillenkoetter could do nothing but accept this outside interference and, despite his mounting anger, had to accept the taunts of skeptical legislators as well.

Fault can be laid at the door of the succession of directors of central intelligence, particularly Hillenkoetter, who did much to undermine CIA's reputation. While leaders like Souers and Vandenberg had not done anything to diminish their own personal authority, they had not done enough (or been around long enough) to establish the organization's. The engagement necessary to build trust with the stakeholders and create a more rounded understanding of intelligence's potential (and limitations) had not been sufficient.

Fault can also be attributed to the demands of President Truman and the friction caused by rivalry between the services and the State Department. Truman did not require anything other than current intelligence, yet it was long-range estimative strategic intelligence that was part of the Agency's mandate. The conditions placed on CIA's intelligence output by Truman, and the constant stonewalling of the other agencies, made it almost impossible for CIA's analysts to deliver what was needed. The temporary loans of staff and the endless meetings where representatives of the other agencies pursued their own agendas meant CIA was being hollowed out from within even as it was trying to grow.

By 1948 CIA's reputation as a warning bell of impending danger was greatly tarnished. The Office of Reports and Estimates was both the primary center of this dissatisfaction and an illustration of how far off course from its original mission CIA had strayed.

Notes

Epigraph: Pettee, *The Future of American Secret Intelligence*, 91.
1. Truman, *Memoirs*, 2:56.
2. US Congress, *Supplementary Detailed Staff Reports*, 2.
3. US Congress, "Ninety-Fourth Congress, Second Session," 15, cited in Prados, *The Soviet Estimate*, 7.
4. Dulles, Jackson, and Correa, *The Central Intelligence Agency*, 70.
5. Johnson, "The Contemporary Presidency," 829.
6. Snider, *The Agency and the Hill*, 11.
7. Later crises—for example, the Mansfield Resolutions of 1953–54—were mostly centered on CIA's covert activities. See Snider, 11–14.
8. Greg Bruno and Sharon Otterman, "National Intelligence Estimates" (Council on Foreign Relations website, last updated May 14, 2008), https://www.cfr.org /backgrounder/national-intelligence-estimates.
9. Kreps, "Shifting Currents," 610.
10. Bruno and Otterman, "National Intelligence Estimates."
11. See Prunckun, *Handbook of Scientific Methods*, 6–7.
12. Lowenthal, *Intelligence from Secrets to Policy*, 61.
13. For an overview of intelligence failures during World War II, see Matthais, *America's Strategic Blunders*, 7–42.
14. See Prados, *The Soviet Estimate*, 4–5. See also chapter 3 of Hogan, *Cross of Iron*, 23–68.
15. Pettee, *The Future of American Secret Intelligence*, 6.
16. Clifford, *Counsel to the President*, 165.
17. Truman, *Memoirs*, 2:56.
18. Troy, *Donovan and the CIA*, 303.
19. Warner, *CIA Under Truman*, 337.
20. Clifford, *Counsel to the President*, 165–67.
21. Adair, "The Quiet Warrior," 2; and US Congress, *Supplementary Detailed Staff Reports*, 10.
22. Weber, *Spymasters*, 3.
23. Clifford, *Counsel to the President*, 165–67.
24. Snider, *The Agency and the Hill*, 3.
25. Jackson and Claussen, *Organizational History of the Central Intelligence Agency*, 1:1–2.
26. Andrew, *For the President's Eyes Only*, 165.
27. Warner, *CIA Under Truman*, 337; and Jackson and Claussen, *Organizational History of the Central Intelligence Agency*, 1:2.
28. Andrew, *For the President's Eyes Only*, 165; and Barrett, *The CIA and Congress*, 25.
29. Truman, *Memoirs*, 1:58.
30. Clifford, *Counsel to the President*, 167.
31. Andrew, *For the President's Eyes Only*, 166.
32. Clifford, *Counsel to the President*, 167–69.
33. Andrew, 169.
34. Vandenberg asked at that meeting for the Intelligence Advisory Committee to approve his definition, which was, "Strategic and national policy intelligence is that composite intelligence, interdepartmental in character, which is required by

the President and other high officers and staffs to assist in determining polices with respect to national planning and security in peace and in war and for the advancement of broad national policy. It is in that political-economic-military area of concern to more than one agency, must be objective, and must transcend the competence of any one department." Warner, *CIA Under Truman*, 117.

35. US Congress, *Supplementary Detailed Staff Reports*, 10.

36. US Congress, 10. See also Jackson and Claussen, *Organizational History of the Central Intelligence Agency*, 1:13.

37. Originally titled the Office of Research and Evaluation, the name changed to Reports and Estimates in October 1946. See Montague, *General Walter Bedell Smith*, 29. Jackson and Claussen, *Organizational History of the Central Intelligence Agency*, 1:23.

38. Jackson, *The DCI Miscellaneous Studies*, 1:97.

39. Montague, *General Walter Bedell Smith*, 29.

40. Andrew, *For the President's Eyes Only*, 164.

41. Montague, *General Walter Bedell Smith*, 30.

42. Richard A. Best and Herbert Andrew Boerstling. *Staff Study Permanent Select Committee on Intelligence House of Representatives One Hundred Fourth Congress. IC21: The Intelligence Community in the 21st Century. Appendix C. CRS Report: Proposals for Intelligence Reorganization 1949–1996.* Permanent Select Committee on Intelligence Staff Study, House of Representatives, 104th Congress, February 28, 1996, 3.

43. Jackson and Claussen, *Organizational History of the Central Intelligence Agency*, 1:27.

44. "Additional services of common concern" is considered a euphemism for espionage and counterespionage. Warner, *CIA Under Truman*, 133–34.

45. Jackson and Claussen, *Organizational History of the Central Intelligence Agency*, 1:28–31.

46. Andrew, *For the President's Eyes Only*, 170.

47. Montague, *General Walter Bedell Smith*, 4.

48. Matthais, *America's Strategic Blunders*, 60.

49. Smith, *The Unknown CIA*, 42–43.

50. Barrett, *The CIA and Congress*, 1.

51. Matthais, *America's Strategic Blunders*, 73.

52. See Jackson and Claussen, *Organizational History of the Central Intelligence Agency*, 2:24n1.

53. Statement of Management Improvement Activities for the Current and Fiscal Years (1949). CIA-RDP80R01731R003400060006-7, CIA, CREST Archive.

54. Possibly Chief of Administration Martin McHugh's or Meredith P Davison's. Prepared as part of the CIA's budget estimates. See Jackson and Claussen, *Organizational History of the Central Intelligence Agency*, 1:57.

55. "Statement of Management Improvement Activities."

56. Prados, *Safe for Democracy*, 39–40. For the full directive, see Warner, *CIA Under Truman*, 213–17.

57. Barrett, *The CIA and Congress*, 32.

58. Barrett, 28.

59. Prados, *Safe for Democracy*, 40.

60. Barrett, *The CIA and Congress*, 41.

61. Barrett, 33. For a history of CIA involvement in the Marshall Plan, see Pisani, *The CIA and the Marshall Plan*.

62. Barrett, *The CIA and Congress*, 33–39.

63. Barrett, 41.

64. CIA went on to correct this estimate in the Intelligence Memorandum 225/1 "Estimate of Status of Atomic Warfare in the USSR," October 25, 1949, DOC_0001117738, CIA, CREST Archive.

65. Atomic Heritage Foundation, "Soviet Atomic Program—1946," June 5, 2014, https://ahf.nuclearmuseum.org/ahf/history/soviet-atomic-program-1946/. See also Nuclear Weapon Archive, "The Soviet Nuclear Weapons Program," last rev. December 12, 1997, https://nuclearweaponarchive.org/Russia/Sovwpnprog.html.

66. Barrett, *The CIA and Congress*, 53–54.

67. Letter from Harry S. Truman to Bess W. Truman, September 22, 1947, Truman Library, https://www.trumanlibrary.gov/library/truman-papers/correspondence-harry-s-truman-bess-wallace-truman-1921-1959/september-22-1947.

68. Letter from Harry S. Truman to Bess W. Truman, 53.

69. Barrett, *The CIA and Congress*, 53–54.

70. Barrett, 56.

71. Barrett, 56–57.

72. Barrett, 54.

73. Barrett, 57.

74. Barrett, 57.

75. Barrett, 59–60.

76. Barrett, 60.

77. Barrett, 60.

78. Barrett, 84.

79. Barrett, 86–88.

80. Barrett, 88–89.

81. Barrett, 88.

82. Vickers and the CIA History Staff, *The History of CIA's Office of Strategic Research*, x.

83. Snider, *The Agency and the Hill*, 43–44.

84. Ranelagh, *The Agency*, 281.

85. Perhaps more. Barrett quotes Leverett Saltonstall claiming that by the mid-1950s the budget was as high as $500–600 million. See Barrett, "Glimpses of a Hidden History," 275–77. Also see the conversation with author and Stephen Aftergood, Project on Government Security, November 27, 2021.

86. Warner, "Sources and Methods for the Study of Intelligence," 20.

87. Snider, *The Agency and the Hill*, 6–7.

88. Barrett, *The CIA and Congress*, 274.

89. Snider, *The Agency and the Hill*, xv.

90. Massachusetts Historical Society, Biographical Timeline, Leverett Saltonstall Papers, http://www.masshist.org/collection-guides/view/fa0272.

91. Snider, *The Agency and the Hill*, 4.

92. Barrett, *The CIA and Congress*, 273–76.

93. Saltonstall and Weeks, *Salty*, 106, 165–66. For the annual appropriation figures for the CIA, see note 85, above.

94. Massachusetts Historical Society, Biographical Timeline.

95. Saltonstall and Weeks, *Salty*, 108.

96. Saltonstall and Weeks, 139.

97. Saltonstall and Weeks, 132–33. For Saltonstall's recounting of the MacArthur hearings, see 149–50.

98. Letter to the Honourable Chan Gurney from Charles C. Cheston, June 2, 1947, CIA-RDP90-00610R000100020020-3, CIA, CREST Archive.

99. State Department, Office of the Historian, Letter from the Director of Central Intelligence (Hillenkoetter) to the Chairman of the Senate Armed Services Committee, in *Foreign Relations of the United States, 1945–1950: Emergence of the Intelligence Establishment* (1947), 575, https://history.state.gov/historicaldocuments/frus1945-50Intel/d217.

100. Snider, *The Agency and the Hill*, 40–41.

101. Saltonstall and Weeks, *Salty*, 165–66.

102. An Interview with Former General Counsel John Warner (1977), CIA, CREST Archive; see also Snider, *The Agency and the Hill*, 41.

103. Leffler, *A Preponderance of Power*, 179.

104. Snider, *The Agency and the Hill*, 41.

105. Hilsman, "Review Essay: On Intelligence," 137.

106. Snider, *The Agency and the Hill*, 95.

107. Snider, 98.

108. Hilsman, "Review Essay: On Intelligence," 137.

109. Snider, *The Agency and the Hill*, 95.

110. Snider, 116–17.

111. Grose, *Gentleman Spy*, 273.

112. Grose, 273.

113. US Congress, "National Defense Establishment."

114. US Congress, 527.

115. US Congress, 528.

116. US Congress, 526.

117. There was an earlier "Eberstadt Report" of 1945; here we discuss the second and main one. Best and Boerstling, *Staff Study Permanent Select Committee on Intelligence.*

118. Best and Boerstling.

119. Montague, *General Walter Bedell Smith*, 124.

120. Leffler, *A Preponderance of Power*, 42–43.

121. Grose, *Gentleman Spy*, 283.

122. Dulles, Jackson, and Correa, *The Central Intelligence Agency*, iii.

123. Dulles, Jackson, and Correa, 4–5.

124. Dulles, Jackson, and Correa, 6.

125. Dulles, Jackson, and Correa, 5, 7–9.

126. Dulles, Jackson, and Correa, 7.

127. Dulles, Jackson, and Correa, 16–17. For more on the underperforming of ORE, see the Church Committee report: US Congress, *Supplementary Detailed Staff Reports*, 15.

128. The Office of Collection and Dissemination was mostly responsible for biographical, library, and other resources as well as coordination collection requests. The three operations offices were the Office of Operations (collection from domestic contacts travelling overseas, and open-source collection), the Office of Special Operations (espionage and counterespionage), and the competing Office of Policy

Coordination, of which the director was appointed by State. See Dulles, Jackson, and Correa, *The Central Intelligence Agency*, 11.

129. Dulles, Jackson, and Correa, 65.
130. Dulles, Jackson, and Correa, 68 (emphasis added).
131. Dulles, Jackson, and Correa, 68.
132. Dulles, Jackson, and Correa, 5.
133. Dulles, Jackson, and Correa, 70.
134. Dulles, Jackson, and Correa, 70, 72–74.
135. Dulles, Jackson, and Correa, 85.
136. Dulles, Jackson, and Correa, 85–86.
137. Dulles, Jackson, and Correa, 86.
138. Dulles, Jackson, and Correa, 86.
139. Dulles, Jackson, and Correa, 86.
140. Dulles, Jackson, and Correa, 76.
141. Grose, *Gentleman Spy*, 324.
142. Grose, 291.
143. Grose, 11.
144. Grose, 290.
145. Mosely, *Dulles*, 246.
146. Montague, *General Walter Bedell Smith*, 44–46.
147. Montague, 43.
148. Jackson and Claussen, *Organizational History of the Central Intelligence Agency*, 1:48.
149. Montague, *General Walter Bedell Smith*, 46.
150. Montague, 125.
151. Montague, 49–50.
152. Jackson, 100.
153. Jackson, 23.

The Failure of the Office of Reports and Estimates, 1947–50

It would not be correct in the view of the record to say that the Office of Reports and Estimates, in the course of three years, had failed utterly to do what it was designed to do. A more accurate statement would be that it had done not only what was planned for it but much that was not planned and need not have been done. In consequence, the Office had unnecessarily dissipated its energies to the detriment of its main function.

—George Jackson (1954)

By 1949 the Office of Reports and Estimates (ORE) was producing five categories of intelligence: basic, current, staff, maps, and other miscellaneous publications. The current intelligence report included the Daily Summary and Weekly Summary for the president, Special Evaluations for rush estimates, weekly oral briefings, the monthly *Review of the World Situation*, and periodical publications for the Office Committee on International Communism as well as inter-branch publications on current topics.[1]

In addition, CIA had three types of report between 1949 and 1950: Intelligence Memoranda, the ORE Special Estimates Series, and Current Situation Reports. Of these, only the ORE Series fit the official definition of national intelligence in that it was created with the coordination of the other agencies. Up until 1949, only a quarter of the ORE reports could be considered a "national" estimate. Instead, the office diverted much of its time and attention to the Current Situation Reports.[2]

The Current Situation Reports became a convenient default for ORE, showcasing the knowledge of the regional branch chiefs without providing the necessary analysis that a long-range estimate would entail. Described as "relatively exhaustive strategic studies of countries and areas," they became, in George Jackson's view, "relatively easy to write" and a "sort of favorite" of the Agency. But they could not ever qualify as a national intelligence estimate, with 80 percent of the content of the situation reports basic intelligence—no more controversial, says Jackson, than the *Encyclopedia Britannica*.[3]

The view that current intelligence was sufficient, and that estimates could be rolled into the daily and weekly summaries, appears to have been the dominant opinion in 1948. When further explanation was needed, the Office of National Estimates produced Special Evaluations.[4] ORE produced around fifty reports that year, which included developing the Current Situation Reports as well as prodding the regional branches to produce proper estimates.[5]

A Lack of Understanding About Estimates

Why was it so hard for ORE to get its head around estimating? It appears that much of the blame can be put on the leadership of Theodore Babbitt, assistant director of ORE from 1948 to late 1950.[6] Babbitt, who was fifty-one in 1948, was a former instructor in romance languages at Yale as well as having been the assistant dean of freshmen. He had served as an Army colonel during the war, acting as a liaison and attaché role in the Mediterranean theater (in Ankara and Istanbul, in particular), and spent some time at the Office of Intelligence Research (OIR), the State Department's intelligence wing, which later became the Bureau of Intelligence and Research.[7]

Babbitt lacked the hard-headedness that William Langer was to later provide. He equivocated over major decisions and, while respecting the work of the most talented of his analysts, Montague and DeForest Van Slyck, never gave them the opportunity to impose a robust framework on ORE's intelligence work.

Another part of the problem appears to have been the question of who owned the project. From 1946, the department was broken up into "branches," later called divisions (in 1949), which included the Western Europe and Northern (Scandinavia and the UK/British Empire) branch; Eastern Europe–USSR; Middle East–Africa (including India); Far East–Pacific; and Latin America.[8] The branch chiefs were area specialists and were largely free from reporting back to the assistant director. Over time they assumed a de facto responsibility for writing and reviewing assessments. This responsibility was jealously guarded and often became a stumbling block for creating a formal estimates group staffed with intelligence analyst generalists. The area specialists had a mindset: "if the intelligence picture—that is, day-to-day events in every country in the world or each country of importance—were kept current, then the makers of policy would have no reason not to be able to deal intelligently with current problems." In other words, in the branch chiefs' view, current intelligence could take the place of long-term estimates.[9]

A third problem was more structural. Between 1946 and 1950 the department went through three name changes: the Central Reports Staff, the Office of Research and Evaluations, and the Office of Reports and Estimates. The first lasted only four months. Each name change was a response to a new directive from above; in the case of the Office of Research and Evaluations, an instruction from the Intelligence Advisory Authority gave the organization slightly more power to conduct its own research.[10] CIA historian Woodrow Kuhns says the Central Reports Staff "was born under a cloud of confusion in January 1946. Specifically, no consensus existed on what its mission was to be, although the president's concerns in creating CIG were clear enough."[11]

The problem was also exacerbated by the rapid growth of the organization under Vandenberg. According to Jackson, the new employees created confusion in the organization. Many of them were brought into CIG "without knowing, except vaguely, what it was, or what their work was to be. There was no opportunity to give them a grounding in the theories of central intelligence on which the Group had been founded nor to disabuse them of the idea . . . that current intelligence was the primary if not sole function of the office."[12]

The Planning and Production of Estimates

Neither was there any formalized leadership to help guide and then approve the work of ORE. The Agency consistently struggled with questions of who was responsible for liaising between departments and between oversight and coordinating boards like the Intelligence Advisory Board (from September 1947, called the Intelligence Advisory Committee).

The Interdepartmental Coordinating and Planning Staff was "an early go-between" to liaise between the director of central intelligence and the Intelligence Advisory Board. CIA historian Arthur Darling says it was "thwarted" by the branch chiefs themselves, who set up alternative committees that undermined the work of the Interdepartmental Coordinating and Planning Staff. Hillenkoetter tried to ameliorate the situation by recognizing the alternative committees rather than confronting the problem they created. This meant the whole process of instructing work through the DCI to the board had become muddled. "In short," says Darling, "the whole procedure had become ridiculous, and almost everybody knew it."[13]

The Policy Advisory Board, which seems to have been in effect from mid-1947, was little more than a water-cooler gang, "an almost social gathering" that had met sporadically on Friday afternoons and had reflected the informal, small size of ORE at that time. By 1949 this purely advisory group had taken on more substance in an Intelligence Production Board, whose job was to review production requirements, create periodic plans centered around production, and act as an arbiter when there were internal issues over who was doing what and when. It was therefore both a planning committee and a board of review and appeal, but not what the Board of National Estimates would later become: a quality control mechanism. Jackson suggests the real role of the Intelligence Production Board was to take the pressure off Babbitt, shifting the responsibility for managing internal fights away from himself as assistant director.[14] It was also a means to curtail the power of the branch chiefs: who didn't have the time to devote to a proper board, and in such a formalized setting might soften some of their criticisms of the estimators' work. Perhaps unsurprisingly, the new Intelligence Production Board only met twice. The first meeting, called for January 13, 1949, was intended to form a plan of the first quarter's work and discussed requirements for national economic intelligence as well as for a government foreign information program. The second meeting, on March 30, was to discuss changes to the Weekly Summary. No record of the results of the first meeting exist, and the changes suggested by the board to the Weekly Summary appear to have never been implemented.[15]

In mid-1949 a new board was set up, the Estimates Production Board, composed of the same members: the branch and staff chiefs. This reorganization was prompted by the release of the Dulles-Jackson-Correa Survey Report, which found that the DCI had failed in producing coordinated national intelligence, and it recommended a small estimates office supported by a larger office that provided basic intelligence. The reaction to this was predictably shortsighted. Hillenkoetter himself thought the Dulles Report's proposals were of dubious merit. At ORE they were reluctant to make the estimates group a stand-alone entity, instead wanting to see it contained within a larger office, not unlike the system they were already running. When it came to working with the other agencies (at State, or the service wings) ORE was openly hostile, seeing itself as having moved on from the shackles of coordination and afraid it might be returned to a mere reviewing and collating role. ORE's cynical institutional response was that the Dulles recommendations might be possible but that such radical changes should not be attempted at once.[16]

CIA was under considerable pressure to respond to the Dulles Report, although NSC-50 had lessened the changes the Agency was required to make. Nevertheless, a direct answer to Dulles had political value because, "in the face of so much clearly expressed dissatisfaction, the Office would be left vulnerable in case of any future intelligence failure."[17] Whether a reform was genuine, however, or was a quick patch-up is arguable. Jackson believes the branches (regional desks) were sufficiently experienced to contribute to a new office of national estimates but were wholesale against the idea as it undermined their own power. Without their cooperation, serious reform was unlikely to succeed. The Agency decided not to take on the power of the branch chiefs but instead to initiate a quick makeover. As described, this involved replacing the old Intelligence Production Board with a new Estimates Production Board, merging the staff intelligence and current groups, and giving each branch its own estimates group. At least in name, ORE had responded to the demands of the Dulles Report.[18]

In reality, ORE had made more work for itself. The merging of current and staff intelligence did not remove the pressure to produce daily and weekly summaries, and they continued to work as two separate groups. Neither did the creation of "baby estimates groups" within the branches mean much; they continued to perform the function they had in the past. The establishment of the new Estimates Production Board, if it were to truly fulfill the role of a board of final review, would pull the branch chiefs away from their regional desks. A repeat of its predecessor's failings ensued: the new board met five times from February 1950 but accomplished little. The reforms, then, of 1949 achieved nothing more than the continuation of the status quo. "It succeeded nevertheless," says Jackson, "in introducing new confusion even into the status quo."[19]

Hillenkoetter's Reaction to the Dulles Report

Darling also recounts the reaction at ORE to the Dulles Report. Babbitt asked Lewis E. Stevens, head of his Plans and Policy Staff, to write a draft response on the report and requested feedback from the branches. Their view was that the branches would, as a matter of course in reporting on their regions, conduct estimates. The branches were led by the chief of the Western Europe section, S. A. Dulany Hunter. Opposing them was Ludwell Lee Montague, who believed that estimating needed to be executed by a dedicated team. Montague saw estimating as "quasi-judicial, an argumentative process." This debate was reflected in Stevens's final report. While acknowledging that ORE was split down the middle, Stevens recommended an estimates division that was big enough to do its own high-level research, with an enlarged reports and research office to support it (and with an economic intelligence unit as well).[20]

Montague wrote to Babbitt on February 11, 1949, agreeing with the substance of Stevens's report but highlighting that the Dulles Report had been "technically naive" on the matter of interdepartmental coordination. This wasn't going to happen anytime soon, thought Montague, without a complete reorganization of the intelligence community. Montague wanted to see an estimating committee that took on board the views of the other intelligence wings and emphasized dissents (which he believed were useful to policymakers). The committee would represent the views of the departments and would be guided by "suitable procedural safeguards" and "authoritative leadership." The responsibility for the estimates would be taken by the Intelligence Advisory Committee (IAC).[21]

Babbitt disagreed that the IAC would bear the collective responsibility, believing the DCI and CIA were ultimately responsible. He also wanted to stop dissents from appearing on estimates from agencies that were raising issues they weren't charged to do—for example, the Navy raising a problem with a political matter if the State Department, which was responsible for political matters, did not have an objection.

It appears that Hillenkoetter made the final decision as to how the ORE report would respond to the Dulles group. He ruled there was no reason to create a separate estimates division outside of ORE but that it could be done within the office. In doing so, Hillenkoetter rejected the recommendations of the Dulles Report. Even Darling (who is pro-Hillenkoetter in most of his history) recognizes this, saying: Hillenkoetter "had not seen fit to carry out the wishes of the Dulles Group for an Estimates Division."[22]

Internally, CIA was understandably sensitive that it might get caught proving some of the Dulles Report's criticisms. In a memo to the DCI from Prescott Childs, who was in charge of interagency coordination, dated February 8, 1949, Childs complained that Babbitt was not letting the State Department see the estimates, even when they were in State's domain. Similarly, the Air Force had complained that they had not been consulted on an estimate titled "Reinforcing and Uncontrolled International Air Traffic." Babbitt's answer had been that State never met its deadlines. So ORE clearly had given up involving the other agencies. Child's concern was that the Dulles Report had made it plain that coordination needed fixing, and CIA shouldn't be seen to be the problem.[23]

Yet the Agency could not help itself. In January 1948 Hillenkoetter briefly gave Babbitt responsibility for the Scientific Branch, taking the job from Wallace R. Brode, who had been humiliated by a call from Vannevar Bush, head of the Research and Development Board, asking CIA to take over nuclear intelligence. As head of the scientific division, Brode was "completely stymied" by the recommendation, as he could not recruit staff and does not appear to have had nuclear security clearance. It is not clear from Darling's history what happened except that Brode resumed the role three months later and the episode reflected badly on Hillenkoetter.[24]

While compiling the Dulles Report in 1948, William Harding Jackson interviewed Babbitt, alongside his deputy, Capt. Clarence L. Winecoff. Jackson was curious what part Babbitt had played in Winecoff's appointment, given the fact he had "no intelligence experience whatever, . . . nor did he appear to have any aptitude at the work." Babbitt said Winecoff was a Naval representative and had been given the job as deputy of ORE, traditionally a Navy appointment, just as chief of ORE was the State Department's domain.[25] So much, indeed, for Dulles's view that the Agency needed to be staffed with "competent and highly trained men and women."

Internal Reviews of ORE

By mid-1949 Winecoff, now promoted to Hillenkoetter's executive assistant, was urging ORE to go back to the drawing board. He wanted a blueprint, and this came in the shape of the Reitzel Report, which Darling says aimed to "learn what kinds of estimates they were supposed to make, and what reports they should file."[26]

The chair of the committee, William Reitzel from the Global Survey Group, was one of the more analytical of the members of ORE. The committee decided to start from scratch and try to determine what ORE's core mission was, going back further than the Dulles-Jackson-Correa investigation had done and looking at the impact of the 1947 National Security Act's directives on the programming of estimates. Their judgment was (and, remember, this was 1949) that "no adequate definition of an ORE mission exists."[27] Instead, the process had evolved over time and in an ad hoc way. In the year to July 1949 the committee noted that ORE had moved from broad, long-range reports for a high-level audience to quite short-term, nonpredictive reports for an audience at a more working level.

Reitzel's committee also wondered about estimates that fit indirectly into assessments of the Soviet intentions, like the 1948 *Soviet and Satellite Grain* paper. Where did it fit in the hierarchy of national intelligence estimates? To make the assessment, CIA would need to coordinate with a number of different agencies, which is what the National Security Act expected the Agency to do. But in itself, it was only one small part of a larger picture of the Soviet economy and could only show a very limited impact on Moscow's intentions. Yet CIA in 1948 had neither the information nor the expertise to gauge what the Soviet grain harvest would achieve, and the paper had been unsatisfactory. Should the estimate have even been attempted? This discussion showed some of the day-to-day problems that beset the shop-floor analysts, whom those at higher levels neither appreciated nor much cared about.[28]

The Reitzel Report was delivered on July 19, 1949. The title, *Analysis of ORE Production, with Conclusions, First Report*, was perhaps a bit optimistic. There was never a second report. Instead, it looks like Babbitt quashed it. While Reitzel had artfully dodged Montague's strong argument for an Estimates Division, he had less artfully implied that ORE's failure to deliver national intelligence lay with Babbitt's management, which had produced haphazard, unrelated, and inconsequential reporting.[29]

In fact, Babbitt was also fielding criticism from the State Department. While Reitzel was writing his analysis of ORE, W. Park Armstrong at State was also pushing for an estimates division, following the Dulles model. Having spent some time at OIR and State before coming to ORE, Babbitt clearly stiffened at this characterization of his office's output as one of confusion and ineptitude, particularly when—in his view—the State Department was less cooperative than Defense.[30]

A second internal investigation came only eight months after the Reitzel committee tendered its findings. This appears to have been prompted after CIA had had time to consider the Dulles Report and NSC-50, and had considered that a reorganization at ORE in October 1947 was needed. The Stout committee, however, added little that was new to a reassessment of the office, nor did it shift things at all. Chaired by Hiram Stout of the Northern branch, the committee was composed of staff selected by the chiefs of the branch offices. An observer at the time wrote: "The report as a whole reflects a Babel of tongues, confusion of purposes, and default of doctrine which unfortunately is characteristic of the Office of Reports and Estimates. From the welter of words it does emerge, however, that two parties exist: (1) those who would do something to remedy the existing situation, (2) those who were opposed to any remedial action."[31]

Babbitt's ineffectiveness as assistant director of ORE was reported in another internal report dated June 9, 1948. This document, Administration and Management, is a comprehensive review of CIA made department-by-department and runs seventy-five pages long. Babbitt is described as "personally agreeable" but "not generally considered to have much force" and as having owed his senior position at ORE to his previous experience at OIR.[32]

According to the report, the regional desk chiefs were probably "the backbone" of ORE, but the quality of their work was considered mixed, and they "figured largely in the controversies which distinguish a number of the working relationships."[33] The Western Europe branch was considered by numerous people to embody everything that was wrong with ORE and was considered the poorest branch but gave as good as it got by claiming ORE was throttling its attempts to add intelligence comments to current intelligence reports. The recently replaced chief of the Eastern Europe and USSR branch was criticized for "carrying all his intelligence in his head." His successor, an Army intelligence officer, ran a branch that was considered weak, or spotty at best, and—as had been the case under the former chief—was guilty of making "a priori interpretations of Soviet intentions and capabilities." To complicate matters, this branch was split into three (overlapping) desks: political, economic, and transportation. The Near East and Africa desk was considered the best and was run by a former archaeologist and naval intelligence officer. The Far Eastern branch was "fair"; the North Europe region, split into Britain and Scandinavia, was run by a former professor (likely Hiram Stout) in public administration, with poor staff and low productivity. The Latin America desk was managed by a former schoolmaster and colonel who had been secretary-general to the Inter-American Board. His reports were considered academic and pedestrian, but the report considered his staff had failed to give warning of the Bogotá incident.[34]

In addition to the regional branches, there were five panels devoted to the global survey, economics, international organizations (United Nations and others), transportation, and military. Of these, the Global Survey Group, run by Ludwell Lee Montague, was the most lauded. Montague was considered "one of the most capable and senior men in ORE," and, despite his friction with the

Western European branch (Montague was critical of its efforts to produce estimates), his monthly *Review of the World Situation as It Relates to the Security of the United States* was considered "the most thoughtful and worthwhile" of ORE publications.[35] Montague and his associate Ray Cline were also the conscience of ORE and took a hand in reviewing and providing quality control on other reports and estimates, and "their influence seems to be rather pervasive and generally good." They had a low opinion of the output of the rest of ORE.[36] In comparison, the military panel, run by three senior officers of the Army, Navy, and Air Force, had failed to impress. Their contribution to ORE's output was minimal, and they produced little intelligence of their own.[37]

The Administration and Management assessment is backed up by one Stephen Penrose, a former employee of CIA. When compiling the Dulles Report in early 1948, Mathais Correa had received a letter from Penrose, passed on from the special assistant to the secretary of Defense, W. J. McNeil. Penrose, who had worked for Special Operations (OSO or SO), had left CIA complaining of inexperienced management, infighting, and a complete lack of respect in the intelligence community. While he had left CIA bitter, "everything," said McNeil, "had a basis in fact."[38] His testimony is worth printing in full:

> In spite of this situation within SO it is still the one branch of CIA which has the respect of outside agencies. OIR in State prefers to receive raw intelligence direct from SO rather than in processed form from OR&E not only for the sake of speed but because the type of processing now given by OR&E detracts from rather than adds to the value of the reports. With rare exceptions the studies put out by OR&E are such as might be written by any well-informed person, and they command little respect from the users of such reports in State, Army or Navy. The Strategic Intelligence Division of the Army recently pointed out that it had received no useful additions to its files since the R&A Branch of OSS had been broken up. It considers its conferences with CIA to be largely a waste of time, particularly as regards Russian matters. Captain Frankel (Navy) of the OR&E Russian division seems content to rest upon his short visits to Russia as sufficient qualification of him as a Russian expert. A report on an aviation subject was recently prepared for OR&E by the Library of Congress. The research people of the Library developed a rather low opinion of the OR&E men with whom they had contact who seemed to be astonished at the quality of the report, which they felt was beyond their capacity. . . . An unduly large proportion of the effort of OR&E is devoted to putting out the daily intelligence summary. This publication, containing chiefly State Department materials, could be put together in short order by a small unit of editorial analysts instead of requiring half the day of many branch heads

and their staffs, as appears now often to be the case. OR&E, which should be the top research and analysis office in the government, is headed by a former assistant military attaché in Turkey who was never distinguished either for research or administrative ability during his pre-war stay on the Yale faculty.[39] His stature is not such as to attract highly qualified research experts. . . . The disturbing situation which has been described is the more alarming because it occurs at a time when, as almost never before, the government needs an effective, expanding, professional intelligence service. On the contrary, CIA is losing its professionals, and is not acquiring competent new personnel who might gain experience in the only rapid way possible, namely by close association with those professionals. It is dependent in most working branches for imaginative and energetic direction upon career military men of a type which is not apt to be either imaginative or energetic as regards non-military intelligence or procedures. As a direct result, CIA has failed to win the confidence of the military services or the State Department and is rapidly losing what confidence they had had in its predecessor organizations. Yet effective cooperation with these departments is a sine qua non of CIA success. Under present conditions such cooperation does not exist to any practical degree. Other departments feel no assurance that they can rely upon CIA to perform intelligence functions which they will privately admit could and probably should be performed centrally. Without that assurance they will continue, as they are continuing, to operate their individual intelligence services in a manner which cannot but nullify the principles of coordination and centralization which were implicit in the establishment of CIA.[40]

Responding to the Korean War Outbreak

The North Korean invasion of South Korea quickly drew attention to the weaknesses of ORE's status quo structure. Here, George Jackson's official history claims, ORE "proved unable to deal satisfactorily with the problems that ensued."[41] When the different branches all delivered opposing assessments, and with no independent board to mediate and make rulings, the weight of responsibility fell on the unwilling shoulders of Babbitt. His answer was to form another committee. The Special Staff was created on July 3, 1950, just nine days after the invasion, in a memorandum that required the Special Staff to advise "on all matters arising from the situation in Korea" and gave the staff "responsibility for preparing reports and estimates bearing on the present crisis."[42] There is a whiff of panic in the wording of the memorandum, which gave the Special Staff authority to call on all the materials it needed from ORE, and gave the eight appointees relief from any current work in which they were engaged. No branch chiefs were invited to the staff, obviating any quarrels that might have come from their entrenched views on the subject. Privately, Babbitt told the staff that they were his personal representatives in dealing with the branches, and he—for the first time—took a very hands-on approach to their work.

By the spring of 1950 inertia had created an ORE with estimating spread over several teams and Babbitt unwilling to do the dirty work of forcing resignations. The Webb Staff Study arrived on Hillenkoetter's desk for comments on July 7, 1950, just after the North Koreans crossed the 38th parallel. The author, John Magruder, now believed that Hillenkoetter and Babbitt were never going to get around to producing estimates.[43]

On October 6, William Harding Jackson, now arrived at CIA, reported that he had been reading the National Security Council's NSC-81, United States Actions with Respect to North Korea (September 9, 1950), and in his view, it could not be described as an intelligence estimate. He said he had been searching but "[I] have been unable to locate any coordinated national estimate dealing with the intentions and capabilities of the North Koreans to attack in the first place."[44]

The Special Staff was dissolved on October 26, 1950. The reason given was that the "emergency" that had prompted the forming of the staff had stabilized, and ORE was now able to assume its duties. But the real reason was probably the imminent arrival of William Langer.[45]

On assuming the job of DCI, General Smith moved to set up the Office of National Estimates as an estimates-dedicated office. Babbitt held the position of assistant director of the Office of Research and Reports until Max Millikan took over on January 16, 1951.[46] On February 9, Deputy Director of Central Intelligence William Harding Jackson spoke to a Mr. J. J. Wadsworth of the Federal Civil Defense Agency who was looking for someone to head their intelligence division. Explaining that the office had been reorganized, Jackson recommended Theodore Babbitt as a highly regarded and available candidate. Wadsworth was interested. Babbitt began his new job with Civil Defense on March 21, 1951.[47]

The Content of the Estimates from 1946–50

Those reports generated by CIG/CIA that met the description of a long-range estimate were few and mostly centered on Soviet intentions. Writing many years later about ORE 1: The Basis of Soviet Foreign Policy (July 1946), veteran analyst Willard Matthias concluded that "it was a good pioneering estimate on the USSR."[48] ORE 1 was the work of the CIG's Office of Research and

Evaluation and was a break from the practice of intelligence being a weekly or monthly report. ORE 1 provided what Matthias believes was the thinking of most Kremlin watchers at the time.

ORE 1, which was written by Montague in just a few days, was not coordinated with the other intelligence agencies.[49] It ran to twelve pages, including just over one page of summary with two enclosures of details in the remaining ten pages, covering Soviet foreign and military policy. Each paragraph was numbered, as most estimates were. It used language such as that Soviet policy would be "grasping and opportunistic" and run by a small clique that was prejudiced, shrewd, ignorant of the world, and led by Marxist dogmatism.

Montague's report predicted the Soviets were preparing for the "inevitable" clash with capitalism that Marxist–Leninism expects, but that the Soviets would avoid conflict for "an indefinite period."[50] The Soviet regime needed to build up its relative power. It would not provoke a major war until ready, yet it would not miss an opportunity to undermine the West and push the boundaries when the occasion permitted. The USSR wanted to preserve its power east of the Stettin-Trieste line and would not permit any blocs that weakened that power. It aimed to increase its influence over Germany and Austria as well as Greece, Turkey, and Iran, but also to the Far East by limiting US reach into China, Korea, and Japan. The Soviets would keep a conventional force of 4.5 million men and pursue air and nuclear forces.

To this point, as Matthias recounts, there appears little here that was not touched upon by George Kennan's opinion piece six months earlier. More detail comes in summaries of Eastern European reactions to Soviet influence: Poland, Romania, and Bulgaria had active oppositions; Hungary was mostly compliant, but Moscow was unconvinced of its reliability and applied coercion.[51] ORE 1, then, demonstrates a good grasp of what was happening behind the Iron Curtain but with little precision in the language used: "an indefinite period" was not that helpful to a policymaker preparing for a Soviet attack.

According to Matthias, this vagueness was not helped by CIG's director, Hoyt Vandenberg. ORE 1 did not, Matthias says, "bear the imprimatur of a politically powerful Director of Central Intelligence (DCI), as was the case of estimates produced after 1950." Vandenberg, Matthias claims, wrote a secret memorandum to Truman on August 24, 1946, that equivocated over the likelihood of near-term Soviet military action. On the one hand, the memo asserted, there was no sign of Soviet military buildup or any break with a plan to strengthen its economy in the short to medium term. On the other, the memo claimed the USSR could, in a very short space of time, overrun Europe and North Asia and "secure those areas without much difficulty." The regime was also vulnerable to a "combination of militaristic marshals and ideologists [who] might establish ascendancy over Stalin and the Politburo and decide on a war of conquest." Climbing down from this rhetoric, the memo had stressed that recent saber-rattling by Tito in Yugoslavia, "atomic diplomacy," and Moscow's demand for joint control of the Bosphorus and Hellespont might really be only "an intensive war of nerves" but argued that "the possibility of direct Soviet military action or irresponsible action by Soviet satellites cannot be disregarded."[52]

Matthias says that the writers of this memo are unknown but that, six months later (in January 1947), a revised estimate was produced titled ORE 1/1 "Soviet Tactics in International Affairs," which he believes was a response to the secret memorandum.[53] While not specifically referring to the memo, the revised estimate acknowledged some softening of the Soviet position and reiterated the earlier view of ORE 1 that the regime would oscillate between opportunism and compromise as it saw fit.[54]

For Matthias, the advice given by CIG is demonstrative of what in the next decade would be an intelligence community busy trying to avoid the pitfalls of Pearl Harbor intelligence and "trying to have it both ways." Donald Steury points out that, although ORE 1 "represented exactly the kind of high level estimate of foreign situations" CIG was created to produce, "it stands out as virtually unique among the crop of estimates ORE turned out." CIG created only four estimates on the Soviet Union in 1946. Too much labor and time, says Steury, was being consumed "answering the mail"—the everyday work of situation reports and daily briefs. The same time that ORE 1 was being written, the Joint Intelligence Committee commissioned a working group of Army, Navy, and Air Force intelligence on Soviet intentions. CIG was not invited. "While ORE-1 was more concise and perhaps more balanced" than the military intelligence estimate, writes Steury, it offered little more. "In short, the new kid on the block still had a lot to prove."[55]

In two later estimates—CIA-1, "Review of the World Situation as It Relates to the Security of the United States" (September 26, 1947) and ORE 41-49, "The Effects of a US Foreign Military Aid Program" (February 24, 1949)—Matthias believed the analysts had stayed true to their assessment.[56] The September 1947 estimate mirrored the policymaker's view that had prompted the Marshall Plan.[57] It claimed the USSR was the only power that threatened the United States and was capable of overrunning Europe, the Near East, China, and Korea but had no power projection outside of that. ORE analysts did not believe the USSR would start a war in the near future but would instead use political, economic, and psychological tools to extend its influence. The United States must guard against financial meltdown in Europe and shore up its economic and political institutions, which would in turn restrain the USSR.[58]

In the second estimate, two years later, ORE 41-49 "The Effects of a US Foreign Military Aid Program," the Agency gave its opinion on the political environment prior to the signing of the North Atlantic Treaty Agreement. Once again, the analysts saw no likelihood of a war with the Soviet Union short of Moscow sensing a direct and imminent attack. The USSR would instead continue the same strategy, which appeared to be showing success.[59] "The question of how great and what kind of military threat was actually posed by the USSR," says Matthias "troubled national estimating from its beginning, as the passages from ORE-1, ORE-1/1 and CIA 1 confirm . . . the problem was not only troublesome but had enormous impact upon US diplomacy and defense budgets."[60]

Matthias adds a further note that probably implicates Montague, as the estimates chief, as much as it does the DCI (in this case, Hillenkoetter).[61] As an example of CIA's lack of influence at the top level, Matthias cites ORE 3-49 "Consequences of Troop Withdrawal from Korea," written in February 28, 1949, less than a year before the North Korean invasion (June 1950). In ORE 3-49, CIA analysts warned that withdrawal of US troops would "probably in time be followed by an invasion," and it was unlikely South Korean troops would have the strength to resist, whereas a "moderate US force" would likely deter any aggression. Within five months the US forces were out of the peninsula.[62] However, the obvious question is what "probably in time" means. For an agency charged with providing policymakers with clarity and prescience in their intelligence reporting, this seems unforgivably vague.

The formats of the ORE reports of 1946–49 are inconsistent, which probably illustrates the mix of approaches between the regional branch chiefs and Montague's Global Survey Group. Most are structured with a summary at the beginning, followed by an enclosure that provides the main argument and details. Technical surveys, like ORE 2 and ORD 2/1 (on Soviet broadcasts) and ORE 3/1 (on Soviet weapon production), usually dispensed with a summary, although ORE 4/1 (Soviet petroleum resources) did include one. Estimates, like ORE 7 (Bolivia) and ORE 6/1 (Greece), kept the same summary and enclosure format. In ORE 53 (Spain) and ORE 8-48 (Argentina), the enclosure was only used for a dissent from State.[63] Many of the 1947 OREs used subsections titled Strategic Importance, Probable Developments, Political Situation, Economic Situation, Military Situation, and Foreign Affairs as part of the summary.

There is no evidence of research questions or hypotheses in any ORE until November 1947's ORE 55 (Palestine), where the report tries to estimate what attitudes the Arab governments might adopt toward a Jewish state and whether they would be favorable to the United Nations, Britain, and the United States, among others. Assumptions begin to be a regular starting point for estimates in 1947—for instance, that the USSR would not sign the Japan peace treaty, with some attempt at counterfactuals.[64] In ORE 49 "The Current Situation in Palestine," CIA writes that there are three possible decisions the UN General Assembly might make, admitting that "it is impossible to predict which of these developments will occur," a phrasing that would later be contentious regarding Soviet aggression.[65] This is ameliorated in ORE 55 "The Consequences of the Partition of Palestine," a month later, where CIA offers six likely outcomes from the General Assembly decision and then puts three questions to be answered in the report: How will the Arab–Jewish conflict develop and with what results; how will the stability of the Middle East be affected; and how will US strategic and commercial interests be affected?[66] The answers, however, are vague and not dealt with in a systematic way. In ORE 9-48 "Succession of Power in the USSR," discussing the possible death of Joseph Stalin, three contingencies are added: that Stalin might disappear from the political scene leaving Vyacheslav Molotov as leader; that Molotov might predecease Stalin, leaving Andrei Zhdanov as leader; or that several members of the Politburo might die simultaneously with some plan of succession in place.[67] (Stalin was, in the end, succeeded by Georgy Malenkov, an interim leader before Nikita Khrushchev defeated him in a leadership contest.)

In ORE 6-48 "Consequences of Communist Accession to Power in Italy by Legal Means," published in March 1948, a new section in the enclosure is titled Assumptions, and three new sections follow: Direct Consequences, Effects on Soviet Strategy and Policy, and Reactions Elsewhere.[68] This format is not repeated. In ORE 10-48 "Consequences of Certain Courses of Action with Respect to Greece," a month later, a new format is introduced in the summary: The Problem (and sometimes Facts Bearing on the Problem), Discussion, and Conclusions.[69] While this format change might be explained by the contingent nature of the topic, the same system appeared in April's ORE 22-48 "Possibility of Direct Soviet Military Action During 1948" and in July's ORE 58-48 "The Strategic Value to the USSR of the Conquest of Western Europe and the Far East (to Cairo)" (with "Assumptions" added); ORE 26-48 "The Prospects for a United States of Indonesia" published in June; and September's ORE 60-48 "Threats to the Security of the United States," which retained "the Problem," but abandoned the others. ORE 29-48 "Possible Program of Future Soviet Moves in Germany" earlier in April dispensed with the format altogether, as did ORE 44-48 "Prospects for Survival of the Republic of Korea," in October, and ORE 27-48 "Possible Developments in China," in November 1948. In May of 1949 the format returned with ORE 17-49 "The Strategic Importance of the Far East to the US and USSR" using "Problem," "Scope" (definition of geographical area), and "Assumptions." But by 1950, in ORE 7-50 "Probable Developments in Taiwan," the format moved to the situations style of "Strategic Importance," "Probable Developments," "Political Situation," "Economic Situation," "Military Situation," and "Foreign Affairs."[70] In ORE 48-49 "The Soviet Position in Approaching the CFM," the analysts offer two alternative interpretations of why the Soviets are reconvening the Council of Foreign Ministers in the wake of the Berlin Blockade stalemate.[71] This format is more conscious of policy decisions that might be impacted by the estimate's conclusions.

Grappling with how to express what "the Problem" was and what "assumptions" to make were features of an estimate like ORE 58-48 "The Strategic Value to the USSR of the Conquest of Western Europe and the Far East (to Cairo)," says veteran analyst Raymond Garthoff. The estimate was to discuss whether a successful invasion would put the Soviets in a stronger position: "The paper failed to achieve its aim. It could not get beyond the problem of what assumptions to make (e.g., if Soviet actions caused a war, would it escalate or end in a negotiated peace?) and it presented its main conclusion that the Soviets would be unlikely to attempt such a conquest, thereby earning a justified US Air Force dissent claiming that, by estimating intent, the paper had gone beyond its announced purpose."[72]

The continuing series of "current situations" in certain states, like ORE 15 "The Situation in Korea" in March and ORE 13-48 "The Situation in Austria" in April 1948, among others, kept to the original 1947 format of "Strategic Importance," "Probable Developments," "Political Situation," "Economic Situation," "Military Situation," and "Foreign Affairs." Yet, oddly, ORE 47-48 "Consequences of Withdrawal of United States Forces from Tsingtao," published in June 1948, kept to the 1947 "Situation" format.

For estimates of future courses of action (those most often titled "consequences of," "possible," or "probable" developments, etc.), there appeared to be no systematic approach to writing them. Other OREs in the same period (1948–49) had no common format at all. While one reason for the lack of standardization of future estimates might be that the topics were diverse and a format restricted the analysts into something too rigid, the number of experiments over the period with different formats suggest attempts were made to standardize the reports.

Dissents: ORE's Estimates Considered "Dangerous"

Perhaps the most telling evidence of the struggles of ORE is in the dissents against the estimates they produced. In the case of ORE 16/1 "Soviet Objectives in Latin America" (1947), the Office of Naval Intelligence complained that the subject had not been explored properly and the "real and latent danger from Communism in Latin America, as expressed in this paper, has been exaggerated." The tenor of the paper, the dissent continued, was based on the assumption of some "inevitable conflict in the unforeseeable future between the Soviets and the capitalist world," so, the ONI concluded, whether the Latin American states could deal with it in the present day "appears not to bear on the problem."[73] In ORE 9-48 "Cuban Political Trends," the State Department's intelligence organization claimed that "the alarming tone of the summary is not justified by the main text of the report, nor by the known facts of the situation."[74] In ORE 58-48 "The Strategic Value to the USSR of the Conquest of West Europe and the Near East (to Cairo)," the Air Force's A-2 complained that, while the estimate had attempted to be objective, it had endeavored to show Soviet intent, of which there was no evidence to discern it. It was also determined on the "basis of Western, not Soviet logic."[75]

Perhaps most disturbing was the dissent against ORE 91-49 "Estimate of the Effects of the Soviet Possession of the Atomic Bomb upon the Security of the US" just seven months before Langer and Kent arrived. Here the Army, Navy, Air Force, and State all dissented. The Army's G-2 felt that ORE had understated Soviet aggression to the point that it could seriously affect the security of the United States. The ONI argued that the estimate was based on "extremely hypothetical speculations on 'what might happen.'" State believed ORE was in no position to assess the intentions of the Soviet Union, which may have changed entirely since it now possessed the atomic bomb. Agreeing, the Air Force claimed the Kremlin had considered itself weaker than the United States prior to getting the bomb but was no longer restrained from aggression. This one point was enough to make "the CIA estimate, ORE 91-49, dangerous as an intelligence basis for national policy."[76] It is difficult to read these dissents today without feeling the unease that the high-ranking policymakers in the White House, the Department of State, or the military must have felt seeing such blatant contempt for the work of their central intelligence organization.

This level of damning dissents was effectively dismissed by ORE's estimates group as well as the branches, who found the system of sitting down with dissenting agencies "tedious and often little more than a discussion of semantics." Instead, ORE argued that their critics did not understand the terms "concurrence" and "substantial dissent" and did not employ them in a way that was meaningful or helpful.[77]

Montague on the Failure of ORE

As someone who was on the ground from the very early days, Montague's views are worth recalling. Montague had been head of the Central Reports Staff under the CIG's first director, Sidney Souers. He had also worked under DCIs Vandenberg and Hillenkoetter. Souers had wanted a small team of professionals running the estimates division, but Vandenberg had grown the staff to a counterproductive size. Despite this, the quality of recruitment was poor: "anyone able to reach the door was admitted," recounted Montague, "but ORE had little success recruiting men of discernment and mature judgement."[78]

Montague cites three other reasons for ORE's failure. One, which was true also of CIG/CIA in general, was a lack of understanding of the mission of the organization. This had been demonstrated in the National Security Act of 1947, where the way in which CIA was to work and its specific duties were left to the NSC to flesh out, and even then with such imprecision that the infighting between the IAC agencies was unchecked. A second reason was a lack of leadership: Montague believed someone with intelligence experience and more forceful in pushing CIG/CIA viewpoints was necessary. Vandenberg in particular had antagonized the representatives of the Agency's governing body, the IAC, who returned the favor, says Montague, with "hostility and obstructionalism." One example was the behavior of Adm. Thomas Inglis, a key member of the IAC. The more Montague pushed Vandenberg to allow him to pursue the primary goal of producing national intelligence estimates, the more Inglis got in the way. As the Navy representative on the IAC, Inglis was not inclined to see Naval Intelligence undermined by the new central intelligence agency, and he insisted that Vandenberg stop Montague from writing estimates. Instead of having the Office of Naval Intelligence contribute to CIG's coordinated reports, Inglis wanted ORE to contribute basic intelligence to ONI. He ruled that Navy intelligence representatives were only "messenger boys." They refused to base themselves in the Office of National Estimates offices, as they were expected to, and refused to meet with Montague's staff to discuss estimates. Instead, they demanded that Montague's people courier their draft estimates to ONI, where they would sit with "intolerable delays" only to be returned with "scornful and captious" feedback to ORE. When the NSC criticized ORE for not doing its job of coordinating between the intelligence agencies, Montague remonstrated, "It was Inglis and his colleagues on the IAC who refused such participation where ORE sought it."[79]

A report titled *Preparation of ORE-1* describes the process of writing an urgent estimate without any of the support that would have been expected. Written by the acting assistant director of ORE (presumably Montague), it tells of a Friday request to produce an estimate by Monday afternoon. The substance of the estimate appeared to already exist in JIS 80/26, which had been coordinated and signed off by the Agency's Joint Intelligence Staff. Montague called the group together on Friday afternoon with the intention of dividing up tasks needed to write the estimate and avoid duplication. He found the Joint Intelligence Staff had no idea how to do this and had instead passed the job on to the regional branches. The branch experts could not then be found so late on a Friday. On Saturday morning Montague again attempted to get confirmation that JIS 80/26 was the right document to be working from. He discovered the branch experts were working on a draft but not using JIS 80/26, instead working impromptu on whatever they thought was relevant. Realizing no one was using the one piece of intelligence that had been coordinated and agreed to,

Montague himself worked until nine o'clock that night, and then Sunday until three in the afternoon, putting together what was needed for the Monday deadline. He presented it to a committee of representatives from State, ONI, G-2, and A-2 on Monday afternoon. While largely complimentary, the G-2 and ONI people took issue with some of the comments Montague had made on Soviet policy: their criticism, Montague says, he and State found "extravagant" and "unanalytical" and irrelevant to the substance of the report. Montague then spent until midnight that night collating his estimate with the one written by the branch experts, which he had managed to wheedle out of them late on the Monday afternoon. Their report Montague considered "a miscellany of random ideas, assertive rather than analytic, in approach" but not contradicting his own arguments in what became ORE 1.[80]

Montague says his team, the Global Survey Group, battled on and did produce some good estimates. But even he concurs that ORE did not produce many, and that the good ones they did produce were few and far between.[81] Steury is more direct:

> Whatever their talents, the CIG's 29 intelligence officers simply lacked the time and the resources to perform analytical work on such a level. In effect, they lacked an institutional basis for the intellectual authority they were expected to wield over the national intelligence process. ORE was perhaps better placed, but it was compounded by the institutional difficulties of inserting itself into a preexisting and bureaucratically entrenched national security establishment.[82]

Part of the blame can be placed with DCI Hillenkoetter, who was unwilling to take responsibility for the estimates and therefore left the approvals process up to his subordinates, the assistant directors at both ORE (Babbitt) and the IAC.[83] Moreover, there was no incentive for the other agencies to make sure the estimates process went smoothly. As Jackson points out, why would they aid ORE when CIA's success "might prove fatal to themselves?"[84]

Kent's Review of ORE

As an outsider, Sherman Kent was invited to inspect and make recommendations on ORE and did so in a report to Hillenkoetter of February 1948.[85] He seems to have confined his thoughts to how ORE worked with other departments and external agencies and did not raise the issue of whether the Agency was producing proper long-range estimates (possibly because he didn't get to review them). In what appears a very nice turn of phrase, Kent described the intransigence of the military and State's intelligence agencies as them having "the weapons and strategic position to resist any intrusive coordinative activities by ORE."[86] And, indeed, without the help of the National Security Council, Kent saw this as an impasse. He also believed ORE needed to be more in control of the planning and dissemination of its work. Internally, ORE had too many competing divisions to exercise any real control over its output. Finally, ORE needed a better relationship with the intelligence collection departments within the Agency, like the Office of Operations. It wasn't enough to ask for information from a distance: ORE needed to cozy up to those in the field overseas and bring them home to Washington for frequent briefings.

There was very little in Kent's report that would have offended Hillenkoetter and Babbitt. It may be that he was hoping it would lead to a job. Yet he did press upon the DCI that there was no one within CIA that was in control—ORE needed an internal "customer." Yet, as we have seen, neither Hillenkoetter nor Babbitt were willing to take ownership of the reports being generated.

Notes

Epigraph: Jackson, *The DCI Miscellaneous Studies*, 1:95.
   1. Jackson, *The DCI Miscellaneous Studies*, 1:93–95.
   2. Jackson, 1:93–95, 101.
   3. Jackson, 1:279.
   4. Jackson, 1:41.
   5. Jackson, 1:44, 94.
   6. In April 1947, as Hillenkoetter was about to join CIG, J. Klahr Huddle was assistant director of ORE. He left for the Foreign Service as Hillenkoetter arrived. His assistant, Capt. A. H. McCollum, replaced Huddle as acting assistant director of ORE. McCollum returned to the Navy in 1948. See Diary Rear Admiral R. H. Hillenkoetter / Schedule for Presentation of their Activities by Office and Staff Heads to Admiral Hillenkoetter, 1947-04-09a, CIA CREST Archive. See Darling, *The Central Intelligence Agency*, 129; and "McCollum, Arthur H., Rear Adm., USN (Ret.) (1898–1976)," US Naval Institute website, https://www.usni.org/press/oral-histories/mccollum-arthur.
   7. See Jackson, *The DCI Miscellaneous Studies*, 2:139. Also Memorandum: Administration and Management, CIA, June 9, 1948, p. 47, CIA-RDP86B00269R00050-0050059-7, CIA, CREST Archives.
   8. Sometimes split, with Western Europe and Northern Europe (Britain and Scandinavia) separate branches. See Memorandum, June 9, 1948, 47.
   9. Jackson, *The DCI Miscellaneous Studies*, 1:40–41.
  10. Jackson, 1: 11–12.
  11. Woodrow J. Kuhns, "The Office of Reports and Estimates," in *Central Intelligence: 50 Years of the CIA*, ed. Michael Warner and Scott A. Koch, 45–74 (Central Intelligence Agency, 1998), 45.
  12. Jackson, *The DCI Miscellaneous Studies*, 1:11, 18.
  13. Darling, *The Central Intelligence Agency*, 414.

14. Jackson, *The DCI Miscellaneous Studies*, 1:45, 47, 50.

15. Jackson, 1:53.

16. Jackson, 1:58–59.

17. Jackson, 1:60.

18. Jackson, 1:60, 63–64.

19. Jackson, 1:69.

20. Darling, *The Central Intelligence Agency*, 340–45.

21. Darling, *The Central Intelligence Agency*, 340–45.

22. Darling, 314–15.

23. Coordination of Intelligence, February 8, 1949, CIA-RDP86B00269R000500020 056, CIA, CREST Archives.

24. Darling, *The Central Intelligence Agency*, 231.

25. Darling, 340–45, 406.

26. Darling, 375–77.

27. Jackson, *The DCI Miscellaneous Studies*, 1:118.

28. Jackson, 1:116–17.

29. Darling, *The Central Intelligence Agency*, 121.

30. Darling, 378.

31. Jackson, *The DCI Miscellaneous Studies*, 1:121–24, 125.

32. Memorandum, June 9, 1948, 47, CIA, CREST Archives.

33. Memorandum, 48.

34. Memorandum, 49–50; and Jackson, *The DCI Miscellaneous Studies*, 1:88–89.

35. Memorandum, June 9, 1948, 54, CIA, CREST Archives.

36. Memorandum, 53.

37. Memorandum, 54.

38. US State Department, Office of the Historian, Letter from . . . Special Assistant (McNeil) to Mathias F. Correa.

39. Penrose appears to be talking about Theodore Babbitt, the chief of ORE, who earned his doctorate at Yale in 1932 and served as a military attaché in both Ankara and Istanbul among other places. See Theodore Babbitt Second World War Correspondence, Box WWII 153, Folder 11, Folder 1, https://chapman.lyrasistechnology .org/repositories/4/resources/749, Chapman University Library.

40. US State Department, Office of the Historian, Enclosure. Memorandum by Stephen Penrose. Washington, January 2, 1948, https://history.state.gov/historical documents/frus1945-50Intel/d338.

41. Jackson, *The DCI Miscellaneous Studies*, 1:69.

42. Jackson, 1:70.

43. Darling, *The Central Intelligence Agency*, 394–95.

44. Director's Diaries, 1950-09-01, pp. 57–58, CIA, CREST Archives.

45. Jackson, *The DCI Miscellaneous Studies*, 1:95.

46. Darling, *The Central Intelligence Agency*, 415.

47. Director's Diaries, 1950-09-01, pp. 154, 157.

48. Matthais, *America's Strategic Blunders*, 47.

49. Steury, "Origins of CIA's Analysis of the Soviet Union," 13n58.

50. ORE 1 "The Basis of Soviet Foreign Policy," July 23, 1946, p. 1, DOC_0000256601, CIA, CREST Archives.

51. ORE 1, 5.

52. ORE 1, 47–48.

53. See ORE 1/1 "Soviet Tactics in International Affairs," RDP79R00971A0003000-50001-8, CIA, CREST Archives.

54. Matthais, *America's Strategic Blunders*, 47–48.

55. Steury, "Origins of CIA's Analysis of the Soviet Union," 2–3, 7.

56. See CIA Series: Memo re Suspended CIA Series, n.d. CIA-RDP84-00022R000 200130005-4, CIA, CREST Archives; and List of Staff Intelligence Projects Completed July 1946 to April 1949, April 30, 1949, CIA-RDP67-00059A000300017 0012-2-2, CIA CREST Archives. See also To the Recipients of All CIA Weekly Summary and CIA Monthly Review of the World Situation, December 1, 1950, CIA-RDP78-01617A002400180001-5, CIA, CREST Archives.

57. Matthais, *America's Strategic Blunders*, 55.

58. Matthias, 55–56.

59. Matthias, 64.

60. Matthias, 58.

61. As an aside, Sherman Kent says that there were times Montague didn't pull his weight on estimate projects and that even Montague admitted he was "an indolent man." Kent and Thacher, *Reminiscences of a Varied Life*, 254.

62. Matthias is quick to point out that, even with an accurate assessment from CIA, this alone would not necessarily have prevented the war. Regardless of this, he says, nobody in the loop took them seriously." Matthias, *America's Strategic Blunders*, 74, 79.

63. From 1948 the OREs are usually suffixed with the year, e.g., ORE 8-48. See ORE 53 "The Current Situation in Spain," November 5, 1947, CIA RDP78 01617A 003000160001, CIA, CREST Archive.

64. ORE 44 "The Japan Peace Treaty; Problems, Issues and Reactions," November 14, 1947, DOC_0000256618, CIA, CREST Archive.

65. ORE 49 "The Current Situation in Palestine, October 20, 1947," CIA RDP78 0161 7A003000120004, CIA, CREST Archives.

66. ORE 55 "The Consequences of the Partition of Palestine," November 28, 1947, CIA RDP78 01617A0003000180001, CIA, CREST Archive.

67. ORE 9-48 "Succession of Power in the USSR," January 13, 1948, 263-a1-22-ORE-9, CIA, CREST Archive.

68. ORE 6-48 "Consequences of Communist Accession to Power in Italy by Legal Means," March 6, 1948, 263-a1-22-ORE-6-48, CIA, CREST Archive.

69. ORE 10-48 "Consequences of Certain Courses of Action with Respect to Greece," April 5, 1948, 262-a1-22-ORE-10-48, CIA, CREST Archive.

70. ORE 7-50 "Probable Developments in Taiwan," March 20, 1950, 263-a1 22-ORE-7-50, CIA, CREST Archive.

71. ORE 48-49 "The Soviet Position in Approaching the CFM," May 18, 1949, 263-a1-22-ORE-48-49, CIA, CREST Archive.

72. Garthoff, *Analyzing Soviet Politics*, 60.

73. ORE 16/1 "Soviet Objectives in Latin America," November 1, 1947, p. 8, DOC_00 00256612, CIA, CREST Archive.

74. Referred to as "the Intelligence Organization, Department of State" in the dissent. ORE 9-48 "Cuban Political Trends," March 26, 1948, 263-a1-22-ORE-9-48, National Archives and Records Administration (NARA), College Park, Maryland.

75. ORE 58-48 "The Strategic Value to the USSR of the Conquest of West Europe and the Near East (to Cairo)," July 30, 1948, 263-a1-22-ORE-58-48, NARA.

76. ORE 91-49 "Estimate of the Effects of the Soviet Possession of the Atomic Bomb Upon the Security of the US," 6 April 1950, 263-a1-22-ORE-58-48, NARA.

77. "Office of Reports and Estimates [review] CIA-RDP86B00269R000500050059-7, CIA, Crest Archive, p. 11.

78. Montague, *General Walter Bedell Smith*, 121.

79. Montague, 120–23.

80. Appendix: The Preparation of ORE-1, September 10, 1946, RDP67-00059A000-200200002-5, CIA, CREST Archive.

81. Appendix: The Preparation of ORE-1," 123.

82. Steury, "Origins of CIA's Analysis of the Soviet Union," 5.

83. Jackson and Claussen, *Organizational History of the Central Intelligence Agency*, 1:41.

84. Jackson and Claussen, 1:57.

85. Darling, *The Central Intelligence Agency*, 408.

86. US State Department, Office of the Historian. Letter from Sherman Kent to Director of Central Intelligence Hillenkoetter, February 9, 1948.

The Intel Intellectual as Administrator and the Reforms of 1950–53

Thanks to our wartime labors we not only possessed a stock of relevant and useful information about the Soviet Union, we also had the makings of a far better intelligence profession than had existed heretofore. The analytical arm of US intelligence was able to identify its principal objectives—and with precision; it had developed some mature doctrine; it had mastered some difficult and important methodologies; it was moving toward a common technical vocabulary; and, most important of all, it had produced a good number of sophisticated practitioners.

—Sherman Kent (1948)

World War II had demonstrated that processes needed to be improved if the United States was going to be able to make better use of the information it collected about the intentions and capabilities of its adversaries. The most far-reaching intelligence failure, the bombing of Pearl Harbor in 1941, prompted investigator Henry Clausen to admit that while US military intelligence had people of "genius" working on the decrypting of Ultra material, "no one had the brains to know what to do with it," and there was "no comprehensive method for either disseminating or evaluating [the] material."[1] Clausen had concluded the attack could have been prevented if American intelligence had a more efficient system in place—a valuable lesson when the United States confronted a new enemy after the war had ended.

This chapter focuses exclusively on two administrators: Gen. Walter Bedell Smith, who arrived at CIA with a reform agenda, and William Langer, whom Smith chose to run the intelligence analysis wing of the Agency. We focus particularly on Langer, the embodiment of the "intel intellectual" as an administrator, developing a strategy that would establish a new civilian peacetime strategic intelligence analyst, a role that stood outside the previous military or diplomatic intelligence function.

Social science promised a way to make national security goals and actions more focused—adding both clarity and forewarning of threats—and thus assist in winning the Cold War. As a direct consequence of that, social science methodologies (what Matthias calls "the pursuit of a rational and non-partisan estimating approach"[2]) were considered key to gaining this understanding and achieving better processes in pursuing this understanding.

Intelligence analysis, says Stephen Marrin, "involves the interpretation of information about the adversary or environment for the purposes of assisting decision making." The process requires specific knowledge about the subject of their inquiry in order to perform the task of describing, explaining, evaluating, and forecasting, but it also includes the ability to understand the nature of the process of analysis itself. It was this dual role—of providing a physical intelligence product in the form of estimates as well as standing back and determining what methods were needed to manufacture the product (what Marrin calls the management, organization, and processes related to the performance of intelligence analysis) in a consistent and reliable manner—that Langer was charged to execute.[3]

Smith and Langer had two primary concerns during this period: to institute a structure and processes to demonstrate that CIA was capable of fulfilling its mission, and to engage with external actors in a way that showed CIA was listening to their concerns and taking appropriate actions. Smith's task was in many ways much simpler: to exert his authority as DCI and ensure that the reform program he was hired to push through was carried out. Langer's role was more difficult. How might the concept of "strategic" intelligence work in the context of determining the intentions and capabilities of the new Cold War adversary? How could CIA's analysts not only provide a clear exposition of the global security environment to policymakers but also give them due warning of future challenges?

CIA's fundamental problem was that policymakers had very little understanding of what a peacetime strategic intelligence agency should be, how it was differentiated from a wartime strategic intelligence agency, how it would be staffed, what product it might create, and how it would sit in the hierarchy of the national security community. Without the founders, funders, and national security community having a clear picture of CIA's role, the Agency would continue to struggle to be respected and valued. This was at the heart of it, a survival issue.

This chapter begins by looking at how the idea of a strategic intelligence agency was reconceptualized as a response to the intelligence failure of Pearl Harbor. It then examines how this drew into CIA's orbit academics like Langer and observes the journey he took to transform strategic intelligence analysis into a process that utilized social science skills. The chapter reviews the new DCI's brief to reform CIA and how he engaged with external actors to demonstrate he was putting into effect their wishes. Finally, it discusses how Langer operationalized the reforms by recruiting people who would understand the rigorous techniques and could embed them into institutional processes. This is the story of how the administrators created a strategy to see CIA through the reform years of 1950–53.

The Wartime Intelligence Intellectuals:
Research and Analysis at OSS

In July 1941 President Roosevelt signed an executive order establishing a new intelligence office, the Coordinator of Information (COI), which had the objective of "collect[ing] and analyz[ing] all information and data which may bear upon national security."[4] This civilian organization ran counter to the military intelligence agencies and recognized what would be a long-running issue for US national security: the difficulty of achieving coordination between the Army, Navy, and (later) Air Force entities with their competing interests and ongoing turf wars. Lawyer William J. Donovan was appointed to the post, at least until Roosevelt's patience ran out with this controversial and empire-building maverick. Donovan set up two offices within the COI: the Research and Analysis Branch (R&A) and the Foreign Information Service.[5] After Pearl Harbor in December of that year, the COI was reconfigured (in June 1942) to become the Office of Strategic Services (OSS), which was further divided into Secret Intelligence and Special Operations functions.[6]

R&A was headed by James Phinney Baxter III, a diplomatic and military historian and president of Williams College, who had in turn recruited academics from over thirty-five universities.[7] When Baxter took ill in 1942, the Harvard diplomatic historian William Langer, whom Baxter had recruited in 1941, took the helm.[8] He ran it from September 1942 until the OSS was disbanded in 1945 (and then returned briefly when, after the war, R&A moved to State).[9] Recognizing the uniqueness of a social sciences approach, a steering committee was set up by the Librarian of Congress, Archibald MacLeish, who convened a meeting that drew together representatives of the American Council of Learned Societies, the Social Science Research Council, and the National Archives as well as key scholars from leading, mostly Ivy League universities. The R&A division was set up in a structure copied by CIA a few years later: with Baxter as chair of a board of analysts, and a staff doing the day-to-day work. The Board of Analysts included leading academics from various social sciences and a representative from both the Army and Navy. Known as the College of Cardinals, it included economists Edward S. Mason (Harvard) and Calvin Bryce Hoover (Duke); Donald Cope McKay, a specialist in modern French history (Harvard); military and diplomatic historian Edward Mead Earle (Institute for Advanced Study at Princeton); and political scientist Joseph Hayden (University of Michigan). They were joined by two military representatives: Lt. Col. J. Y. Smith (Army), Cdr. Frances C. Denebrink (Navy), and Treasury official John C. Wiley. The board met regularly, on Tuesday and Thursday mornings.[10]

The Library of Congress became the first workplace of the new OSS R&A team, and where it stayed until 1943.[11] In his autobiography Langer says R&A

made little use of human intelligence in its studies, apart from agents providing it with newspapers, journals, and books from Germany and the Soviet Union. "Donovan's hunch that most of the needed information could be obtained from printed materials (often from quite aged books) was proved altogether correct," Langer argued. "The strength of R&A lay in the research training and experience of its personnel."[12]

One example of the academic approach R&A immediately took was that of Wilmarth "Lefty" Lewis, who ran the Central Information Division. Lewis, a graduate in English literature from Yale, knew all about indexing, having compiled while at the university a forty-eight-volume annotated edition of Horace Walpole's works.[13] "The [Central Information Division] catalog that Lewis built was so good," says Robin Winks,

> it would make you cry; the State Department wound up coming to R&A to find out what State itself had by way of consular reports. In the end there were over a million of those little filing cards. . . . When the War College, having surveyed all filing and indexing systems in Washington, chose the Central Information Division as its model, no one was surprised. Lewis's system was, as an admirer remarked, overpowering in "its detail and complexity."[14]

It closely fit Sherman Kent's description of the centralized function of intelligence collection as "a vast and living encyclopedia of reference set apart from all such departments and agencies, and devoted to their service."[15]

Robert Lee Wolff, another Harvard professor who worked for OSS, was a specialist in Balkan history. He described R&A as being like the faculty of a large university. Langer drew on a wide range of social scientists, some of them very young postgraduates. They included geographers, economists, political scientists, historians, linguists, anthropologists, and sociologists.[16]

> Like all university faculties, it worried incessantly about the effectiveness of its work. What was the use? the analysts moaned, of laboriously compiling a study that reported on all the port facilities of Morocco, or that ingeniously located and closely estimated the strengths of various German army units by using the obituaries of officers published in the current German newspapers specially flown in from Stockholm, or that evaluated the morale and intentions of rival guerrilla groups in occupied Yugoslavia, if there was no immediate audible applause for the product? Complaints flooded Langer's desk. "I don't understand all the gripes," he would occasionally explode to his assistants, "aren't they doing exactly what they like best?" But his juniors had neither the nerve nor the wisdom to reply that one of the things that university faculties like best is to grumble.[17]

An early project for R&A was a bulletin called *The War This Week*, a publication sourced from State Department dispatches, newspaper reports, foreign radio broadcasts, and the military. This proved popular among policymakers until the Joint Chiefs of Staff pulled the plug on it. Langer says the criticism was that the authors were privy to a good deal of sensitive information that they were not considered discreet enough to have access to, but that interforce rivalry was just as much a factor in its demise.[18]

R&A was frustrated by its mandate, which OSS scholar Bradley F. Smith described as "diffuse and confusing."[19] It was Langer himself who had decried the United States' slow start on developing an intelligence analysis skillset: having arrived in Washington Langer found that "we were badly hampered by our own ignorance about the details of our mission. No one would enlighten us as to what we should do and how to go about it. . . . We decided before long that our wisest course would be to collect and evaluate such information that came to us from the State Department cables, the newspapers, radio intercepts and military."[20]

With a staff of 950–1,000 by 1944, R&A recruited academics who champed at the bit to be given proper long-range intelligence estimates to write. They were frequently unsure who the intended audience for their research was. With few staff receiving even basic military training, research was often pursued for the sake of academic interest only. Even Langer, who one would have thought would have enough on his hands managing the unit, at one point took on a commission of writing a report on US policy toward Vichy France ostensibly because, as an academic, his curiosity to see classified files got the better of him.[21]

The R&A academics learned their craft along the way. Charles Kindleberger was an economist who worked on the European section:

> It was a very distinguished group of scholars organized in OSS to do, not the hokey-pokey, not the fancy spying, but simple straight analysis to see what brains could do. I was asked to come over to start something called the Military Supplies Section. I knew nothing about military supplies; that didn't make any difference. The hypothesis was, a good one I think, that any economist who put his mind to something could learn it. We could create instant experts.[22]

Much of R&A's work involved basic intelligence, collecting information about the enemy's ports and railway networks and supplying up-to-date maps. The bombing of Germany brought into focus the lack of topographical knowledge available to the Allies, with many towns often having the same name. This called for a gazetteer of German industrial towns.[23] Arthur M. Schlesinger Jr.

says that Langer widened the range of assessments R&A took on so that it "covered most of the planet, clarified political and strategic quandaries and perhaps made a modest contribution to military victory."[24]

Langer's role took him to England in September 1942. He traveled with Lefty Lewis and the head of the British Empire desk, Conyers Read. Intelligence was in its infancy in the United States, and Langer believed they had much to learn from the British. He spent a good deal of time on this trip discussing intelligence analysis with the local OSS people and their British allies.[25] One of the centers of intelligence research was at Oxford, largely empty now of students and dons but the home of the Inter-Service Topographical Department, which played a similar role to R&A in the provision of maps and area expertise. He also visited the press-reading group at All Souls. Langer was surprised to see top academics assigned to the quite menial tasks of poring over foreign newspapers and listening in to enemy broadcasts. "I have never understood," he later recounted, "why the British failed to assign these men to crucial posts in the war effort. Clearly Donovan had a higher opinion of scholarship and made far greater and better use of the country's academics than did our British allies." It was in England that Langer first met his future employer at CIA, Walter Bedell Smith.[26]

Social Science at OSS

Schlesinger had known Langer while studying as an undergraduate at Harvard, although he never attended the diplomatic historian's lectures.[27] Schlesinger also knew Langer's boss, James Phinney Baxter III, who had been head at Adams, his undergraduate house.[28] Baxter offered to be Schlesinger's referee for a job at R&A and introduced him to Langer, who offered him a role as an analyst.[29] In the first volume of his memoirs Schlesinger says the choice was between joining the Board of Economic Warfare or at R&A. He had been offered both jobs. "I thought hard about the choice," he says.

> I was attracted by the activism of [the Board of Economic Warfare]. People were rushing about doing things—imposing blockades, buying up scarce materials, blacklisting Axis-controlled firms, plotting to deny the enemy strategic materials. R&A/OSS would be almost a return to academic life— "depressing," I wrote to my parents, "to be in the middle of a lot of PhD's once again." But I chose OSS in the end because I felt a good deal more at home with politics than economics.[30]

Schlesinger started at R&A on May 8, 1943. Having resigned from the Office of War Information over disagreements with the direction it was taking, he initially kept to a small clique of old colleagues who had traveled with him to R&A. His first impressions were not good: He described R&A as an ivory tower far removed from the day-to-day politics of Washington. He was put into Current Intelligence under the direction of the medievalist Everett Gleason.[31] Schlesinger was given the task of editing *PW Weekly* (*Psychological Warfare Weekly*). "I was skeptical about the thaumaturgic qualities of psychological warfare," he later wrote. "Economists, geographers and topographers, I argued in a memorandum toward the end of the first month, supplied hard information of operational value in winning the war. . . . But psychoanalysis of Nazi propaganda, a current PW enthusiasm, was not likely to furnish clues to German intentions. . . . There were just too many variables to lay a basis for forecasting the moves of the enemy."[32]

As we can see by his inclusion of the social science concept of variables, Schlesinger was determined to impose a robust framework upon R&A reports. Within three months of arriving, he wrote a paper titled *The Need for Intellectual Guidance in Psychological Warfare Research*. Schlesinger's main complaint was the idea, firmly embedded in the intelligence process today, that analysts should not cross the threshold between assessing fact and making policy recommendations. For the Harvard historian, this was "founded on the crude conception of the intellectual processes which go into analysis. . . . Fact, judgment and value are inextricably entangled."[33] This conception, Schlesinger argued, was epistemologically naive: The very act of selecting which facts to include and which to ignore meant the analyst made a value judgment. And value judgments were exactly what R&A regional desks were letting creep into their own reports anyway. The Central European desk believed that the German people should be absolved of responsibility for Nazi crimes, whereas the Low Countries desk believed they should be held accountable. The Scandinavian desk was disapproving of Danish sabotage, while the Central European desk actively encouraged it. These disagreements overflowed into interagency disputes. R&A sided with the Charles de Gaulle faction, while the State Department favored Gen. Henri Giraud. For Schlesinger, this choosing of sides was part and parcel of the analytic process. "Since most decisions have to be made on imperfect data," he argued, "the obligation of the expert to participate in making them becomes all the greater."[34]

Schlesinger had a second concern, and that was the problem of objectivity in R&A. While professors are almost duty-bound to argue with each other, he argued, at the OSS division there were too many biases evident in their work. One of the most extreme cases, Schlesinger believed, was that of Maurice Halperin, a University of Oklahoma professor heading the Latin American desk. Halperin was a card-carrying Communist and was later alleged to have been a spy for the USSR. In several reports written for R&A, Halperin defined would-be American friends as American enemies. In a coup in Bolivia in 1943 against a corrupt regime propped up by mining companies, Halperin had sided with *The Daily Worker*, who claimed the coup members were a "bridgehead of German Nazis, the Italian fascists, and Spanish falangists in the Americas." In Schlesinger's view, the coup members were not Nazis. Instead, the new government was made up of mining workers who quickly committed to the ideals of the United Nations, began to supply war materials to the allies, and sent a Dartmouth College–educated envoy to Washington.[35] In another example Halperin had painted two well-known anti-Nazis as "a group of foreign Trotskyites." Halperin appeared to be waging a different war: a war of Marxist in-fighting and unforgivable crimes against doctrine.[36]

For Schlesinger, the levels of bias creeping into research reports, particularly those tackling major wartime and national security issues, were a concern. For the department's reports to be intellectually consistent, there needed to be agreement on what processes should be followed. This he termed "intellectual unity."[37]

Sherman Kent, who was then the head of the Europe-Africa Division at R&A, took Schlesinger's report seriously enough to incorporate it into his own methodology.[38] Kent scribbled his own thoughts on a copy of the report and passed it on to Langer.[39] Langer was impressed and began to apply the problem of objectivity to the reports he was preparing on postwar German policy.

Having been blocked from writing estimates, R&A had focused instead on area studies of the theaters of war. Bradley Smith says, "its foundation lay in its ability to obtain useful information from routine documents and published materials."[40] One example was a project on Germany's foreign workers given to Harold Deutsch in 1943.[41] This had gained R&A no small reputation among decision-makers, particularly in the planning of psychological warfare. As the war progressed, R&A focused less on theaters of war and more on the policies that would be needed for postwar occupied territories, with Hajo Holborn's Civil Affairs section assigned to work with State and the War Department. Langer was, according to Bradley F. Smith, setting his sights on making R&A useful once hostilities ended.[42]

"The first steps in the organized application of new ideas are always crude," says George Pettee, "but the OSS, with all its faults, represented . . . the initial step toward a broad strategic intelligence function in the United States Government."[43] In his *War Report of the OSS*, Kermit Roosevelt claimed that the analysis methods developed by R&A "served to influence, if not revolutionize, intelligence processing throughout Government."[44]

The Lessons of Pearl Harbor:
The Need for a Social Science Framework

One postwar account of the failure of Pearl Harbor was George S. Pettee's 1946 book *The Future of American Secret Intelligence*, which Sherman Kent described as "a trail breaker in the literature of strategic intelligence."[45] Pettee, a political scientist from Amherst College, defined "strategic intelligence" simply as intelligence that has an impact on strategic decisions. In wartime, these are policy-level decisions that inform "the overall conduct of war, the scale and timing of major operations, the scale and scheduling of production and transport, and the evaluation of all relevant military, economic, political, psychological, logistical and technical factors."[46] In peacetime, strategic intelligence was just as integral to national policymaking but aimed at preserving peace rather than waging war. Pettee saw the role of peacetime intelligence as interdisciplinary. This meant not only the idea of coordination of intelligence from many sources but also doing away with the conceptual separation of disciplines in data collection and analysis. "The characteristic of strategic intelligence will be the comprehension of the situation as a whole, whether it be a national or international situation. . . . It will therefore be concerned with the economic consequences of political occurrences, and the political consequences of economic developments, and with the social-psychological matrix in which such equations work their calculus."[47]

This was a very different approach from the collection and analysis of old, where economic intelligence was siloed into product from solely economically focused agencies, political from diplomatic sources, or technical information from scientific organizations. The compartmentalization of intelligence was counterproductive and failed to see the bigger picture.

"The new methods of obtaining information in great bulk, and of analyzing this flood of material," argued Pettee, "necessitated the growth of complex staffs of analysts, engaged in discovering the most essential details, combining them by large-scale calculations into meaningful conclusions, and arriving at a picture of the enemy system vastly more elaborate than was possible with the older methods."[48] Yet there was a failure, Pettee argued, to acknowledge the shift in requirements that large-scale collection and the need for a new and effective organization had brought about, and this fundamental misreading of needs persisted right up until late 1945.[49]

The emphasis not only on the intelligence process but on the *administration* of the intelligence process was a key idea. Reviewing the role of intelligence during World War II, Pettee acknowledged that what had been a "rudimentary" business had grown fast but had experienced growing pains along the way. This was partly due to the inexperience of those directed, for the first time, to run government intelligence. "The administration of intelligence," he wrote, "has been backward partly because the administration of research has been backward. In spite of shining examples to the contrary, there are extraordinarily many of those who are engaged in research, and even of those who direct it, who cannot see the task as a series of operations."[50] Pettee was highly critical of the military intelligence organs. The task of strategic intelligence in the world of 1941 was a new one, he argued. It required "organized brainwork, not off-hand flash judgment."[51] The problem, he believed, was well beyond the scope of either the War or Navy or State Department intelligence wings. Pettee cited four factors that needed to be addressed to overcome the failures of Pearl Harbor: First, that intelligence would provide warning of a surprise attack before actual declaration of war; second, that modern intelligence was a big job that needed coordination; third, that technological breakthroughs needed to be embraced; and, fourth, that none of the military intelligence agencies were up to the job. "Each one of these four factors required adaptation of methods and procedures." Pettee stated. "No adaptation of intelligence organization had yet [as of 1946] become effective to meet any one of them."[52]

For Pettee, the constant intelligence failures of the war were rooted in poor methodology. For instance, he claimed that measuring enemy casualties had been calculated using World War I statistics and had underestimated German losses.[53] War production estimates had assumed that Germany had peaked in 1939 and that, since 1941, the effect of Allied bombing, labor and material shortages, and inflation had seen it sink to below 1939 figures.[54] US estimates had predicted German locomotive and tank manufacturing would slow after 1943, and fighter production after 1944, and that the acute labor shortage would prevent pyrites mining for sulfuric acid, an essential chemical. None of these production estimates were correct, and sulfur production increased by three times in the period. This was a measure of "our lack of understanding of their economic and productive situation," claimed Pettee. Ignoring the fact that British morale had not broken after the bombing of Britain, US analysts believed the German public spirit had been crushed by the continued aerial firebombing of their cities. The US Strategic Bombing Survey conducted after the war showed instead that morale had held firm. "A study of the question based on our knowledge of modern social psychology," Pettee wrote in 1946, "might have easily predicted this result."[55]

Langer and the Intelligence Problem

By the beginning of the Cold War, Langer had determined what would be required in order to have a globally competitive strategic intelligence organization. In early 1948 he published a short think piece called *Scholarship and the Intelligence Problem*. This was an outline of where the intelligence analysis product was by 1948. First, Langer confirmed that before the war, except for State, no one was doing the kind of broad, long-ranging surveys that were necessary. Up until 1939, intelligence collection was inadequate, but political analysis was almost nonexistent. "From time-to-time some academically-minded official in the Department of State might essay an historical survey or systematic analysis, but such cases were exceptional." The Treasury, Federal Reserve, and Department of Commerce had been more active in international finance, but not outside of that. The armed services, thought Langer, had been too casual in their approach and appointed people they considered unfit for combat. They were not professionals, and "the estimates and conclusions of the service intelligence staff were notoriously inadequate and sometimes mistaken to a dangerous degree."[56]

This had changed with R&A. The idea had been to bring together specialists in foreign countries who were capable of assembling, selecting, evaluating, and presenting evidence. "This unpublicized research staff consisted of scholars drawn from all the social science fields—economists, political scientists, historians, geographers, psychologists, archaeologists and even philologists. The great objective was to get these specialists to work together, to pool their knowledge of the materials and literature and to focus their techniques on specific problems in the hope of coming up with the best-informed, most comprehensive, and most critical estimates of particular situations."[57]

This had been much more difficult to do than it was first thought. The United States lacked specialists who knew the Russian or Near or Far East regions, but those who did were far too narrow in their knowledge, and interdisciplinary work in fields like psychology or economics was spartan. Arguments sprang up between academics: Russian economists claimed the field for themselves, whereas Russian area specialists countered that the economists knew nothing of conditions on the ground or the materials available. Yet Langer's department had overcome the initial problems and had worked to dispel bureaucratic skepticism of "procedures and conclusions arrived at by unfamiliar techniques."[58]

Langer felt the initial arrival of the professors had been greeted in Washington with derision and suspicion—even downright hostility. Yet the proof of the success of R&A had been that it was not disbanded when the war ended but had been moved to the State Department. While the ranks of scholars had been depleted (with so many returning to their universities), R&A had continued uninterrupted in its work, which was to study the intentions and capabilities of adversaries. Langer believed they had achieved that far beyond anything the United States had done previously and even better than achieved elsewhere—even in Germany.

> What we have, then, in the government is something like a huge social science research institute devoted to the exploration of certain types of problems bearing on national security. . . . In the social science fields results are of course less concrete and spectacular than in the fields of science and invention. Furthermore, the exact preparation is difficult to define and organize.

FIGURE 4.1. Harvard diplomatic historian William L. Langer.
Shutterstock/Life Magazine

But it is, I am convinced, very necessary that encouragement be given and that concerted efforts should be made to get training in less familiar fields, as well as to study and live abroad. . . . My hope is that, as appreciation of the problem spreads, something larger and more systematic will be undertaken and that, ultimately, it will be realized that the country has a real stake in the type of study that is clearly essential for any nation which, whether it likes it or not, is called upon to play a major part in world affairs.[59]

Langer simultaneously called for an investment in a social science–driven central intelligence agency and the formation of a career for strategic intelligence analysts. But he warned that it would be an inexact science of procedures and techniques the policymakers might not always fully understand. The template for such a national security research institute he clearly believed was R&A, and the work of CIA must prioritize the broad and long-ranging reports that would become the national intelligence estimates (NIEs).

"Beetle" Smith's Brief

Langer moved with R&A to the State Department after OSS was dissolved in 1945. He was transferred along with five hundred analysts (from a high of around nine hundred), returned briefly to Harvard, but was summoned back to State to fill what was considered a temporary position. He stayed on as special assistant for research and intelligence.[60] From his office at State he watched and thought about CIG/CIA's problems, and he disapproved of what he saw. At a meeting of the National Intelligence Authority in 1946, which Langer had been invited to, he questioned the rapid growth of personnel under CIG Director Vandenberg's leadership. He told the National Intelligence Authority he believed there should be a review before the money was spent.[61]

The most comprehensive call for reform, the Dulles-Jackson-Correa Survey Report, was rubber-stamped with NSC-50 in July of 1949.[62] Of all the reports provided to fix the problem, the Dulles report was the most comprehensive, running to over two hundred pages and guiding both internal reform and how CIA should manage its external relationships.[63]

NSC-50 had taken the Dulles-Jackson-Correa report's fifty-seven conclusions and recommendations and distilled them down to twelve main points. It was satisfied with the legal provisions that made CIA accountable to the NSC but wanted the DCI to work more closely with the secretaries of Defense and State. It believed that CIA had "not fully discharged" its responsibility to coordinate with the other agencies and that the DCI must display "forthright initiative and leadership" in chairing the Intelligence Advisory Committee (IAC).[64] As far as specific changes that related to intelligence analysis went, NSC-50 demanded better coordination between the agencies to deliver prompt NIEs in crisis situations, saying there had been confusion at CIA over its responsibility to produce national intelligence and its role carrying out basic and current intelligence. The directive argued that the committee and dissents process had created poor NIEs and that the DCI and IAC needed to fulfill their responsibilities of producing "the most authoritative [estimates] available to policy makers."[65] Finally, the NSC instructed CIA to create a "small estimates division which would draw upon and review the specialized intelligence product of departmental agencies in order to prepare coordinated national intelligence estimates" as well as an office of research and reports to handle intelligence of common interest.[66] The NSC directive stipulated that the report's "recommendations should be put into effect at once and the [NSC] should plan to have a suitable review of the progress made after a reasonable period of implementation."[67]

It only remained for a suitable leader to implement the recommendations. CIA's DCI, Roscoe H. Hillenkoetter, had initially been welcoming of Dulles' criticisms, although a little abashed by the comments that the failures of CIA could be put down to poor leadership. Yet with the publishing of NSC-50, Hillenkoetter became increasingly psychologically withdrawn and bitter and went through only the motions of reorganization.[68]

In May of 1950, with the Dulles-Jackson-Correa Survey Report now curling up at the edges and little or no reform having been actioned, Truman suggested to Sidney Souers that Gen. Walter "Beetle" Bedell Smith might be the right man. The president had confidence in him. He had been Eisenhower's chief of staff during the final days of the war, followed by an ambassadorship to the Soviet Union. It was Truman who had called Smith home from his Moscow ambassadorship during the early stages of the 1948 Berlin Blockade to brief the president on Stalin's mood and the likelihood of war.[69] Souers agreed with Truman's choice. It made sense to have a good organizer running CIA, and someone with sufficient rank to bring the other agencies into line. Smith was confirmed by the Senate in late August. But the new DCI was recovering from major stomach surgery and did not start his new job until October 1950.[70]

Smith was "a tough-minded, hard-driving often intimidating" man whom Winston Churchill had nicknamed the "American Bulldog."[71] The qualities that made Smith such a good foil to Eisenhower also made him a good director of CIA. Ray Cline says in addition to having no tolerance for fools he "was a perfectionist . . . [and] had a photographic memory, encyclopedic knowledge, and a shrewd judgement about people and ideas."[72] The new job also required a man who Smith's biographer, D.K.R. Crosswell, described as being "not afraid to go out on a limb, who never avoided a fight, and who at least gave the appearance of having a thick skin."[73] When he had been appointed US ambassador in Moscow, his old boss, Eisenhower, had muttered "serves those bastards [the Soviets] right."[74]

Just prior to arriving at CIA, Smith was sent a memo by the Agency's legal counsel, Lawrence Houston, who reiterated NSC-50 and warned Smith that up until then CIA's estimates had been "watered-down compromises, replete with loopholes, in an attempt to secure complete IAC support."[75] They were not the recommendations that CIA had been instructed to produce by law. Instead, the "refusal of the IAC agencies to honor the requests for necessary intelligence" had contributed to inadequate assessments.[76] The IAC agencies had, according to Houston, begged off cooperation, saying their intelligence was operational and for their eyes only. As CIA had no powers to enforce cooperation, its ability to produce the necessary work for the president, the NSC, and others was "hampered by the lack of complete material." There were no limits restraining the IAC agencies from making dissents, which were "frequently insubstantial, quibbling or reflective of departmental policy," and they could not "free themselves from departmental bias or budgetary interests."[77] The concept of coordinated and centralized intelligence was failing, and rather than respond to urgent requests for information, CIA's estimates were being slowed down by the IAC agencies—taking months to produce and watered down at the very end of the process.

Houston believed the answer to this was a strongman at the head of CIA. The relationships with the president and NSC must be redefined and clarified. Smith must ensure his authority as DCI and CIA's as an organization. He must "achieve the necessary coordination by direction rather than placing reliance in a spirit of cooperation and good will."[78]

Smith was just the man for the task. With an outstanding reputation in both the military and government, Smith had the clout that CIA badly needed to overhaul its practices. And his experience as chief of staff prepared him for that. Crosswell says, "Chiefs of staff translate the will of the commander into practical plans; they harmonize and integrate the actions of headquarters, issuing succinct guidance to their principal staff subordinates while coordinating actions with higher, lateral, and lower staffs. Chiefs of staff must possess not only intelligence and a thorough grasp of detail but also tact and diplomatic skills."[79]

Montague says Smith was shown seven reports that had called for changes to CIA, but he concentrated on NSC-50.[80] This meant concentrating on repairing the coordination problem; separating national, current, and basic intelligence; creating a small, dedicated team that would concentrate on long-range estimates; and focusing on delivering the most authoritative intelligence possible.

While NSC-50 had also wanted changes to the psychological warfare and espionage departments, Smith—like Hillenkoetter before him—was not a covert operations enthusiast.[81] Moreover, as Tracey Barnes remembered, the Agency was "a group of warring factions," particularly between the covert operations departments of the Office of Policy Coordination and the Office of Special Operations.[82] Faced with mounting criticism of the Office of Policy Coordination's covert operations role much later on (1952), Smith reminded his staff that the Agency's "primary mission" was intelligence, and he would "approve nothing that mitigated against accomplishing" this function.[83]

In late November 1950, George Marshall (now secretary of Defense) wrote to Smith. It was an odd letter. Citing the importance of intelligence to national security, Marshall returned to the Pearl Harbor directive. CIA was to provide:

> (a) A 7- to 10-day warning of the imminence of hostilities, during which period our defense systems could be alerted and forces deployed or positioned as required.
>
> (b) Provide additional warnings at least 12 to 48 hours prior to the initiation of hostilities which will indicate the location of bases on which atomic

attacks are mounted and which will report the approximate time of launching of these attacks.[84]

Marshall acknowledged this was a big ask. It was something Smith could work toward. But as far as Marshall was concerned, the standard of estimates CIA was producing on Soviet intentions and capabilities was "dangerously inadequate." In this, he recognized that the services' intelligence wings had no special inside knowledge on the USSR. As far as Marshall was concerned, it was up to CIA to get this intelligence, and this was Priority One.[85]

Smith knew that in order to steer the Agency back into good favor, he had to recruit the right people. According to Lyman Kirkpatrick, "Smith did not try to get too deeply into the details of what was going on, but he tried to organize the agency and to select the people who were competent to do the job he wanted done. . . . He changed just about the entire top echelon of the agency in a couple of months."[86] When Kirkpatrick, newly promoted to the position of Smith's personal assistant, was struck down with polio, Smith visited him in hospital. "Don't worry about the fact your legs won't work," he told his employee. "All I care about is your brains."[87]

Smith's first step was to call William Harding Jackson and ask him to become his deputy.[88] Jackson agreed, on the basis that the Dulles-Jackson-Correa report (which he had co-written) would be followed to the letter.[89] Jackson had dealt with British intelligence during the war and understood how they went about the estimates process, so he was well suited to act as Smith's deputy in the administration of CIA as well as keep an eye on the analysts.[90] At the same time, after consultation with Donovan, Smith asked Allen Dulles to come to CIA for a six-week consultation. Kirkpatrick says Smith rang Dulles and demanded his presence: "You wrote the report—now come to Washington to implement it."[91] This ended up becoming a more impactful decision than the one to hire Jackson. Dulles stayed on and eventually succeeded Smith in 1953. Jackson only stayed a few months.[92] This was clearly a second factor of Smith's strategy: to neutralize the influence of the outsiders (Jackson and Dulles) by bringing them inside the organization.

He made rapid and deep changes to the infrastructure of CIA. Kirkpatrick remembers an advertising slogan for a Washington removals company by the name of Smith: "Don't make a move without calling Smith" evolved at the Agency to become "If you can't find your desk you've been moved by Smith!"[93]

In keeping with the instructions of NSC-50, a major change was the dissolution of the old Office of Reports and Estimates (ORE) and the establishment of the Board of National Estimates (BNE) and the Office of National Estimates (ONE), alongside a new Office of Research and Reports that would include the economic intelligence wing. Theodore Babbitt had been retained at the Office of

Research and Reports, but it was now recognized that a first-rate economist was needed. DCI Smith was going to fire him on the evening of October 10, 1950. This was the night of Smith's first meeting with the IAC, when he had been asked by Truman for six estimates to take to McArthur at Wake Island.[94] Babbitt had failed to produce a coordinated estimate on Korea. William Jackson asked Sherman Kent to find someone to replace him: Kent recommended Max Millikan.[95]

The BNE would be made up of an influential and respected group of military, diplomatic, academic, business, and law worlds. It was the overseeing committee of CIA and men from the military staff that decided on estimate topics and signed them off to be forwarded to the NSC. The staff of ONE would be drawn from outside as well as the pick of those already working at CIA.

> [Smith's] first step was to create a new organization for the production of national intelligence estimates and to provide it a stature and environment that ensured his success. This was an important step, because it took the estimating process out of the large research organization that then existed and placed it in an "ivory tower" atmosphere, as Smith himself called it. He went further and said that the men in this office should not concern themselves with day-to-day developments, which would be handled separately, but should devote their attention exclusively to what might happen in the future. Smith was very conscious of the fact that quality of personnel was the most important element for success and he intended to get the best brains for this organization.[96]

The day-to-day work would be handled by a new Office of Current Intelligence, which Smith established in early January 1951.[97] Smith saw the value in continuing to provide the president with what he wanted and believed in the Army system where the commander was briefed fully at the start of each day.[98] This enhanced product meant the replacement of the old daily and weekly reports with a new daily *Current Intelligence Bulletin* and weekly *Current Intelligence Weekly Review*. The first daily report was published on February 28, 1951, and the weekly edition in August. Another, the *Situation Summary*, was created to focus on the Korean War.[99] Vacationing at "the Little White House" in Key West, Florida, in March of 1951, Truman wrote to Smith to express his approval. "Dear Bedel [*sic*], I have been reading the intelligence bulletin and I am highly impressed with it. I believe you have hit the jackpot with this one. Sincerely, Harry Truman."[100]

Smith also set up a new organizational system based on the general staff of the Army, which Kirkpatrick understood as being "responsible for seeing that all staff work was completed on all matters before they got to the chief of staff, and to insure all paper work was in order before it reached his desk." Murray

McConnell, who had a business background, was asked to be deputy for administration, a role specifically created by the new DCI.[101]

The general considered it his responsibility to manage the external relationships.[102] There had been a history of dysfunctional relationships between intelligence chiefs and the president. Roosevelt had been a one-man band in foreign policy, shunting the State Department off to irrelevancy, relying on his generals but otherwise running a very uncoordinated, top-down decision-making regime.[103] Moreover, CIA's wartime predecessor, the OSS, had never managed to create a direct line to Roosevelt: "Roosevelt relied on informal conversations and a retinue of personal aides in his decisions. The orderly procedure of reviewing, evaluating, and acting on the basis of intelligence was simply not part of his routine."[104]

Truman was aware of the problems this loose structure might cause for the new Cold War order, and building a national security state was his response to that. He also had no illusions about his lack of expertise in foreign policy matters. He drew on all the advice he could muster, and his military advisers were much more frequently present at his decision-making conferences than they had been under his predecessor. Much later still, Eisenhower concentrated much of his presidency on systems, building a foreign policy machine that would "bring information to him in an orderly way, engage in long term planning, and provide for the systematic consideration of policies."[105]

Smith worked hard at establishing good relations with the president, Congress, and intelligence community and made weekly personal appointments with the president.[106] He invested heavily in the IAC, reinvigorating it from one that had virtually atrophied before his arrival to one that now met weekly (almost one hundred meetings between Smith's arrival and his departure two years later.)[107] CIA had also attempted to transform its more testy relationships with the intelligence community. William Jackson and his assistant, Loftus Becker, spent a good deal of 1950–51 negotiating a "treaty of peace" between CIA, State, and Defense (even though Smith himself had a good relationship with George C. Marshall, the new secretary of Defense), setting the parameters of who would do political, economic, and scientific research. Smith also helped heal a rift between CIA and FBI when ex-Bureau staff at the Agency began actively recruiting from their old employer and belittling FBI among their new and old colleagues.[108]

Smith focused, too, on improving the coordinating and cooperation environment by placing a number of military friends on interagency committees over the next three years.[109] Montague recalled meetings where Smith's appointee, Lt. Gen. Ralph Huebner shut down any criticisms or noncompliance: "If any IAC representatives from the Pentagon ever got out of hand, a growl from General Huebner was sufficient to restore good order and military discipline."[110]

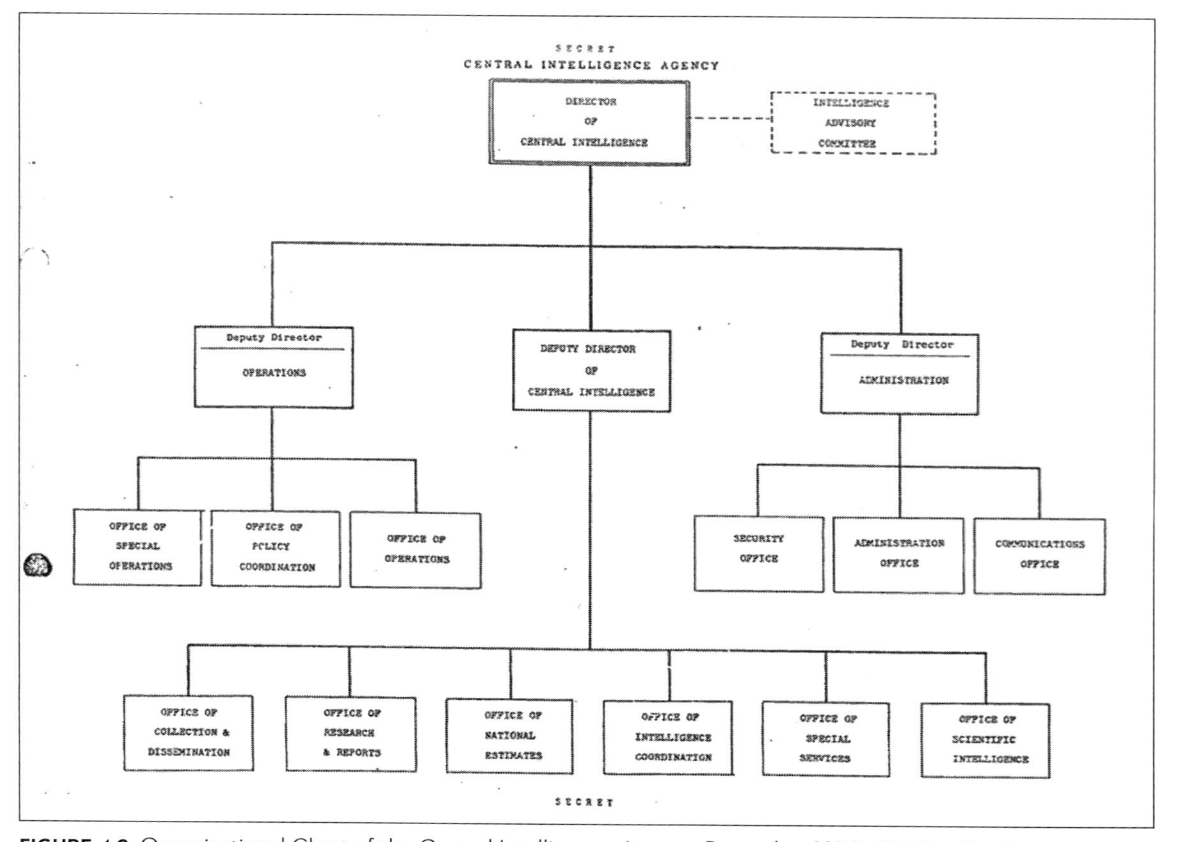

FIGURE 4.2. Organizational Chart of the Central Intelligence Agency, December 1950. *CIA Reading Room*

Finally, Matthew Baird from the Air Force was brought in to run an in-house training program. Baird had degrees from Princeton and Oxford, had been a headmaster at a boys' school, and was chief of the 13th Air Force Service Command during the war in the Pacific. Training was a key focus for Smith, says Kirkpatrick, "One of the offices created after the war had started its own training effort, with considerable success, but some offices didn't bother at all with training their personnel—operating on the philosophy that they would hire their own personnel already trained."[111] Baird and his deputy, Barnaby C. Keeney, visited industry, universities, and government departments before building their own training program. In February 1951 Baird reported on an interdepartmental meeting regarding the Social Science Research Council. CIA had been funding the council to train area specialists.[112] In early December 1951 CIA's Office of Training began a new half-day indoctrination course, to be run weekly. The first class was given to 120 recent (mostly covert operations) employees and included an introduction to the basic ideas and language of intelligence in general and the scope, mission, and internal organization of CIA.[113] Training was considered so important that it was the subject of a direct report to Smith.[114]

Smith was also quick to consider how CIA's institutional history and public face might work. In early 1951 a historical branch was created to write the history of CIA. It was also to be the interface with the national press and would help put together presentations to other government agencies. In May 1951 Col. Chester B. Hansen was made its first director.[115]

Smith's appointment had come at a critical juncture—as the war in Korea was intensifying. It fell to Smith not only to brief Congress on the war but also to keep the CIA-focused subcommittees informed of the Agency's operational activities in support of the war effort. Having someone of Smith's stature and demeanor in charge of the Agency at this point lent credibility to both its analysis and its operational achievements. Indeed, Smith's tenure awakened many in Congress to the existence of CIA.[116]

The war in Korea put pressure on CIA for intelligence related to the war effort, particularly as the national security community became worried about what else was happening in the Communist Bloc. A lack of staff in all of the intelligence agencies was heightened by the difficulty of training people in a hurry. "The Central Intelligence Agency was still a young organization," wrote Lyman Kirkpatrick, "and still suffering from bureaucratic pains. While it cannot be said that we were as poorly equipped as at the time of Pearl Harbor, our intelligence organizations had not yet fully matured."[117]

Smith recognized that the structure of the Agency had been created as a patchwork of solutions to the demands of the external actors. The Agency's research side had grown to eight hundred people inside of a few short years but was only really delivering current and basic intelligence reports.[118] The greater

FIGURE 4.3. Gen. Walter Bedell Smith, 1946. *NARA*

part of the work being done at CIA was in liaising with, and second-guessing the needs of, the intelligence customers. The warring factions of the Office of Policy Coordination and the Office of Special Operations, which duplicated services, were a legacy of the OSS's maverick power and State's wish to have covert operations within its jurisdiction. CIA was not in control of its destiny, and Smith needed to correct that.

Finally, the new DCI recognized that the functions of estimates and current and basic intelligence needed to be separated. Smith prioritized the strategic intelligence analysis function of CIA over everything else. He acknowledged that analysts working on predictions could not be tied up with the day-to-day demands of collating cables from the military, State, and the world's press. Smith was determined to make ONE the best-resourced department but not to interfere in how it was run. That job would fall to Langer.

Langer Moves to CIA

Langer moved over to CIA in November 1950, a month after Smith. He was hired by Smith to assume full responsibility for the findings of the NIEs.[119] It was probably former OSS chief Donovan's recommendation to bring in Langer.[120] Smith and Jackson needed someone to set up and run the BNE and ONE, and Langer was the obvious choice. While there is no record of Smith reading Langer's *Scholarship and the Intelligence Problem*, Langer's experience running a "huge social science research institute" must have appealed to the general.[121]

Sherman Kent, for many years Langer's junior in both the COI/OSS and, from 1950, at CIA, described his boss as capable of kindness and generosity, but—when he felt he had been let down—abrasive to the extent of inflicting terror and hurt. In the four years Kent worked for Langer at R&A, he saw firsthand the drive that made him a great scholar and exacting administrator. "The drive that he showed as an administrative chief was a talent transferred from the 'attaque' of his scholarly writing," recounted Kent. "When he got into a subject matter, God help it; he ripped its clothes off irrespective of difficulties."[122] "Langer sure must be an able man," Kent recalled a former colleague in R&A saying, because "it was through ability alone that he had arrived, not, for example, through his personal charm."[123] Schlesinger thought him "sardonic."[124] With a "nasally and grainy" voice and a slight lisp, Langer's Bostonian accent could deliver bons mots or acerbic comments that cut like a knife.[125]

Langer had little experience with critical evaluation of the raw intelligence produced by collecting agencies like OSS's Secret Intelligence division. Kent says the main difference for Langer was that he had been head of an intelligence research operation prior to his arrival at CIA and then became head of an intelligence estimates operation.[126] Furthermore, Langer was a scholar's intelligence analyst, and he rated books more highly than he did human intelligence. This was partly reflected in the difficulty of placing anyone in a high enough position in the Kremlin to get good information. By the close of World War II the Soviet Union had over six hundred spies working within the United States, Canada, and the United Kingdom. The West had no one working in the Soviet Union.[127] In a memo to the British permanent secretary of state for foreign affairs, Alexander Cadogan, in January 1946, the Foreign Office's Harold Caccia spoke of the future plans of MI6 (Secret Intelligence Service): "The main target is, of course, Russia, and in view of the difficulty of piercing the iron ring of Russian controlled territory . . . it may take years to get an agent into the position of trust from which alone he can supply the information required."[128] Peer de Silva, who had learned Russian in Germany after the war and had been a diplomatic courier traveling between Helsinki and Moscow, offered his services to CIA in 1949. "I came to realize the newly formed agency had no plans for intelligence work within the Soviet Union nor indeed any idea of what might be done. This was confirmed to me when I was assigned to CIA headquarters in 1951. I had thought a great deal might be accomplished, if I had known what some of the requirements were."[129]

Heading up ONE was a role Langer took very seriously. In an early battle of words with one of the members of the BNE, Langer reminded him that he had personal responsibility for the estimates given to him by the DCI.[130] "The fact that Langer was willing to even contemplate assuming personal responsibility for the sort of judgments and reasoned speculations on subjects of highest national importance with which the NIEs were laden," remembered Kent, "says much of his quotient of self-confidence."[131]

Within just two months of starting his new role, Langer was asserting control over both the process and the product of the NIEs. Langer reported on the progress of ONE to a CIA staff conference on January 2, 1951.

> Dr. Langer said that the organization of the Office of Estimates was well along toward completion. He pointed out that the Board of National Estimates now consisted of a very high-powered group who would keep all of the estimators on their mettle. General Huebner has joined the Board of Estimates; Dr. Raymond J. Sontag of the University of California and Dr. Maxwell Foster will shortly be added to the Board. Dr. Langer stated that he was worried about the ability of the IAC agencies to keep pace with such a high level group. Dr. Langer said that he thought it would be desirable to alternate members of the Board of Estimates [redaction] where they would be working with [redaction] for a two-month period. He stated he felt any additional time would result in their getting out of touch with the thinking of O/NE.[132]

Writing in mid-1951, Langer claimed the board was made up of "outstanding scholars of national repute, experts in the field of strategy, political science, economics and other social sciences, and individuals having the broadest experience of intelligence at the highest level."[133]

Board member and ONE analyst Raymond Sontag was a German diplomatic historian and holder of the prestigious Ehrman Chair at the University of California, Berkeley. Prior to that he been head of the History Department for seventeen years at Princeton. He had studied initially at the University of Illinois, receiving a BS and an MA in 1920 and 1921, respectively, and in 1924 earned a PhD from the University of Pennsylvania. Sontag had had no previous experience in intelligence work.[134] He sat on the Board of Estimates for two years from 1951.[135] CIA was often writing to universities requesting their scholars to continue their leave of absence. In November 1951, for example, CIA wrote to the president of the University of California, Dr. Robert Gordon Sproul, asking for Raymond Sontag's leave to be extended until the end of June 1952.[136]

Maxwell Evarts Foster was not a professor but a businessman who joined the board at the behest of William Jackson to "to cross examine you professors, give you a hard time, put you on the spot."[137] During the war he had worked with a leading semanticist, I. A. Richards, to translate a manual on US destroyers for the Chinese navy, who were being gifted them.[138]

Another addition to the board (for only eight months) was Calvin Hoover, professor of economics at Duke University. Hoover had earned his PhD at the University of Wisconsin and written a book, *The Economic Life of Soviet Russia*, in 1931.[139] He had worked with Langer at R&A on the old Board of Analysts and then moved to the Secret Intelligence section of OSS.[140] He also served the US Control Council in Germany before spending 1948 as chief of economic intelligence for the Economic Cooperation Administration (which administered the Marshall Plan).[141] Sherman Kent evidently held him in high regard, telling Hoover in one letter that "I am big enough to punch anybody in the nose—even Joe Louis—as soon as he begins to query the correctness of your analysis and conclusions."[142]

The board would meet with the staff of ONE each morning at nine o'clock to review the work in progress and discuss what was happening in the world as it related to the reports in hand. It was also responsible for deciding which areas of study were worthwhile, determining the questions that needed to be asked and what information was required to answer them. The completed estimates would then return to the board for review. Throughout this process the board consulted members of the IAC and other agencies.[143] Of the eight members of the Board of Estimates, five of them had PhDs in history: "excellent training," said Montague, "for the exercise of critical judgement on the basis of incomplete evidence."[144]

Langer immediately set about determining who he needed on the "ivory tower" estimates team. CIA had inherited about three hundred analysts from CIG, not the small, dedicated team Langer believed he needed.[145] And CIG had not come up with the goods Langer thought necessary either. Already at CIA were two historians who had suffered the humiliation of the Dulles-Jackson-Correa report: Ludwell Lee Montague and DeForest Van Slyck. Montague's PhD was from Duke University. He had been an assistant professor of history at the Virginia Military Institute, served with the Air Force intelligence unit G-2 initially and then the Joint Intelligence Service, was assistant director at CIG, and finally was chief of the Global Survey Group during the ORE years.[146] Van Slyck had been his deputy and had a PhD from Yale, teaching history there for nine years before becoming an investment banker. While at ORE, Van Slyck had chaired a working group that had produced an NIE in 1948 on Soviet intentions over the Berlin Blockade. Convened on a Saturday by Hillenkoetter (who contributed not by attending but by "bustling in and out with trays of coffee and sandwiches"), the interagency group struggled for days to agree on a statement. After an impatient Truman exhorted them to arrive at an estimate, the group settled on estimating that the Soviets would not "resort to military action

within the next 60 days." An NSC study later commented that the Berlin Blockade group was "the most significant exception to a rather general failure . . . in
national estimates."[147]

Both Montague and Van Slyck would have been understandably prickly
about the new regime.[148] Writing in 1970, Kent was diplomatic:

> Both had served in the O/RE [Office of Reports and Estimates] of CIA writ-
> ing the pre-November 1950 national estimates; both were accomplished
> practitioners of the art and knew ten times as much about it as the rest of
> us put together. But there they were, the veterans, outnumbered and out-
> ranked by the newcomers. I think we in our innocence annoyed them, and
> the way Langer ran things must have been doubly hard to take. On our
> part, we got a bit miffed at being treated too often as new boys and second
> formers by these two sixth-form senior prefects. But no matter, we held
> their talent and experience in high regard and I think they did admirably in
> getting used to us so speedily.[149]

There were others who had arrived before Langer and now stayed on. Ray
Cline, who gained his PhD in international relations and history at Harvard in
1949, had joined CIA in early summer the same year.[150] Recruited by R. Jack
Smith, another former OSS man, Cline had been working initially on the
monthly *Review of the World Situation* under the eye of Montague.[151] Langer
asked Cline to draw up a list of around thirty people, stipulating that "every man
[be] a broadly qualified intelligence officer and all capable of writing a review
of evidence and a summary of critical findings on a very broad strategic plane."
He promoted Cline, then only thirty-two years old, to be the first chief of the
estimates staff.[152] Cline is credited as one of the key people who later grew the
White House's confidence in CIA.[153]

Willard Matthias, who had come to CIA in 1947 from wartime experience
at G-2 military intelligence, had earned an MA first from the University of
Minnesota (1938) and then a second as a Litauer Fellow at Harvard (1938–39).
He was on the staff of the Brookings Institution the following year and then
taught briefly as an assistant professor at Miami, Oxford, and Ohio Universities, in government and international relations.[154] Matthias spent over twenty
years writing and directing estimates.[155]

Robert Komer was another of the pre-Langer ONE staff. He had studied
history at Harvard and served in the Fifth Army's G-2 shop. At the cessation of the war, he returned to Harvard to earn an MBA on foreign trade and
resources.[156] Arriving in 1947, he was assigned to ORE's European desk on mul-
tilateral institutions such as the United Nations. Komer thought his bosses were
uninterested in this and only wrote one analysis while there. Langer, however,

considered Komer to have potential and moved him to the newly established ONE. Promoted to the Western European, then to the Africa, the Middle East, and the Far East Asia desks, he (according to Tim Weiner) wrote reports on "everything from Morocco to Malaysia." He became the chief of the estimates staff in 1955, then CIA representative on the NSC in 1958, finally ending up as an adviser to the Kennedy administration during the Vietnam Era.[157] He was known as "Blowtorch Bob," a nickname given to him by the senator (and historian) Henry Cabot Lodge, who said that arguing with Komer was like having "a flamethrower aimed at the seat of your pants."[158]

Other analytical staff included the historian Abbot E. Smith (who succeeded Kent as director of ONE on his retirement in 1967), Richard P. Stebbins (ex-R&A), historians George Jackson and Paul Borel (both, like Montague and Van Slyck, from ORE), Sovietologist John Whitman, Asia specialist James Graham, historians and Middle East specialists Charles Cremeans and Keith Clark, military Sovietologist Ted Walker, William P. Bundy, and historians John Huizinga (who also became a ONE director) and Harold "Hal" P. Ford.[159] Ford joined in 1950 with an undergraduate degree in history from the University of Redlands, California, and a PhD in political science from Chicago.[160] He had also held a postdoctoral fellowship at St. Anthony's, Oxford. Among other senior roles in CIA and the intelligence community, Ford went on to head the national estimates team and to write one of the discipline's key texts, *Estimative Intelligence*.

Perhaps the most lasting recruitment success was the hiring of Sherman Kent, a historian from Yale who had worked with Langer at R&A on the European and North African desk. Kent's story, and the in-depth story of the NIE, is told in the next chapter. Ray Cline remembers him in those early days and emphasizes his most durable achievement, the creation of a new workforce and respected intelligence product:[161]

> Finally Langer brought onto his board as his Deputy—after January 1952 his successor—an old colleague from OSS, Yale Professor Sherman Kent, whose just published book on strategic intelligence made him the outstanding academic expert on a new profession. . . . We sat in one of those bare little offices in the old South Building looking at each other across a scarred old wooden desk inherited from OSS, and I told him that so few people in the CIA knew what intelligence was all about and such threatening situations existed in the world that he was needed. I do not know if this influenced him but he came, he stayed, and built the National Intelligence Estimates into a significant element in decision-making.[162]

In addition to this roll call of professors, a panel of consultants was created, which included Vannevar Bush and George Kennan. The Princeton Consultants effectively peer-reviewed the estimates and would meet with selected members of the board and ONE about once a month.[163]

Recruitment from universities became more structured as CIA embedded the idea of the scholar as intelligence analyst. In early December 1951 the Agency discussed with Professor Alfred Raymond Bellinger of Yale the possibility of him setting up contacts between CIA and academia for the recruitment of high-level graduates.[164] Bellinger, an archaeologist, who was chair of the Department of Classics at the time, would talk to fifty or more colleges and universities.

Conclusion

As an administrator, Langer had developed a strategy to raise CIA out of the organizational morass it had found itself in. Langer's strategy was rooted in his belief that social science could provide a firm basis for strategic intelligence. Langer had called for a huge social science institute devoted to the problems of national security. He believed he had the ingredients for it at R&A, where economists, political scientists, historians, geographers, psychologists, archaeologists, and even philologists worked together in a multidisciplinary fashion. The work of CIA must prioritize the broad- and long-ranging reports that would become the NIEs. This was not work that Langer was familiar with: R&A had been an intelligence research operation focusing on the present, where CIA was an intelligence estimates operation looking to the future.

Together with DCI Smith, Langer imposed a new structure on CIA, giving the estimates team plenty of room to think while peeling away the day-to-day work that had distracted his predecessors. It was an ivory tower to be sure, but it was one committed to creating a robust research method staffed by some of the very best social scientists available. It was DCI Smith who created this environment through soldierly brute force, but it was Langer who created the academic community that would slowly transform into a strategic intelligence analysis discipline.

Smith had gone further still; he had silenced two of his most vocal critics. By taking Dulles and Jackson into the organization, he had effectively made them willing accomplices to the CIA's organizational reform. When Jackson left CIA in 1951, Smith made Dulles deputy DCI, making him even further a "CIA man."[165] In an interview in 1953 Dulles confirmed this:

> Bill Jackson and I sat down and spent a good bit of a year in 1948 with such experience as we had behind us in outlining the kind of organization we felt should produce intelligence. . . . That general blueprint is, I believe, sound. General Smith and Jackson, and to some extent myself, during the past two years, with the able help of many others, have been trying to put

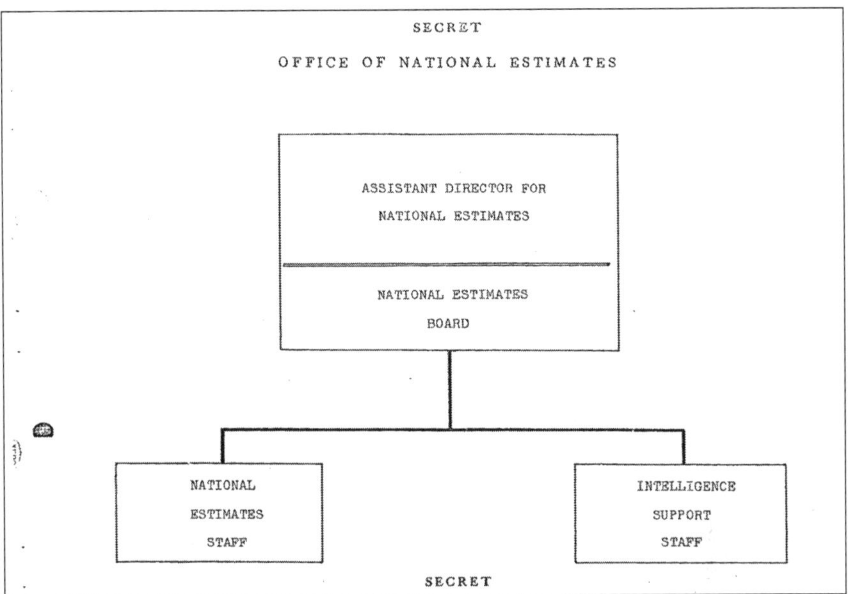

FIGURE 4.4. Organizational Chart of the Office of National Estimates, December 1950. *CIA Reading Room*

that blueprint into effect. Naturally we have changed it here and there, but by and large, we have today, I believe, a working organization.[166]

By late 1952 CIA had begun work on institutionalizing the social science–based intelligence method. On November 25 of that year, a CIA memo titled "Intelligence Research Program" outlined the intention to create a "program of directed research" that would build a database of CIA's institutional knowledge. This would include (a) a master comparative chronology, presumably a charting of historical events that could be viewed across continents to discover patterns and links; (b) a list of problems, or titles, that would not be too big or unwieldy; (c) the breaking down of these major titles into smaller ones that were more achievable for the unit; (d) the "formulation of specific hypotheses and their analysis into historically verifiable propositions. Assembly and analysis of evidence, and analysis of subsequent events, for upholding or refutation of hypotheses"; (e) and detailed case studies "from all relevant points of view" of events, episodes, and sequences of events, and the inclusion of analytical and historical monographs.[167] The research design itself would get to the heart of the CIA intelligence mission. It would include:

(a) analysis of problems into small and manageable component solutions within the capability of our shops; and (b) problems amenable to empirical or historical test. In the philosophy of science (elaborated most highly in logical positivism) questions amenable to empirical test are called "operational" all others are called "metaphysical." We must avoid all so-called "metaphysical questions." (c) Problems would be either major questions of Soviet policy and intentions, or analytic components of such major problems; they could be reconstruction, trend analysis or description problems.[168]

The intention was to produce papers that would then be circulated to all the CIA "shops" for criticism, and to bring about a meeting of minds on the most serious problems the Agency was considering. "All personnel would thus be brought to think about the same problems, important omissions would be discovered, discussion and mutual assistance would be stimulated, all persons would be jointly educated in some important respect." Once agreed to, these would be issued as Strategy Staff working papers.[169] The social science method had now reached its apogee at CIA. Not only was there a desire to bring all of the problems facing the Agency under one umbrella, but it was also now a CIA way of tackling problems, and it was couched in the language of the social scientist.

Langer left CIA for Harvard in February 1952.[170] In an interview shortly after for the *Harvard Crimson*, he played down his work, saying, "I went down there very suddenly in November of 1950 to organize the office of national estimate [*sic*] in the CIA. I wasn't so much concerned with research—rather to pull together the results of all the various agencies." The university newspaper told its readers the professor was now teaching History 132b.[171]

Notes

Epigraph: Kent, *Strategic Intelligence for American World Policy*, xv.
1. For an overview of intelligence failures during World War II, see Matthais, *America's Strategic Blunders*, 14. Ultra (from ultrasecret) was the name given to decrypted signals intelligence gathered mostly from the German Enigma cypher machine during World War II.
2. Matthais, 4.
3. Marrin, *Improving Intelligence Analysis*, 1–2.
4. Katz, *Foreign Intelligence*, 3.
5. For a fuller story of the Research and Analysis section of OSS, see Winks, *Cloak and Gown*.
6. Katz, 2–3.
7. Ford, "The US Government's Experience," 35–36.
8. Langer, *In and Out of the Ivory Tower*, 184.
9. Langer, 189.
10. Katz, *Foreign Intelligence*, 4–8.
11. Katz, 5. See also Langer, *In and Out of the Ivory Tower*, 188.

12. Langer, 187.
13. *History of the Library: Lewis, Walpole, and the Library*, Yale University website, accessed April 15, 2020, https://walpole.library.yale.edu/about/history-library/. See also Liebert, *Wilmarth Sheldon Lewis (1895–1979)*, 198–200.
14. Winks, *Cloak and Gown*, 100, with Winks quoting Hammond, "Intelligence Organizations and the Organization of Intelligence," 694.
15. Hammond, "Intelligence Organizations and the Organization of Intelligence," 699.
16. Wolff, "William L. Langer," 191.
17. Wolff, 191.
18. Langer, *In and Out of the Ivory Tower*, 182–83.
19. Smith, *The Shadow Warriors*, 209.
20. Langer, *In and Out of the Ivory Tower*, 182.
21. Smith, *The Shadow Warriors*, 209–10.
22. Richard D. McKinzie, Oral History Interview with Charles P. Kindleberger, Truman Library (1973), https://www.trumanlibrary.gov/library/oral-histories/kindbrgr.
23. Pettee, *The Future of American Secret Intelligence*, 20.
24. Schlesinger, *A Life in the Twentieth Century*, 300.
25. Langer, *In and Out of the Ivory Tower*, 183.
26. Langer, 184–87. Langer says the All Souls press-reading group included Charles K. Webster, Alfred Zimmern, H.A.R. Gibb, and David Mitrany.
27. Schlesinger, *A Life in the Twentieth Century*, 174.
28. See chapter 4 in Aldous, *Schlesinger*.
29. Schlesinger, *A Life in the Twentieth Century*, 295.
30. Schlesinger, 35.
31. Gleason never returned to academia, going on to run the secretariat of the National Security Council in the 1950s. Schlesinger, 297.
32. Schlesinger, 297.
33. Schlesinger, 299.
34. Schlesinger, 300.
35. This event is disputed by Halperin's biographer. There is possibly some confusion here, with Schlesinger specifying Bolivia and Halperin telling a slightly different story about the Sinarquistas of Mexico. Schlesinger's memory may be serving him wrong or there may be two stories. In the Mexico case, Halperin argues it was a collective assessment made by the Latin American desk. The report found "the movement in the class relationships of a volatile nation and, more specifically, in the effort to 'evolve a modern democratic nation out of an essentially feudal agricultural society.' The Latin Americanists . . . were convinced that the *Sinarquistas* were connected with the Nazis and the fascist *Falange* of Spain. It was an indigenous movement," writes Halperin's biographer, "but it employed the techniques and slogans of the European Right, and was spreading what amounted to Nazi propaganda." Halperin says OSS knew of his political leanings and Donovan had no problems so long as he delivered. See Kirschner, *Cold War Exile*, 70–71, 76–77.
36. Schlesinger, *A Life in the Twentieth Century*, 301–2.
37. Schlesinger, 209–300.
38. Schlesinger, 300.
39. Winks, *Cloak and Gown*, 90.
40. Smith, *The Shadow Warriors*, 210.

41. The Central European desk was composed of German scholars who had fled Nazism: Franz Neumann, Felix Gilbert, Hajo Holborn, Herbert Marcuse, and Otto Kirchheimer.
42. Smith, *The Shadow Warriors*, 211.
43. Pettee, *The Future of American Secret Intelligence*, 30.
44. Quoted in Ford, "The US Government's Experience," 36.
45. Kent, *Strategic Intelligence for American World Policy*, xi; and Olcott, "Revisiting the Legacy," 28.
46. Pettee, *The Future of American Secret Intelligence*, 65.
47. Pettee, 67.
48. Pettee, 34.
49. Dean Acheson had appeared before the House Appropriations Committee on November 26, 1945, and claimed that, up until the beginning of the war, there had been no changes in the way the State Department collected intelligence since John Quincy Adams was in St. Petersburg and Benjamin Franklin in Paris—short of the use of the telegraph and typewriter. Pettee, *The Future of American Secret Intelligence*, 36–37.
50. Pettee, vii–viii.
51. Pettee, 7.
52. Pettee, 7.
53. Pettee, 5.
54. Pettee,13.
55. Pettee, 12–21.
56. Langer, "Scholarship and the Intelligence Problem," 43–45.
57. Langer, 43–44.
58. Langer, 43.
59. Langer, 45.
60. Kent, "The First Year of the Office of National Estimates," 151. See also Warner, *The Office of Strategic Services*, 7.
61. See National Intelligence Authority: Minutes of the Meeting Held in Room 212, Department of State Building, on Wednesday 24th July 1946, at 10:30 am, CIA-RDP10-01569R000100060017-7, CIA, CREST Archive.
62. Warner, *CIA Under Truman*, 295–313.
63. Jackson and Claussen, *Organizational History of the Central Intelligence Agency*, 2:29.
64. Warner, *CIA Under Truman*, 298.
65. Warner, 304.
66. Warner, 305.
67. Warner, 296.
68. The choice of his replacement might have been Allen Dulles (Montague seems to think so) if it had not been for Dulles's association with Truman's Republican challenger, Dewey. See Montague, *General Walter Bedell Smith*, 43–50, 13.
69. McCullough, *Truman*, 665.
70. Montague, *General Walter Bedell Smith*, 55–56.
71. U.S. Congress, "Ninety-Fourth Congress, Second Session, Senate: Elect Committee to Discover Government Operations with Respect to Intelligence Activities" (hereafter cited as Church Committee), 11.
72. Cline, *The CIA Under Reagan, Bush, and Casey*, 130–31.

73. Crosswell, *Beetle*, 5.

74. Crosswell, 18.

75. Memorandum for the Record, August 29, 1950, CIA, CREST Archive, in Warner, *CIA Under Truman*, 343.

76. Warner, 343.

77. Warner, 344.

78. Warner, 345.

79. Crosswell, *Beetle*, 4.

80. Although Jackson, according to Montague, did not believe Smith had ever actually read NSC-50, Montague says he was familiar with all seven and must have read NSC-50. The seven reports were the follow up to NSC-50, NSCID1, in two revisions and a supplementary legal memo, another memo interpreting the National Security Act of 1947, the Webb Staff Study written by Magruder, and JIC 445/1 covering CIA's status and responsibilities during wartime. Montague, *General Walter Bedell Smith*, 112.

81. Barrett, *The CIA and Congress*, 28.

82. Ranelagh, *The Agency*, 191.

83. Matthais, *America's Strategic Blunders*, 47.

84. US State Department, Office of the Historian, Memorandum from Secretary of Defense Marshall to Director of Central Intelligence Smith, 56.

85. Memorandum from Theodore Babbitt, Ludwell Montague, and Forrest Van Slyck, 56.

86. Ranelagh, *The Agency*, 191.

87. Kirkpatrick, *The Real CIA*, 118.

88. *The New York Times* reported that Averill Harriman of the White House had suggested Jackson's appointment and had also originally suggested Smith to Truman as being a good candidate for DCI. See footnote in Jackson and Claussen, *Organizational History of the Central Intelligence Agency*, 2:51fn1.

89. Jackson ended up being more flexible on the execution of the Dulles Report than he first intended. When General Magruder (Defense) and W. Park Armstrong (State) suggested an umbrella "national intelligence group," Jackson thought it worth considering, despite it not having featured in the Dulles Report. This was an indication that—as Jackson was now working within the organization—he was longer working as an external actor. See Jackson and Claussen, 2:43.

90. Kent and Thacher, *Reminiscences of a Varied Life*, 249.

91. Kirkpatrick, *The Real CIA*, 89.

92. Kirkpatrick, 89.

93. Kirkpatrick, 95.

94. Montague, *General Walter Bedell Smith*, 151.

95. Montague, 151. In a letter to Kent from Max Millikan dated March 29, 1950, Millikan says MIT is "expanding our social science staff in fields of history, economics, sociology, psychology, etc., of the modern industrial and technological community." Millikan then adds "Why don't you and Beth come up for a weekend sometime?" MS 854, Box 18, Series 1, Correspondence, 1920–1980, Folder 391: Wolfers, Arnold, 1942–1947, 1965, Sherman Kent Papers, Manuscripts and Archives, Yale University Library (hereafter, SKP).

96. Kirkpatrick, *The Real CIA*, 104.

97. Helgerson, "Truman and Eisenhower," 65–77.

98. Kirkpatrick, *The Real CIA*, 106.
99. Helgerson, *Truman and Eisenhower.*
100. Helgerson. See also Knutson, "Truman Beach."
101. Kirkpatrick, *The Real CIA*, 95–96.
102. Montague, *General Walter Bedell Smith*, 59–61, 55–56.
103. Neu, "The Rise of the National Security Bureaucracy," 88. See also Eisenhower, *The White House Years*, 2:114–35.
104. Church Committee, 5.
105. Neu, "The Rise of the National Security Bureaucracy," 87, 114–35.
106. Jackson and Claussen, *Organizational History of the Central Intelligence Agency*, 2:3.
107. Jackson and Claussen, 2:61.
108. Kirkpatrick, *The Real CIA*, 117–18; and Jackson and Claussen, *Organizational History of the Central Intelligence Agency*, 2:58–59.
109. Jackson and Claussen, 2:65.
110. Montague, *General Walter Bedell Smith*, 133.
111. Kirkpatrick, *The Real CIA*, 95–97.
112. Minutes of Meeting held in Director's Conference Room, Administration Building Central Intelligence Agency Monday March 26, 1951, CIA-RDP80B01676R-002300010016-1, CIA, CREST Archive.
113. Director's Log, 8.30 am November 17–8.30 am November 18, 1951-09-01, CIA, CREST Archive.
114. Kirkpatrick, *The Real CIA*, 97–98.
115. Jackson and Claussen, *Organizational History of the Central Intelligence Agency*, 2:52–54.
116. Snider, *The Agency and the Hill*, 45.
117. Kirkpatrick, *The Real CIA*, 88.
118. Kirkpatrick, 97–98.
119. Kent, "The First Year of the Office of National Estimates," 151.
120. Kent, 151.
121. Langer, "Scholarship and the Intelligence Problem," 43–45.
122. Kent, "The First Year of the Office of National Estimates," 44.
123. Kent, 44.
124. Schlesinger, *A Life in the Twentieth Century*, 35.
125. Kent, "The First Year of the Office of National Estimates," 144.
126. Kent, 146.
127. Pringle, "Guide to Soviet and Russian Intelligence Services," 52. A major of the KGB, Peter Popov, provided CIA with Warsaw Pact secrets from 1953 to 1958. See Prados, *The Soviet Estimate*, 26.
128. Minutes, to Alexander Cadogan from Harold Caccia, 1946, FO 1093/400, National Archives, Kew, United Kingdom.
129. de Silva, *Sub Rosa*, 17.
130. This was an interesting position for Langer to take: It assumed that the final responsibility for the NIE was delegated to him from the DCI. The argument over whether the DCI or the IAC was ultimately responsible had been raging since Vandenberg's time. Vandenberg demanded the authority, Hillenkoetter refused it, and Smith made it one of his first rulings. See Montague, *General Walter Bedell Smith*, 67–68, 70–71; and Jackson and Claussen, *Organizational History of the Central Intelligence Agency*, 2:39–40.

131. Kent, "The First Year of the Office of National Estimates," 146.
132. Staff Conference—Minutes of Meeting held in Director's Conference Room, Administration Building, Tuesday, January 2, 1951, at 1100 hours, Mr. William H. Jackson Presiding, CIA-RDP80B01676R002300010003-5, CIA, CREST Archive.
133. Activities of the Office of National Estimates, July 9, 1951, p. 2, RDP84-00022-R000200160046-6, CIA, CREST Archive.
134. Kent and Thacher, *Reminiscences of a Varied Life*, 250.
135. *Raymond James Sontag, History: Berkeley*, Online Archive of California, UC Libraries, accessed April 25, 2020, http://texts.cdlib.org/view?docId=hb9t1nb5rm&doc.view=frames&chunk.id=div00063&toc.depth=1&toc.id=. See also Cline, *Secrets, Spies and Scholars*, 121; and Kent, "The First Year of the Office of National Estimates," 147.
136. Director's Log, 8.30 a.m. November 17–8.30 a.m. November 18.
137. Kent, "The First Year of the Office of National Estimates," 152–53.
138. Kent and Thacher, *Reminiscences of a Varied Life*, 252.
139. Hoover's impressions of the Soviet economy mirrored those of other economic Sovietologists at the time. Talking of his sources, Hoover had written, "In some cases I feel they are subject to discount, on account of the fact that Soviet statisticians are subjected to considerable pressure, and are, therefore, not free to interpret their own data. This pressure is due to a kind of self deception which renders Party members unwilling to face unpleasant facts, and which causes them to see other data through rose-colored spectacles." Hoover, *The Economic Life of Soviet Russia*, vii.
140. Kent and Thacher, *Reminiscences of a Varied Life*, 250.
141. Kent, "The First Year of the Office of National Estimates," 133.
142. "Letter to Prof. Calvin B. Hoover from Sherman Kent, October 4, 1965," MS 854, Series 1, Box 6, Folder 158, SKP.
143. Byrnes, "Harvard, Columbia and the CIA," 93–114.
144. Kent also mentions board members James C. Cooley and Wayne G. Jackson (both lawyers and OSS veterans) as well as military representatives Gen. William Morris and Lt. Gen. Harold R. (Pinky) Bull. See Kent and Thacher, *Reminiscences of a Varied Life*, 268; and Montague, *General Walter Bedell Smith*, 134.
145. Vickers, and CIA History Staff, *The History of CIA's Office of Strategic Research*, x.
146. Kent, "The First Year of the Office of National Estimates," 152–53; and Montague, *General Walter Bedell Smith*, 132.
147. "Learning to Estimate 1948," CIA website, https://www.cia.gov/news-information/featured-story-archive/2008-featured-story-archive/learning-to-estimate-1948.
148. Darling, *The Central Intelligence Agency*, 110–11.
149. Kent, "The First Year of the Office of National Estimates," 148.
150. Bart Barnes, "Ray Cline Dies at 77," *Washington Post*, March 16, 1996, https://www.washingtonpost.com/archive/local/1996/03/16/ray-s-cline-dies-at-77/4831cbd4-2f4b-4631-a89c-bc2addccf24c/.
151. Weber, *Spymasters*, 180–81.
152. Jones, *Blowtorch*, 20.
153. Kent and Thacher, *Reminiscences of a Varied Life*, 250.
154. Prabook, *Willard C. Matthias*, n.d., accessed November 19, 2020, https://prabook.com/web/willard_c.matthias/513376; and Willard C. Matthias and Reid Graham, Veterans History Project, and Library of Congress, Willard C. Matthias Collection, 1943, Personal Narrative, https://www.loc.gov/item/afc2001001.24789/.

155. Matthais, *America's Strategic Blunders*, 315. Cited in Coogan, Review of *America's Strategic Blunders*, 275.

156. Jones, *Blowtorch*, 13.

157. Jones, 24; see also Trahair, *Encyclopedia of Cold War Espionage*, 196; and "Robert W. Komer—2018," Clayton Education Foundation, accessed November 12, 2020, https://www.claytoneducationfoundation.org/s/1537/17/interior.aspx?sid=1537&gid=1&pgid=696&cid=1569&ecid=1569&crid=0&calpgid=598&calcid=1312.

158. Tim Weiner, "Robert Comer, 78, Figure in Vietnam, Dies," *New York Times*, April 12, 2000, https://www.nytimes.com/2000/04/12/world/robert-komer-78-figure-in-vietnam-dies.html.

159. For Abbot E. Smith, George Jackson, Paul Borel, Ted Walker, William P. Bundy, John Huizinga, and the economists Edgar Hoover and Harold F. Linder, see Kent and Thacher, *Reminiscences of a Varied Life*, 250, 269–72; and Consultations with People about the Intelligence Process (1979), CIA-RDP98S00099R000501010011-1, CIA CREST Archive. For Richard Stebbins, see Winks, *Cloak and Gown*, 65; and Montague, *General Walter Bedell Smith*, 136. See also "John Whitman, CIA Analyst, Dies at 72," *Washington Post*, November 14, 1998, https://www.washingtonpost.com/archive/local/1998/11/14/john-whitman-cia-analyst-dies-at-72/dd2d0fb9-daeb-49bb-a60d-b69aa8a718e6/; US Congress, House Select Committee on Intelligence, "U.S. Intelligence Agencies and Activities," 1719; "Charles Cremeans, CIA Official," *Washington Post*, August 28, 1996, https://www.washingtonpost.com/archive/local/1996/08/29/obituaries/a63a783b-bdc1-419e-84b9-d71023514490/; and "Keith Clark, 58, Dies," *Washington Post*, November 1, 1981, https://www.washingtonpost.com/archive/local/1981/11/01/keith-c-clark-58-dies/cf6387aa-a43c-4f65-8244-431cc0d48348/.

160. Scott Shane, "Harold P. Ford, C.I.A. Analyst, Dies at 89," *New York Times*, November 12, 2010, https://www.nytimes.com/2010/11/12/world/12ford.html.

161. Cline's praise of Kent was not reciprocated: In his memoirs Kent recognizes Cline's ability but says he was only interested in himself. See Kent and Thacher, *Reminiscences of a Varied Life*, 275.

162. Cline, *Secrets, Spies and Scholars*, 122.

163. Activities of the Office of National Estimates.

164. Director's Log, 8.30 a.m. November 17–8.30 a.m. November 18.

165. Jackson and Claussen, *Organizational History of the Central Intelligence Agency*, 2:52–54.

166. See CIA History 1950-53-2 (1957), fn1, II.37, CIA, CREST Archive.

167. Intelligence Research Program (1952), CIA-RDP91T01172R000400130015-9, CIA, CREST Archive.

168. Intelligence Research Program.

169. Intelligence Research Program.

170. Jones, *Blowtorch*, 20.

171. "Langer, Former Intelligence Expert in C.I.A., Returns to Old Post—Teaching History," *Harvard Crimson*, February 8, 1952, https://www.thecrimson.com/article/1952/2/8/langer-former-intelligence-expert-in-cia/.

The Intel Intellectuals and the Emergence of a Strategic Intelligence Discipline

I was sitting at my desk in the Office of National Estimates (ONE) at the Central Intelligence Agency (CIA) when the phone rang. "Ray, how big is the Soviet army?" It [was] the late Robert Amory, Deputy Director for Intelligence. The call, and still more the question, were unexpected. I began to reply that the answer depended on whether certain marginal categories, such as border guards and construction troops, were counted, and did he want divisions and major arms, or manpower. Before I had gotten very far, Amory interjected impatiently, "Don't give me a dissertation, Ray, just the answer."

—Raymond Garthoff (1960)

The intel intellectuals came to a struggling CIA with the brief to reform it into an organization that would meet its mission. The task was to provide clear and prescient information about the intentions and capabilities of the new Communist adversary. Yale historian Sherman Kent was at the forefront of shaping this new discipline as well as recognizing the strengths and weaknesses of his academic craft. The intentions and capabilities of the Soviet Bloc would not be gleaned simply by research. In the search for some sort of objective truth as it pertained to the enemy, a new approach was needed. Kent wrote in 1948:

> Research is the only process which we of the liberal tradition are willing to admit is capable of giving us the truth, or a closer approximation to true, than we now enjoy. A medieval philosopher would have been content to get his truth by extrapolating from the Holy Writ, an African chieftain by consultation with his witch doctor, or a mystic like Adolf Hitler from communion with his intuitive self. But we insist, and have insisted for generations, that truth is to be approached, if not attained, through research guided by a systematic method. In the social sciences, which very largely constitute the subject matter of strategic intelligence, there is such a method. It is very much like the method of the physical sciences. It is not the same method, but it is a method none the less.[1]

Kent had taken on board the need for a multidisciplinary approach (that blended history, political science, economics, geography, sociology, anthropology, and psychology) and was now transforming it from a strictly social science method to one that could be truly called a strategic intelligence discipline—with its own expertise. He gave special consideration to objectivity, consistency of methods, preciseness of definitions and language, source selection, and hypothesis making. But social science would only provide the foundations of intelligence analysis. The nature of working with such a secretive enemy would require leaps into the unknown that even social science, which attempted to understand the vagaries of human behavior, might not be fully equipped to meet.

Kent Lays the Groundwork for a Strategic Intelligence Discipline

Kent was born in Chicago in 1903. The son of a congressman, the family moved to Washington, DC, where he lived until he was sixteen.[2] He attended Yale, graduating in 1926, and was awarded a PhD in history in 1933. His dissertation topic was the electoral procedure under French king Louis Philippe.[3] Kent was made a professor in 1935.[4] His salary as a professor at Yale had climbed to $8,000 a year in 1948.[5] In 1949 his net worth included cash holdings of $7,360, government bonds worth $43,000, and common stocks of $70,537. He received dividends and interest on his shares of $6,489.20, royalties from his books of $836.55 and lecture fees of $300.[6] By 1952 CIA was paying him $14,800 per annum.[7] By 1960 he was earning $18,500 from his investments alone, with a handsome 17.5 percent return.

As befitting an Ivy League professor, Kent bought his seersucker suits, shirts, and socks from J. Press on York Street, New Haven, and had business suits made both in Hong Kong and on Savile Row. He wore a vintage Patek Phillipe watch, and in the later part of his life bequeathed two paintings (by the Russian-born surrealist Pavel Tchelitchew) to the Yale University art museum. He regularly gave money to family and friends and was an active member of the Democratic Party.

In 1941, at the age of thirty-eight, he joined the Office of the Coordinator of Intelligence, which became the Office of Strategic Services (OSS) shortly after Pearl Harbor.[8] In 1943 he was promoted to chief of OSS's Research and Analysis Europe-Africa division.[9]

The Europe-Africa division was a major contributor to the success of OSS. Kent's researchers provided information on North African ports and railways in time for the Allied invasion. They worked around the clock in what was described as an undergraduate "final exam culture."[10]

Kent was a meticulous scholar. Before the war he published a textbook for undergraduates called *Writing History* (1941).[11] Kent approached it as a "how-to" guide, including how to select the perfect topic, research techniques, keep track of your sources, write bibliographies, and prepare an index. "No detail of composition, punctuation, or typography is too trifling for notice; nothing is common or unclean; every need of the beginner seems sensed," wrote A. B. White of the book in the *American Historical Review*.[12] This attention to detail was carried through to his work at OSS where, according to Jack Davis, "the most potent weapon was the index card crowded with information and insight for understanding and defeating the enemy."[13] It was social science best practice that underscored Kent's approach to intelligence.

He was not a natural administrator. Kent was interested in the intellectual challenge of analysis and not the paperwork. His management style appears to have been quite organic: he simply wanted to recruit the best team and then work them to the bone. Dressed in colorful red braces, Kent was known by his staff as "Buffalo Bill the Cultured Cowboy"—a sobriquet he had picked up as an undergraduate.[14] His language was also colorful: according to former DCI Richard Helms, Kent once assessed the chances of a tin-pot dictator's promise to reorganize his government as similar "to gathering piss with a rake."[15]

As chief of R&A's Europe-Africa division, Kent had been instrumental in bringing Hajo Holborn into the OSS. Holborn was one of several German émigrés who fleshed out the OSS's understanding of contemporary Nazi Germany. This list included Holborn's close friend Felix Gilbert, who, like Holborn, was trained by Frederich Meinecke, the leading German historian of the day. Holborn's historical training was founded in the modern tradition of Leopold von Ranke, which emphasized "rigorous objectivity, the critical examination of original documents, the banishing of philosophical predispositions from the territory of the historian, [and] the assumption that the past is a unified field and history a unified process."[16]

As detailed by Barry M. Katz, the German émigrés had mixed influence on Allied planning, particularly in managing postwar Germany. But they would have been deeply instructive to Kent in thinking about the task. Katz says, "Without [any] models, precedents, or even the framework of American policy, they had to proceed with a judicious admixture of close empirical research and disciplined extrapolation if they were to help military and diplomatic policy makers to anticipate developments rather than simply respond to them."[17] Holborn was important in another way to the OSS's R&A department: He was a key figure in bridging the gap between the Pentagon as a customer and the academic suppliers who developed the hundred-odd civil affairs booklets that instructed the US occupying forces on managing postwar Germany. The Pentagon, it appears, was not an easy client, and the administration was uncertain as to what policy to pursue in denazifying Germany in particular. This meant Holborn had the job of reconciling competing policy views in an environment that presaged the combative interagency committee structure of the early national intelligence estimate process for CIA.[18] It was an experience Kent and his boss,

William Langer, would have been well familiar with when they arrived at CIA in late 1950.

Henry L. Roberts was another historian who worked with Kent during the war. He joined R&A in the spring of 1942, shortly after earning his PhD at Yale.[19] Roberts was also involved in the groundwork that R&A did in preparation for the Allied landings in North Africa. Yet it was not just a daily grind of identifying ports and transportation links for the Army: R&A was a fertile learning ground for the young scholar. "Both the nature of his work with that body, and the colleagues with whom he worked in it, appear to have been intellectually formative," argues his former student Joseph Rothschild.[20] Working alongside Herbert Marcuse and Franz Neumann gave him important insights into Marxist thought, which—coupled with the common cause of fighting totalitarianism—had a lasting impact on his belief in defending democracy and delivering policy-oriented research. Roberts returned to academic life after the war, teaching first at Columbia, where he both ran the Russia Institute and was founding director of the university's Institute for East Central Europe.[21] He continued to contribute to policy papers, in 1958 personally sending a report on the USSR to the then-DCI Allen Dulles.[22]

Kent was also instrumental in persuading economists to work under him, a forerunner to the interdisciplinary teams he put together later at CIA. One example was Edgar Hoover, who was chief economist at R&A and later joined CIA's Board of National Estimates for a short period in 1951.[23]

Writing in 1965, Kent summed up the progress US intelligence had made during World War II:

> Thanks to our wartime labors we not only possessed a stock of relevant and useful information about the Soviet Union, we also had the makings of a far better intelligence profession than had existed heretofore. The analytical arm of US intelligence was able to identify its principal objectives—and with precision: it had developed some mature doctrine; it had mastered some difficult and important technical methodologies; it was moving toward a common vocabulary; and most of all it had produced a good number of sophisticated practitioners.[24]

However, Sherman Kent warned, the influx of new collection methods had meant the intelligence discipline needed to change with the times. Nevertheless, he argued, "there is no substitute for the intellectually competent human—the person who was born with the makings of a critical sense and who has developed them to their full potential; who through firsthand experience and study has accumulated an orderly store of knowledge; and who has a feeling for going about the search for further enlightenment in a systematic way."[25]

After the war ended, Kent spent a brief time at the State Department, which had absorbed OSS Research and Analysis, as acting director of the Office of Intelligence Research.[26] Jack Davis considers State to have been willfully neglectful of the OSS research powerhouse, saying the diplomatic foreign service officers had low regard for the academics (particularly those who were foreigners) and considered their embassy-derived intelligence more than sufficient.[27] Kent chose to move on, but not just back to Yale. He also accepted a job at the National War College, teaching alongside George Kennan and Bernard Brodie.[28]

In late 1946 Kent was invited by the publishers of the *American Political Science Review* to apply for the job of director, replacing Waldo G. Leland. The job was based in Washington, DC, with a salary of $12,000. Kent wrote back saying he was honored to be considered but was "thoroughly committed to returning to Yale next fall. The University has done in my behalf everything that one could possibly ask and I could not in honor further inconvenience the President and my Department chairman by forcing them to reconsider the case of my replacement."[29]

In fact, Kent was unresolved about returning to Yale full-time. Between 1946 and 1954 a series of letters crossed the desks of Kent and his department bosses. In September of 1946, having left State's intelligence organization in June, Kent told Harvard president Charles Seymour he was keen to teach at both Yale and the National War College (which he joined that autumn) and had "no stomach for government work, even intelligence."[30] In 1949 he told History Department head William Dunham that he was keen to take up teaching again, but the National War College still wanted him.[31] (It wasn't until early 1954 that Kent finally made his mind up and resigned from Yale.[32])

What was driving Kent was his need to get his ideas down on paper, and to try to change the way the United States was thinking about strategic intelligence. An early attempt was for the *Yale Review*, "Prospects for the National Intelligence Service," published in the autumn 1946 issue. At the same time, he offered a piece on "Is Intelligence Possible?" to *Harper's Magazine*.[33]

The *Yale Review* article was very much a forerunner to Kent's later book, *Strategic Intelligence for American World Policy*, but, given the time of writing, it had a more urgent edge. "We have just won a war, and we are currently trying to win a peace," Kent asserted. He was acerbic about the intelligence capability prewar: The main task of American intelligence agencies like the Office of the Coordinator of Information after Pearl Harbor had been to make up "for the derelictions of the past twenty years." Kent gave a quick history and brought the reader up to date where things stood now. The State Department had squandered the opportunity it had with acquiring R&A and, along with CIG, was likely to reflect the derelictions of duty in 1941. He held out hope that the appointment of Vandenberg would turn things around.[34]

FIGURE 5.1. Sherman Kent, the "father of modern intelligence," in 1961. *SKP*

The article prompted a quick response from William Langer. "The only point in which I would differ would be in your evaluation of Vandenberg," Langer noted. "I liked him very much and enjoyed my contacts with him, but I am not at all sure that his program is as moderate and reasonable as you seem to think. Indeed, I am a little bit afraid that he might try to do too much too quickly, and in that way he may injure the cause rather than benefit it."[35]

Kent remained bitter about the way State had handled R&A. In late 1946 he wrote to the British diplomat and man of letters Harold Nicolson, who had just written an article in *Foreign Affairs* on the Paris Peace Conference. "There are many things which contributed to the Department's attitude [toward R&A]," opined Kent, "but one is, I think, worth of special mention. It is my hunch that the Department never recovered from the Enquiry. . . . Never again would the old guard permit an outside organization . . . to muscle into the task of peacemaking."[36]

The idea to write a book on intelligence had come from Yale as early as 1945. In a letter from Frederick S. Dunn at Yale's Institute of International Studies, dated October 9, Dunn told Kent that he had heard OSS had "folded up shop" and wondered if Kent was interested in a paid job, "devoting a few months to making a study of intelligence for us. We are primarily interested in the function of intelligence in relation to the carrying on of foreign affairs and I hear from Arnold [Wolfers] that you have some ideas on the subject."[37] Kent replied two days later, agreeing it was an interesting proposition, but with R&A having moved to State, a merger he was tied up in, he didn't know when he would be free to undertake the job.

The project took on momentum when Kent applied for a fellowship with the John Simon Guggenheim Foundation, which would give him time to sit down and write his magnum opus. His former boss at State's intelligence organization, a veteran of the Military Intelligence Corps, Alfred McCormack, wrote to Guggenheim director Henry Allen Moe supporting Kent's application for *Strategic Intelligence.*

> It is [a task] that only a few men would be capable of doing, or have the experience to do, and of those who might be capable I know of no one but Dr. Kent who is able and willing to take the time to do it. I emphatically endorse Dr. Kent's statement that if he or some other qualified person had been able to write such a book in the past "the present intelligence resources of the country might not have been so wastefully dissipated as they have in the year just gone by." You know, I am sure, that the matter of foreign intelligence is of prime national importance. What perhaps you do not know, since not many know it, is that the intelligence activities of the Government are now largely in the hands of the armed services, who are floundering around without any clear idea of their objectives, without adequate resources of money or personnel, gradually returning to the miserable pre-war condition of foreign intelligence. I hope your Foundation will find it possible to sponsor the constructive work that Dr. Kent is proposing to do.[38]

Kent was granted the Guggenheim fellowship in April of 1947, for the period of nine months and with a $2,500 stipend. He thanked Henry Allen Moe enthusiastically. "The title of this book will probably be "The Intelligence of Grand Strategy," he wrote, "and the content will, as I have noted, deal almost exclusively with the overt sides of the business. Furthermore, as the war recedes, I find myself much more concerned with the intelligence problems of the grand strategy of peace than those of war."[39]

It was only five days later that he heard from William Donovan, offering help with the new book. A week later, a second letter arrived from Donovan, wanting to discuss Kent's criticisms of CIG. And a fortnight later, Donovan asked Kent if he had read his own proposal on how to improve the organization. Kent was achieving the influence he wanted on shaping US strategic intelligence future, and he had not written the book yet.[40]

The Framework for Strategic Intelligence Analysis

Sherman Kent's *Strategic Intelligence for American World Policy* was even more influential than Pettee's *The Future of American Secret Intelligence*. Thanking him for any "unconscious or otherwise unacknowledged borrowings" in the preface of the book, Kent praised Pettee's book as a "trailblazer in the literature of strategic intelligence."[41] While claiming not to agree with many of his views, Kent largely built upon the former book and emphasized Pettee's distinctions on how strategic intelligence needed to be shaped around social science methods—a departure from the strategic intelligence of the past. Mindful perhaps that this rather dry book on intelligence analysis was written with some academic rigor and might have some influence not only at the policymaking level but also in the new international relations departments opening in the universities, Princeton University Press agreed to publish it.[42]

Kent began with a definition of strategic intelligence. He indicated that strategic intelligence was purposeful, with the goal of obtaining knowledge that was "vital for the national survival." These included problems that "involve[d] long-range speculations on the strength and intentions of other states, [and] involved estimates of their probable responses to acts which we ourselves plan to initiate." Strategic intelligence would be a discipline that required expertise, clandestine work, and—because of the sheer bulk of information needed to be processed—an organizational structure to support it. Kent also made clear that intelligence was there to serve the wider field of foreign policy–making rather than the narrower wartime view of intelligence being for military combat goals. This differentiation was important: "never before in our peacetime history have the stakes of foreign policy been higher," stressed Kent; "never before was it so important that the intelligence mission be properly fulfilled."[43]

In defining strategic intelligence, Kent further refined it to be "high-level foreign positive intelligence," meaning that it was knowledge needed so that the state's interests and actions would not fail through the ignorance of its leaders, and that it was not "negative" in the sense that it hunted out spies (counterintelligence or counterespionage). For Kent, the work he was specifying was foreign-focused and not domestic intelligence. It was "high level" because it was critical to the security and welfare of the state and therefore excluded operational, tactical, and combat intelligence.[44] It was also positive because it worked toward peace and prosperity, an aim that agreed with Pettee's understanding of the subject.

By creating a separation between peacetime and wartime (military) intelligence, Kent was ushering in a need for a new type of expertise and organizational structure, one that within two years he would be directly responsible for implementing. And he was quite specific about the kind of expertise that would be required. Strategic intelligence required two kinds of "operation," Kent argued. The first was based on "close and systematic observation" of the contemporary world, which he called the surveillance operation. The second, the research operation, attempted to "establish meaningful patterns out of what was observed in the past and attempts to get meaning out of what appears to be going on now." Kent was taking strategic intelligence thinking even further into the realm of the social scientist, into the field of the scientific method. While acknowledging that in its totality it would ultimately require knowing everything about humanity and nature—that is, all the aspects of human behavior and the environment it operates in, and this would require lists which would in turn require systems of categories—Kent took a more functional approach from the beginning. Policymakers needed to know the answers to some very practical questions:

I. *how* the other country is going to receive the policy in question and what it is prepared to use to counter it;
II. *what* the other country lacks in the way of countering force (i.e.) its specific vulnerabilities;
III. *what* it is doing to array its protective force; and
IV. *what* it is going, or indeed can do, to mend its specific vulnerabilities.[45]

These questions demonstrated a social scientist's interest in causation, separating out variables—in this case, "the other country" (dependent variable) and the effect of the United States' policies upon it (independent variable). While, ostensibly, strategic intelligence referred to variables a military analyst would traditionally be focusing on—for example, its defensive and offensive capabilities and any vulnerabilities that might be exploited—Kent kept the concept of the US "policy in question" open rather than specifically frame it as a US military action.

Kent then drilled down further. Acknowledging that the questions above needed to be answered as completely as possible, as well as accurately, timely, and in a way that could be actionable, he also specified categories that the intelligence ought to cover. "The other country," thought Kent, should be treated as an "objective entity" and studied in a methodical way. The kind of knowledge needed would be twofold: first the analyst would need to compile an encyclopedic amount of research that was descriptive and would include the country's topography and climate; cities; agricultural and industrial resources; transportation and communication links; demographics; political, economic, and social systems; and organizational and technological capabilities. A second kind of knowledge was reportorial: it looked at current news about the country. A third kind of knowledge took in the country's intentions and abilities to successfully meet those goals. This third category was estimative in that it considered possibilities and was future looking. As a class of knowledge, it was evaluative and speculative, not easily pinned down to facts, and prone to conflicting assessments. These three categories of strategic intelligence Kent classified as the basic descriptive form, the current reportorial form, and the speculative-evaluative form, or "the established things, the presently going-on things, and probable things of the future."[46] In intelligence parlance, they boiled down to basic research, current intelligence, and estimative intelligence. In chronological order, the OSS's Research and Analysis unit had focused on basic research during the war; its postwar successor, the CIG and early CIA, mostly on current intelligence; and CIA post-1950, estimative intelligence. Each institution had largely gained or lost its reputation based on achieving those tasks: OSS had been lauded for its basic research work, primarily on North Africa and postwar Germany; CIG and early CIA had been found wanting for concentrating mainly on current intelligence; and the Korean War, the development of the Soviet bomb, and the loss of China had prompted reform at CIA in 1950 based on a perceived need for better coordinated estimates.

More than this, Kent was focused on creating a sound intelligence analysis process. He reminded his reader that strategic intelligence wasn't just a product, it was an activity. "My primary concern will be the large number of methodological and other problems which are characteristic of the intelligence process," he wrote. Intelligence, he argued, was at its heart a research activity. "Sometimes research is formal, highly technical, and weighty: sometimes it is informal, untechnical, and speedily arrived at. Sometimes a research project requires thousands of man-days of work, sometimes it is done in one man-minute or less." This appears to be acknowledging that an analyst might have to conjure up something overnight or even on the spot, given the urgency of the problem or the demands of the anxious policymaker. But it was also Kent trying to make sense of the new discipline of strategic intelligence analysis: as he himself admitted, two sorts of methodological problems arose: "One sort is characteristic of all systematic research in the social sciences, the other derives from the peculiarities of intelligence research activities. To put it another way," Kent postulated, "strategic analysis has a set of methodological problems all its own which are relatively unknown to the social scientist at work in his university."[47]

So how did Kent describe this process? He distinguished between the substantiative problem and the methodological problem. The former was the research question: What did you want to know? The latter was a procedural question: By which means would you decide what was worth researching? Yet, for Kent, the methodological problem could easily take you down "one of the main roadways of epistemology."[48] It was not a road he was willing to walk down. The metaphysical was not a fruitful journey for a positivist like Kent.

Instead, both the substantiative and methodological problems could be approached in relatively simple ways. An analyst—one who knew his subject well, such as an area specialist on the Middle East—could simply be paid to set his mind to think of the most pressing issues of the day. Similarly, he could spot something unusual happening and wonder what it was and what caused it. In both cases he could not only devise the research question but he could also simultaneously pick it apart and phrase it so he was asking it the right way as well as judge whether the answer it elicited was what he really wanted to know. A social scientist should be skilled at this process and implicitly understand how minor changes in the structure of a question produce very different answers. More routinely, rather than ruminate on what questions to ask, the intelligence analyst might be asked a direct question by the policymaker. Whether the policymaker created the question or the analyst did, the most important consideration was whether the answer would be accurate in broad terms and, hence, relevant to the policy being pursued.

Once the substantive question was decided on, the analyst must then go about the process of collecting the data. This might be an easy task of consulting a library or index system, it might require asking another researcher to collaborate, or it might require prying secrets from another state. When the data came from another analyst, the original analyst then had to evaluate it. "He criticizes it, judges its importance, mixes it with other data he received yesterday and the week before, [and] gives it background and point."[49] If the data has been collected through a clandestine process, it may be handled first by a middleman to protect the source. This environment requires an additional process of rating the data for reliability. Again, the analyst is vulnerable to mistakes being made along the way that compromise the integrity of his material. Without some criticism of what has been collected, it is impossible to proceed to the next stage: formulating a hypothesis.

The hypothesis was, according to Kent, a supposition created from both quantity and quality. Quantity, because the more explanations the better. "What is desired is a large number of possible interpretations of the data, a large number of inferences, or concepts, which are broadly based and productive of still other concepts," he stated. Equally important was the quality of the data. This extended to access to all relevant information even when the problem being addressed was critical to the nation's security (intelligence analysts were frequently denied access to secrets bearing on national security).[50]

This shows that the basic precepts of a social science technique could be identified in any deconstruction of the intelligence analyst's craft. The formation of a research question, the sorting of reliable and comprehensive sources (the historical method), the systematic classification or categorization of new information, the creation of a holistic range of hypotheses and the presentation of verifiable evidence are all elements of the social scientist's rulebook. "Unless the kind of knowledge here under discussion is complete, accurate and timely," Kent exhorted, "and unless it's applicable to a problem which is up, or coming up, it is useless. In this proposition it is recognized that intelligence is not knowledge for knowledge's sake alone, but that intelligence is knowledge for the practical matter of taking action."[51]

Kent was writing for an audience he was trying to persuade to consider his treatise as a manual for a new type of intelligence agency. Thus, mindful of needing an academic approach to intelligence analysis, he was at the same time delivering what he saw as an applied and very policy-friendly reasoning of what was needed and how. But the approach could also work in reverse: Kent was able to speak the policymaker's language, but he could also use the authority of scientific reasoning. He knew that shaping strategic intelligence into a scientific process would give the new agency's product a great deal of persuasive power. Kent's social science methodology offered a cut-through capacity to the intelligence process that it previously lacked. As a result, Kent could promise a method that was robust and could withstand academic scrutiny. This was very different from the "my opinion is just as good as yours" problems Leonard Doob had faced at the Office of War Information, where the findings of his social science team were often trumped by the real-world experience of the journalists, advertising men, and German refugees also serving the propaganda department. Unlike Doob, Kent could simply point to the rigorous processes he employed and the logical machinery of science over personal opinion.

How influential was Kent's book? Reviewing the book for *Political Science Quarterly* in September 1949, Columbia University's Lawrence Chamberlain said Kent "demonstrates clearly that intelligence work depends chiefly upon sharply disciplined intellectual analysis and alert diagnosis . . . [and that] no amount of complex organizational structure or elaborate formulae could take the place of top-grade men."[52] In *Public Opinion Quarterly*, Bruce Lannes Smith called it a "brilliant and orderly analysis," with a broad theoretical approach grounded in practical knowhow.[53] In *American Political Science Review*, Hans Morgenthau of the University of Chicago highlighted the previous lack of constructive criticism on intelligence operations, particularly regarding personnel and organization. This he believed was Kent's great contribution. Kent had been instructive on organizational reforms, but when it came to the relationship between intelligence producers and consumers, Morgenthau somewhat grumpily complained, "the author is sometimes in danger of losing himself in details and academic exercises."[54] The influential *New York Herald Tribune* columnists Joseph Alsop and Stewart Alsop declared it "the most important postwar book on strategic intelligence."[55] Asked in 1989 why he was still quoting Kent when so many books on intelligence had been written since, Harvard presidential historian Ernest May said, "Yes, but with concept after concept, in 40 years nobody has ever stated things as smartly as Kent."[56]

The Dissenting Voice: Willmoore Kendall

If there was an early dissenting voice over Kent's ideas about strategic intelligence, it was from his Yale colleague and sometime intelligence analyst Willmoore Kendall. His story is worth recounting, partly because—if his intellectual ability to wound and offend had not been so acute—he might well have become a leading figure at CIA.

During the 1930s, Kendall had studied Spanish at the University of Illinois Urbana–Champaign and, armed with a Rhodes Scholarship (Modern Greats at Oxford), had worked briefly as a journalist in Spain prior to the civil war before returning to earn a PhD in political science at the University of Illinois. Originally leaning to the left, Kendall was outspoken and made enemies easily. Characteristic of his polemicist views and his unconventional approach to research are the letters he wrote to his father in 1936 and 1937. In these, he criticized the Political Science Department at Illinois, saying it "lays great emphasis upon detailed mastery of the subject, does not encourage criticism or original thinking as such, and attempts to place its 'stamp' on the men who pass through it." Kendall told his father he had never before had "so many brutal facts at [his] fingertips" and would soon be "lousy with 'em."[57]

By 1942 Kendall was looking for a job in government but worried his left-wing past and commitment to isolationism would be noted at FBI and undermine his chances of a civil service career.[58] He worked briefly for State, and then at CIG, but from around 1947 was scaled down to a part-time, one-and-a-half-days-a-week job at the Agency. His ambition was to run ONE.

Kendall's review of Kent's book in *World Politics* was one of the most considered. He did not agree with much of what Kent wrote but did consider his general theory of intelligence function instructive: "*Strategic Intelligence,*" wrote Kendall, was "a book that every social scientist should lay in his heart and ponder."[59] Those practitioners who had been involved in intelligence had little ability to step outside the idea that strategic intelligence was for war, and yet its new role was to carve out "United States' destiny in the world as a whole, as contrasted to the conduct of United States policy toward a congeries of nation-states."[60] Kendall felt Kent had erred in thinking about strategic intelligence in the same wartime manner, and that he was concentrating too much on the need for prediction, particularly in a Pearl Harbor–warning sense.

For Kendall there was a difference between absolute prediction and contingent prediction—the job of the intelligence analyst was to think about possibilities, not foretell actual crises. The political scientist complained that, even though he had talked about hypotheses, Kent had not discussed theory and theorists. A social science approach to intelligence that looked to the theory-building skills of economics, sociology, and (hopefully one day, thought Kendall) political science would be a better discipline than the one Kent described.

He also took issue with the idea of assigning regional desks to analysts (which Kent had discussed and not been completely convinced of). "For, if it is regional units you are building, and it is social scientists specialized to specific countries and areas you wish to staff them with, what you end up with is an extremely high percentage of historians, who with the best will in the world communicate to the operation the characteristic vices (and virtues) of their kind of research."[61] Kendall wanted to see analysts freed of the deluge of already-out-of-date documents that a historian like Kent arguably valued most. He wanted them to be able to pick up the telephone and call anywhere in the world for on-the-ground information. He wanted them to be free to *think*.

The review of Kent's book hurt the political scientist's chances at CIA. Despite being friends with Langer, by 1950 Kendall had become persona non grata at the office. Sherman Kent was considerably offended, having thought Kendall a model intelligence officer. Kent had also been instrumental in getting him into Yale. Arnold Wolfers, who was one of Kent's closest friends on the New Haven campus (his letters were usually addressed to "Shermo"), also ostracized Kendall. He fell out, too, with George Kennan at State for criticizing Kennan's containment concept in a 1947 book. For someone who had at one time harbored ambitions to lead ONE, the path was now blocked.[62]

Instead, Kendall turned to psychological warfare. In 1950 he applied for a job with George Pettee, now running the Army's Operations Research Office. He got the job and was assigned Project POWOW, a psychological warfare study of USSR radio broadcasts and Nazi propaganda. Kendall argued, too, with Pettee, but they agreed enough on the role of analysts that they put aside their differences on the direction of POWOW. Sent to Korea, Kendall was an avowed supporter of Gen. Douglas MacArthur and his intelligence chief, Gen. Charles A. Willoughby. When Willoughby's intel reports on Chinese intervention to MacArthur and Washington were found to be disastrously wrong, Kendall blamed it on the G-2 man's lack of political science training. This meant he had never been able to put military intelligence to work solving political problems, Kendall argued.

Kendall's work at the Operations Research Office allowed him to test out some of his theories on intelligence. Now a fervent anticommunist, he believed that a hot war was imminent and that the United States was unprepared for such a crisis. His academic hires included the literary critic Cleanth Brooks, poet and novelist Robert Penn Warren, and political scientist John Ponturo (later at the Institute for Defense Analyses)—all from Yale—and Charles

Hyneman, a political scientist from the University of Illinois. Kendall edited two publications at the Operations Research Office, *China: An Area Manual* (1953) with political scientist David Rowe, and Wilbur Schramm's *The Nature of Psychological Warfare* (1954). Of the first, the message was that Truman had lost China due to policy blunders; of the second, that psychological warfare was an art employing science.[63]

He continued to make enemies. Pettee fired Kendall in 1953 when his coworkers rose against him. He was turned down for a job at the State Department, which he attributed to his support for Senator Joe McCarthy. Perhaps even less attractively, he described his second wife, Anne Brunsdale, who worked at CIA, as the opposite of his ideal woman, who would be both rich and good-looking. Brunsdale, Kendall claimed, was neither and was what he did not require: intellectual and a career woman. Kendall returned to Yale, which was willing to be more tolerant of his outspoken behavior. Having helped William F. Buckley Jr.'s first work: *God and Man at Yale: The Superstitions of "Academic Freedom,"* he went on to become one of America's foremost conservative thinkers.[64]

Applying Social Science Methodology to a Strategic Intelligence Approach

In the meantime, *Strategic Intelligence for American World Policy* came to the attention of General Smith, who Agency historian Jack Davis says "ordered" Kent to an interview.[65]

Kent met William Jackson for breakfast on a Saturday morning, October 21, 1950. The two had met several times already: once while Kent was at State after Research and Analysis had moved there, once at a cocktail party in New York, and a third time at Jackson's club. At the third meeting Jackson had wanted to canvas Kent over the review he was writing of Kent's *Strategic Intelligence* for *The New York Times Book Review.* Jackson wanted to discuss the review but made it clear he would not be influenced by Kent's objections. According to Kent, he was pleasantly surprised that the book "had smelled so little of the lamp." It was an expression the Yale scholar had never heard before.[66] The next day he met with DCI Smith and was offered a job. Kent seems to have been relieved to finally be back in the intelligence business: "I must confess that, with the outbreak of the war in Korea, I rather expected to be asked to return to intelligence work. By September with no invitation, I began to think that some of my run-ins with the Security people in the State Department had blighted my record."[67]

During his seventeen years at CIA (he joined in 1950 and on William Langer's retirement was chair of the Board of National Estimates from 1952 to

1967), Kent set about changing strategic intelligence into a professional, career-oriented discipline that could be "taught" to new analysts.[68] He did so by applying his understanding of social science methods such as the historical method, hypothesis making and testing, employing objectivity in analysis, precision in language and definitions, and inductive and deductive reasoning. While these approaches are not always apparent on the surface of the national intelligence estimates, Kent discussed them openly in his lectures and writings about the discipline. This survey of his writings is anachronistic, as some were published later than the timeline dealt with here; they are included because there is evidence he was employing these methods during the 1950 to 1953 period.

Precision in Language

Kent explored the idea of using more precise language (what he called "estimative vocabulary") in an article he published in CIA's in-house journal *Studies in Intelligence* in 1964.[69] In the article, Kent recounted a misunderstanding he had encountered over NIE-29 51 "Probability of an Invasion of Yugoslavia" thirteen years earlier (in 1951). In the conclusion ran the following sentence: "Although it is impossible to determine which course the Kremlin is likely to adopt, we believe that the extent of Satellite military and propaganda preparations indicates that an attack on Yugoslavia in 1951 *should be considered a serious possibility*" (emphasis added). A few days after the NIE came out, Kent says he saw the chair of the Department of State's Policy Planning Staff in what appears to be a chance meeting. Talking about the NIE, the chairman asked Kent what CIA had meant by the words "serious possibility." Kent thought about it and said he thought the chances of an invasion of Yugoslavia were reasonably high: a 65 to 35 chance. The other man was taken aback. He had read "serious possibility" to mean a much lower likelihood. And others on the Policy Planning Staff had read it differently too. Kent went back to his office and asked his co-writers what they had meant by "serious possibility" and found none of them shared his opinion.[70]

Paul Nitze claims to be the person that Kent spoke to. His story is worthy of being printed in full:

> I called up the boys at the CIA and asked them to give us some estimation on this. They gave us a report in which they said *it was possible* that Moscow might invade Yugoslavia. I called in Sherman Kent, who was then running the National Board of Estimates [*sic*], and told Sherman that "*it was possible* that wasn't good enough." We had to make up our minds in the Policy Planning Staff as to whether we would recommend to Mr. Acheson and whether

he would recommend to Mr. Truman that we increase our stockpiles of military equipment in Italy, in order to be able to support Tito with military equipment in the event he was attacked by Moscow. We didn't really think that ought to be done unless the prospect of Moscow attacking Yugoslavia was of a certain probability. And what probabilities did they think an attack by Moscow would be? Sherman Kent said, "Well, you see, I don't do that sort of thing." They avoided attaching percentages to adjectives and adverbs of that kind. I said, "Well, you know, we've got to make a decision, and so I'll tell you what I'll do. I'll tell you what I think the percentage chance is; I think the percentage chance is about twenty percent. I'll tell you further that if I'm right it's about twenty percent, then our recommendation to Mr. Acheson will be that we not build up the military supplies in Italy. It is a very expensive thing to do, and on a twenty percent chance we don't think it ought to be done. Now, since you've got from me that way in [*sic*] interpret your report, you tell me whether I am high or low. And if you don't tell me anything, why, I'll consider that you haven't got any better judgment than I have; that it's about twenty percent." Sherman Kent went back horrified by this. I think a year or two later he wrote a deep thinkpiece for the CIA on the question as to whether they should or should not give percentages when they gave estimates as to probabilities.[71]

This is an interesting example of the policymaker making clear his needs to the intelligence analyst. It is a lesson Kent clearly took to heart. It's demonstrative of the learning process that was going on at ONE in the 1950–53 period. While Kent had arrived with a prescriptive manual on how to operationalize strategic intelligence, he was still learning on the job how to apply his craft to the new discipline.

Kent was honest that he never managed to get his "words of estimative probability" off the ground. He and his colleague Max Foster did go to the trouble of drawing up a chart of words of estimative probability, but this was not adopted by ONE. "I didn't feel that I had the right to cram this word chart down the throats of my unwilling colleagues, but did for years carry on a rear guard action, and, in the end, did at least succeed in preventing the use of such horrible built-in conflicts of sense, such as 'serious possibilities.'"[72] In a April 1952 memo the idea is discussed at a joint meeting of the Board of National Estimates and the NSC Steering Group. The reaction was "mixed," although there was agreement that ONE's papers had become much clearer than they had in the past. James S. Lay, then executive secretary of the National Security Council, "seriously questioned whether or not the ultimate consumers could ever be educated as to the meaning of estimative terms."[73]

Employing the Historical Method

In the 1965 edition of *Strategic Intelligence for American World Policy*, Kent responded to a criticism of US methods that had been published in 1963 by Gen. Alexander Orlov, a former member of Soviet intelligence who had defected in 1938. According to Kent, Orlov believed that the only proper means of pursuing strategic knowledge was through espionage, and that the stealing of secrets unveiled all an intelligence agency needed to know about its adversary. While Kent admitted that spy work was useful, Orlov's philosophy attacked the very heart of the former Yale professor's beliefs. Kent understood the future of US intelligence depended on "the intellectually competent human—the person who was born with the makings of a critical sense and who has developed them to their full potential: who through first-hand experience and study has accumulated an orderly store of knowledge; and who has a feeling for going about the search for further enlightenment in a systematic way."[74]

For Kent, the leaps made by intelligence practitioners during the war were in the fields of collection and analysis. "In the one no less than the other the thoughtful effort of bright and studious people conducting their business within the very broad limits of the scientific method, is the thing that did the work."[75] The value of intelligence lay in the application of the historical method. The method has three distinct parts: the search for sources of information; an appraisal of the value of the sources; and the assembling of the sources in a formal statement, including a discussion of their objective truth and significance.[76] As far as Kent was concerned, Orlov's dependence on espionage laid bare the weaknesses of Soviet intelligence. Kent wrote, perhaps rather angrily: "did every [stolen] document proclaim on its face: 'I am *not* the off-beat thoughts and recommendations of a highly placed but erratic advisor; I am *not* a draft from high quarters intended solely as a basis for discussion; I am *not* one of those records of decision which will be rescinded orally the next day, or pushed under a rug and forgotten, or nibbled to death by disapproving implementers. *I am the real McCoy; I am authoritative and firm; I represent an approved intention and I am in effect'*" (emphasis added).[77]

Kent believed the historical method mattered. He wrote this in 1965, but it was a view that was consistent with his book of sixteen years earlier. Kent believed if Soviet intelligence had gotten things wrong, it was because of their dependency on stolen secrets. The Cuban Missile Crisis, he argued, might owe its origins to a stolen document that Moscow had read as approved intentions; similarly, the USSR might not have backed North Korea's invasion of the South had it not misread the United States' intentions that the peninsula was not of strategic value. The historical method as he understood it meant not taking any document at face value. It was up to the intelligence analyst to interrogate its worth and then to discuss its objective truth and significance.

Hypotheses

In his autobiography, Kent says that writing estimates meant assessing three different phenomena: "knowable information which we knew for certain; unknowable information which we could not state for certain but about which we could make reasonable conjecture; and unknowable information which was virtually impossible to prove and when presented had to be couched in varying degrees of probability or improbability."[78] This is an acknowledgment that there was a distance between social science research questions and the kind of national security questions CIA was being tasked to answer. While all scientists are capable of stumbling on the "unknown unknown," they prefer to work in environments where evidence already exists or there is a process to discover it. ONE, on the other hand, could be held responsible for not anticipating the un-anticipatable. This put enormous pressure on Kent and his staff to create hypotheses that covered every possible eventuality and then rank them in terms of the evidence available and their probability. The big questions would be asked in a planning meeting, where the terms of reference would be debated and decided upon. Getting the terms of reference out to the collaborating intelligence wings of the military and State was an additional safeguard, so if an angle had been missed, another agency might pick it up.[79] Good hypotheses did not always lead to good conclusions. Deciding what an estimate was going to say was still a committee process, and the other agencies were free to express their dissent, although the ultimate responsibility rested with DCI Smith. Yet any analyst guarding against bias entering his assessments needed to develop hypotheses to cover as many bases as possible.

Objectivity and Consistency of Methods

Kent had been influenced at OSS by the historian—and future presidential adviser—Arthur Schlesinger Jr. At a critical time when intelligence reports were making their way into the postwar planning rooms of the nation, Schlesinger had worried about bias creeping into the reports of OSS analysts, particularly those Marxist professors who were making judgments on who should be supported by the United States in the future and who might be a potential enemy. Kent remembered the fighting clearly: the "battles between the pro-Mihailovitch and pro-Tito factions, between the champions and opponents of aid to China, between the defenders and detractors of the Jewish national home in Palestine."[80] In *Strategic Intelligence for American World Policy*, Kent discussed how intelligence might guide policymakers and how it could avoid accusations of subjectivity or even prejudice. Intelligence provided a service to the policymaker or, as Kent called them, "the doers." "Its job is to see that the doers are generally well-informed: its job is to stand behind them with the book opened at the right page, to call their attention to the stubborn fact they may be neglecting, and—at their request—to analyze alternative courses without indicating choice."[81] This spoke not only to the analyst's evaluation of the right books to have open and the right hypotheses that could suggest options but also to a close relationship between intelligence provider and consumer that imbued the analyst with a sense of responsibility for the project.

Schlesinger had argued that intelligence analysis and policymaking were entwined. In making decisions on what to study and what sources to use, the analyst was already making choices about policy direction; it was unavoidable. For Schlesinger this meant that the two practices must work together: The analyst needed to know what the policymaker's intent was and what problems he was trying to solve. Kent agreed with this. Yet there were practical considerations why policymakers shared so little with their intelligence analysts. First was the question of hierarchy: Leaders did not tell their staffs everything because knowing the full picture might prejudice the analyst's objectivity. Second, leaders did not always share their intentions for reasons of secrecy: The more people who knew the plans (particularly of war) the greater the chance the enemy would learn them too.[82]

For Kent, the role of the intelligence staff was to produce reasoned and impartial analysis: "The main difference between professional scholars and intelligence officers on one hand, and all others on the other hand, is that the former are supposed to have had more training in the techniques of guarding against their own intellectual frailties."[83]

It was Kent who developed Schlesinger's ideas from R&A about consistency in methods and consensus in intelligence reporting. The objective was to deliver clear estimates to policymakers in such a way that how the conclusions were developed couldn't be challenged. You might disagree with the conclusion, but you could not disagree with the methodology. Pettee had wanted these to be based on premises uncovered through "mental operations" that were the final conclusions of intelligence operations. "In order to be effective as premises," Pettee believed, "these conclusions must be presented in a most lucid and serious form to the highest officials whose decisions govern the conduct of war."[84]

Inductive and Deductive Approaches

In an article written in 1968, Kent discusses the difficulty of approaching research questions concerning the great imponderables of a nation's intentions or capabilities. While this was written fifteen years later than our timeline of 1950 to 1953, and therefore possibly not a process Kent was quite so conversant with at the time, it is the case that others at CIA were talking about it in a similar way during the reform years (see chap. 7 on the "Inventory of Ignorance"). Moreover, the concepts of inductive and deductive reasoning were not new in the early 1950s. Therefore, it is appropriate to include them here.

Writing estimates on the future of Greece or Communist China's military capabilities was not an easy task. "Knowing" about China's readiness for war was not something you could ever be certain about, and "knowing" was the wrong word entirely, it was more like "approximating." "In pursuit of this you evoke a group of techniques and ways of thinking, and with their help you endeavor logically and rationally (you hope) to unravel the unknown or at least roughly define some area of probability by excluding a vast amount of the impossible. You know that the resultant, while still a lot better than nothing at all, will be some mix of fact and judgment."[85]

Kent thought of this thinking process as being like a pyramid. At the base of the pyramid were all the facts you needed for the foundation of the argument. You knew that this base was the widest part of the pyramid and covered a lot of research ground. At the apex of the pyramid was the conclusion you made, a simple, but supportable answer. Because the pyramid was the model of this process, and because you knew that a pyramid was always this shape, you knew that to reach your answer you would start with a very great amount of information, and that the sides of the pyramid represented you distilling that information down to smaller and smaller amounts until you reached the apex. This was a process that started out as inductive (your understanding that you needed to collect information on many possible angles of the problem) and then became deductive (as you refined that information toward a conclusion). This was your model for approaching an intelligence problem, but it was not always the model adopted. "Let me not even seem to pretend that all conceptual pyramids in our area of work are constructed as described," confessed Kent. "The procedure that moves from the unknown to the known with a certain amount of tentative foraying as new hypotheses are advanced, tested and rejected is merely the most respectable way. Its very opposite is sometimes employed, though usually with a certain amount of clandestinity."[86] This process requires a great deal more aplomb, as the analyst knows the answer he wants but can see only the apex of the pyramid. Working downward toward the base, he has no feeling for where it ends. He risks being found out. "Without an artfully contrived joint," said Kent, "the whole structure can be made to proclaim its bastardy, to the chagrin of its progenitor."[87]

The apex of the pyramid can be sharp or, like a weatherworn Giza pyramid, may have the sharp end broken off. The sharp apex ends with a conclusion where the analyst is confident that his assessment has been proved; the broken apex, where more research may be needed and the answer is inconclusive. The final shape of the apex is often an undefined one, what Kent calls the "look before you leap" answer. Here the analyst hesitates before he makes the assessment: he is unsure if the conclusion is a palatable one (Kent suggests a conclusion that is "too soft" on Communism is one example) or if it will be used by the policymaker in a way the analyst had not intended. Then the options are open whether to abandon the estimate or start all over again and work toward a conclusion that is safer or better suited to your policy preferences.

Institutionalizing the New Processes

This new thinking about strategic analysis methods manifested itself as long-term institutional knowledge. It was integral to the establishment of the new approach to intelligence assessment that new analysts joining CIA could be indoctrinated in these methods and thus transition from highly skilled academics into strategic intelligence analysis professionals.

George S. Pettee had discussed the difference between wartime recruiting and what would be called for in the postwar era. Complaining that the "civil service principle" had operated with only a superficial matching of qualified people to important jobs, he warned that this could easily continue in Washington as people with wartime experience were low-hanging fruit as far as recruitment was concerned. Those with military backgrounds and existing security clearances would stultify the new civilian intelligence industry and be prone to the "diseases of bureaucracy."[88] To become a career intelligence analyst required excellent training and the recognition of good work when it was performed. Pettee called for a much more careful recruitment process in the future. He wanted internships set up to bring young graduates out of the universities, who might then go on to other careers but would in time "provide an accumulated corps whose further experience outside would be assimilated to minds trained to strategic considerations, and who as needs arose might be called back for service."[89] Once these conditions were met, the civilian intelligence career would become "an important national institution."[90]

Under Kent, CIA did move to embed institutional knowledge into the organization, including training in the new intelligence analysis methods, creating a database of basic knowledge about the world, and starting an in-house magazine that celebrated the newly established career path and passed on the experiences of analysts from one generation to the next.

In 1952 the Agency appointed a chief of intelligence training: Hiram Stout (of the Stout Committee). Having received a BA degree at DePauw University and an MA and PhD in political science at Harvard as well as a diploma from

Oxford, Stout had been a journalist as well as professor before joining Army's G-2 intelligence unit between 1942 and 1945. After the war he worked at the Bureau of the Budget and the State Department before joining CIA in 1947 as chief of the Northern Division of ORE. He had also represented the Agency on the National Security Council.[91] His role was specified thus: "The Chief, Intelligence Training will have under his direct control both the Analysis Training Branch and the Information Science Center and will be better able to bring about a more direct linkage between behavioral and technical aspects of analysis methodology."[92] By appointing both a wartime intelligence officer and an ORE veteran, CIA had an analyst training program that linked an understanding of the military and bureaucratic intelligence consumers with experience of ORE's problems before 1950. The job description recognized that the methodology to be taught was grounded in social science as well as the growing need for scientific and particularly weaponry expertise.

In his book *Strategic Intelligence for American World Policy*, Kent described the idea of a peacetime Baedeker, a "handbook which would contain the knowledge for peace and the knowledge necessary to meet aggression with dynamic defense."[93] This would be based on the blue books created for the British delegation to the Paris peace conferences after World War I, which provided regional background material on the Austro-Hungarian Empire (particularly the lands that would become Czechoslovakia), Germany and its colonies, Alsace-Lorraine, and Turkey. "No one who read them," says Kent, "could possibly have remained in ignorance of the main ethnic and economic problems which were to beset the men responsible . . . and no one who read them would fail to acquit himself better at the peace table."[94] Kent saw this project as part of the descriptive function of CIA and as the more basic accompaniment to the deeper-delving national intelligence estimate. The *CIA World Factbook* was not published until 1962, initially as a classified project, but it was grounded in the JANIS (Joint Army–Navy Intelligence Studies) reports begun in 1943 as part of the war effort, which Gen. Forrest Sherman claimed became "the indispensable reference work for the shore-based planners."[95] In 1947 CIA took over stewardship of JANIS, and the following year it was formally confirmed by NSC directive No. 3.[96] It was replaced by the National Intelligence Survey program in 1948 and an annual compendium, the *Factbook*, was created twenty years later. It is another illustration of a key initiative prescribed by Kent and put into effect to deliver a more robust intelligence product.

Pettee had foreseen a journal of strategic intelligence dedicated to its methods, a professional association, and a strategic intelligence school. "It is indispensable" he argued, "that intelligence be recognized, at least by its own people, as itself a special field, involving problems not actively covered on a professional level by any other modern profession, and involving methods in the solution of problems from imperfect data which are systematically avoided by the other professions."[97] The in-house magazine *Studies in Intelligence* remains to this day an integral part of CIA's institutional knowledge and commitment to development.[98] While the first issue didn't arrive until the autumn of 1955, the contributors to the first three issues included Kent on the need for an intelligence literature, Abbot E. Smith on capabilities in national intelligence, and Max Millikan on the nature and methods of economic intelligence. These articles were not only of strong historical value (Millikan's is a how-to guide to his craft), but they also saw Kent thinking ahead on how to develop the strategic analysis discipline in a way that was systematic.[99] Writing in 1955, Kent said:

> Intelligence today is not merely a profession, but like most professions it has taken on the aspects of a discipline: it has developed a recognized methodology; it has developed a vocabulary; it has developed a body of theory and doctrine; it has elaborate and refined techniques. It now has a large professional following. What it lacks is a literature. . . . What I am talking about is a literature dedicated to the analysis of our many-sided calling, and produced by its most knowledgeable devotees. The sort of literature I am talking about is of the nature of house organ literature, but much more. You might call it the institutional mind and memory of our discipline.[100]

An institutional memory is key to any organization that is creating processes, standards, and conceptions of quality that signify a "profession" and that it needs to communicate to future generations of the workforce. It is also critical that stakeholders—particularly customers—see this legacy as enduring and reliable. Kent's comments show it was a deliberate strategy instituted at CIA in the mid-1950s.

Conclusion

Writing in 1993, Harold P. Ford claimed that "our present national estimating system was basically formed at that time, the autumn of 1950. It has since been altered and improved in detail, but remained substantially unchanged to this day."[101] Kent's role was much less about recruiting social scientists to CIA than establishing the foundations of how to apply social science methods to a new civilian-based strategic intelligence analysis process. In determining this process, he was thorough and, as Ford states, sufficiently consistent and effective in his approach to embed these processes into CIA estimative work for nearly the next three decades. Methods did evolve—the arrival of computers had an effect on the storage and retrieval of data, and advanced techniques like Bayesian statistics ushered in new ways of assessing probability.[102] The foundations, however, concentrated on source selection and evaluation to (or attempt to) remove bias, on precision in language to avoid ambiguity, on the willingness to postulate many hypotheses to cover every possible explanation of a situation, and on the desire to give impartial analyses that assisted policy decision-making without actually prejudicing it. Kent's long tenure at CIA could have created an environment where one man's view on "doing it right" ran roughshod over the views of others. But it seems that this did not occur—Kent appears to have been a modest leader who welcomed his staff's opinions. Yet there is no question he became the guardian of CIA's estimates process.

Kent, then, was at the center of this reform of the intelligence process. Over his many years working at the Agency, Kent helped determine a "CIA way" of producing intelligence analysis. He recognized that peacetime strategic intelligence analysis would be an expertise distinct from traditional military or diplomatic intelligence and that it not only would require a new set of processes but also had the potential to become a career that would pull it away from traditional intelligence jobs.

Kent was a considered thinker who had had extensive experience applying social science methods to intelligence before he arrived at CIA. He knew, too, the parameters and limits of its application. He was attuned to many of the growing hurdles that intelligence analysis would have to face, problems that social science for the most part did not have to reckon with or could parcel into smaller packages to make it less arduous. Not the least of these was the sheer volume of collection and analysis CIA would need to deal with in order to inform the United States' new role in the world.

Kent's contribution was twofold. First, by applying social science methods to intelligence analysis, Kent used concepts that could imbue the strategic intelligence process with scientific rigor. While these methods were not always understood by the layman policymaker, they could be accepted as scientifically sound. It would be part of Kent's legacy that he left behind very clear writings on how these worked, and the fact Nitze knew Kent wrote about their conversation suggests some degree of interaction: Not only did Kent learn more about strategic intelligence creation from the policymakers, they did too.

His second contribution was embedding of this thinking into the institution. Kent actively managed the career development and expertise strategies, ensuring that future generations of analysts could lay claim to legitimate careers and expertise. While Kent knew that strategic intelligence analysis was not perfect, he was open and frank about this in his search for constant improvement.

Kent's reputation was somewhat mythologized by CIA, whose analysts and in-house historians may have felt psychologically in need of traditions and a founding father.[103] Yet there is no question that his work warrants the high position attributed to him. "Of the many individuals who paved a pathway for the development of intelligence analysis as a profession," says Jack Davis, "Kent stands out—both for his own contributions to analytic doctrine and practice, and for inspiring three generations of analysts to build on his efforts to meet changing times. Kent's tools for leadership once again were tough standards, color and wit, and enthusiasm for drawing lessons from intelligence challenges. If intelligence analysis as a profession has a Founder, the honor belongs to Sherman Kent."[104]

Notes

Epigraph: Raymond L. Garthoff, "Estimating Soviet Military Force Levels: Some Light from the Past," *International Security* 14, no. 4 (1990): 94.

1. Kent, *Strategic Intelligence for American World Policy*, 155–56.
2. Steury, *Sherman Kent and the Board of National Estimates*, x.
3. Collection overview, Sherman Kent Papers (MS 854), Beinecke Rare Book and Manuscript Library, Yale University (hereafter, SKP), https://archives.yale.edu/repositories/12/resources/4475.
4. Davis, *Sherman Kent and the Profession of Intelligence Analysis*, 14.
5. Larbaree, Leonard W., 1937–48, Folder 252, Correspondence, 1920–1980, MS 854, Box 12, Series 1, SKP. See also Yale University, 1903–1974, Folder 396, Correspondence, 1920–1980, Box 18, Series 1, SKP.
6. Hunter, Miller and Fleming (Hunter, Turrell & Dahl), (Hunter & Dahl), 1942–1949, Folder 166, Correspondence, 1920–1980, MS 854, Box 7, Series 1, SKP. See also Hunter, Miller and Fleming (Hunter, Turrell & Dahl), (Hunter & Dahl), 1950–63, Folder 167, Correspondence, 1920–1980, MS 854, Box 7, Series 1, SKP.
7. United States Central Intelligence Agency 1947–60, Folder 361, Correspondence 1920–1980, MS 854, Kent MS 854, Box 16, Series 4, SKP.
8. United States Central Intelligence Agency 1947–60, SKP.
9. Steury, *Sherman Kent and the Board of National Estimates*, x.
10. Winks, *Cloak and Gown*, 84.
11. Davis, *Sherman Kent and the Profession of Intelligence Analysis*, 3.
12. White, Review of "Writing History," 824.
13. Davis, *Sherman Kent and the Profession of Intelligence Analysis*, 4.
14. Davis, 3, 6.
15. Helms, *A Look Over My Shoulder*, 237.
16. Katz, *Foreign Intelligence*, 62–64.
17. Katz, 68.
18. Katz, 72.
19. Interestingly, he married another research analyst at OSS, Deborah Hathaway Calkins, in 1945. Rothschild, "Henry L. Roberts," 210.
20. Rothschild, 207.
21. Rothschild, 210.
22. Letter to Mr. Henry L. Roberts from Allen W. Dulles (1958), CIA-RDP80B01676-R003800180042-8, CIA, CREST Archive.
23. This is not J. Edgar Hoover of the FBI. Davis, *Sherman Kent and the Profession of Intelligence Analysis*, 4. See Kent and Thacher, *Reminiscences of a Varied Life*, 267.

24. Kent, *Strategic Intelligence for American World Policy*, ix. See also Davis, *Sherman Kent and the Profession of Intelligence Analysis*, 15.
25. Kent, *Strategic Intelligence for American World Policy*, xxi.
26. A letter to Robert Wolff, dated March 28, 1946, has Kent signing off as "Acting Director Office of Research and Intelligence." A reply from Wolff on April 21, 1946, is stamped in red ink with a "Received" mark, which reads "Chief's Office, Research and Analysis Branch." See Wolff, Robert Lee, 1946–1950, 1970–1976, Folder 392, MS854, SKP. See also Steury, *Sherman Kent and the Board of National Estimates*, x.
27. Davis, *Sherman Kent and the Profession of Intelligence Analysis*, 4–5.
28. Davis, 5.
29. Letter Kent to Frederic A. Ogg, November 18, 1946, Folder 1, MS854, Series 1, Box 1, SKP.
30. Seymour, Charles, 1937–49, 1969, 1977, Folder 334, Correspondence, 1920–1980, MS 854, Box 15, Series 1, SKP. See also Yale University, 1903–1974, Folder 396, Correspondence, 1920–1980, MS 854, Box 18, Series 1, SKP.
31. Dunham, William Hux Jr. 1944–73, n.d., Folder 94, Correspondence, 1920–1980, MS 854, Box 4, Series 1, SKP.
32. Yale University, 1903–1974, Folder 396, SKP.
33. Correspondence "F" (Fa–Fi), Folder 103, Correspondence, 1920–1980, MS 854, Box 4, Series 1, SKP.
34. Kent, Sherman, "Prospects for the National Intelligence Service," *Yale Review*, Autumn 1946, copy 1, Pforzheimer Intelligence 7377, Walter L. Pforzheimer Papers, General Collection, Yale University, Beinecke Rare Book and Manuscript Library.
35. Langer, William L. (Mrs. William L. Langer) 1943–1969, 1978, Folder 253, Correspondence, 1920–1980, MS 854, Box 12, Series 1, SKP.
36. Kent to Nicolson, December 1, 1946, Foreign Affairs 1946–1947, 1952–1968, Folder 112, Correspondence, 1920–1980, MS 854, Box 5, Series 1, SKP.
37. Correspondence, "D" (Dr–Du), Folder 84, Correspondence, 1920–1980, MS 854, Box 4, Series 1, SKP.
38. Correspondence M (Mac–MC), Folder 260, Correspondence, 1920–1980, MS 854, Box 12, Series 1, SKP.
39. John Simon Guggenheim Memorial Foundation, Folder 182, Correspondence, 1920–1980, MS 854, Box 7, Series, SKP.
40. Correspondence, "D" (De-Dh), Folder 83, Correspondence, 1920–1980, MS 854, Box 4, Series 1, SKP.
41. Kent, *Strategic Intelligence for American World Policy*, xi.
42. Davis, *Sherman Kent and the Profession of Intelligence Analysis*, 5.
43. Kent, *Strategic Intelligence for American World Policy*, xxiii–xxiv.
44. Kent, 3.
45. Kent, 4–5.
46. Kent, 7.
47. Kent, 151, 158.
48. Kent, 160.
49. Kent, 169–70.
50. Kent, 174–75.
51. Kent, 180.

52. Chamberlain taught government at Columbia and had been assistant to the director of the Naval School of Military Government and Administration during the war. See Chamberlain, "Review: [Untitled] Reviewed Work." See also Michael Mukasey, "Lawrence H. Chamberlain," *Columbia Daily Spectator*, March 6, 1962, http://spectatorarchive.library.columbia.edu.

53. Smith had served as a propaganda expert at the Department of Justice early in the war, before moving to economic intelligence and finally the OSS's Research and Analysis division. Together with Harold Lasswell, Smith had written *Propaganda: Communication and Public Opinion* (1946). See Smith, Review of "Kent, Sherman," 524; and Smith and Lasswell, *Propaganda, Communication and Public Opinion*.

54. Morgenthau, Review of "Strategic Intelligence."

55. Joseph Alsop and Stewart Alsop, "We Underestimate the Russians," *New York Herald Tribune*, January 8, 1956, quoted in *Congressional Record*, Proceedings and Debates of the 84th Congress, 2nd Session, vol. 102, pt. 14 (1956), appendix, January 12, A246, https://www.congress.gov/84/crecb/1956/01/05/GPO-CRECB-1956-pt14-1.pdf. Also see Scoblik, "Beacon and Warning," and taken from Bart Barnes, "CIA Official Sherman Kent, 82, Dies," *Washington Post*, March 14, 1986, https://www.washingtonpost.com/archive/local/1986/03/14/cia-official-sherman-kent-82-dies/e22ef6e0-a118-42be-b529-7e39f2babaaa/.

56. Davis, *Sherman Kent and the Profession of Intelligence Analysis*, 7.

57. Owen, *Heaven Can Indeed Fall*, 59, 60. See also Olcott, *Revisiting the Legacy*.

58. Owen, *Heaven Can Indeed Fall*, 71.

59. Kendall, "The Function of Intelligence," 547; see also Davis, "The Kent-Kendall Debate of 1949," 94.

60. Kendall, "The Function of Intelligence," 548.

61. Kendall, 548.

62. Owen, *Heaven Can Indeed Fall*, 108. See also Wolfers, Arnold, 1942–1947, 1965, Folder 391, Correspondence, 1920–1980, MS 854, Box 18, Series 1, SKP.

63. Owen, *Heaven Can Indeed Fall*, 108.

64. Owen, 112–14.

65. Davis, *Sherman Kent and the Profession of Intelligence Analysis*, 15.

66. Kent, "The First Year of the Office of National Estimates," 153. The *Collins Dictionary* says "smell of the lamp" is an expression meaning "to give evidence of laborious study or effort."

67. Kent had battled a rule that non-Americans could not serve, and he believed the German Jews on his team were among his best staffers. When he left State, Langer made him rewrite his overly critical resignation letter, saying it would end up on file and might prevent a government job in the future. Kent, "The First Year of the Office of National Estimates," 154; and Letters to William Langer, May 21–31, 1946, Folder 253, MS854, Series 1, Box 12, SKP.

68. Kent resigned his professorship at Yale in 1953 and retired from CIA on December 31, 1967. Davis, *Sherman Kent and the Profession of Intelligence Analysis*, 5. Also Steury, *Sherman Kent and the Board of National Estimates*, xii.

69. *Studies in Intelligence*, the Agency's classified in-house journal, was founded by Sherman Kent and produced by the CIA's Office of Training. The first issue was September 1955. See Dujmovic, "Fifty Years of Studies in Intelligence."

70. Kent, "Law and Custom," 75–77.

71. Richard D. McKinzie, Oral History Interview with Paul H. Nitze, August 4, 1975, Harry S. Truman Library and Museum, https://www.trumanlibrary.gov/library /oral-histories/nitzeph2#oh3, italics added.
72. Kent and Thacher, *Reminiscences of a Varied Life*, 264.
73. DDI Diary Highlights for 1952. September 24, 1952, CIA-RDP79B00970A000-100050027-9, CIA, CREST Archive.
74. Kent, *Strategic Intelligence for American World Policy*, xvi.
75. Kent, xvi.
76. Garraghan, *A Guide to the Historical Method*, 34.
77. Kent, *Strategic Intelligence for American World Policy*, xvi.
78. Kent and Thacher, *Reminiscences of a Varied Life*, 257.
79. Kent and Thacher, 258.
80. Kent, *Strategic Intelligence for American World Policy*, 199.
81. Kent, 182.
82. Kent, 184–92.
83. Kent, 199.
84. Pettee, *The Future of American Secret Intelligence*, 87.
85. Kent, "Estimates and Influence," 35.
86. Kent, 37.
87. Kent, 37.
88. Pettee, *The Future of American Secret Intelligence*, 93.
89. Pettee, 93.
90. Pettee, 94.
91. *CIA Office of Training, July 1951–January 1966*, vol. 2: *Growth and Development* (n.d.), 53. CIA, CREST Archive.
92. Memorandum for the Deputy Director for Administration from the Director of Training and Education: Proposed OTE Organizational Alignment (1952), CIA-RDP84B00890R000800010066-9, CIA, CREST Archive. See also Stout, *Stout and Allied Families*, 409.
93. Kent, *Strategic Intelligence for American World Policy*, 25.
94. Kent, 24–25.
95. The War Department's Strategic Index program began in 1919. See "A Brief History of Basic Intelligence and the World Factbook," n.d., https://www.cia.gov/the -world-factbook/about/history; Kent, *Strategic Intelligence for American World Policy*, xvi; and Rios-Bordes, "When Military Intelligence," 105–32, xii–xiv.
96. "A Brief History of Basic Intelligence."
97. Pettee, *The Future of American Secret Intelligence*, 98–100.
98. The Center for the Study of Intelligence was created in 1973 with a charter that warranted the study of intelligence "and profession as a theory, process merits vigorous study." This included long-range issues of professional doctrine and institutional policy, safeguarding institutional memory, accepting constructive criticism and "professional enrichment of the individual officer through research, reflection and the articulation of ideas." See Charter for the Center of Intelligence Studies (1973?), CIA-RDP85M00364R002003810015-5, CIA, CREST Archive; and Memorandum for the Acting Director of Central Intelligence, from Harry E. Fitzwater, Director of Training. Subject: Assignment of Personnel to Study Attached Problems, August 5, 1977, CIA-RDP81B00493R000100010011-0, CIA, CREST Archive.
99. Kick and National Security Counselors, *CIA's Studies in Intelligence*.

100. Westerfield, *Inside the CIA's Private World*, xiii.
101. Ford, *Estimative Intelligence*, 8.
102. See Zlotnik, "Bayes Theorem for Intelligence Analysis."
103. Jack Davis also makes the observation that when it came to recording the successes of historians at OSS, this was largely left to the same historians to write. Davis, *Sherman Kent and the Profession of Intelligence Analysis*, 4.
104. Davis, 2.

The National Intelligence Estimates of Soviet Strategic Intentions and Capabilities

Let me first be quite clear as to the general and the particular meaning of the word "estimate" in the present context. In intelligence, as in other callings, estimating is what you do when you do not know.

—Sherman Kent (1968)

On September 15, 1950, under United Nations Security Council Resolution 83, 40,000 US Marines landed at Inchon, successfully driving the North Korean forces back over the 38th parallel. By September 30 China was warning the United States that it would intervene if the United States went any farther. The United States continued to push into North Korea. On October 1 the Soviets told the Chinese to send five to six divisions into Korea, and by October 19 the Chinese People's Volunteer Army had crossed the Yalu River into North Korea. On November 1 the People's Volunteer Army encircled the 8th Cavalry Regiment during the Battle of Unsan, in North Korea, with heavy losses to man and machine. By December the UN forces had been pushed back below the 38th parallel.[1]

The involvement of the People's Republic of China, as well as the covert backing of the Soviet Union, made the Korean conflict much more than just a regional war. It meant that at any time the conflict on the peninsula could explode into an all-out war between the Communist Bloc and the West. The Soviet Union now possessed the atomic bomb and was rearming its conventional forces at an alarming rate. Now more than ever, CIA needed to be able to determine the intentions and capabilities of this formidable adversary, and it needed to do so when the organization was arguably at its most vulnerable, transitioning between leaders and amid a restructure.

Not surprisingly, the Cold War had by now passed into a hot ideological war. NSC-68 had been approved in April 1950, and it clearly set out that the Soviets were bent on world domination and were developing their military to force the free world to submit. Although probably not of sufficient strength to strike yet, the USSR could launch a major attack in 1950, which could include the invasion of Western Europe, air attacks on the United Kingdom, and nuclear weapons deployed against Alaska, Canada, and the mainland United States. Historian Melvyn Leffler says there were no new goals set by NSC-68, only "rhetorical flourishes and ideological fervor."[2] Yet the rhetoric and ideology clearly established a language of war. In his memoirs, Charles "Chip" Bohlen agrees. He says both he and Secretary of State George Marshall had thought Truman's speech to Congress in 1947 (the Truman Doctrine) had been too flamboyant in its anticommunist language: "Marshall and I felt that Truman was using too much rhetoric. Marshall cabled our thoughts back to Washington. He received a reply that in the considered opinion of the executive branch, including the President, the Senate would not approve the doctrine without the emphasis on the Communist danger."[3]

This built upon a similar language already established by George Kennan in his so-called Long Telegram of 1946 and "Mr. X" article a year later.[4] It became the established narrative for how to talk about the new enemy. Leffler says:

> Kennan's analysis was appealing because it provided a unifying theme to US foreign policy. Rather than tackle deep-seated problems in disparate parts of the globe, Kennan urged policymakers to view Soviet Russia as their enemy and to approach all other issues from the viewpoint of competition with the Kremlin. Moreover, Kennan disavowed all legitimacy to Soviet policies and portrayed Russian fears and insecurities as irrational. . . . Policy makers need not scrutinize avenues for compromise, it was futile.[5]

CIA was effectively being instructed how to talk about the Cold War by their policy masters. As social scientists accustomed to taking value-free, objective positions in their writing, this would provide a major challenge to their approach to the national intelligence estimates.

As part of the reforms of the 1950–53 period, CIA was charged with setting up a small team of analysts who would coordinate and write estimates that were an "authoritative interpretation and appraisal that will serve as a firm guide to policy makers."[6] The *Cambridge Dictionary* gives three related meanings for "authoritative": "showing you are confident, in control and expect to be respected and obeyed," "containing complete and accurate information, and therefore respected," and "having the power of special knowledge, or (of a person) showing the confidence of special knowledge."[7] There is little evidence that, prior to 1950, CIA's estimates were respected, or that the director of central intelligence, the organization's leader, was respected or obeyed. On the contrary. It was General Smith's task to correct its lack of leadership authority and Langer's and Kent's job to earn the estimates respect. The other dimension to the Cambridge definition is special knowledge, and knowledge that is complete and accurate and demonstrates some control over the subject. This chapter sets out to tell the story of how CIA's early estimates were approached after Langer and Kent arrived in late 1950.

The chapter first reviews what a national intelligence estimate is, including Sherman Kent's commentary on how they were created. It then reviews the estimates created during the reform period of 1950–53. Both Kent and Langer had written extensively before their arrival at CIA concerning what was needed and what the best way would be to approach a new discipline of peacetime, civilian-led strategic intelligence analysis. Next, the chapter investigates to what extent they were able to impose social science methods on the estimates process once they arrived. It is accepted that not all methodologies will necessarily translate into national security documents, so to what extent does the policymaker need to know everything you have considered or which tools you have used to arrive at your conclusions? Kent himself said, prior to 1950, that social science was just the beginning and that strategic intelligence analysis would be a progression from those methods. To investigate this, the chapter reviews the terms of reference process as a better way of seeing the workings "laid bare," the dissents lodged against the estimates by the competing intelligence wings of the military and State Department, the postmortem system set up to look at weaknesses in the analysis of estimates, the caveats CIA put into their assessments in order to educate policymakers on the limitations of their methodology, and the growing confidence in making predictions even when social science was cautious about doing so.

The National Intelligence Estimate

The national intelligence estimate (NIE) is "a multidisciplinary assessment of the facts and implications of an important topic, taking into account all available sources."[8] Kent explains that the word "estimate" meant they were writing about something of which they were not certain.[9] The subject matter was the future, and the content was intended for the highest levels of policymaking: the president and National Security Council.[10] "In short," he says, "if there was any office in the United States Government which was and should have been perpetually worrying about the future and where its perils or the opposite lay, [ONE was it]."[11]

The NIE was outlined originally in the NSCID-3 directive of 1948, which stated that "national intelligence is integrated departmental intelligence that covers the broad aspects of national policy and national security, is of concern to more than one Department or Agency, and transcends the exclusive competence of a single Department or Agency or the Military Establishment." The directive also insisted that the director of central intelligence was ultimately responsible for each NIE, a role that Smith and the Agency read as a legal responsibility and that William Langer, as the new assistant director of ONE, had assumed for himself in his dealings with the Board of National Estimates (BNE). (The previous DCI, Roscoe Hillenkoetter, had renounced that responsibility early in his directorship.)[12]

The title "National Intelligence Estimate" appears to have been coined by General Smith.[13] In one of his first meetings with the Intelligence Advisory Committee, in October 1950, Smith made it clear that CIA's emphasis would be "seeing to it that the United States has adequate central machinery for the examination and interpretation of intelligence, so that the national security will not be jeopardized by failure to coordinate the best intelligence opinion in the country, based on all available information."[14] Estimates would be prioritized for production in five categories: crash, urgent, high, routine, and deferred.[15]

Truman described the process in his memoirs:

> Tied in with the National Security Council staff, as an adjunct, is the Central Intelligence Agency, which operates in this way: Each time the Council is about to consider a certain policy—let us say a policy having to do with Southeast Asia—it immediately calls upon CIA to present an estimate of the effects such a policy will have. The Director of the CIA sits with the staff of the National Security Council and continually informs [them] as they go along. The estimates he submits represent the judgment of the CIA and a cross-section of the judgments of all the advisory councils of the CIA. These are G-2, A-2, ONI, the State Department, the FBI and the Director of Intelligence of the AEC [Atomic Energy Commission]. The Secretary of State then makes the final recommendation of policy, and the President makes the final decision.[16]

Kent described both the physical and intellectual process of writing an NIE in 1964. Published originally in the house organ *Studies in Intelligence*, it reviewed the failure of CIA's initial assessment of the Cuban Missile Crisis.[17] The NIE was approached with three goals in mind: to meet the needs of the policymaker; to use every relevant piece of information available to the intelligence community; and as "an attainment of the best agreed judgement of imponderables, or lacking unanimity the isolation and identification of dissenting opinion."[18] In other words, the estimate was intended to get as close to the truth as possible, and to do that by making sure other explanations or objections were not made invisible. For Kent, this meant postulating a range of hypotheses, expanding the analyst's imagination for possible explanations so that no scenario was not considered. In *Strategic Intelligence for American*

World Policy, he explained it as "checking on the accuracy of sources, comparing divergent accounts, and gaining perspective by broadening the field of inquiry, finding new leads—out of which emerges a proposition which seems the truest of all possible propositions. . . . This research is a systematic endeavor to get firm meaning out of impressions, . . . truth is to be approached, if not attained, through research guided by a systematic method."[19]

Each estimate was approached with a great deal of thought and planning. Information was sourced in theory from both the military and State Department intelligence wings and the report assembled and written by the "ablest staff in the business."[20] Finally, it was scrutinized by a "painstaking" number of interagency meetings and sent to up to eight stations (presumably CIA stations abroad) for their input. It is therefore fair to say that each estimate was the combined work of perhaps thousands of intelligence people around the world. Yet responsibility for the estimates came down to a small number: those who worked on the staff of ONE and the BNE itself. For Kent, this meant that the estimate had the benefit of the best information available and had been constantly checked and rechecked by those responsible for supplying the information. This was much more than the work of one scholar.

But when it came to writing the estimate, Kent spoke in language familiar to most social scientists, particularly those who had been trained in the historical method.

> After a confrontation of the problem and some decisions as to how it should be handled, there is a ransacking of files and minds for all information relating to the problem; and an evaluation, analysis, and digestion of this information. There are emergent hypotheses as to the possible aggregate meaning of the information; some emerged before, some after its absorption. No one can say whence came these essential yeasts of fruitful thought. Surely they grow best in a medium of knowledge, experience, and intuitive understanding. When they unfold, they are checked back against the facts, weighed in the light of the specific circumstances and the analysts' general knowledge and understanding of the world scene. Those that cannot stand up fall; those that do stand up are ordered in varying degrees of likelihood.[21]

A 1974 internal CIA document suggested the task of intelligence in relation to policy making was fourfold: (1) alerting policymakers to events abroad; (2) estimating future developments; (3) appraising the likely consequences of possible US courses of action; and (4) monitoring conditions that affect US policies or agreements with foreign governments.[22] This reflects the basic categories of the NIEs as we saw them in the late 1940s and early 1950s: the situation report, estimates that dealt with the consequences of US actions, those that looked at potential adversary actions, and those that scrutinized how allies would react or the capabilities they had to withstand actions by the Communists.

A 1977 CIA study recommended that the estimate should emphasize analysis rather than description; show the relationships among data, analysis, and conclusions; and describe the thought process by which the estimators came to their judgments. The writer should flag contentious issues and dissents, describe the history behind previous related estimates and how things had changed, and highlight what relevance the conclusions had to current US policy.[23] In this respect, the intention of the study appeared to be to provide the reader with a lot more background to the estimate than the early CIA estimates—and, indeed, the Langer and Kent documents ever provided. This does not mean, however, that such issues were not top of mind at ONE or were not discussed at some length in personal accounts by the intel intellectuals. Indeed, they provided the content for many years in *Studies in Intelligence*.

Small Success: Montague and Van Slyck and the Global Survey Group

Prior to the arrival of Langer and Kent, the Global Survey Group, under the leadership of Ludwell Lee Montague, appears to have been the only component of ORE working specifically toward social science–founded estimates. In particular, the CIA *Review of the World Situation* largely sidestepped the painful coordinating process and, George Jackson says, "boldly stated the theoretical basis for its analysis, a procedure potentially more 'dangerous' than any individual estimate."[24]

Originally accompanying a one-off oral briefing commissioned by Admiral Souers, the *Review* became a monthly, using the prefix "CIA-"[25] At least twenty-nine were published, from CIA-1 in September 1947 to CIA-11-50 in November 1950.[26] Generally thought of in good stead, a *Review* of March 16, 1948, was praised as "the most significant exception to a rather general failure to coordinate intelligence opinion."[27] Yet the CIA series was largely uncoordinated, with the usually unhelpful service and diplomatic intelligence branches mostly excluded from the process ostensibly because of timing issues but more probably because Montague and Van Slyck wanted it that way.

The *Review*, says George Jackson, was a sustained NIE written in a way that demonstrated Montague and Van Slyck knew what one was. It dealt with the major issues of the day, responded in a timely fashion, and was usually written by just one analyst. Montague wrote the first issue, CIA-1 *Review of the World Situation as It Relates to the Security of the United States*, published September 26, 1947. He was responsible for most of the series until mid-1948 (with

Van Slyck taking over during occasional absences), when authorship passed to William Reitzel, with Montague overseeing. Reitzel was succeeded by Ray Cline in 1950, who was replaced for the final issues by George Oakes.[28]

The use of theory in the reviews included discussions on the balance of power and polarity. A definition of the concept of "security interest" was employed as a basis for all analysis of US policy and grouped "security situations" into three categories: geographical, sociological, and domestic. CIA-1 argued that the balance of power had shifted against the United States and that any economic collapse in Europe would exacerbate this even further. The Soviets would behave in the way of all traditional land-based powers by slowly absorbing the states around them. CIA-0-49 stated that the shift in polarity from a multipolar to a bipolar environment meant that the Soviets would endeavor to consolidate the power resources of Europe and Asia into one single authority. While middle and smaller powers existed, they would always be drawn to one of the two major blocs. Psychological warfare would primarily take the place of physical conflict. The concept of time was also a valuable lens, and Soviet power expansion did not need a major global war and could be achieved incrementally.[29]

CIA-0-49 was written as the theoretical basis for the rest of the series, which lasted until Langer and Kent arrived in late 1950. Jackson says that, despite (or perhaps because of) the application of theory, the CIA estimates seemed "forever to be frustrated by the failure of events to happen."[30] In fact, Reitzel appears to have moved away from a theoretical framework and had begun to analyze global politics according to his own interpretation of them.[31]

Montague, Van Slyck, and the Global Survey Group were an isolated case in ORE. They were largely left to their own devices. Theodore Babbitt, according to Jackson, "seldom offered any comments. [The] Director had time to study the draft, but if he made changes in it they were never brought to the attention of the producers."[32]

The National Intelligence Estimates After Langer Arrived

With his arrival on November 8, seven days before the Inchon landings, Langer's first appointments were to earmark ORE veterans Montague and Van Slyck as members of the BNE and Ray Cline as chief of the Office of National Estimates staff.[33]

Sherman Kent reported for duty five days later, overwhelmed by the task ahead. He knew the option of replacing Langer was open to him but was unsure whether—like Langer —his might be only a one-year secondment. At his interview with Walter Bedell Smith and William Jackson in 1949, Kent had stressed he had very little experience in writing estimates. He also felt that, while his wartime duty for OSS had made him well-versed in North African and European affairs, he was not knowledgeable enough to take on estimates for the whole world. Arriving at CIA he found himself intimidated by the "rarified intellectual atmosphere" at ONE, admitting years later that his feelings of impostor syndrome never left him.[34] It is not surprising, then, that Kent did not take an active hand in the estimates tackled in his first few weeks. Analyst Ray Cline seemed to be the main drafter, with Langer making sure that nothing was said without his approval.[35]

The task that Kent and Langer faced was daunting. Kent was deeply concerned about the crisis in Korea and believed the United States had a 50/50 chance of losing every soldier and all the equipment stationed on the peninsula. "The US was confronted," in his opinion, "with the prospect of a staggering defeat."[36]

The first estimates, NIE-3 "Soviet Capabilities and Intentions" and NIE-2/2 "Soviet Participation in the Air Defense of Manchuria," led with a simplified "Problem," "Discussion," "Conclusion" format.[37] This format became the standard template for NIE's from 1951 to 1953, with SEs (Special Estimates) following the same style but often substituting "Estimate" for "Conclusion." The Problem consistently kept to a short sentence; for example, NIE-3 stated that its task was "to estimate Soviet capabilities and intentions with particular reference to the date at which [the] USSR might engage in a general war." NIE-2/2 specified "to estimate whether, in the event of UN air attacks on targets in Manchuria, the Soviet Air Force would participate in the defense of such targets." This contrasted with ORE's estimates that would often begin with "we have been directed to estimate the likelihood . . ." or "by direction of the National Security Council we estimate herein the consequences of the following . . ."[38] Langer appeared to be taking responsibility for the research question, and the master/servant relationship of old was gone. The matter-of-fact approach to stating the problem probably reflected the terse formality of Langer's style, but it emphasized to policymakers that each report needed to succinctly sum up the parameters of the research: a vague reason for writing the report or unstated problem to be solved might translate into an equally vague answer. It also meant a decision had finally been made as to how an assessment should be presented.

While estimates were mostly short, the use of more detailed appendixes was quickly established. Recalling the reforms at ONE twenty years later, Abbot E. Smith said a distinction had been made early on between "national" estimates—destined for the very highest levels of the president, the NSC, and his advisers—and "departmental" reports, which covered everything below that. "Fine and dandy," claimed Smith, "but some people thought that the conclusions presented to the President should be supported by something more substantial than mere assertions by the DCI with the advice and concurrence of the IAC. . . . So NIEs came to have appendices containing the (estimated to be) factual data on which the conclusions of the NIE were based."[39] This academic discomfort with presenting conclusions without comprehensive citations was illustrated by a point that Kent made to DCI Smith in 1952, when he—perhaps cheekily—wrote, "In the past the DDCI (Mr. Jackson) and the DDI have advised the Board of National Estimates that in their opinion the conclusions of some national estimates should be more strongly supported by facts and reasoning from facts. The Board concurs in this view."[40]

An Analysis of ONE's Estimates on Soviet Intentions and Capabilities

As Kent later admitted, the Soviet estimates were those that most mattered.[41] In 1951 there were seventeen estimates directly referencing Soviet intentions and a further ten on the Chinese. Soviet estimates drilled down further from NIE-3, on Soviet action in Germany (NIE-4), Yugoslavia (NIE-29), the Far East (NIE-43), Austria (NIE-21), and Spitzbergen (NIE-38). General war was discussed in NIE-18 "Probability of Soviet Employment of BW and CW in the Event of Attacks upon the US"; NIE-31 "Soviet Capabilities for Clandestine Attack Against the US with Weapons of Mass Destruction and the Vulnerability of the US to Such Attack (Mid-1951 to Mid-1952)"; and SE-10 "Soviet Capabilities for a Surprise Attack on the Continental United States Before July 1952."[42]

Chinese Communist estimates included SE-20 "The Probable Consequences of Certain Possible Courses of Action with Respect to Communist China and Korea"; NIE-20 "Consequences in Mainland Southeast Asia (Thailand, Malaya, Burma) of Communist Control of Indochina"; NIE-27 "Chinese Communist Capabilities and Intentions with Respect to Taiwan"; and NIE-32 "Effects of Operations in Korea on Communist China." There were also estimates showcasing the work of the new economic intelligence unit of the Office of Research and Reports, including NIE-22 "Vulnerability of the Soviet Bloc to Economic Warfare" and NIE-14 "The Importance of Iranian and Middle East Oil to Western Europe Under Peacetime Conditions."[43]

From 1952 to 1953 there were over forty Soviet or Communist Bloc–related estimates, with long-range projections like NIE-65 "Soviet Bloc Capabilities Through 1957." There were also new assessments on the capabilities of allies, like NIE-63 "France's Prospective Ability to Play a Major Role in the Western Security System." In addition to the Communist Bloc estimates, there were reports on Yugoslavia, Albania, Panama, Guatemala, Argentina, Venezuela, Chile, Denmark, Italy, Sweden, Iran, North Africa, and South Africa.

The Content of the First Soviet Estimates

The first NIEs on the USSR (NIE-3 "Soviet Capabilities and Intentions," published November 15, 1950, followed by NIE-11 "Soviet Intentions in the Current Situation," on December 7, and NIE-15 "Probable Soviet Moves to Exploit the Present Situation," less than a week later) are representative of the nuances that began to appear under the new ONE.[44]

NIE-3 argued that the window of opportunity for Moscow existed between 1952 and 1954, the former date being when Soviet power would peak and the latter date when the buildup of the new NATO forces would have had sufficient time to resist a Soviet invasion. ONE believed that the Soviets thought a Sino-American war would be in their interests. The chance of a general war in 1950 was a "grave danger," and the Korean situation alone was sufficient cause for a conflict. Stalin was in an aggressive mood and was not as shy of conflict, as the earlier estimates under Montague had suggested. Unlike the "misleading" seven-page ORE-32 50 "The Effect of the Soviet Possession of Atom Bombs on the Security of the United States," published just five months earlier, NIE-3 was a full twenty-seven pages long, demonstrating a considerable effort that was probably designed to show the new office in a good light. It was not political intelligence that gave ONE reason to think the Soviets were preparing for war but economic and military intelligence. The USSR had already mobilized and had "a great preponderance of military stocks," which the United States and its allies would take months to catch up with. While the Soviet people did not want war, they considered any possibility of one an existential matter, while the people of the West had no taste for another war at all. NIE-3 was immensely detailed in what courses of action the enemy might take. It reflected Langer's familiarity with fighting a war in several theaters at once and (while it drew on already published data), it took an encyclopedic approach to strategic intelligence estimates. NIE-3 listed nine pages of possible Soviet strategies against the West, including capturing Northern Europe (as a base of operations), Western Europe (preemptively); Berlin (to control all of Germany); Yugoslavia (in a coup against Tito); Greece (to isolate Turkey); Turkey (for control of the Straits), Iran (as a bulwark to defend Baku oil); Afghanistan (as another bulwark); Pakistan (to prevent US airbases being established); and South and East Asia (to foment the spread of Communism). Japan was seen as a likely Soviet military base. As the first Soviet estimate produced under the new Langer-led ONE, no stone was going to be left unturned.

The second analysis of the Kremlin's intentions, NIE-11 "Soviet Intentions in the Current Situation," in December 1950, was a much more succinct two pages, as was NIE-15, at just over two. (ONE kept the "11" suffix from there on, and NIE-11 became the vehicle for all assessments of Soviet strategic objectives.) NIE-11 stated that Moscow was determined to get UN forces out of Korea and would look favorably upon a Sino-American war. It accurately argued that the Soviets were using the Chinese to shoulder the brunt of the Korean War, supplying them with matériel, technical personnel, and "volunteer" units where necessary, and were most likely willing to defend China if the UN forces decided on a direct attack. NIE-15 "Probable Soviet Moves to Exploit the Present Situation" took public statements coming out of Moscow as the basis of some assumptions about intentions. NIE-15 returned to NIE-3 in detailing areas of weakness for the West, citing Berlin and Germany, Indochina, Yugoslavia, and Iran, among others. The Soviets were turning the screws on the West, relying on "a continuation of pressures rather than upon negotiation."[45] The USSR had decided that China would become the leading Communist power in the Far East, and it would undermine US control over Japan and seek to remove the United Kingdom from the Middle East. In Indochina, the Chinese were supplying and training the Viet Minh in an effort to drive out France. No intelligence was available to suggest the Soviets had made any decision regarding a general war.

Harold P. Ford summed up the early Soviet estimates by saying that it became clear to Washington that Moscow intended to expand its influence wherever it could but would not do so at the risk of precipitating a total war with the United States. Therefore the aim of the estimates was to focus particularly on where the openings lay for Soviet opportunism.[46] The threshold for this new way of thinking was NIE-25 "Probable Soviet Courses of Action to Mid-1952" (1951), says Montague, when it was agreed by the IAC that the Soviets would not resort to nuclear war if they could avoid it.[47]

A 1957 "validity study" says NIE-3 was a stopgap as ONE learned the terminology of the task at hand. The idea of an annually updated estimate of Soviet intentions and capabilities did not take hold until NIE-64, in late 1952, and subsequently with the NIE-11 series.[48]

How the Terms of Reference Briefs Illustrated the Thinking Behind Estimates

Once an estimate had been commissioned, either by the IAC or by the NSC, the first step was to draw up a terms of reference (TR, sometimes TOR), which was essentially a brief to ONE written by the BNE laying out the scope of the research. Kent puts it like this: "The object was at least two-fold: it aimed to define the subject matter of the estimate, its scope, and time frame; it aimed to focus the forthcoming estimate on the few major points that were discerned as the principal concern of the requester; it aimed to ask those questions (irrespective of anyone's ability to provide factual answers) which would direct research and cogitation to the general area of these major points."[49]

Kent says that, while the other intelligence agencies participated in their production, they were generally skeptical about estimating that they considered "feckless speculation of unknowns and unknowables."[50] This would clearly put any researcher on their guard when writing a scoping brief. Therefore, we should be able to see some examples of careful planning in the early TRs, planning that might otherwise not be included in the final NIE.[51]

One such example is from SE-1, originally titled "The Scope and Nature of Soviet Military Preparations in the Far East," dated March 17, 1951, which puts it nine months into the Korean War and five months after Langer and Kent's arrival.[52] The two-page document appears to have originated from the Air Force Intelligence Directorate A-2, but this is crossed out and "Central Intelligence Agency" is written in ink below it. This is clearly designated a TR and begins with a heading "The Problem" followed by "Questions Bearing on the Problem."

The problem is stated as "to determine the scope and nature of Soviet military preparations in the Far East during the past six months and to estimate the significance of such preparations." There are seven questions in the original, the last of which is blacked out and too difficult to read. The first six questions are (1) What Soviet military preparations have taken place in the last six months and where have these been most pronounced? (these are listed as changes in training, equipment, morale, leadership, logistical support and deployment and repeated for land, sea and air); (2) What percentage increase (or decrease) in Soviet military activities and strength in the Far East is estimated to have occurred in the last six months?; (3) To what extent have these affected Soviet offensive capabilities against (a) United Nations forces in Korea; (b) United States forces in Japan, Ryuku Islands, Alaska, and the continental United States?; (4) To what extent have changes affected Soviet defensive capabilities?; (5) Have there been any changes in Soviet military capabilities or potential [word crossed out, perhaps "activities"] in Europe or the Middle East that might indicate Soviet intentions in the Far East?; (6) Are the changed Soviet military capabilities in the Far East related to the Japanese Peace Treaty, Japanese rearmament, or the pending Council of Foreign Ministers, or other items of Soviet interest?

This TR for SE-1 is heavily annotated, presumably by a writer who felt the Central Intelligence Agency should have had the job of writing it, not the Air Force. The writer amends the problem to "examine" rather than "determine," sets the time frame for the preceding three rather than six months, takes in Soviet satellites, and specifies "activities" rather than "preparations." The writer also changes the questions around. Rather than being interested in the percentage change in Soviet activities, there is a focus on political and economic changes. Chinese Communist activities are also a focus, as well as requesting information on Taiwan and Southeast Asia. The question about the Japanese

Peace Treaty is deleted, and the final question is made "what is the probable purpose of the developments?"

The amendments to the terms of reference for SE-1 show how the estimate evolved over the first few weeks of development. The writer changes the title of the estimate to Current Soviet Activities, with Particular Reference to the Far East, thus changing the direction of the estimate from one looking at the Far East to one looking further afield to see if the Soviets are shifting emphasis to the Far East. It is telling that the writer differentiates between "determining" and "examining"—determining bears a heavier responsibility. However, it is also telling that the terms of reference show a belief that "activities" demonstrate purpose, whereas "preparations" are much harder to prove and are contingent.

Another example is NIE-25 "Probable Soviet Courses of Action to Mid-1952," originally titled "Soviet Intentions with Respect to General War."[53] This NIE started out as a comparative study of relative power, as seen in the diagram in figure 6.1. ONE analysts would build a picture of each superpower's objectives, capabilities, and vulnerabilities and then determine the options for action available to each. From this, an assessment would be made as to how each might respond to the first action. A distinction would be made between the most "feasible" option available to the United States and the most "probable" option for the USSR.

NIE-25 was also created through the established division of labor among the intelligence agencies: with the Bureau of Intelligence and Research at the State Department looking at the comparisons between the United States and USSR in the political realm; CIA, Defense, and State working together on the psychological; the Census, State, and Labor Departments working on sociological factors; CIA and Defense on geographic; CIA's Office of Scientific Intelligence on scientific matters; the National Security Resources Board, Commerce, State, and CIA on economic; Commerce and Defense on transportation; and Defense on military. Questions asked by Langer included the status of Soviet morale, readiness for war, and resilience to psychological warfare (State); the USSR's economic strength compared to the United States and the West (State); the strength and combat efficiency of Soviet forces compared to the West's total NATO forces (Army); the logistics of supplying the Soviet army for any length of time in battle (Army); the strength of the Soviet Navy (including submarines) relative to the West's (Navy); the same for the Soviet air force compared to NATO's (Air Force); plus two requests for CIA: one to the Office of Research and Reports for industrial mobilization to war of both sides as well as the economic effects of war on the population and another to Office of Scientific Intelligence on weapons of mass destruction.[54]

Writing to the BNE in April 1951, along with an enclosed draft of NIE-25, the likely author, Montague, explained how he had thought through the

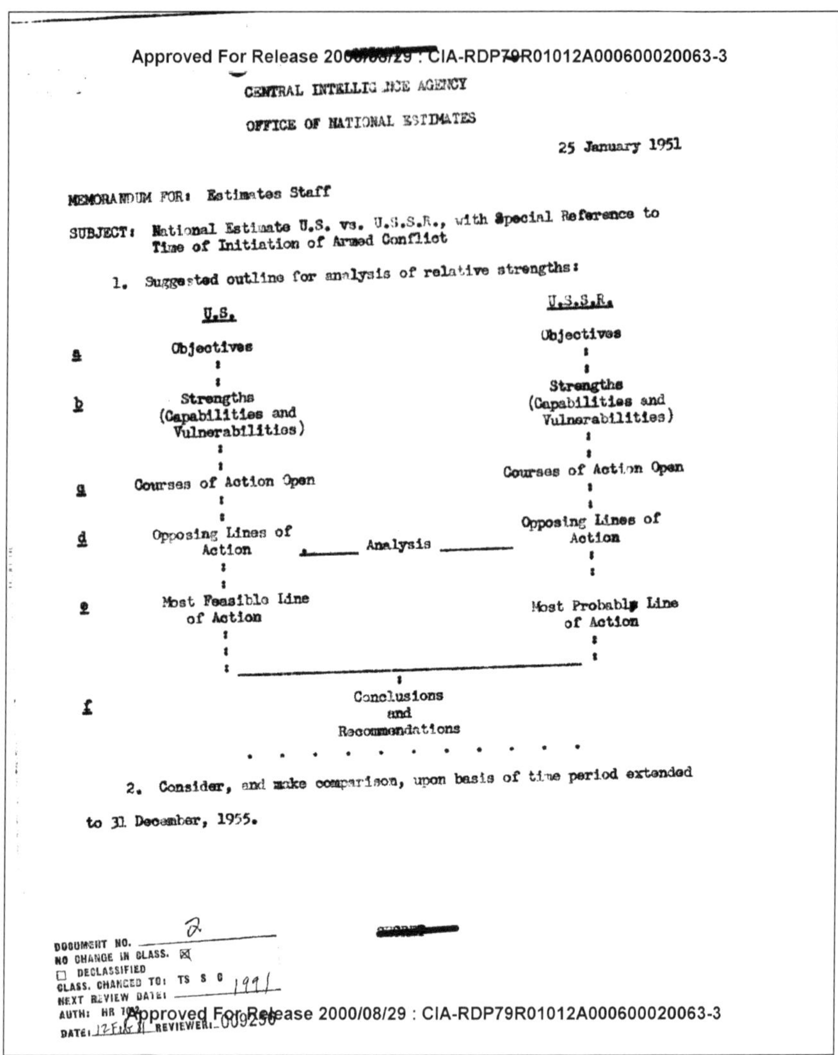

FIGURE 6.1. A comparison of the relative strengths of the United States and USSR from NIE-25 (1951). *Memorandum NIE-25 Soviet Intentions with Respect to General War, February 1 Gen.0, 1951, CIA-RDP79R01012A000600020044-4, CIA, CREST Archive*

estimate.[55] Here he discusses how a military format has constrained the Soviet estimates so far:

> I understood that I was merely to revise the 26th March draft (Possible Sources of Soviet Action) but when at last I was able to get to it I found it desirable to adopt a radically different approach to the subject and submit

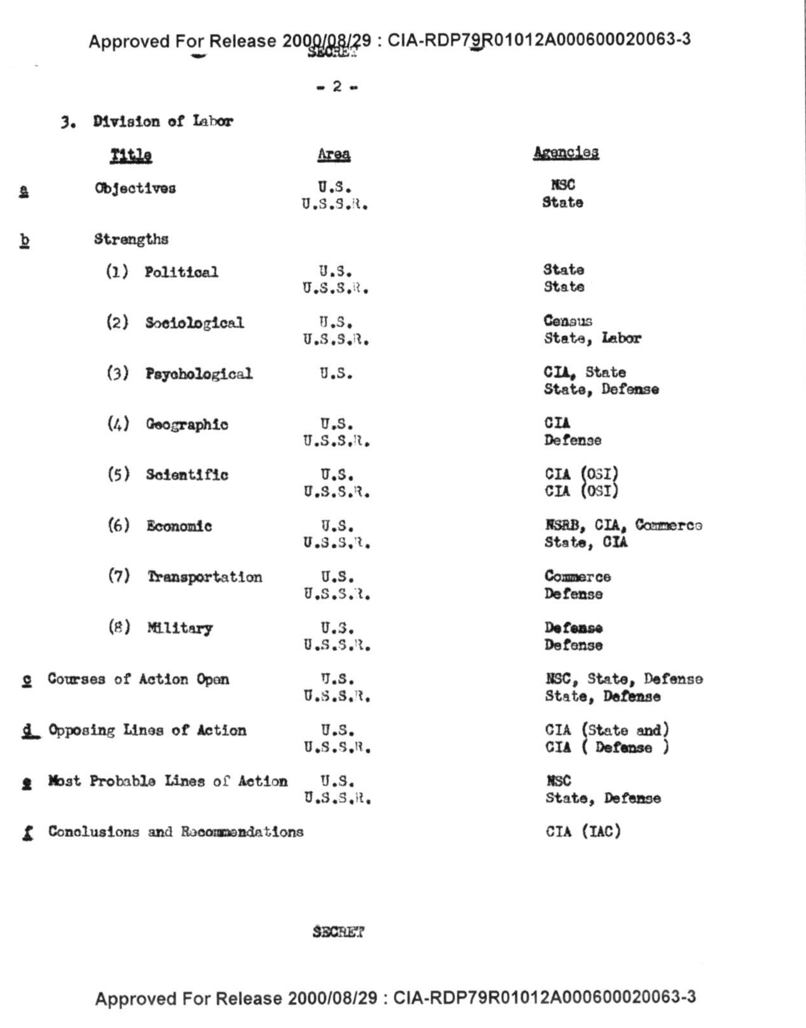

Approved For Release 2000/08/29 : CIA-RDP79R01012A000600020063-3

SECRET

- 2 -

3. **Division of Labor**

	Title	Area	Agencies
a	Objectives	U.S. U.S.S.R.	NSC State
b	Strengths		
	(1) Political	U.S. U.S.S.R.	State State
	(2) Sociological	U.S. U.S.S.R.	Census State, Labor
	(3) Psychological	U.S.	CIA, State State, Defense
	(4) Geographic	U.S. U.S.S.R.	CIA Defense
	(5) Scientific	U.S. U.S.S.R.	CIA (OSI) CIA (OSI)
	(6) Economic	U.S. U.S.S.R.	NSRB, CIA, Commerce State, CIA
	(7) Transportation	U.S. U.S.S.R.	Commerce Defense
	(8) Military	U.S. U.S.S.R.	Defense Defense
c	Courses of Action Open	U.S. U.S.S.R.	NSC, State, Defense State, Defense
d	Opposing Lines of Action	U.S. U.S.S.R.	CIA (State and) CIA (Defense)
e	Most Probable Lines of Action	U.S. U.S.S.R.	NSC State, Defense
f	Conclusions and Recommendations		CIA (IAC)

SECRET

Approved For Release 2000/08/29 : CIA-RDP79R01012A000600020063-3

FIGURE 6.1. (*continued*)

a new draft of the estimate as a whole. That was necessary to take due account of the [Princeton] Consultants' just criticism of NIE-3/1 which is equally applicable to A-BI 14 and all its progeny. Indeed, as one of the joint authors of A-BI 14 and of previous examples of that form of literature I have felt strongly that ONE should break out of the straitjacket of that form and make a radical new departure in its approach to the subject.

The faults of A-BI 14 and papers like it are attributable to a misapplication of a rigid military form designed for another purpose, the estimate of a specific limited situation as a means of reaching a definite decision regarding an immediate course of action. As such that form has a snapshot static effect and is unsuitable for the estimation of a complex and moving situation having a past and a future full of contingent possibilities.

In this draft I have endeavored to introduce historical perspective, as called for by [name redacted] without going back to Ivan the Terrible or Karl Marx, and have also endeavored to indicate the contingent aspect of Soviet intentions, as suggested by Dr. [name redacted, presumably both from the Princeton Consultants panel or BNE]. I have omitted quantities of descriptive matter, order of battle and war gaming, as inappropriate to this level of estimation. There is no formal catalogue of capabilities as such in the abstract, but they are referred to in broad terms as they naturally occur in the discussion of the situation and the possible courses of Soviet action.

Having completed my draft, I find that it bears scant resemblance to the standard literature on "Capabilities and Intentions." I have therefore ventured to change the title and statement of the problem.[56]

The 1957 validity study records that the process of writing NIE-25 was "torturous," and it passed through many hands as each draft was rejected and another took its place. Montague's memorandum does not indicate that he was the final author. Yet it is interesting to see the sensitivity shown to writing "first-cause" type histories (like going back as far as Ivan the Terrible) and the suggestion that he had been told to do so. More importantly, Montague is grappling with the problem of introducing too many variables to project a future course of action. The format he has been used to working with, the A-BI series, is too constricting as it assumes a very simple causal explanation but an overview of possible actions by the USSR takes in many possible theaters and a very wide range of actors, interests, and possible responses.

Whereas ORE-91 had implied that as the Soviets grew more confident in their military superiority the chances of them precipitating a general war would grow, NIE-25 was more concrete in its causal factors. Moscow, it argued, had shorter-term goals and would prefer these "actions short of war."[57] These more achievable goals included dividing the West; preventing Western, German, and Japanese rearmament; and preventing the establishment of US overseas bases. As a result, the estimate predicted that in the period up to mid-1952, the USSR would concentrate on readying for war and growing its capabilities, warding off any threat to its interests or that would undermine control of its satellites, expanding its territories where it could, growing its influence on those countries not yet under its control, and pushing those countries it couldn't control into neutral positions, thus denying the United States from putting bases there (see appendix A.1 of NIE-25).

By breaking Soviet goals down into smaller pieces, Montague and ONE avoided looking into the collective mind and intellectual history of the Soviet Politburo. Instead, Montague focused on the tools at their disposal, like political warfare, to wedge Western relationships apart and undermine democracies in weak or small states. Or like using proxy wars through the Chinese. NIE-25 therefore saw opportunities for Moscow in Indochina and Burma, but the risks of taking on Taiwan, Hong Kong, and Macau were too high. While ONE estimated the Soviets could overrun Europe, the Middle East, and the Far East in a short period, Moscow would prefer small regional wars, perhaps undertaken by satellite armed forces rather than its own. The Soviets' relative inferiority to NATO forces would rule out Greece and Turkey as targets. Iran was politically fragile, but it would be the British who would more likely invoke a war, in which case the Soviets could justifiably occupy the northern regions. The USSR would continue to offer clandestine aid to the Chinese and North Korean forces and would increase that if the war turned in the South's favor. When it came to the danger of general war, NIE-25 flipped the argument, saying it "will continue to exist as long as the USSR is in a position to take action which threatens, wholly or in part, the interests of the Western Powers."[58] This idea may well have been generated by thinking about the links between "courses of action open" and "opposing lines of action" illustrated in the diagram (fig. 6.1) outlined in the terms of reference.[59] When it came to general war, it took two to tango. Montague had built on the argument entailed in CIA 0-49, but this "call and response" approach—of actions sparking reactions—was new.

In 1967 Abbot Smith penned a think piece on how TRs should be structured.[60] As one of the early ONE team members, Smith was well positioned to consider a new way forward. He began by saying TRs were often confused with three different tasks: (1) a terms of reference proper, (2) an outline of an NIE, and (3) a list of questions on which information could be sourced and a line of argument built. What we saw with SE-1 compared with NIE-25 shows how Smith's differentiation could produce two very different TRs even though they were created within a month of each other.

Instead, he called for a TR structured in two parts. Part 1 would be a proper TR, which he emphasized would be what the NIE needed to cover. This was an elastic concept that could entail an outline, perhaps a brief essay of a few paragraphs covering the main points, a prefatory note (an introduction or background), or a scoping document. This would be discussed with the BNE, who would concern themselves not only with the structure of the estimate but also its coverage. Smith believed there were two factors a TR needed to encapsulate: why the NIE was being written and what it was *not* going to cover. Whether a statement of the problem was required was up to the drafter.

Part 2, Smith argued, would be questions bearing on the problem. Regardless of whether other intelligence agencies would be contributing to the estimate, some detail on what information would be needed was valuable, and this was best put as a series of questions. If contributions were called for, then this was a specific brief. Not everything in the estimate needed to be covered in the Questions section, but sometimes it was useful to ask questions about matters that were not to be included in the final report. This harks back to Kent's musings earlier about estimate writing being a "ransacking of files and minds for all information relating to the problem" and that an active imagination was needed to hypothesize all possible scenarios. The question determines not only the focus but the peripheral interests that must be considered before the research begins.

Finally, a few words on the timeline for an estimate produced in a crisis, normally called a special estimate (SE or SNIE). This example gives some idea of how ONE responded to urgent requests and considered the relationship between speed and quality. In a December 1950 meeting, Park Armstrong, the State Department representative on the BNE, requested a special estimate on Soviet intentions for Germany, Iran, and Indochina. Armstrong argued that it was likely that Moscow would turn its attention from Korea to these regions, and there were signs already in Germany of that happening.[61] Langer acknowledged the need for a crisis report but argued that estimates required a great deal of preparation and that quality might be sacrificed if the assessment was rushed. A draft report of NIE-4 "Soviet Courses of Action in Germany" was with the IAC for approval before January 11 and published on February 1, 1951.[62] Terms of reference for NIE-20 "Consequences in Mainland Asia (Thailand, Malaya, Burma) of Communist Control of Indochina" were agreed to on January 17, and after an extension requested by the Army, it was published on March 20.[63] (A further report solely focused on Indochina was rushed through between April 18 and April 20, 1951.[64]) "Position in the East–West Conflict" was produced on April 5.[65] That Armstrong's request was not produced as an SE but was broken into at least three dedicated NIEs suggests that Langer both got his way on the project and managed to deliver comprehensive and timely answers to the State Department's concerns. Yet timely delivery was often at odds with the urgency of the request: the 1957 validity report says some estimates were published within a few months of the forecast period (NIE-25 was published in August, 1951, four months after Montague's memo, the forecast period being mid-1952).

Dissents: The Peer-Review Process of Strategic Intelligence Analysis

Dissents from the other intelligence wings, which had been damning during the ORE years, were much less critical between late 1950 and 1953, despite institutional differences.[66] There were no recorded dissents in 1951, and nine in 1952, but these were mostly word changes. For example, in NIE-12 the Air Force dissented over the size of the Chinese Nationalist forces.[67] In NIE-25 "Probable Soviet Courses of Action to Mid-1952," the estimate ended by saying, "We recognize the desirability and importance of concluding this estimate with a simple and direct statement of the likelihood or unlikelihood that the Kremlin will directly precipitate or provoke general war between the US and USSR during the period here covered. Existing intelligence does not allow us to make such a precise forecast." A dissent came from the Director of Naval Intelligence, who preferred, "It is recognized that precise information on enemy intentions is rarely available and that enemy counteraction cannot be accurately predicted. However all aspects of the Soviet problem considered, we believe it unlikely that the USSR will deliberately choose to precipitate or undergo the hazards of general war." While the ONE report argued the Soviets had the capability to start a general war and that tensions were high and might spill over to war, the Office of Naval Intelligence preferred to emphasize that Soviet power would continue to build without necessarily risking a war with the United States.[68] Matthias contrasts the tensions between CIA and the Pentagon as being between "a rational approach, with its commitment to keeping Soviet behavior under review," and an ideological approach "that simply identified the USSR as an implacable and changeless enemy determined to enslave the world."[69] Yet Kent was probably a lot closer to the mark in saying, "Some of us believed that the purpose of dissent was not merely to identify a difference of opinion, but to define that difference as precisely as possible."[70]

One question is why, after a particularly pointed attack from State in 1950 regarding the inability to read intentions in ORE-91 "Estimate of the Effects of the Soviet Possession of the Atomic Bomb upon the Security of the US," there should be no criticism in late December of the same year of NIE-11 "Soviet Intentions in the Current Situation." But in writing NIE-11, ONE had steered clear of any Kennan-esque analysis that attributed future Soviet actions to Marxist-Leninist ideology or Russian history. As an argument, ORE's analysis in ORE-91 that "no Communist—with his concept that the end justifies the means—can have any scruples regarding the use of force, including military aggression, to advance the world revolution" led its analysts to one conclusion that, should the USSR overtake the West in terms of capability, the United States would be tempted to resort to force, "for if the USSR could decisively defeat the United States, no power on earth could resist its domination."[71] It was this kind of causal logic that would have upset the diplomatic intelligence analysts at State. In contrast, ONE's assessment in NIE-11 eight months later was much simpler. Eschewing ideological motivations, ONE concluded that it made sense for Moscow to push further in East Asia with Chinese backing, particularly as it considered the West unlikely to escalate to a general war.[72] Almost a year later, ONE revisited the question of another Pearl Harbor in NIE-31 "Soviet Capabilities for Clandestine Attack Against the US with Weapons of Mass Destruction and the Vulnerability of the US to Such Attack (Mid-1951 to Mid-1952)." This time there were no dissents to the report, partly because ONE kept NIE-31 to capabilities only and not intentions.

The same appeared in NIE-64, published in four parts (including appendixes) in late 1952 as General Smith "wrathfully demanded" that capabilities and intentions be treated separately.[73] Part 1 was titled "Soviet Bloc Capabilities, Through Mid-1953." It was the first estimate to combine the Communist Bloc's capabilities rather than limit it to Russia's. Part 2 was titled "Probable Soviet Bloc Courses of Action, Through Mid-1953." There were no dissents for NIE-64, although some cautious caveats from Army, Air Force, and Navy on their estimates of numbers of ground forces, air strength, ships, and submarines.[74]

One reason dissents trailed off initially and returned to make only minor points may have been the iron hand of DCI Smith and his hand-picked generals on the BNE. Smith had stipulated early on that the other intelligence agencies would not simply contribute to the NIEs when they were available but every time.[75] This meant the military and diplomatic intelligence wings were compelled to be team players rather than criticizing from the outside looking in. Langer expressed it as a more agency-wide venture than experienced in ORE days: "The important advance is that active cooperation has replaced reluctant and marginal participation, with the result that top policy makers now attach real importance to the estimates produced, whereas this was not formerly so."[76] He gave an example of SE-8, which had been held up from printing so that General Ridgeway could be briefed on it by G-2; at the same time, the secretary of State waited eagerly to read it. While this also demonstrates the success of CIA in turning their detractors around, it also suggests that the more rigorous approach to the estimating process was paying off.

The Postmortems: Checks and Balances on the Estimates

The first review of a previous NIE was also published, for NIE-29 "Probability of an Invasion of Yugoslavia in 1951," which had been produced two months earlier (and was the subject of the discussion about precise language with Paul Nitze.) While this process started with the best possible intentions, Kent says the postmortems became a nightmare for ONE staff. NIE-29 was reviewed based on an observed military buildup in Hungary, Bulgaria, and Rumania as well as on some movements of troops along the Yugoslav border. The postmortem decided that, while a war of nerves may still be taking place between the Tito regime and Soviet satellites, the military buildup was more likely evidence of an investment in Warsaw Pact force strengths.[77] It seems likely that, rather than test assumptions made in earlier estimates, the postmortems became a tiresome effort in justifying them.

Overall, ONE estimates became more balanced in their assessments, with the language recognizing the difficulty of making precise predictions and a willingness to look at all sides of the issue demonstrated. A special estimate written in July 1951, SE-8 "Possible Communist Objectives in Proposing a Cease-Fire in Korea," concluded that the Kremlin believed it would cause a general war if it pushed things too far in Korea, and that a cessation of hostilities would free their hand in East Asia and help forestall a final treaty on Japan. However, the report was prepared to look at alternative explanations, creating a new format that ended every section on possible objectives with a bullet-pointed "arguments for this course of action" contrasted by an "arguments against this course of action." Once again, like NIE-25, ONE analysts were prepared to consider a complex series of actions and responses in their assessments, consistent with Kent's view that multiple hypotheses were an integral part of estimate making.

Caveats and Overpromises: Growing the Understanding of the Limits of Social Science for Policymakers

ONE staff were also wary of estimates that became too speculative, might become difficult to measure, or might give wrong impressions. NIE-61 "Consequences of Communist Control of South Asia," produced in 1952, had been proposed by Deputy Undersecretary Harrison Freeman Matthews in the State Department. It began with his assumption that India, Pakistan, Afghanistan, Nepal, and Ceylon (Sri Lanka) would fall to Communism. This assumption did not sit well with Kent, who considered that the report—regardless of what it concluded—might be misinterpreted by policymakers. He even tried to cancel the project.[78] The terms of reference the BNE wrote for NIE-61 was therefore wary: "No attempt will be made to estimate the likelihood of a Communist assumption of power in the Indian subcontinent," it cautioned.[79] Kent recommended that it be published not as an NIE but as an SIE, to in some way give it less credence.[80] In a letter to Matthews, Park Armstrong (the State Department representative on the IAC) said, "CIA has twice come back to us with difficulties over this. They now specifically ask us to withdraw our request, mainly because such an estimate—particularly if couched in terms of 'the con-sequences of the loss'—will present great difficulties in the doing and when completed will be of dubious value."[81]

Making Predictions: Thinking Fifteen Years Ahead

In mid-1953 ONE was asked to look into the future and determine where the balance of power would sit by 1968. The special estimate produced, SE-46 "Probable Long Term Development of the Soviet Bloc and Western Power Posi-tions," showed a growing comfort with forecasting—so long as it was couched with the circumspection of a social scientist looking for patterns, not predic-tions.[82] This was despite an ongoing awareness that there were serious deficien-cies in the information available on the Communist Bloc, and despite strategies that had been put in place to identify gaps in collection.[83]

CIA had been requested to investigate whether "time was on our side," a vague question that received the usual caveats from the estimates team. The Agency was also asked to start with two assumptions: that there would be no general war, and that there would be a continuation of the present general trend of policies by both the Eastern Bloc and the Western powers. The final esti-mate addressed these two assumptions with concern: "We believe it essential," it said, "to state at the outset that there is no unequivocal answer to the ques-tion 'is time on our side?' Even assuming a 'continuation of the present trend of policies of both the Bloc and the Western Powers' (itself an assumption of doubtful validity) there are so many accidental or unpredictable factors which will materially affect the world situation."[84] This made any "firm estimate" of what might happen in the next fifteen years difficult. ONE was becoming more skillful and confident when communicating to policymakers what social science could do as well as what it couldn't.

A six-page analysis followed, broken up into four categories of comparison: the probable economic growth of the Soviet Bloc and the West, probable sci-entific capabilities, probable trends in military capabilities, and probable trends in political and social strength and cohesion of the two blocs.

A draft dated a week earlier shows how conclusions could be amended and a more sophisticated understanding of Soviet intentions was being formed. In the draft of June 26 there are only two paragraphs of conclusions.

The language still betrays some of the jingoistic tone of NSC-68:

> We believe that over a period of time the possibility exists of internal decay
> or collapse of the totalitarian bloc, and if the Western Powers maintain their
> strength and unity, and no general war occurs, then time may be on the side
> of the West. However it would be unsafe to assume that a collapse of the

Soviet system will take place in the next fifteen years. Until the process of disintegration sets in, the totalitarian nature of the Soviet system and the Kremlin's pervasive control or influence over its Bloc partners will continue to provide it with many advantages in a power struggle with a looser coalition led by the US. Moreover, trends now seem to be running against the West in the underdeveloped areas. If these trends cannot be arrested, the constant growth of instability and Communist interference in these areas may eventually have serious effects on the economic stability and pro-Western orientation of Western Europe and Japan.[85]

In the final estimate, this paragraph is almost completely rewritten. Gone is the "free world" style of rhetoric of the draft, and instead we see something more like the sober assessment of the political scientist.

While there is no reason at this time to predict the Bloc's decay or collapse, the possibility exists of certain changes adverse to its present strength and stability. Internal rigidity may deprive the USSR of that flexibility and vitality which contribute to a political system's survival and growth. Alternatively, the Kremlin may decide to modify and relax its previous policies, only to find that this relaxation adversely affects continuing Soviet economic growth, Satellite stability, and Sino-Soviet cohesion. It would be unsafe, however, to assume that the problems which are inherent in the Soviet system will of themselves have reached critical positions within the next fifteen years. Unless they do, the totalitarian nature of the Soviet system and the Kremlin's pervasive control of influence over its Bloc partners will continue to provide it with many advantages over the less cohesive coalition led by the US.[86]

In the final version, approved July 3, the draft's two paragraphs are expanded to six.[87] In the early draft, the remaining conclusion was that there were too many accidental and unpredictable factors to say anything conclusive about future trends, and it was impossible to say whether time was on the side of either power. In the final version, ONE believed that the economic and technological gap between the Soviet Bloc and the United States would decrease, with the United States still maintaining sizable superiority. In this respect, time was on the side of Moscow. If, however, the United States and the West decided to pursue this, then in the next fifteen years' time the West's military capabilities, both with conventional rearmament and the tactical use of unconventional weapons, would continue to increase. Time in this case was on the side of the West. The final version retained the earlier point that there were trends within the West that might undermine stability and cohesion, and that time was possibly running against the West when it came to the pro-Western orientation of Western Europe and Japan. In the final version of the concluding paragraph, the estimate retained the caveat that it was difficult to project "with fair confidence" the relative power positions of the Soviet Bloc and the West, but with the addition of the rewritten paragraph above, the tone of the caveat is much less vacillating.

The differences between the two texts may demonstrate the value of having the BNE as overseer. By this time Kent was chairing the board, with Langer having moved on. Interestingly, Kent says that when drafting the early NIEs, his analysts would invariably include a conclusion, but this was changed so often by the BNE that his staff eventually abandoned the practice.[88]

As a forward-looking estimate of the relative power positions of the Eastern and Western blocs in 1968, the conclusions hold up well. By 1968 the Kremlin's pervasive control over its satellites had been recently demonstrated in Prague but also previously with the construction of the Berlin Wall in 1961 and the invasion of Hungary in 1956. Communist growth and instability had spread to Vietnam and Laos, most notably, and the United States had responded by shoring up its influence over Japan, the Southeast Asian states, and Western Europe. The result that a Soviet collapse might be precipitated by internal rigidity or the relaxation of its policies in Eastern Europe, was yet to come.

Determining Intentions

As we have seen, the problem of determining both Soviet intentions and Soviet capabilities was of consuming interest at CIA in the early Cold War, as indeed it was throughout the conflict.

This prompts two questions with respect to the work of the intel intellectuals: First, why were they so quick to avoid using history, culture, and psychology to explain Soviet intentions when the promise of social science had so clearly expounded the use of a synthesized methodology combining these with political, economic, and military explanations? Keren Yarhi-Milo has looked at the NIEs from the period 1977–80, specifically, the time of the Carter administration. She found that the intelligence analysts avoided determining Soviet intentions and instead focused on estimating existing and future military capabilities. At best, the NIEs dedicated only two paragraphs to intentions. "Consistently throughout this period, the single most important indicator that US intelligence used to infer Soviet intentions was the material capabilities of the USSR."[89] Leffler agrees with this, saying power for both the NSC and CIA was defined in physical terms: "According to CIA," he says, "nations could not become powerful if they did not have adequate supplies of mechanical energy (coal, water power or petroleum), raw materials for basic industries, skilled technicians, experienced managers and a sophisticated social structure accustomed to producing surpluses beyond consumption for military purposes."[90] The role of historical or current actions did not play a significant role in their assessments. This is consistent with our findings for the NIEs of the 1950–53 period, although ORE's analysts in the pre-Langer period did make more of possible intentions than its successor did.

This gives us some insight into why Montague says, regarding NIE-25, that he has played down the historical narrative, offering a background "without going back to Ivan the Terrible or Karl Marx."[91] Like Kent's experience with Nitze, learning on the job that policymakers wanted clear assessments of whether the Soviets would act or not, even to the point of assigning percentage values of probability, historians like Montague were discovering that evidence for policymakers meant observable examples of intentions—actual actions— not possible intentions. Writing in 1973, Kent recalled that traditional military intelligence doctrine was that enemy intentions were not the purview of analysts and was strictly the job of the commander to assess. At CIA, however, General Smith was adamant that any national estimate of the Soviet Union "would not be complete unless we had given the reader our best thoughts on how it was likely to use its vast military apparatus."[92] On whether ONE was actually capable of determining intentions, Kent was chary.

Kent remembered three estimates where Soviet intentions had been the focus: NIE-3 "Soviet Capabilities and Intentions" (November 1950); Montague's NIE-25 "Probable Soviet Courses of Action to Mid-1952" (August 1951); and a request for "Likelihood of a Soviet Attack on Japan." Of the first, the fact that "Intentions" was in the title was testament to the forcefulness of General Smith's powers of persuasion. Remembering that NIE-25 had originally been titled "Soviet Intentions with Respect to General War," Kent says that ONE danced around the problem by talking about the courses of action open to the Soviet government, which he said, "on balance was about as far a prudent man would wish to probe into probable intentions."[93]

He is remarkably frank about what to some might be an admission of failure. Of the Japan estimate, he says the smart thing to do (and the course most military analysts would take) would be to list Soviet military "strengths-in-being" in the Far East and then talk about the logistics of getting reinforcements positioned in the West over to join them. While this would in no way answer the original question, it was a safer approach and a "far less heinous offense than getting into the business of Soviet intentions."[94]

Kent recognized that the Soviets themselves would not arrive at their own intentions without first surmising US intentions. In 1950 this was still taboo, with the Army, Navy, and Air Force bridling at the possibility of CIA assessing US military strengths. Kent says that CIA would try to engage the military representatives in conversations—a sort of "what would Stalin do?" approach that they hoped might prompt them to let their guards down. In the end, Langer wrote a memorandum that took the issue head on:

> Many National Intelligence Estimates deal with the probable intentions of the Kremlin. It may be assumed that in deciding upon a course of action, the Kremlin is influenced by its estimate of the US power available to counter that course of action and by its estimate of how US policy makers are likely to use that power. An NIE on the intentions of the Kremlin cannot be written without ONE's having an estimate of the Kremlin's estimate of US capabilities and intentions. To procure such an estimate is the problem.[95]

Langer then stated that he wanted to see an estimate written on a Soviet view of US capabilities for September 1951. He wanted a second assessment written on a Soviet view of US global intentions. For this, Langer suggested an outside team from Yale and perhaps Columbia. The central idea here was around open-source intelligence: Whatever was publicly available to the university would also be available to the Soviets. In the end, the capabilities assignment went to Yale, who put fifteen academics to the task: from history, biology, chemistry, the classics, English, mathematics, and physics. Headed up by William H. Dunham, the multidisciplinary project took just over two months.[96] The result stunned Kent:

> The section devoted to the army, for example, totaling some 120 pages with its appendix, begins with paragraphs on the state of mobilization, the army field forces, continental commands, overseas commands, tactical organization of the regimental combat team (the smallest unit under scrutiny), the division, corps, field army, and army group. The bulk of the material presented is devoted to the order of battle of army units of the zone of the interior, far eastern command, ground forces in Europe, and other overseas commands. In the appendix the structure of divisions and RCT's in combat in Korea is cited down to the level of specialized companies, along with their tables of organization and equipment. The final pages are devoted to the geographical whereabouts of a strange mix of some 251 army units ranging from the First Infantry Division in Darmstadt and the Seventh Infantry Division in Korea to the 8111 AU signal service in Okinawa and the 764 AAA gun battalion in the Canal Zone. For all of them there is an APO number [giving location]. The dozen and a half pages devoted to army weapons hit the high spots of the new automatic small

arms and machine guns, mortars, recoilless rifles, artillery, tanks, liaison aircraft, and helicopters.[97]

The Yale Report provided a similar level of detail for the Navy (80 pages) and Air Force (200 pages). In one section the academics described the Navy's Heavy Attack Wing 1, which Yale said was capable of delivering atomic weapons and which was classified "Secret." The report also assigned 150 pages to discussions on atomic, biological, and chemical warfare capabilities, including a guesstimate on the size of the US nuclear stockpile (around 1,500 of Hiroshima strength) and lists of biological warfare weapons including the places of manufacture and universities studying them.[98]

The estimate had used no more than information that was in the public domain. It unsettled the military services, who hadn't realized how much could be made of material that was declassified and, in most cases, they had publicly released. For Langer, it proved his point: An assessment of US capabilities was possible, and the military thinking they were holding their cards to their chest was ridiculous. "To come back to the origin of the whole project," said Kent, "one would be justified in assuming that the Soviet leaders had very precise notions as to the inventory of US forces in being at the end of 1951 and were in a position to make confident estimates as to the capabilities of those forces in any of several possible war situations."[99]

Kent believed that around 90 percent of the Yale Report was accurate. The exercise reiterated two further things: first, that assembling a team of academics, armed only with library cards and a few weeks of forensic study, could produce incredible results; and, second, as was shown in the terms of reference for NIE-25, that the key to understanding possible courses of action was in reviewing your own probable moves.

However, the project had still only really dealt with capabilities. The bigger job—determining intentions—was still being reckoned with. Kent recalls that, as with many of General Smith's dicta, the military representatives' opposition to writing an estimate as speculative as the "Likelihood of a Soviet Attack on Japan" had melted away, and the report had been no more painful than any other estimate. Yet the theoretical exercise remaining did produce a second report, although the authors of it are not known (presumably, it was not Yale). The "Intentions" survey, produced by a team of Sovietologists, arrived a few weeks later: "It fell a good distance short of our hopes," says Kent, "and we decided to file it without reproducing and circulating it."[100]

Kent concludes the story by saying the intentions problem never really went away. ONE continued with its struggle to divine what the Soviet leaders thought about the world and how they might respond, but the problem was simply one of disagreement among analysts and no longer a fear of crossing into forbidden turf.

Conclusion

As Matthias points out, there is little wrong with the conclusions of earlier estimates like ORE-1 when it came to determining Soviet actions over the short-to-medium term. It was evident that, prior to success with its atom bomb tests in 1949, Moscow would be opportunistic but not take any risks that might lead them into a general war with a more powerful competitor. Once the nuclear threshold had been crossed, however, likely actions were a little more difficult to ascribe. The Pentagon was far more wary than CIA about the Soviets' growing power, but this was a necessary vigilance in a postwar environment where funding was being diverted away from the military sector and the armed forces had organizational concerns about diminishing resources and status. This meant that any suggestion on CIA's part that the Soviets presented less of a threat was a direct threat to the military—and nuances of wording mattered.

While CIA's analysts might have been sensitive to the politics of growing military budgets, this was hardly what they were created to do. Taking a neutral stance on the Soviet threat, however, was not going to work if the methods CIA used to justify their conclusions were not sound. NSC-68 had established a rhetorical norm of using emotive words like "the Free World" and "Soviet world domination," and although this language may have been both acceptable and even encouraged by the containment-minded national security community, it was not the objective language of the social scientist. Similarly, while Kennan had used ideological, historical, and even psychological arguments to put his case for "counterforce" forward, the Long Telegram was not an NIE, coordinating "the best intelligence opinion in the country, based on all available information."[101] The early estimates produced by ORE earned the opprobrium of the other intelligence agencies, and this cannot be put down to interagency rivalry. What we see, rather, is ORE struggling to find a voice of its own and convince the IAC agencies of its skills at estimate writing.

This is also obvious in the inconsistency of the formats of the early estimates. Acknowledging, as Abbot Smith does, that formats need to be flexible to the situation being discussed, ORE's estimates were constantly changing and demonstrated a lack of academic rigor, if not a complete befuddlement about what worked and why. Kent and Langer, who had been alerted to the need for consistency of voice by Schlesinger at OSS, appear to have moved very quickly to standardize the estimate template.

Notions of causality are mostly absent in the pre-1950 estimates. ORE could argue that the Soviet ideology anticipated world domination and might therefore leap into a general war the moment they discerned the balance of power was in their favor. Under Kent and Langer, ONE was much more careful with causal arguments, particularly with linking ideology to future actions. Instead, we find ONE analysts experimenting and refining their techniques in order to get closer to what Talcott Parsons had described as rational actions that conformed to a law of maximizing utility.[102] So, in SE-1's terms of reference you see "preparations" being replaced with "activities" in what seems to be a deliberate attempt to spurn the speculative for the observable. As we see with the terms of reference for major Soviet estimates, ONE analysts were also focused on the interplay of responses between the USSR and the United States. Wars were not simply started by one player but rather a series of actions that were contingent and might rope in many states with competing interests and varying abilities to make trouble.

We also see an attempt to make estimative language more precise after 1950, particularly around words of probability. Here Kent seems to have learned the hard way, through the acerbic demands of people like Nitze. ORE's language had often been vague, even vacillating. ONE was much more careful not to fall into any traps that might be laid by their hypercritical intelligence competitors at State, G-2, A-2, and ONI. This wasn't just self-preservation: the success of a social science approach was predicated on demonstrably more careful arguments.

There is less evidence of the use of hypotheses, at least the way we would expect to see them in a scholarly work. Writing in the late 1970s, Richards J. Heuer Jr. described an initiative pushed by then-DCI William Colby, which saw CIA develop methodology. He put it like this:

> Since theory is the basis for all explanation and prediction, one might argue that the intelligence analyst is just as concerned with theory as the academician, the only difference being the intelligence analyst normally does not make his theories explicit enough to be systematically tested and critiqued by others. This is, of course, true, but it glosses over very real differences in perspective between the researcher searching for patterns and the government analyst focusing on individual events. While these two perspectives seem to be complementary in theory they tend to be contradictory in practice and to require different skills and methods.[103]

Kent would have agreed with this. It would be understandable if ONE's analysts thought that too much intellectual handwringing would frustrate their readers: Garthoff's quote at the beginning of chapter 5 is one of several where

PhD thinking is considered a major turn-off (Arthur Schlesinger makes similar disparaging remarks). Yet there is plenty in the writing of Kent, and in the range of options and scenarios covered in many estimates, to suggest it was an important part of the process.

The reforms to the NIEs undertaken between late 1950 and 1953 therefore seem to be a work in progress. We see some quick moves to standardize the format of the estimates, and then a good deal of work on developing more robust arguments. The conclusions themselves about Soviet intentions and capabilities differ in very minor ways from the pre-1950s estimates, except for Montague's claim that NIE-25 was a decisive estimate that Moscow would not consider a preemptive nuclear attack. Later estimates, like SE-46, show a growing confidence in discussing long-range trends and an increasing sophistication that moves away from the rhetoric of earlier assessments. The decrease in the number of major dissents over this period suggests that intelligence competitors had less justification to criticize and undermine the work of ONE.

We see some excitement initially with the idea that social science methods will make an impressive mark on the NIE. Montague complains in NIE-25 that the military report format is too monocausal—a snapshot rather than a broad picture—and says he will create an entirely new way of looking at intentions. He excitedly hints of a revolution in analysis—"a radical new departure"—but there is little evidence of it. What we are really talking about is an evolution.

Notes

Epigraph: Kent, "Estimates and Influence," 35.

1. See chap. 2, "Phases and Campaigns," in Lee, *The Korean War*.
2. Leffler, *A Preponderance of Power*, 314.
3. Bohlen, *Witness to History, 1929–1969*, 262.
4. Written from the US Embassy in Moscow, the Long Telegram was the origin of Washington's containment policy toward the USSR; the anonymous article in *Foreign Affairs* was a follow-up written by Kennan.
5. Leffler, *A Preponderance of Power*, 108–9.
6. Dulles, Jackson, and Correa, *The Central Intelligence Agency*, 1949.
7. *Cambridge Dictionary*, "authoritative," https://dictionary.cambridge.org/dictionary /english/authoritative.
8. Walton, "Lessons Learned from the CIA's Assessment," 469.
9. If they were reporting on something they were certain about, they would use a different format, like a memorandum or a statement. See Kent, "Estimates and Influence," 35.
10. Kent and Thacher, *Reminiscences of a Varied Life*, 257.
11. Kent and Thacher, 258.
12. National Security Council, National Security Council Intelligence Directive No. 3. See also Kent, "The Law and Custom," 47; and Jackson and Claussen, *Organizational History*, 1:12.

13. Kent, "The Law and Custom," 46.

14. Kent, 48.

15. See *Intelligence Advisory Committee Progress Report*, March 1, 1951, p. 1, CIA-RDP 85S00362R000200140015-8, CIA, CREST Archive.

16. Truman, *Memoirs by Harry S. Truman*, 60.

17. In a memo sent to Dean Acheson, Kent apologized for the classified nature of the topic and jokingly suggested he could at least read it in the privacy of his own sanctuary. See Sherman Kent, "A Crucial Estimate Relived," *Studies in Intelligence* 8, no. 4 (1964): 4. Also published in Steury, *Sherman Kent and the Board of National Estimates*, 173–78.

18. Kent, "A Crucial Estimate Relived," 3.

19. Kent, *Strategic Intelligence for American World Policy*, 155.

20. Kent, "A Crucial Estimate Relived," 3.

21. Kent, 4.

22. William J. Barnds, *Intelligence and Policymaking in an Institutional Context* (1974), CIA-RDP80M01133A000900160045-4, CIA, CREST Archive.

23. *National Intelligence Estimates: An Assessment of the Product and Process*, Intelligence Monograph (1977), 17–18, CIA, CREST Archive.

24. Jackson, *The DCI Miscellaneous Studies*, 2:281.

25. Jackson, 2:268.

26. The full title is *Review of the World Situation as It Relates to the Security of the United States*, CIA Series. Memo re Suspended CIA Series, n.d., CIA-RDP84-00022R00 0200130005-4, CIA, CREST Archive; and List of Staff Intelligence Projects Completed July 1946 to April 1949, April 30, 1949, CIA-RDP67-00059A000300170017-2-2, CIA, CREST Archive. See also To the Recipients of All CIA Weekly Summary and CIA Monthly *Review of the World Situation*, December 1, 1950, CIA-RDP78-0617A002400180001.5, CIA, CREST Archive.

27. Jackson, *The DCI Miscellaneous Studies*, 2:270.

28. Jackson, 2:276.

29. Jackson, 2:302–12.

30. Jackson, 2:295.

31. Jackson, 2:287. See also CIA-0-49 *Review of the World Situation* (Preface to CIA-49 Series) 19 January 1949, CIA-RDP67-00059A000500080014-3, CIA, CREST Archive.

32. Jackson, *The DCI Miscellaneous Studies*, 2:276.

33. Kent, "Estimates and Influence," 35.

34. Kent and Thacher, *Reminiscences of a Varied Life*, 243–45.

35. Kent and Thacher, 250.

36. Kent, "The First Year of the Office of National Estimates," 154.

37. NIE-3 "Soviet Capabilities and Intentions," November 15, 1950, NIE-3-15-NOV-1950, CIA, CREST Archive; and NIE-2/2 "Soviet Participation in the Air Defense of Manchuria," November 27, 1950, DOC_0000269239, CIA, CREST Archive.

38. ORE 46-49 "The Possibility of Direct Soviet Military Action During 1949," May 3, 1949, 263-a1-22-ORE-46-49, CIA, CREST Archive; and ORE 10-48 "Consequences of Certain Courses of Action with Respect to Greece," April 5, 1948, 263-a1-22-ORE-10-48, CIA, CREST Archive.

39. "The Reform of the NIE," the enclosure to Abbot's memo dated 9 March 1970, March 10, 1970, CIA-RDP79R00967A001400010017-8, CIA, CREST Archive.

See also IAC Policy on Approval of Appendices in NIEs, October 1, 1953, CIA-RDP79R00904A000100040025-2, CIA, CREST Archive.

40. Memorandum for the Director of Central Intelligence, September 2, 1952, CIA-RDP79R00971A000100030011-1.pdf, CIA CREST Archive.

41. Kent and Thacher, *Reminiscences of a Varied Life*, 276.

42. War was also discussed in SE-15 "Possible Psychological Reactions to a US Air Offensive Against the USSR"; SE-16 "The Strength and Capabilities of Soviet Bloc Forces to Conduct Military Operations Against NATO"; SE-14 "Soviet Capabilities for a Military Attack on the United States Before July 1952"; NIE-39 "Psychological Impact of a Strategic Air Offensive Against the USSR"; and NIE-40 "Strategic Effects of a Soviet Acquisition of Western Europe and the Near East Before 1953."

43. Additional estimates are NIE-60 "Soviet Programs to Disperse Industry and Stockpile"; NIE-59 "Relative Effects of a Complete Severance of East–West Trade on the Economic Capabilities of the Sino-Soviet Bloc and the West"; and SE-37 "Probable Effects on the Soviet Bloc of Certain Courses of Action Directed at the Internal and External Commerce of Communist China."

44. NIE-3 "Soviet Capabilities and Intentions"; NIE-11 "Soviet Intentions in the Current Situation," December 5, 1950, DOC_0000269236, CIA, CREST Archive; and NIE-15 "Probable Soviet Moves to Exploit the Present Situation," December 11, 1950, DOC_0000269237, CIA, CREST Archive.

45. "NIE-15 Probable Soviet Moves," 1.

46. Ford, *Estimative Intelligence*, 21.

47. Montague, *General Walter Bedell Smith*, 141.

48. "A Study of National Intelligence Estimates on the USSR 1950–1957" (1957), 7–8, CIA-RDP70R00971A000300050001-8, CIA, CREST Archive.

49. Kent, "The Law and Custom," 64.

50. Kent, 65.

51. Montague says that, before Langer's arrival, he had fought to keep the estimates short and bare of any detail, which he felt would sidetrack policymakers from the real gist of the report, the conclusions "without the recitation of the basic data itself or step-by-step exposition of the analytical process." See Montague, *General Walter Bedell Smith*, 141.

52. "Terms of Reference [number crossed out]: The Scope and Nature of Soviet Military Preparations in the Far East," March 17, 1951, CIA-RDP79S01011A00010029-7, CIA, CREST Archive.

53. Memorandum NIE-25 Soviet Intentions with Respect to General War, February 10, 1951, CIA-RDP79R01012A000600020044-4, CIA, CREST Archive.

54. Memorandum NIE-25.

55. Although Willard Matthias claims that he, Ray Cline, and a board member all wrote drafts of NIE-25 TR, and although Matthias also wrote military estimates, Montague is the likely author because he refers to being a coauthor of A-BI 14 "Soviet Intentions and Capabilities 1950–53," which is detailed here. Director's Diary, 1950-09-01, p. 28, CIA, CREST Archive. See also Matthias, *America's Strategic Blunders*, 102–3.

56. NIE-25 "(Draft for Board Consideration) Apologia," April 25, 1951, CIA-RDP79R01012A000600020039-0, CIA, CREST Archive.

57. NIE-25 "Probable Soviet Courses of Action to Mid-1952," August 2, 1951, p. 2, DOC_0000269243, CIA, CREST Archive.

58. NIE-25 "(Draft for Board Consideration) Apologia."

59. "Memorandum NIE-25 Soviet Intentions with Respect to General War."
60. "Terms of Reference for NIEs," March 17, 1967, Abbot Smith, CIA-RDP79R00 967A001100020008-0, CIA, CREST Archive.
61. Intelligence Advisory Committee, Minutes of Meeting, December 7, 1950, CIA-RDP82-00400R000100010011-3, CIA, CREST Archive.
62. Intelligence Advisory Committee, Preliminary Agenda, Thursday January 11, 1951, CIA-RDP85S00362R000200120007-9, CIA, CREST Archive; and NIE-4 "Soviet Courses of Action in Germany," February 1, 1951, DOC_0000269247, CIA, CREST Archive.
63. Intelligence Advisory Committee, Progress Report, January 31, 1951, CIA-RDP-85S00362R000200140006-8, CIA, CREST Archive; NIE-20 "Consequences in Mainland Asia (Thailand, Malaya, Burma) of Communist Control of Indochina," March 20, 1951, DOC_0001166377, CIA, CREST Archive.
64. "Estimates Staff Planning Project No. 13," April 18, 1951, CIA-RDP79R01012A00 1000020049-4, CIA, CREST Archive.
65. NIE-6 "Iran's Position in the East–West Conflict," April 5, 1951, CIA-RDP98-009 79R000100130001-6, CIA, CREST Archive.
66. Dissents number around ten for late 1950 to 1953 and are usually minimal, emphasizing aspects of conclusions rather than rejecting them.
67. NIE-12 "Consequences of the Early Employment of Chinese Nationalist Forces in Korea," December 27, 1950, DOC_0000874161, CIA, CREST Archive.
68. NIE-25 "Probable Soviet Courses of Action to Mid-1952."
69. While noting Matthias's one-sided view that ONE could do little wrong, Robert Jervis notes that "[his] discussion of the pre-Korean War years is particularly interesting, because he can compensate for his lack of first-hand involvement by his knowledge of the changing processes and organizational arrangements, which remain obscure in most histories of the period." Jervis, "Review: America's Strategic Blunders," 638. See also Matthias, *America's Strategic Blunders*, 315. Also cited in Coogan, Review of "America's Strategic Blunders: Intelligence," 275–76.
70. Kent, "The Law and Custom," 96.
71. ORE-91 "Estimate of the Effects of the Soviet Possession of the Atomic Bomb upon the Security of the US," April 6, 1950, 15, 263-a1-22-ORE-91-49, NARA.
72. NIE-11 "Soviet Intentions in the Current Situation," December 5, 1950; and NIE-15 "Probable Soviet Moves to Exploit the Present Situation."
73. "A Study of National Intelligence Estimates on the USSR 1950–1957," p. 11, CIA-RDP70R00971A000300050001-8, CIA, CREST Archive.
74. NIE-64 "(Part I) Soviet Bloc Capabilities, Through Mid-1953," November 12, 1952, 263-a1-29-Box-1-NIE-64-PARTI, CIA, CREST Archive; and NIE-64 "(Part II) Probable Soviet Bloc Courses of Action, Through Mid-1953," December 11, 1952, 263-a1-29-Box-1-NIE-64-PARTII, CIA, CREST Archive.
75. Kent, "The Law and Custom," 74.
76. Activities of the Office of National Estimates, July 9, 1951, p. 4. CIA-RDP84-000 22R000200160046-6, CIA, CREST Archive.
77. NIE-29/1 "Review of the Conclusions of NIE-29 Probability of an Invasion of Yugoslavia in 1951," May 4, 1951, DOC_0000269244, CIA, CREST Archive.
78. Memorandum for the Director of Central Intelligence, Subject: NIE-61: Consequences of Communist Control over South Asia, September 24, 1952, CIA-RDP79S01011A000800010008-3, CIA, CREST Archive; and *Intelligence Advisory*

Committee Progress Report: Projects Completed, March 12, 1952, CIA-RDP85S00-362R000200140021-1, CIA, CREST Archive.

79. Terms of Reference, NIE-61, Consequences of Communist Control of South Asia, March 25, 1952, CIA-RDP79S01011A000800010024-5, CIA, CREST Archive.

80. Memorandum for the Director, September 24, 1952.

81. Memorandum: G - Mr. Mathews, Subject: NIE on India-Pakistan, February 8, 1952, CIA-RDP79S01011A0008000100004-7, CIA, CREST Archive.

82. Koch, *CIA Cold War Records*, 155–62.

83. Memorandum for the Intelligence Advisory Committee, Post-Mortem for 1953 Production, April 30, 1954, CIA-RDP79R00971A000500010011-9, CIA, CREST Archive.

84. Koch, *CIA Cold War Records*, 157.

85. Subject: SE-46 Probable Long Term Development of the Soviet Bloc and Western Power Positions, June 26, 1953, p. 15–16, CIA-RDP79S01011A001000080011-9, CIA, CREST Archive.

86. Koch, *CIA Cold War Records*, 162.

87. Subject: SE-46 Probable Long Term Development.

88. Kent, "The Law and Custom," 73.

89. Yarhi-Milo, *Knowing the Adversary*, 174.

90. Leffler, *A Preponderance of Power*, 12.

91. NIE-25 "(Draft for Board Consideration) Apologia," April 25, 1951.

92. The DCI Miscellaneous Studies MS 10: Military Secrets in An Open Society, by Sherman Kent, April 1973, pp. 1–2. CIA-RDP86M00886R002100140005-2, CIA, CREST Archive.

93. DCI Miscellaneous Studies MS 10.

94. DCI Miscellaneous Studies MS 10.

95. DCI Miscellaneous Studies MS 10.

96. Estimates of Capabilities of the US Combat Forces in-Being, September 1, 1951, CIA-RDP79R00971A000300020002-0, CIA, CREST Archive.

97. DCI Miscellaneous Studies MS 10.

98. Information on the nuclear weapons stockpile was restricted at that time, and neither Kent nor Langer knew whether the Yale physicist's assessment was right. Twenty years later Kent did find out, and the physicist was wrong, but only because he did not consult two other publicly available datasets that could have steered him in the right direction. The DCI Miscellaneous Studies MS 10, 34–37.

99. DCI Miscellaneous Studies MS 10.

100. DCI Miscellaneous Studies MS 10.

101. Kent, "The Law and Custom," 48.

102. Parsons, *The Structure of Social Action*, 36.

103. Heuer, *Quantitative Approaches to Political Intelligence*, 5.

Soviet Economic Capabilities and the Inventory of Ignorance

Rubles, dollars / computers, collars,
Engineers, chemists / male or femist,
Capital and labor / for plough or saber,
Opportunity cost / steel capacity lost;
We'd choose a measure if we knew how!
Burden, burden, who's got the burden now?

In August of 1953, having left CIA as its head of the Office of Research and Reports (ORR) eighteen months earlier, Max Millikan wrote the introduction to his friend Walt Rostow's *The Dynamics of Soviet Society*.[1] Describing the book as one of a series "dedicated to bring to bear the resources of the academic community on problems of action confronting the United States," Millikan believed one of the most important issues was that of Soviet Russia. He wondered aloud what questions the government "operator" who "must plot daily moves in the chess game" against the USSR might ask of the academic. What would the Kremlin do next, why did they take one step or another, what made them tick, and what changes in the Soviet system might bring the Cold War to an end? "We concluded," said Millikan, "that just because the facts on the Soviet Union were hard to come by, the illusory impression had grown that if only you could get some more information the whole exasperating puzzle would somehow be solved."[2]

For Millikan, what was needed was an "interpretive framework" suitable for informing non-academics about the Soviets. "Nobody can devote his life to the study of a society without developing a set of hypotheses as to the prime motivating forces within it," Millikan claimed.[3] Rostow's thesis was that Soviet society was not something static and unchanging but instead was a result of historical evolution. While it had not been Rostow's intention to supply a formula that helped in the daily analysis of what was read in the newspapers, Millikan still felt the thesis needed to be tested against current events, and, "if valid, new developments should be at least partly explainable in terms of those forces."[4] Yet the presentation of one thesis must be measured against others that also sought to explain Soviet behavior. As an economist and international relations scholar, he kept returning to the question: what can we "know" of such a closed and secret society?[5]

Millikan's role at CIA between January 1951 and March 1952 was to lay the intellectual foundations of a new discipline: civilian peacetime economic intelligence analysis. Noel Firth and James Noren, who have written one of the most in-depth studies on CIA and Soviet defense spending, believe that CIA's delivery of economic analysis from 1946 "makes a fascinating case study in organizational behavior and public administration."[6]

There are four critical components to any new organization's success, according to theorists of institutional legitimacy.[7] CIA would need a strategy to prove itself to the executive, Congress, and national security community by developing those components. It would require a product that no competing agency could deliver, intelligence processes that were demonstrably unique, and a workforce that could be recruited and trained as civilian intelligence analysts. So long as these held true, and the national security machine still required the outputs they manufactured, CIA's role as a peacetime strategic intelligence producer would prosper.

This chapter shows how the new assistant director of ORR, Max Millikan, systematically worked through a strategy of a differentiated product, developed new processes and recruited a new workforce of civilian economic intelligence analysts. This shows that Millikan's social science approach to intelligence analysis during his brief stay was a critical part of CIA's reforms. We begin by looking at Millikan's qualifications for the job, then we trace how Millikan determined the research design for the new economic intelligence unit. We investigate how ORR drew on the research of outside academics on assessing the strengths and weaknesses of the Soviet Bloc economies and then how Millikan implemented the strategy: the analytical processes that were created; the people he recruited; the training and institutionalization of knowledge that transformed social science practices into CIA analytical processes. Finally, we explore whether the new product created by ORR was considered valuable by policymakers, and whether the strategy and processes were durable.

Yale and the War Years

Millikan was thirty-seven at the time of his arrival at CIA. He had been born in Chicago on December 12, 1913, to a brilliant father who was a Nobel Laureate in Physics. Rostow says the younger Millikan also began as a physicist before switching to economics. The two friends worked together in the 1930s at a competitor to the *Yale Literary Magazine* called *Harkness Hoot*, and then between 1930 and 1934 penned a column in the *Yale News*, with Millikan taking

FIGURE 7.1. MIT economist Max Millikan in New England, 1967. *Shutterstock/Life Magazine*

the pseudonym "Gog" and Rostow, "Magog."[8] Millikan's economics PhD was earned at Yale in 1941.[9] His thesis was titled "The Framework of the Theory of Producers' Sales Policy with Special Reference to Duopoly."[10] He was an assistant professor at Yale from 1941 to 1942.[11]

At Yale during the mid-1930s, Millikan had been exposed to Richard Bissell, a recent graduate of the London School of Economics who had studied under Friedrich Hayek.[12] Each Thursday night Bissell convened an "informal seminar" where he gave talks that Rostow described as "a formative part of my education during my sophomore year and beyond."[13] The regulars were Millikan, Lyman Spitzer (then editor of *Yale News* and later a designer of the Hubble telescope), lawyer William Hull, and Walt Rostow—who was some years the junior of the other members. Bissell claims that these lectures converted Millikan from physics to economics. Millikan later helped Bissell teach macroeconomics at Yale.[14]

When the United States became involved in the war after 1941, Millikan signed up first for the Office of Price Administration, then at the War Shipping Administration (WSA) with Bissell.[15] Bissell describes the work of the WSA, and particularly the Requirements Division, for which he worked, as being to forecast how much cargo needed to be shipped and the number of ships needed to move it. Bissell found the calculations to achieve this were logical but cumbersome, meaning they took too long to be useful.[16] As shipping became crucial to the war effort, the WSA gained more power and was vocal during 1942 as to the limitations of the merchant fleet to deliver.[17] Bissell himself developed sophisticated forecasting skills, each month updating a three-month projection of shipping capabilities, claiming a 5 percent margin of error on his estimates.[18] For Millikan, his time at WSA would have shown him the political power that good economics could provide the public official.

Millikan's first job in intelligence proper was in the State Department immediately after the war.[19] His title was chief economist, research for Europe.[20] A year later (1947) he moved to become the assistant secretary for the President's Committee for Foreign Aid.[21] He was a consultant on the (Marshall Plan's) Economic Cooperation Administration from 1948 to 1950, and a consultant to Gordon Gray, executive office to the president in 1950.[22] In 1949 he was promoted to associate professor of economics at MIT.[23]

The Intel Intellectual and Economic Intelligence

As a direct outcome of the Korean War, President Harry Truman wanted economic forecasting from the CIA. The decision was made to make ORR focus on Soviet Bloc capabilities and intentions.[24] In January of 1951, at the suggestion of Sherman Kent, CIA director Gen. Walter Bedell Smith brought in Millikan.[25]

Millikan had already put a lot of thought into the relevance of social science to national security policymakers, and he practiced what he preached by strictly following a social science methodology in founding the economic intelligence unit. He treated Truman's directive as a research question: defining the problem, addressing methodology, and creating a research program that would identify the gaps in Soviet economic knowledge.

The directive from the president's National Security Resources Board to determine the scope of a foreign economic intelligence committee was outlined in a memo to the National Security Council (NSC) on February 2, 1950. It tasked the NSC and CIA to conduct a study determining the requirements for economic intelligence, including those government agencies already supporting economic intelligence efforts, and determining a means for improving the process. Particular emphasis was placed on how foreign economic intelligence supported mobilization planning. Such information would be useful for peacetime stockpiling; wartime procurement and planning; wartime trade agreements; assessing foreign labor; export and import controls; and economic assistance to allies and accurately determining the capabilities and vulnerabilities of allies, neutrals, and adversaries. This would help in the formulation of policies and programs relating to national security.[26] The request for CIA to prepare a study was forwarded from the NSC a month later. Directive NSC 282 added nothing that hadn't already been requested by the president's National Security Resources Board. It was very similar to the National Security Act in that it was a brief that was very light on thinking on the policymakers' part. Like the 1947 act, the directive wanted central coordination of intelligence, despite the interagency rivalry that had frustrated cooperation in the past. And like the act, there was a sense of urgency that placed a high degree of expectation on CIA. But little else. It was up to the Agency to determine how the new economic intelligence project would work and—as much as possible—to claim itself as the authority on how it should be pursued.[27]

The guidelines provided by the Dulles Report of 1948–49 were that ORR had originally been specified as a more generalist service to its counterpart at CIA, the Office of National Estimates (ONE). It would be a research unit that included scientific, economic, and geographical intelligence and would house the library and indexing system, among other functions.[28] This still held, with ORR responsible for big encyclopedic compendia like the National Intelligence Survey. But within ORR there would be a specialist economic intelligence function, one with its own mission to look at Soviet Bloc intentions and capabilities but one that still fed much of its research into ONE reports like the national intelligence estimates.[29]

The study took just over a year to complete. In its report back to the NSC in April 1951, CIA responded with a clear plan for ORR's organization. By this time Millikan had already been with CIA for three months, and he seized on the opportunity to take a lead.[30] The report noted that twenty-two branches of government currently collected economic intelligence but that this information was skewed toward the needs of each department. What analytical work that was done was ad hoc and not executed by analysts who understood the national security dimension and its requirements. Despite the flow of information coming in, CIA clearly saw there were significant limitations. There was a need to give attention to "major gaps and weaknesses in data, the means for filling these gaps, and the allocation of resources for filling gaps."[31] This is what came to be known as Millikan's "inventory of ignorance."

CIA's report recommended centralizing information as well as a collaborative supervising committee, not unlike the job the IAC (Intelligence Advisory Committee) did for ONE. This would include representatives from the Army, Navy, Air Force, Joint Chiefs of Staff, State, and CIA, with the ability to co-opt others as needed. The new Economic Intelligence Committee (EIC) would have the assistant director of ORR (Millikan, at the time) as secretary. It would have the role of reviewing and monitoring what knowledge they had, looking for gaps, and commissioning new collection through IAC and the NSC. It is evident that, in setting up the EIC, CIA was working to address some of the issues it had struggled with between 1947 and 1950: regarding accessing information from the other intelligence agencies, initiating the collection of new data when required, and flagging priorities to be enforced by the NSC. The committee would "define and arrange" what was needed. A key phrase—that the committee should "make such special reviews of economic intelligence processing procedures as may appear useful"—implies that Millikan wanted to have a strong grip on both the collection and tradecraft practices of analysis.[32]

"The gravest threat to the security of the United States and the free world in the foreseeable future," the report read, "stems from the hostile designs and formidable power of the USSR, and the nature of the Soviet system."[33] This meant the priority of any foreign economic intelligence unit was the conflict between the Soviet and non-Soviet worlds, and its mission would be to produce intelligence "relating to the capabilities, the intentions and the probable courses of action" of the Soviet Union and its satellites (including China), US allies in Europe and Asia, and all those who could swing one way or the other.[34]

The work of the early economic Sovietologists, says David Engerman, attempted to achieve two different policy goals: to turn third-world leaders away from the Soviet economic model and to determine the enemy's economic and military capabilities.[35] The nub of the problem for Millikan was how to assess the Soviet economy and military purchasing power when data was almost impossible to come by. "In general our present knowledge of particular industries and segments of the Soviet economy, while weak, is better than our knowledge of the aggregate resources and capabilities of the economies as a whole, either of the USSR proper or of the whole Soviet bloc," the report confided.[36] It then detailed four priorities:

1. to analyze the economic capabilities of the Soviets and their allies to engage in military action, or employ cold war against the US and its allies or neutrals[37]
2. an analysis of the economic vulnerability of the Soviet Union to economic warfare, psychological warfare, military attack including strategic bombing[38]
3. an analysis of economic indications of probable Soviet and satellite courses of military, and political action and analysis of all indications of probable economic action
4. economic analysis relating to the principal European and Asiatic allies of the United States[39]

The last two entries were perhaps the most contentious. Any analysis of military intentions firmly placed CIA's inquiries inside the territory of military intelligence, a boundary the Agency had previously been forbidden to cross. CIA would determine whether there were any economic indications of the

Soviets' intention to military action, whether resources were being channeled into war, and even what kind of air target systems the Soviets were likely to adopt in Europe. This domain was still fiercely guarded by the Pentagon. And while information on the economies of US allies was for the most part easier to collect, CIA was placing a high priority on whether its allies had the ability to withstand military attack, sabotage, and economic warfare. This concern for the vulnerabilities of allies may have come from Millikan's earlier experience working for the Economic Cooperation Administration. In a letter to Millikan dated three months earlier, Richard Tyner of the Economic Cooperation Administration (the agency in charge of the Marshall Plan) suggested it was not a Soviet invasion of Europe that the United States need be worried about, it was "fifth column" movements within it.[40]

The intended effect of the report to the NSC must have been to demonstrate that, even if the policymakers didn't know what the program of a foreign economic intelligence unit would be, CIA certainly did. This was evident in the report's preempting the EIC by recommending five estimates that needed to be tackled immediately. First, CIA wanted to concentrate on the economic capabilities of allies to engage in hot and cold wars. How useful would allies be in the fight against the Communist powers? This estimate would include a comprehensive review of the strategic importance of Europe and the Middle East for the United States in waging war. Second, CIA wanted to know the capabilities of allies to maintain and grow their economies. This would include Britain, France, and Germany's ability to rearm, to grow capital and profitability while doing so, and to supply essential resources like copper, iron, coal, lead, and manganese. Third, CIA wanted to understand the consequences of cutting all trade with the Soviets and the importance of economic assistance to Italy, Turkey, Greece, and (most likely) postwar Korea. A fourth urgent estimate was a study of the effects of economic and psychological warfare as well as military attack on allies, including their ability to withstand strategic bombing and the effects of sabotage on strategic raw material production. CIA also wanted to conduct studies of probable allied support of US security policies, particularly their support of sanctions against the USSR. Finally, CIA recommended a report into the economic intentions of states not allied to either bloc, like Sweden, Switzerland, Yugoslavia, Iran, or India, who "are likely to be the principal battlegrounds of ideological and economic warfare" conducted by both sides.

The report also added a long list of uses for economic intelligence: to support military plans and operations by producing intelligence related to the logistics of a Soviet counter plan; to identify primary targets for a US operation; to provide logistics for joint US and Allied operations; to consider the economic conditions relating to the maintenance of law and order and prevention of disease in areas under Allied control; and to supply economic intelligence for propaganda uses, for use in diplomatic negotiations, in support of covert operations, and for wartime or prewar conditions like preemptive buying, stockpiling, foreign funds control, and joint mobilization.[41]

Millikan was simultaneously laying claim to almost every aspect of cold war planning. It was a bold move that was predicated on social science being able to bring the economic, political, military, and sociological considerations together. It was firmly founded on one very basic assumption: The United States knew too little about the perceived adversary it faced. The organization that could overcome that ignorance would be at the forefront of all national security planning henceforth. The morning after CIA presented, those who had been at the meeting gathered around to discuss the previous day's effort. The feeling was one of surprise: The IAC had raised no objection to their plan to become the main coordinator of Soviet economic intelligence.[42]

Assessing the Strength of the Soviet Economy

The years after World War II saw the Soviet Union concentrating on modernizing its industry at the expense of the average citizen's standard of living. With the Soviet Union demanding reparations from the defeated Germany, German factories were broken down and shipped East to rebuild the metals, fuels, and machinery industries in the Soviet Union. This was the intention of the centralized economy—not so much to determine who got what but where emphasis was to be placed on sectors that would contribute to an industrialized economy with new factories and industries. Success was defined by output— how much was produced as opposed to how much was consumed.[43] Yet growth came at a cost; in order to achieve outputs, the Soviet government needed to put more and more investment into the capital stock. This growth continued up until 1958, when it slowed.[44] The key questions for economists specializing in the Soviet economy centered around (1) the impact that investment in factories and decisions about resource allocation had on the gross national product (GNP) (and whether you could trace the impact individual sectors had on the overall economy); (2) what impact did defense spending have on standards of living for the ordinary Soviet citizen (and whether spending too much in a totalitarian state much might cause domestic instability); and (3) how to measure the GNP of the Soviet Union in a way that was comparable with the Western economies (so it could be communicated in a meaningful way to policymakers making national security decisions).

When it came to assessing the strength of the Soviet economy, Millikan wasn't working in a vacuum. The rise of economic Sovietology had been predominantly in the 1940s and by the end of that decade was centered mainly at the Russian Research Center at Harvard and the Russian Institute at Columbia.[45] The first generation of economic Sovietologists struggled primarily with access to good data. Writing in 1930, Calvin Hoover, who later served in OSS's Research and Analysis division and on CIA's Board of National Estimates, acknowledged that most of his figures came from the Soviet government. "In some cases," he said, "they are subject to discount, on account of the fact that Soviet statisticians are subjected to considerable pressure, and are, therefore, not free to interpret their own data. This pressure is due to a kind of self-deception which renders Party members unwilling to face unpleasant facts."[46]

The discipline grew slowly. In his survey from its early years to its post–Cold War decline, James Millar counted only nine Americans working specifically in Soviet economic studies prior to 1949, of whom two (Abram Bergson, originally at Columbia and later Harvard, and Alexander Gerschenkron at Harvard) trained just over half of the next generation of Soviet economists.[47] The focus of the early years was one of data collection and sorting the good from the bad. This was to be an ongoing problem: Engerman says, "Release of only summary data (often simply one line in the government budget), bizarre and misleading categories for economic statistics, and, of course, outright deception made the task of estimating Soviet defense expenditures and economic capacity two of the major intellectual challenges of Cold-War Sovietology."[48] Engerman says CIA's work had its roots in Bergson's research after the war.[49]

Bergson received his PhD in 1940, a year before Millikan was awarded his. Bergson served in OSS's Research and Analysis, in the Russian Economics section, first under Wassily Leontief and then as the chief.[50] His *Soviet National Income and Product in 1937*, originally published in two parts in 1950, introduced the formula of Adjusted Factor Theory Cost.[51] Here the national income of the Soviets was determined first through prevailing ruble prices and then revalued using Bergson's new method. While he acknowledged the reevaluation was only "a partially satisfactory basis" for assessing the national income, Bergson felt it was getting closer to a "real" appraisal. The "famous Soviet policy of withholding information necessitates frequent resort to estimation and guesswork," he admitted.[52] Bergson's Adjusted Factor Theory Cost method was highly important to CIA's own estimative work.[53]

Leontief is largely remembered for his input–output method.[54] This assumed that the national economy was a system of mutually related industries. The interrelation, claimed Leontief, was manifested in the mostly steady stream of goods and services that linked all the sectors of the economy together. When assessing the growth of an economy, particularly a rapidly industrializing economy like the Soviet Union, an analyst would look at as many as fifty sectors including agriculture, extractive and manufacturing industries, and trade service industries. Trade with foreign countries would also be factored in as well as households and government departments.[55] Leontief's input–output method became another important tool for the CIA economists at ORR.

Bergson and his team had begun their analysis of the Soviet economy by fixing their study from the year 1928, almost ten years after the Bolsheviks attained power and after a tumultuous decade of revolution, war, and famine.[56] During 1921–28 the Soviets relaxed to some degree their ideology and allowed a free market economy known as the New Economic Policy, with the period after 1928 being the first Five-Year Plan. Bergson found that, depending on what years the researcher focused on, there are very different skews. This became one of the key discussion points for all economic Sovietologists for the next fifty years. Gregory argues that the economist's decision whether to employ 1928 or 1950 constant prices makes an appreciable difference to the per annum growth rate, the difference being 11 percent growth for the former and 4.5 percent for the latter. The overriding question is which year pinpoints industrialization as affecting the Soviet economy. The choice of 1928 constant prices assumes preindustrial; the choice of 1950 constant prices, postindustrial.[57]

Similarly, in reviewing Bergson's work in the 1960s, the British economist Phyllis Deane pointed out the difficulty in not only establishing growth rates of the Soviet Union but also comparing them with those of Western Bloc states like the United States. An assumption could be made that all economies industrialized in the same way, but it was not necessarily true that all states concentrated on manufacturing the same products. Deane demonstrated that using two different methodologies the Soviet Union could either be shown to have grown in the years Bergson surveyed (1928–55) or shown to have shrunk. "There seems no reason in principle to prefer one method to the other," Deane argued.[58]

The work, then, of the early economists studying the Soviet Union was concerned with data availability and constructing methodology. The best scholars working on the Soviet economic enigma also had experience working on economic intelligence during the war. So why was Millikan chosen to run ORR over more obvious candidates like Leontief and Bergson? Langer and Kent would have known both at OSS. Both were tied to Harvard, where Langer hailed from, with Bergson having done his PhD there and Leontief teaching there from 1932.[59] (Alexander Gerschenkron, another possible candidate, although he did not serve at OSS, was teaching at Harvard from 1948).[60] Geroid Robinson and Simon Kuznets are two other possibilities.[61] It is interesting that Sherman Kent appears to have made the suggestion regarding hiring Millikan directly to DCI Smith.[62] Kent had recruited Millikan to work at State in 1946, where Millikan ran the European economic desk.

A possible reason is that Millikan was a generalist, where Bergson and Leontief were concerned with the minutiae of Soviet number-crunching. Langer and Kent wanted someone to steer ORR, to set the parameters for its research and not get too immersed in the day-to-day work. Another possibility is that Langer or Kent had not got on with Bergson and Leontief, or that they were considered too senior and expensive.[63] When Millikan was set to leave CIA in early 1952, a director's meeting reviewed possible replacements. Looking at the candidates, General Smith harrumphed: "The Director stated that we could not accept the first individual mentioned and doubted seriously whether we could pay the second individual enough money."[64] Who the two people were is unknown, but it is possible Smith was referring to two of the Harvard professors.

The Inventory of Ignorance

"During the first half of 1951," Millikan wrote very plainly a few years later, "ORR was engaged in taking an inventory of its ignorance concerning the economy of the Soviet Bloc. The main purpose of this inventory was to establish a basis for planning a program of basic research to which ORR should address itself."[65] Millikan resolved to be thorough when determining the role of ORR. What did the customer (the policymakers) want from a foreign economic intelligence unit; what exactly was economic intelligence; where did ORR fit in the overall picture; and, most importantly, how did the peculiar character of the Soviet economy and the information available influence the methods ORR would use?

On the one hand, Millikan admitted there was much they did not know about the communist economies, and a systematic intellectual stocktake of what was on the "shelves" and what was missing was sorely needed. On the other hand, Millikan recognized that other economists had already determined that assessing Soviet strength required different tools from those used to assess the West. Millikan was not a Soviet specialist, but he was an economist, and, in the words of OSS veteran Charles Kindleberger, "any economist who put his mind to something could learn it."[66] Millikan would create Soviet experts.

Like any good social scientist, Millikan began with trying to formulate a precise definition. Economic intelligence was "intelligence relating to the basic productive resources of an area or political unit, the goals and objectives those in control of the resources wish them to serve, and the ways in which, and the effectiveness with which these resources are in fact allocated in the service of these various goals."[67] However, economic intelligence was not just an inventory of knowledge; it was also purposeful. To record all of the adversary's potential labor force, knowing what raw materials were at their disposal and what factories they possessed was not enough. What was required was an understanding of the adversary's goals because only then could the inventory begin to tell a story of the Soviet Union's intentions and true capabilities. Moscow determined which priorities were important and which could be downplayed: this was not the case in the mixed economy of the United States, except in times of war. And while pulling the strings of a centralized economy sounded simple, it was actually a very complicated system. Bottlenecks could easily form that would choke output further down the supply chain. Therefore, any understanding of an adversary's strengths and weaknesses, and any research program that was created to provide it, would require a focus not only on the economic but also the social, military, and political facets of the problem.

Ludwell Lee Montague described the inventory of ignorance as "a systematic inventory of what was reasonably known about the Soviet Bloc economies and what more was needed to be learned in order to complete the picture."[68] The inventory worked on the principle that what was known about Soviet production was imperfect: it listed all of the blanks that needed to be filled in to reach the objective and which would then be improved by "the method of successive approximations," which Montague likens to estimations. It would guide both collection and research.[69] Having established at least a benchmark "approximation," Millikan would refine his estimation from there or, as Montague says, would "work to narrow the difference between the two extremes."[70] This was a "bottom-up" approach. It became one of two methodological approaches CIA employed to understanding Soviet economic capabilities.[71]

The Building-Block Method

Millikan then set ORR two tasks: to survey the economic potential of the Soviet Union and to determine how much it was spending on its military. The first task was not a from-scratch project: the groundwork had already been laid at Columbia, RAND, and Harvard. The second task, to pinpoint how much the Soviets were putting into defense, required new methods of discovery, and it was Millikan's job to create them.[72] Firth and Noren say that, aside from needing to understand the question of Soviet military capabilities, the United States wanted to know whether the Soviet economy could sustain a major military effort. That came down to two very basic questions: the size of the military budget and the burden on the Soviet economy. This led to the question of which methodology would best interrogate the "dense fog of secrecy and unfamiliarity" that exemplified the Soviets' closed, nonmarket economy.[73]

The economic Sovietologists had to assume that the annual accounts that the USSR published were cooked, but with some careful forensics, a real figure could be reached. Each year, among the full accounts of the Soviet state, a single figure was made public for all defense spending, unlike the US budget, which broke it down in over one hundred pages of detail. The view of many economists was that the USSR hid many military costs—like nuclear warheads, security forces, and military research—in the civilian parts of the budget. If one could deduct the true civilian component from these statistics, one would arrive at the hidden military spending. This was called the residual method.[74]

The second, and newer, CIA method did not take the Soviet statistics at face value. Instead, it took a much more laborious approach, which was to cost each item directly, comparing it to US prices for an equivalent item and then pricing it in rubles (for what it cost the Soviets) and US dollars (so that policy-makers could more quickly get an idea of how it compared with US spending). "It begins with the smallest identifiable pieces of military activity," say Firth and Noren, "estimates their costs, and then combines the costs into analytically useful aggregates. It is a straightforward approach: price (p) times quantity (q) equals spending. Then spending for individual items is summed into totals and subtotals." This was the building-block method, which was the "method of choice" for the early CIA economists and a benchmark against which to check more sophisticated models as the Agency's techniques improved. (It is also known as the "direct costing method.") The residual method continued to be used by CIA and was the preferred route for the Department of Defense and university economists.[75]

The benefit of all this hard work was that the total defense expenditure could be arrived at independently of what the Soviets claimed it was. It was also much easier to deconstruct and rebuild datasets to provide information for the different needs of policymaking. Planners looking at the impact of defense structure on Soviet internal politics could ask ORR to extrapolate a snapshot of how much was, for example, being spent on ground forces versus the navy. Military analysts might be more interested in defensive versus offensive capabilities. Millikan's approach allowed the basic information to be reconfigured to provide many insights into the Soviet defense system, which the residual method couldn't deliver.[76]

Millikan also gave an example of his method in the industrial sector. If you wanted to determine Soviet chemical production, you could start with a fact: what is known about US chemical production as a proportion of its total resources, or wartime Nazi Germany's chemical production as a proportion of its total. Both of these figures were readily available to ORR analysts. Then you would consider ways in which USSR chemical production might differ: for instance, it was known that soap was rare in the Soviet Union and that households did not have easy access to DDT spray.[77] By deducting soap and household DDT from production figures (or any other category of chemical production), it was possible to arrive at an educated guess for the total category. Over time, as more was known about chemical use and availability, this technique would improve and become more accurate. The building-block system would expect Soviet "facts" to follow some relationship with US and wartime German "facts."[78] It was, as economist Paul Krugman has said, "small models applied to real problems, blending real-world observation and a little mathematics to cut through to the core of an issue."[79]

Building an "inventory of ignorance" as well as a model for calculating Soviet defense spending was a slow process. Firth and Noren say the early estimates produced by ORR were shy of giving out any precise figures. NIE-3 "Soviet Capabilities and Intentions" (1950) said little more than "the Soviet Union is already largely mobilized for war." NIE-64 "Soviet Bloc Capabilities through Mid-1953" (1952) was a little more confident, estimating that Moscow was spending a fifth of its national product on the military and that by 1952 the USSR would be spending the same amount on defense as it had been in 1944, in the later stages of the war. In NIE-65 "Soviet Bloc Capabilities Through 1957," six months later in June 1953, the estimate changed to say one-sixth of the national budget was going to defense. There were still no real numbers or calculations shown until NIE-11-54 (1954), demonstrating that ORR was very gingerly entering the estimates business.[80] It seems the method took time to establish itself, with the other IAC agencies not understanding how it worked.[81]

A good example of the building-block method being used is in a much later (1959) research aid titled "Military Expenditures in the Soviet Budget: Selected Years 1950–1957."[82] By the time of this report, CIA seemed much more comfortable using the method and explaining their findings. The conclusion is that the figure the Soviets had publicized for defense in 1950 could not have bought the equipment and labor that CIA believed the Soviets had purchased. Between 1951 and 1957 the publicized figures were even murkier: a higher percentage of defense spending comprised allocations that were unspecified. This, on the one hand, confirmed that the figures the Soviets were showing were not helpful in assessing their real budget and were only useful as a benchmark to compare with CIA's independent assessments. But it also, on the other hand, made the figures achieved through the building-block method more difficult to affirm as fact. The best CIA could say was they had a minimum and maximum cost.

CIA economists also worked to determine where individual items were placed within the budget. For example, officers' pensions were an item of defense spending, but nuclear weapons were placed within the national economy budget. The table below shows CIA's assessment from the 1959 report. The figures in column 1 are calculated through the residual method: the Soviets' publicized defense spending minus what CIA could surmise were nondefense (civilian) costs. The figures in column 2 are CIA estimations of additional expenses, like military-oriented research and reservists. Finally, column 3 represents CIA's own calculations using the building-block method. While the years 1950 and 1955 show a shortfall (the Soviets were underestimating their defense costs), the years 1952 and 1957 show CIA's estimates as being in between the Soviet figures.[83]

S-E-C-R-E-T

Table 1

Military Program of the USSR
Selected Years, 1950-57

Billion Current Rubles

Year	(1) Available Budget Funds	(2) Available Nonbudget Funds	(3) Estimate of Military Outlays Based on Pricing Physical Output and Services
1950	98 to 132	5	144
1952	123 to 161	5	153
1955	119 to 156	5	162
1957	110 to 178 a/	5	153

a. Based on plan budget.

FIGURE 7.2. Photograph of the declassified CIA assessment of the Soviet Union's defense budgets from 1950 to 1957. *Military Expenditures in the Soviet Budget: Selected Years 1950–1957, CIA/RR "RA 59-6 April 1959," CIA, CREST Archive*

ORR was also busy with the big-picture research: the Soviet economy itself. Rush Greenslade says Morris Bornstein of Michigan State University compared the USSR and US gross national products during a Senate hearing in 1959, and the methods he used "were identical to those used by intelligence analysts and the data and results were essentially the same."[84] Bornstein had first priced both countries' goods and services in US dollars and then in rubles. There was a wide discrepancy between the two calculations: for 1955, the Soviet economy was 53 percent of the US economy when priced in US dollars, or 27 percent of the size of the United States' when priced in rubles. Then Bornstein calculated again using the geometric mean, which applied the square root of the product of the two. This averaged out the difference to a more comfortable figure: the Soviet economy was 38 percent the size of the American economy. Greenslade says that, while the geometric mean had been widely used until then, this was the first time there had been public disclosure of the dollar-and-ruble comparison.[85]

The Bornstein story shows how important it was to ORR that the work it was doing was academically robust. A CIA working paper distributed in early 1953, "Trends in Economic Policy of USSR Since 1945," shows that ORR followed the research of other economic Sovietologists closely. This document was a summary of the issues facing those working on assessments of the Soviet GDP and defense expenditure. It was followed by a detailed summary of Soviet trade, particularly with non–Eastern Bloc countries. A literature review cited Norman Kaplan, Abram Bergson, Gregory Grossman, Alexander Gerschenkron, and Wassily Leontief. These references sat side by side with the Agency's own work: "The Economy of the Soviet Bloc: Production Trends and 1957 Potential" (CIA-RR-23), where changes in the size and composition of the Soviet workforce were detailed; and "ORR Contribution to NIE-90: Economic Factor [*sic*] Affecting Bloc Capabilities Through Mid-1955" (CIA-RR-1P-333), where ORR discussed "rudimentary" production estimates. Kaplan's RAND article, "Capital Investments in the Soviet Union 1924–1951" (RM-735), was considered a good source on Soviet investment. Some of the problems addressed were how to select variables that independently showed percentage increases in the Soviet GDP, how to determine Soviet national income (Bergson and Grossman were considered the best sources, with Gerschenkron and Leontief's views considered of interest), and a more precise definition of "economic war potential," which was promised in a forthcoming paper, Munitions Producing Capabilities of the USSR (ORR Research Project 13.2).[86]

The processes involved, as the concepts of an inventory of ignorance and building-block method implied, were painstaking in the extreme, particularly without access to computers. This had an enormous impact on staff resources at ORR. Firth and Noren claim the use of the building-block calculations put an "astronomical" strain on ORR's human resources.[87] A (university-based) economist, Donald Green, has talked about the hard slog of pre-computer calculations: "I estimated production functions when I was younger," he told a 1984 conference, "and I never want to endure such pain again."[88]

In the first year, July 1951 to July 1952, EIC/ORR provided analysis for three ONE-created national intelligence estimates, including NIE-33 "Soviet Control of the European Satellites and Their Economic and Military Contributions to Soviet Power Through Mid-1953" and SE-16 "The Strength and Capabilities of Soviet Bloc Forces to Conduct Military Operations Against NATO."[89]

For the period July 1952–July 1953, EIC/ORR produced nine major studies on matters directed to them by the NSC, IAC, or ONE, each one coordinated with other members of the intelligence community.[90] It produced five other studies at the request of other member agencies and another four to fill gaps (in the "inventory of ignorance") deemed necessary by the EIC. In addition, EIC/ORR wrote survey reports on concerns within the community itself, such as whether there were enough economists engaged on Communist China, and three reviews on the quality of economic intelligence available from all sources for the US government on the Soviet Bloc. Another six survey reports were written on what EIC considered priority research and concerns over the collection of economic intelligence. This included a further series of (three or more; much of this is redacted) reports for the IAC that dealt with economic intelligence collection, some which advised the State Department on what was needed from foreign posts.[91] Millikan's claim about an inventory of ignorance was not overstated.[92]

The Recruitment and Training of Economic Intelligence Analysts

Millikan intended to stay at CIA for one year, so he lodged with Bissell rather than find a permanent home, and he worked long hours. He did the rounds of ORR during the day and paperwork at night.[93] His arrival had immediately lifted morale at ORR, which had had no assistant director for three months.[94] Montague says Millikan "gave the leftover personnel at ORR a sense of commitment to a well-defined and important mission pursuant to a well-conceived plan and under an able and forceful but considerate leader."[95] It took Millikan just a year to get ORR up to a standard he was satisfied with.[96]

The new EIC and its staff at ORR originally determined that it needed fourteen subcommittees or working groups, each composed of the "outstanding Government specialists in each of the major foreign economic fields."[97] Millikan had rationalized these into five divisions: Analysis (contributing to ONE's national intelligence estimates), Budget and Plans (Soviet national accounts and five-year plans), Capabilities (probably industrial and military capacity), Economic Defense (trade, sanctions and withstanding economic warfare), and Surveys (responsible for the national intelligence surveys). There were also two library services: Geographic Research (maps) and Economic Accounts (indexing of basic economic intelligence). Finally, there was a department that managed workflow, Requirements and Control.[98]

The office in 1950 employed 150 analysts.[99] By July of 1952, it employed 856 people (including administrative staff). For basic and industrial research, Millikan had asked for 1,222 staff but thought 2,000–3,000 more likely would be needed to keep up with the demand.[100] ORR's early key staff included Warren Nutter, Douglas Diamond Jr., and Rush Greenslade.[101] They are examples of the quality of economic expertise CIA managed to attract in the reform years of 1950–53.

Warren Nutter completed his PhD at Chicago in 1949 and was hired by Yale in 1950. He was an assistant professor there when hired by CIA in mid-1951. Nutter was quickly promoted from special assistant to Millikan to acting chief of the Economic Capabilities division at ORR. He was involved in a working paper on the Soviets' ability to wage a general war, titled "Project 11-051," and contributed to NIE-59 "Relative Strategic Importance of the East/West Trade to the Soviet Orbit and to the Rest of the World" and NIE-65 "Soviet Bloc Capabilities Through 1957."[102] Nutter appears to have been instrumental in applying Leontief's input–output method to ORR's early calculations. By April 1952 he had moved from Economic Capabilities to the EIC's Economic Analysis Subcommittee, which he chaired. This put him right at the center of the theory program: Analysis was using "fairly advanced analytical tools and techniques of economic theory, including input-output analysis, national income accounting, the construction of index numbers, price and cost theory, and the like."[103] While Nutter's stay at ORR was brief, he appears to have made a major impact on its working processes. He was later cited as being one of the first economists to challenge the idea that the Soviet economy was a powerhouse.[104]

Douglas Diamond Jr. joined in 1949, starting as an agricultural analyst and eventually working his way up to deputy director of the office of Soviet Analysis, retiring in 1988. Diamond had bachelor's and master's degrees in agricultural economics from the University of Maryland and had served in the Navy during World War II. He is credited with being one of the first to note the 1980s energy crisis, which is now seen as one of the catalysts of Soviet decline.[105] As an example of the unusual research ORR undertook, in March 1952 Diamond traveled with an associate on a train to Charlottesville "for the purpose of determining the types of transportation intelligence which can be obtained and recorded on a rail trip."[106]

Rush Greenslade joined CIA in 1951 and from 1953 was supervisor of economic research into the Soviet Union and Eastern Europe. Born in Tulsa, Oklahoma, he gained his BA at Princeton and his PhD at the University of Chicago (1953). He served in the Army Air Corps during the war and earned a Silver Star for his service in the Pacific.[107] Greenslade married another economist, Gertrude Schroeder, who joined CIA in 1954 and stayed until 1967.[108] They are considered the mainstay of CIA's Soviet economic studies during that period. Greenslade was a key player in the creation of an analytical framework at ORR. His contributions during the 1950s included an index of Soviet industrial production and estimates of its GNP. During the 1970s he responded to criticisms of CIA's assessments of the Soviet economy by converting the GNP to 1970s prices and reworking its analytical processes. Greenslade retired from CIA in 1973 and continued to consult for the Agency until his death five years later.[109]

In a February 1951 meeting of the IAC discussing a national intelligence survey, Millikan suggested that a program be initiated to alleviate the shortage of qualified personnel. He felt that intelligence demands tended to create competition over who got the best people, and the national intelligence surveys program ought to be given priority over other concerns.[110] Also in February, Millikan told a director's meeting that he would engage with the director of training, Colonel Baird, to address the personnel problem, and he would talk with the academic community to see whether parts of the national intelligence surveys could be farmed out to universities.[111] He became even more concerned as the Korean War began calling up the young men he needed for ORR. CIA's policy was to release staff members to the military only when a replacement could be found. At a director's meeting on March 26, 1951, Millikan argued this would cripple his new office, which required students who were both trained economists and Russian speakers. Of the fifty to one hundred qualified graduates the colleges produced each year, the Agency would need at least half.[112]

ORR also developed specialist skills within the department. For instance, in November 1951 a team of aeronautical consultants met with CIA for a four-day conference on better ways to evaluate the economic input capabilities and vulnerabilities of Soviet air power. This thirty-two-person panel included aircraft industry experts and representatives of the air research and development sector, the US air power program, the US Weapons Systems Evaluation Group, the US Air Force, the Office of Naval Intelligence, and CIA Air Intelligence.[113]

An example of the porousness of talent between ORR and the universities is a letter dated June 20, 1951, where CIA legal counsel Lawrence Houston wrote to Duke University that he regretted that a staff member must return to the university but had been told Langer and Millikan want to retain his services at a fee of $1,200 per month. The request is for "advice on problems involving the Agency which come within your sphere of special knowledge, presentation of reports and estimates for critical appraisal by you, possible requests for special reports on economic problems and for assistance in planning in the economic intelligence field."[114]

The cross-fertilization worked both ways. In a letter to Millikan in January 1952, Abram Bergson, then at Columbia, invited him as a panelist to discuss Norman Kaplan's paper, "Capital Formation and Allocation as a Conditioning Factor." "It has occurred to me," wrote Bergson somewhat coyly, "that this topic might be one of the more appealing from your standpoint."[115]

CIA's outreach to the universities and think tanks continued. A 1960 list featured 180 academics destined as recipients for projects of ORR unclassified studies. The names included Abram Bergson, Alexander Gerschenkron, Richard Moorstein, Abraham Becker, Jerzy Karcz, John Hardt, Joe Berliner, Donald Hodgman, Frank Holzman, and Holland Hunter as well as Max Millikan, Warren Nutter, and Walt Rostow.[116] It also included Thomas Schelling, Klaus Knorr, and Kenneth Arrow. While the role of academics within CIA morphed into permanent civilian intelligence analysts, the idea of the intel intellectual consulting to CIA continues to the present day.[117]

How ORR's Efforts Were Received

Perhaps the best evidence of success for any organization is the promise of more work. It seems the building-block method was well received by Sherman Kent and Robert Komer at ONE. They recognized its value and that the model needed time to work well. They were prepared to invest in the success of the method and employ the extra staff that were needed.[118] In June 1953 ORR was authorized to set up a five-person Military Economics branch to focus entirely on the estimation of the Soviet military budget.[119]

In early December 1951 the possibility of ORR reports being disseminated to the Office of International Trade, a part of the Department of Commerce, was discussed at CIA. This is perhaps an early indication that ORR was beginning to be considered of more widespread value in government circles. At that time the Office of International Trade was receiving raw intelligence support but no finished product. As the Department of Commerce was not part of the IAC, CIA was not bound to share any product with it but decided to supply appropriate information in the future, once clearance was given.[120]

ORR's work was also recognized by the National Security Council. Late in 1954 CIA was formally given the role of "production of all economic intelligence on the Soviet Bloc."[121] While the wider job of military economic intelligence for the rest of the world became the Department of Defense's responsibility, which was consistent with the earlier view that this was military intelligence, CIA continued to work on questions concerning the Soviet Union's economy. This remit was broadened to include all of the Sino-Soviet bloc in 1958.[122]

Conclusion

In a letter dated October 29, 1951, Millikan wrote to an associate offering him a possible job. Having been at CIA for eight months, Millikan recommended it as having "a good deal smaller frustration than is common with Government agencies." He had been reluctant initially to take on the role of putting together an organization to do economic research but had been persuaded to leave MIT "on the ground [*sic*] that there was a particularly urgent job to be done in this Agency on which we might depend in some measure on our success in the international conflict in which we are now engaged."[123] On November 26, 1951, Millikan wrote (to presumably the same associate) saying the organization of the office had been rearranged, and there was no further need for his talents.[124] This is indicative of the rather furious speed at which Millikan had worked to recruit top people, build up the capacity of ORR, and impose robust intellectual processes on the Agency's economic analysis. Millikan himself seemed pleased with the turnaround at ORR. "The agency's economic analysis contributed to a better understanding of the threat posed by the Soviets in both economic and military spheres," he believed, "and restrained a general tendency to exaggerate that threat."[125]

The exaggeration to which Millikan is alluding was primarily the opportunism of the military intelligence agencies, for whom every ruble of growth shown in the Soviet military budget corresponded to a dollar or more to spend on US defense. This was not helped by the enthusiasm many social scientists had for the Soviet system. Economist Holland Hunter claimed—as late as 1955—that the USSR's rapid industrialization was "mysterious in its contours and awesome in its results."[126] Millikan himself was later criticized by former DCI Stansfield Turner for saying that the USSR was an "economic powerhouse."[127] There is evidence of this in some of the early reports, like CIA-RR-23, "The Economy of the Soviet Bloc: Production Trends and 1957 Potential," where ORR concluded that the Soviet GNP had grown by as much as 11 percent between 1948 and 1951 and was poised to grow 35–50 percent between 1951 and 1957 (or 5–7 percent per year at an average annual rate), "nearly double the prewar level."[128] This was published in May 1953, and Millikan is unlikely to have had much of a hand in it. It demonstrates as much the paucity of real economic data available to the West on the Soviet Bloc, and the first tentative steps of the inventory of ignorance, as it does any failings of CIA's calculations.[129]

Millikan can rightly be considered one of the most important intel intellectuals in that he built the economic intelligence function at CIA through an investigation of social science lacunae embodied in his inventory of ignorance. It was not enough to have access to probably the world's best knowledge repository in the United States; he needed to make it better by identifying the gaps and using ignorance as a systematic means to knowing more.

He also worked with tools of analysis, the building blocks he had described in his review of Vilfredo Pareto's *Mind and Theory* in 1936. He dovetailed contemporary economic practices like the input–output method in ways that not only furthered academic understanding of the Soviets' closed society but also grew CIA's intelligence analysis skills.

Millikan's year at CIA was spent imposing intellectual coherence on the measuring of the economy of a closed, authoritarian state. He had a lasting value in converting economists with PhDs into peacetime civilian intelligence analysts and, thus, into a career that gave CIA a reason for existence as an organization. Millikan did this by the selection and promotion of key thinkers like Warren Nutter, Rush Greenslade, and Douglas Diamond Jr. Millikan's outreach to the universities also built a second tier of consultants for CIA that would continue after he left.

Finally, Millikan laid the groundwork for the creation of a distinct methodology—CIA-owned skills and expertise—that had no equivalent in the general US intelligence community. This was the ability to measure with more accuracy the economic strengths and weaknesses of the Soviet Bloc and, from that, US adversaries' capacity to wage war. It was rewarded by making CIA the primary center for Soviet and Chinese economic studies and giving access to—and influence over—military weapons intelligence. In one year, Millikan created processes that could be truly labeled the beginning of a civilian intelligence analysis tradecraft.[130] He also, according to Philip Zelikow, "propelled its ascent to the status of a major source of intelligence analysis to the US government."[131]

He returned to MIT to establish CENIS (the Center for International Studies), a CIA-funded international relations think tank, but continued to consult for the CIA for years to come as one of a group called the Princeton Consultants, headed by William Langer.[132]

Notes

Epigraph: Greenslade, "The Many Burdens of Defense."
1. Rostow, *The Dynamics of Soviet Society*, written in collaboration with Alfred Levin and with the "assistance of others at the Centre for International Studies" at MIT, with an introduction by Max Millikan, director of CIS, dated August 10, 1953.
2. Rostow, ix.
3. Rostow, x.
4. The news that confronted Millikan on the morning of writing the foreword was the Soviet's success in building the hydrogen bomb (August 12, 1953). Rostow, x–xi.
5. Firth and Noren, *Soviet Defense Spending*, 13.
6. Firth and Noren, 10.
7. Zucker, *Institutional Patterns and Organizations*, 14–15.
8. Rostow, *Concept and Controversy*, 15.
9. Montague, *General Walter Bedell Smith*, 151. See also "Max Franklin Millikan: 1913–1969."
10. Max Millikan, "The Framework of the Theory of Producers' Sales Policy with Special Reference to Duopoly," 1941, Max Millikan Personal Papers (hereafter, MMPP), John F. Kennedy Presidential Library & Museum.
11. US Congress, *Third Supplemental Appropriation Bill for 1951*, 228.
12. Bissell was much later one of the CIA planners who lost his job over the botched Bay of Pigs operation. See Bissell, *Reflections of a Cold War Warrior*, 10.
13. Rostow, *Concept and Controversy*, 14.
14. Bissell, *Reflections of a Cold War Warrior*, 10. At one of Bissell's informal seminars, Julian Ripley gave a lecture on the scientific method in the social sciences. Rostow, *Concept and Controversy*, 14.
15. Montague, *General Walter Bedell Smith*, iii.
16. Bissell, *Reflections of a Cold War Warrior*, 29; and Price, "Gregory Bateson and the OSS."
17. Bissell, *Reflections of a Cold War Warrior*, 76.
18. Bissell, 17–18.
19. A 2019 history of OSR says he worked for OSS. This seems like a simplification: the Research and Analysis division of OSS moved to the State Department after the war ended. Millikan worked there from 1946 to 1947 and was recruited by Kent. While William Langer, Sherman Kent, Abram Bergson, and Wassily Leontief all appear on the OSS Personnel Files, Millikan's does not. See Vickers and CIA History Staff, *The History of CIA's Office of Strategic Research, 1967–81* (2019), p. x, CIA, CREST Archive. See also OSS Personnel Files, https://www.yumpu.com

/en/document/view/13698629/oss-personnel-files-from-excel; and Montague, *General Walter Bedell Smith*, 151.

20. MMPP.
21. Montague, *General Walter Bedell Smith*, 151.
22. US Congress, *Third Supplemental Appropriation Bill for 1951*, 228.
23. Montague, *General Walter Bedell Smith*, 151.
24. Montague, 152.
25. Vickers and CIA History Staff, *The History of CIA's Office of Strategic Research*. See also Turner, *Burn Before Reading*, 80.
26. *Report to the National Security Council in Compliance with NSC282*, April 1, 1951, Appendix A: Memorandum for the Executive Secretary, National Security Council, 4, CIA-RDP79-01084A000100070004-7, CIA CREST Archive.
27. *Report to the National Security Council in Compliance with NSC282*, 4.
28. Jackson and Claussen, *Organizational History of the Central Intelligence Agency*, 2:31–32, 86.
29. For more on how ORR research was commissioned and how it worked with ONE and other departments, particularly the working papers produced for the Intelligence Working Group and Economic Defense Advisory Committee, see "Economic Intelligence Initiation and Control Throughout ORR: December 8, 1952," CIA-RDP61-00274A000200100017-7, CIA, CREST Archive.
30. Montague, *General Walter Bedell Smith*, 153.
31. *Report to the National Security Council in Compliance with NSC282*, 5.
32. *Report to the National Security Council in Compliance with NSC282*, 6–8.
33. *Report to the National Security Council in Compliance with NSC282*, 17–18.
34. Underlining in the original. *Report to the National Security Council in Compliance with NSC282*, 17–18.
35. Engerman, "The Price of Success," 252.
36. *Report to the National Security Council in Compliance with NSC282*, 22.
37. This includes materials needed like electronics, precision instruments, tooling, copper, tin, ferro-alloying metals, aviation fuel, and rubber; the economic capabilities to produce certain weapons including atomic weapons and missiles, germ weapons, radar, long-range bombers, tanks, and submarines; the economic effect on the Soviet Union of a prolonged war and acquisition of certain territories in Europe, Middle East, Japan, and Southeast Asia; the effect of Western sanctions on China over the Korean War; and the capability of Soviet satellites intervening in Yugoslavia; and the possibility of the Soviet Bloc waging economic warfare against non-Soviet states.
38. This includes vulnerability to an A-bomb attack; susceptibility to both covert and overt economic warfare; China's weakness to export and shipping controls; how the Soviet Union would cope with the defection of key technical talent; and whether food supplied would withstand biological warfare.
39. *Report to the National Security Council in Compliance with NSC282*, 20–26.
40. Cable from Richard Tyner to Max Millikan, March 17, 1951, CIA-RDP79;040-84A000100070006–5, CIA, CREST Archive.
41. *Report to the National Security Council in Compliance with NSC282*, 20–26.
42. Montague, *General Walter Bedell Smith*, 153.
43. Bergson et al., "Soviet Economic Performance and Reform," 223, 232.

44. Bergson et al., 238.
45. Engerman, "The Price of Success," 224.
46. Hoover, *The Economic Life of Soviet Russia*, vii.
47. Of thirty-nine students, Bergson taught thirteen and Gerschenkron, seven. Millar labels them Generation I of the Soviet economists, including Peter Swanish (PhD Chicago, 1930), Lazar Colin (PhD Michigan, 1931), Arnold Z. Arnold (PhD Columbia, 1937), Abram Bergson (PhD Harvard, 1940), D. Gale Johnson (PhD Iowa State, 1945), Joseph Kershaw (PhD Columbia, 1948), and Chee-Hsein Wu (PhD Harvard, 1948). He also includes the émigrés: Naum Jasny, Wassily Leontief, and Alexander Gerschenkron. See Engerman, "The Price of Success," 234–60. See also Millar, *Rethinking Soviet Economic Studies*, 226.
48. Engerman, Review of *Soviet Defense Spending*.
49. "Abram Bergson spearheaded a remarkable research effort to reconstruct national income accounts since 1928, an approach that became the basis of classified CIA estimates." Engerman, "The Price of Success," 252, 255.
50. Guglielmo, "The Contribution of Economists"; and John Hardt, "Abram Bergson's Legacy."
51. Bergson, "Soviet National Income in 1937, Part 1"; Bergson, "Soviet National Income in 1937, Part 2"; and Bergson, *Soviet National Income in 1937*. See also Gregory, "Economic Growth and Structural Change," 25.
52. Bergson and Heymann, *Soviet National Income and Product*, 5.
53. "Professor A. Bergson had cultivated the special method of estimation of factor productivity and compared this indicator for the USSR with other countries. According his calculations, the level of factor productivity in the USSR in 1960 was 35% in compare with USA. The share of scientific and technological progress in rates of soviet economic growth was less than in capitalist countries and rates of factor productivity growth were also less. All of these Professor A. Bergson connected with totalitarian system, centralized directive planning, with the absence of real innovative motivation in the Soviet economy. This method was used and developed by other sovietologists and CIA." Kudrov, *American Sovietology and the Soviet Economy*.
54. See, for example, Leontief and Harvard Economic Research Project, *Studies in the Structure of the American Economy*, 8–11; and Bergson, "Wassily Leontief," 466.
55. Leontief et al., 8.
56. Gregory, "Economic Growth and Structural Change," 26.
57. Gregory, 41.
58. "All we can say," says Deane, "is that the capacity of the Russian economy to produce the 1937 product-mix was growing less rapidly in the 1950s than it had done between 1928 and 1937; but that its capacity to produce the changing product-mix of the 1950s, evaluated at 1937 or 1950 constant prices was apparently improving more rapidly at the later date." Deane, "Measuring Soviet Economic Growth."
59. Bergson, "Wassily Leontief," 466.
60. My thanks to David Engerman, who pointed me to Marcel van der Linden's article in *Critique*, 2012: "Gerschenkron's Secret: A Research Note," which suggests the economist's political leanings in pre-war Vienna may have disqualified him in General Smith's eyes (if he knew of it). For a biographical note, see "Gerschenkron, Economist and Scholar, Dies at 74," *Harvard Crimson*, October 31, 1978, https://

www.thecrimson.com/article/1978/10/31/gerschenkron-economist-and-scholar
-dies-at/.

61. Robinson, according to Engerman, was a perfectionist and poor manager. He headed up the USSR Economics Division at Research and Analysis, OSS. His overbearing style caused many economists to quit, including the future Nobel Prize–winning (1971) Simon Kuznets, who became a major figure in assessing the United States' own economic capability to prosecute World War II. See Engerman, *Know Your Enemy*, 98–99.

62. Montague, *General Walter Bedell Smith*, 151.

63. A more sinister explanation, which might be chronologically wrong, is that Leontief says he was "accused" by FBI and CIA in 1956 (or as late as 1959, he couldn't remember) of pro-Communist sympathies. He says he spent two years fighting the accusation, which was a misunderstanding. See Dietzenbacher and Lahr, *Wassily Leontief and Input-Output Economics*, 144–45.

64. Director's Meeting, Tuesday, January 29, 1952, CIA-RDP80B01676R00120003-0019-8, CIA, CREST Archive.

65. "The Nature and Methods of Economic Intelligence, by Max F. Millikan," *Studies in Intelligence* 1 (1956), CIA, CREST Archive.

66. Richard D. McKinzie, Oral History Interview with Charles P. Kindleberger (1973), Harry S. Truman Library and Museum, https://www.trumanlibrary.gov/library /oral-histories/kindbrgr.

67. "The Nature and Methods of Economic Intelligence."

68. Montague, *General Walter Bedell Smith*, 152.

69. Montague, 13.

70. Montague, 152.

71. Firth and Noren, *Soviet Defense Spending*, 13.

72. [Redacted], "Analyzing Soviet Defense Program, 1951–1990."

73. Firth and Noren, *Soviet Defense Spending*, 6.

74. Firth and Noren, 10–13.

75. Firth and Noren, 10–13; quote at 12.

76. Firth and Noren, 10–13.

77. Presumably as a pesticide. DDT was banned in the United States from 1972. See US Environmental Protection Agency, "DDT: A Brief History and Status," last updated March 12, 2024, https://www.epa.gov/ingredients-used-pesticide -products/ddt-brief-history-and-status.

78. "The Nature and Methods of Economic Intelligence."

79. Krugman is referring to the MIT economics "house style," cited in an article about Paul Rosenstein-Rodan and his work with Max Millikan at CENIS, MIT. See Alacevich, *Paul Rosenstein-Rodan*.

80. Firth and Noren, *Soviet Defense Spending*, 29–30.

81. In the second annual EIC report, the chairman complains that some projects were unnecessarily long and drawn out. He claims, "It appears that efforts to use the 'input-output' technique were premature in terms of inter-agency capabilities." *Second Annual Progress Report of the Economic Intelligence Committee*, August 17, 1953, CIA-RDP82-00400R000200040002-9, CIA, CREST Archive.

82. "Military Expenditures in the Soviet Budget: Selected Years 1950–1957," CIA/RR RA 59-6 April 1959, CIA-RDP79S01046A000600150001-9, CIA, CREST Archive.

83. "Military Expenditures in the Soviet Budget."

84. Greenslade, "Rubles vs. Dollars." See also Becker, *CIA Estimates of Soviet Military Expenditure.*

85. The argument persisted up until the 1990s as to why CIA had chosen the year 1955. See Becker, *CIA Estimates of Soviet Military Expenditure,* 1980; and Greenslade, "Rubles vs. Dollars."

86. "Trends in Economic Policy of USSR Since 1945," CIA/RR IP-342 (WP) (ORR Project 0.12.), February 24, 1953, Office of Research and Reports, CIA-RDP79-T01049A000800140001-7, CIA, CREST Archive.

87. Firth and Noren, *Soviet Defense Spending,* 29–30.

88. Green developed a later method of calculating the Soviet economy—the Wharton SOVMOD model. See Hildebrandt, *Rand Conference on Models,* 31.

89. The basic intelligence (not economic) department also worked on a high-priority national intelligence survey NIS-27 "Turkey," as well as NIS-29 "China" and NIS-27 "USSR." An example of a report produced by the technical side of ORR was FIR-1 "Geodetic Gravimetry in the USSR." ORR Diary, March 13, 1952, CIA-RDP67-00059A000400290076-3, CIA, CREST Archive; *First Annual Progress Report of the Economic Intelligence Committee* (July 1951–July 1952), August 6, 1952, CIA, CREST Archive; Memorandum for General Counsel, Notes on Briefing, February 13, 1952, CIA-RDP61-00274A000200100034-8, CIA, CREST Archive; and List of all EIC Studies Completed or in Progress, July 1951–June 1953, January 1, 1953, CIA-RDP61S00750A00070052-9, CIA, CREST Archive.

90. *Second Annual Progress Report of the Economic Intelligence Committee,* August 17, 1953, CIA, CREST Archive.

91. List of all EIC Studies Completed or in Progress.

92. For a more detailed survey of the processes involved in assessing Soviet economic capabilities, see Procedure for D/S Analysts in Preparing Service Output and Input Estimates for NIE-65 (1952), CIA-RDP79-01157A000200100018.6, CIA, CREST Archive.

93. Montague, *General Walter Bedell Smith,* 151.

94. Jackson had called Babbitt back to Washington after he spoke to J. J. Wadsworth, so he may have been on vacation or garden leave. "DCI Lt. Gen. Walter Bedell Smith, October 7, 1950, to March 31, 1951," 1950-10-07 (1950), pp. 154, 157, CIA, CREST Archive.

95. "DCI Lt. Gen. Walter Bedell Smith," 151.

96. "DCI Lt. Gen. Walter Bedell Smith," 152.

97. *First Annual Progress Report of the Economic Intelligence Committee.*

98. This appears to be the correct breakdown of the divisions. Montague says there were five divisions under Millikan and does not say that Amory (Millikan's replacement) changed that number. Amory did make it three divisional chiefs. See Montague, *General Walter Bedell Smith,* 154–55; Office of Research and Reports, Monthly Reports, December 1952, CIA-RDP75-00662R000300100001-0, CIA, CREST Archive; and Geographic Division, O/RR, Current Status and Plans, January 15, 1951, CIA-RDP63-00314R000100350014-0, CIA, CREST Archive.

99. Vickers and CIA History Staff, *History of CIA's Office of Strategic Research,* xi.

100. Memorandum for General Counsel.

101. Another well-known economist who was briefly at CIA, Stanley Harold Cohn, earned his MA (1948) and PhD (1952) at Chicago. He was at CIA until 1951.

"Obituary: Stanley Harold Cohn, '47," *Reed Magazine*, August 2005, https://www
.reed.edu/reed-magazine/in-memoriam/obituaries/august2005/stanley-harold
-cohn-1947.html.

102. Kuehn, *Before NBER*. See also Nominations to the EIC Working Group on the JIG
Capabilities Project, November 26, 1951, CIA-RDP92B01090R000200120027-7,
CIA, CREST Archive; and Director's Log. 8.30 a.m. December 26–8.30 a.m.
December 27 (1951), 1951-09-01, CIA, CREST Archive.

103. Kuehn, *Before NBER*. See also Economic Intelligence Committee Minutes of Meet-
ing Held in Room 2101, Temporary "M" Building 26th and Constitution Ave., N.W.
December 18, 1951. December 20, 1951, CIA-RDP82-00283R000100180001-7,
CIA, CREST Archive.

104. Nutter joined the National Bureau of Economic Research (NBER) in 1954. See
Kuehn, *Before NBER*; and Engerman, *Know Your Enemy*, 120–24.

105. "Douglas Diamond Jr., 76, Dies," *Washington Post*, October 6, 2001.

106. ORR Diary, March 13, 1952.

107. "Rush V. Greenslade, 61, Employee of CIA for More Than 20 Years," *Washington
Post*, May 7, 1978.

108. "Obituary: Stanley Harold Cohn."

109. CIA, *USSR: Measures of Economic Growth and Development, 1950–80*, ix.

110. Intelligence Advisory Committee, Minutes of Meeting Held in Director's Conference Room, Administration Building, Central Intelligence Agency, on February 8,
1951, IAC-M-19, IAC_Minutes_8_Feb_1951, CIA, CREST Archive.

111. Minutes of Meeting held in Director's Conference Room, Administration Building Central Intelligence Agency, on February 8, 1951, CIA-RDP82-00400R000100
020007-7, CIA, CREST Archive.

112. Minutes of Meeting held in Director's Conference Room, Administration Building Central Intelligence Agency, Monday March 26, 1951, CIA-RDP80B01676R00
2300010016-1, CIA, CREST Archive.

113. Director's Log, 8.30 a.m. November 13–8.30 a.m. November 14, 1951-09-01, CIA,
CREST Archive.

114. Letter from Lawrence Houston July 20, 1951, CIA-RDPS7-00384R000700120837-4,
CIA, CREST Archive.

115. Millikan's response can be found in Bergson, *Soviet Economic Growth*; and Letter
to Max Millikan from Abram Bergson, January 11, 1952, CIA-RDP75-00662R000-
300160010-4, CIA, CREST Archive.

116. Recipients for ORR Unclassified Studies (1960), CIA-RDP63-00314R0001001800
07-7, CIA, CREST Archive.

117. Thomas Schelling was influential from an earlier date. A 1954 review of Schelling's assessment of the Soviet economy finds ORR conducting a literature review
and recommending new pathways for research. It also includes a long list of ORR
reports. See Memorandum for Mr. Robert B. Wright, Chairman, Evaluation of
Schelling Report, November 8, 1954, CIA-RDP79-01203A000100100002-2, CIA,
CREST Archive.

118. Firth and Noren, *Soviet Defense Spending*, 30–31.

119. Firth and Noren, 31.

120. Director's Log, 8.30 a.m. November 17–8.30 a.m. November 18, (1951), 1951-09-
01, CIA, CREST Archive.

121. Firth and Noren, *Soviet Defense Spending*, 10.

122. Memorandum from the Chairman, Economic Intelligence Committee for the Secretary, Intelligence Advisory Committee, Proposed DCID-3/1 (Formerly DCID 15/1), May 20, 1958, CIA-RDP85S00362R000600050005-5, CIA, CREST Archive.

123. Dear Dan Letter from Max Millikan, October 29, 1951, CIA-RDP79-01157A0002000200002-2, CIA, CREST Archive.

124. Letter from Max Millikan, November 26, 1951, CIA-RDP80R01731R003000200096-6, CIA, CREST Archive.

125. Haines and Leggett, *Watching the Bear*, x.

126. Gilman, *Mandarins of the Future*, 69.

127. Turner, *Burn Before Reading*, 80.

128. *The Economy of the Soviet Bloc: Production Trends and 1957 Potential*, May 20, 1953, CIA-RR-23, CIA-RDP79R01141A000200060002-0, CIA, CREST Archive.

129. For a more recent exploration and more comprehensive look into CIA's history of Soviet economic estimates, see Kontorovich, *Reluctant Cold Warriors*.

130. Robert Amory replaced Millikan as assistant director of ORR in March 1952. As a manager, Amory was respectful of the expertise the economists had and left them alone, putting an economist in each of the divisional chief roles. He went on to become assistant director of Intelligence in 1953. Jackson and Claussen, *Organizational History of the Central Intelligence Agency*, 2:54.

131. Zelikow, "American Economic Intelligence," 167.

132. For example, see Panel for Review of Chinese Communist Capabilities, 1(7) January 1962, CIA-RDP66B00560R000100100164-3, CIA, CREST Archive. On CENIS, see Cline, *Secrets, Spies and Scholars*, 148.

The Princeton Consultants

Kent believes guidance becomes rare as intelligence mounts in augustness.

—Robert Amory

William Harding Jackson had a very poor opinion of professors. Even Sherman Kent, whom he evidently trusted, believed the Princeton Consultants were set up by Jackson to "give you professors a run for your money."[1] The Consultants were meant to be Jackson's response to the Board of Estimates, and to ONE itself, a way of keeping the academics honest. He thought it important enough that the first meetings were held at his home in Princeton. Later they moved to a hotel nearby.

Jackson graduated from Princeton in 1924. Leonard Mosley describes him as "a hard-driving, hard-drinking man."[2] He earned his law degree at Harvard Law School in 1928. He practiced at the New York firm of Cadwalader, Wickersham & Taft; followed by Carter Ledyard & Milburn, becoming a partner in 1934. When the war broke out, he was commissioned in the US Army Air Force as a captain. In 1943, as assistant military air attaché for antisubmarine intelligence, he went to London, where he became acquainted with British intelligence, writing a report on it that helped consolidate his reputation as an intelligence specialist. He became chief of strategic intelligence for Gen. Jacob L. Devers in August 1943 and then joined Gen. Omar Bradley's 12th Army Group as a deputy G-2. He ended the war with the rank of colonel. On his return to New York, he joined J. H. Whitney & Company, an investment firm, as managing partner.[3]

In 1948, with Allen W. Dulles and Mathias F. Correa, he was asked to produce a survey of national intelligence. Jackson's task in the Dulles Report was to concentrate on CIA's role in counterespionage and the restructuring of its administration, while Dulles looked at intelligence gathering and special operations. Correa, who had worked for James Forrestal, played little part in the surveying or writing.[4] Jackson reported for duty at CIA on September 26, 1950.[5]

FIGURE 8.1. William Harding Jackson. *Wikimedia Commons*

On October 1 he was appointed deputy director of central intelligence.[6] He left CIA in August 1951 and became a consultant to the Agency until February 1956, when he became national security adviser under President Dwight Eisenhower.[7]

Jackson, therefore, is the counterpoint to the intel intellectuals. He provides a skeptical view of their usefulness: one that used outsiders like lawyers and businesspeople to rein in any perceived excesses committed by the academics. And he does this in an interesting milieu: that of Princeton, his home both as family man and an alumnus. This chapter reviews the role of the consultants: first as a board and then for those who crossed over from Agency insider to outsider: George Kennan who was very close to ONE, and Max Millikan and William Langer after their retirement from CIA.

The Consultants

Jackson lost no time in setting up his sounding board to ONE and the BNE. The Director's Diary of November 12, 1950, records a conference with Frank

Wisner and George Kennan over the creation of a group of consultants for national estimates.[8] Kennan, himself a Princeton man, was now at the university's Institute for Advanced Study, not far from Jackson's house.[9] He had been invited there by Robert Oppenheimer in August 1950. Kennan would have been pleased to have joined the Consultants. Still licking his wounds after resigning from the State Department's Policy Planning Staff a year earlier, he agreed to serve and recommended a number of people. In his memoirs he says, "I was inclined to wonder whether the day had not passed when the government had use for the qualities of persons like ourselves—for the effort at cool and rational analysis in the unfirm substance of the imponderables—for an estimate of our Soviet adversaries based on their possible weaknesses as well as their possible strengths."[10]

Despite a much less amicable relationship between Jackson and Langer, the Harvard professor was a supporter of the Princeton group. By late November, Langer made arrangements to meet with Kennan in Princeton and suggested Hamilton Fish Armstrong as another possible consultant.[11] According to Kent, Jackson, along with business associate Barklie Henry, added Vannevar Bush and C. Burton Fahs, director of the Rockefeller Foundation and a Far East expert.[12] Fahs had gained his PhD at Northwestern and worked in OSS during the war as chief of the Far East desk for Research and Analysis.[13]

The first meeting of the Estimates Advisory Group was on November 24, with Abbot Smith, Jackson, Kennan, Armstrong, Langer, Henry, and Edward S. Mason present.[14] The meeting was to run from 12:15 p.m. until 5:30 p.m. Kent says the meeting didn't go according to plan. Instead of being a counter to the academics, Langer chaired the meeting and "ran it pretty much as he must have run his seminar in the Harvard Graduate School."[15] Langer laid down the law that it was his show and didn't ask for comment. The non-academics had nothing to say, including Jackson's colleague Barklie Henry. Only Kennan and Armstrong, who were, Kent says, "academics at heart," contributed. This set the tone of the meetings until Langer's departure in early 1952.

A 1959 CIA report on advisory committees by Sherman Kent detailed the mechanics of the group.[16] It was composed of nongovernmental members (although there was some hair-splitting as to whether retired or active military officials were nongovernmental). The group usually met five times a year between late September and late May, and the meetings usually took two days. They were chaired by a member of the BNE and often attended by the DCI. The agendas were set by the chair in consultation of ONE. Each of the consultants had a security clearance, and the premises themselves, always in Princeton, were checked beforehand by the Office of Security, who also had someone at the meetings and protected classified documents. The meetings were designed to receive the comments of the panelists on the format, presentation, and substance of the national intelligence estimates. The discussion was steered by the chair, who wrote up the minutes of the meeting and delivered them as a ONE staff memorandum. The consultants' activities were entirely advisory, and it was up to the chair to decide whether any action would be taken on their advice. They were paid: a letter from Jackson in December 1950 to an unknown recipient included a money order for travel expenses and a consultant's fee for the meeting, totaling $95.76.[17]

As the chair succeeding Langer, Raymond Sontag shifted the Princeton Consultants to a more in-depth focus on the estimates, yet not always very different from the rubber-stamp format his predecessor had initiated. Sontag would use the expertise of the academics to steer support for his ideas back in the office. The consultants got their papers delivered to their homes early, so they could read them thoroughly before the meeting. The meetings would often be bolstered by a "large Washington contingent" of CIA analysts engaged on the particular estimate under discussion.[18]

Sontag expanded the group to take on Philip Mosely (Soviet specialist, Columbia); Samuel Bemis (diplomatic historian, Yale); Joseph Strayer (medieval historian, Princeton), Cuyler Young (Near East specialist, Princeton); and Max Millikan. Non-academics included Gordon Gray and two ambassadors, Norman Armour and Joseph Crew. Richard Bissell and Jackson represented CIA. Those names remained constant for the next few years, with Langer included as a member.

Sontag was replaced as chair of the Princeton Consultants in mid-1953 by Abbot Smith. Like Sontag and Langer, Smith saw the consultants as instruments of ONE. A 1954 meeting had Abbot Smith in the chair, with members Armstrong, Calvin Hoover, Langer, Col. George A. Lincoln, Mosely, Strayer, and Young, with two names redacted.[19] A meeting in February 1956 included the same names (with the exception of Hoover) as well as William H. Dunham, George Kennan, Klaus Knorr, Edgar Hoover, Millikan, and William Reitzel, with James Cooley as chair and Sherman Kent, Robert Komer, Robert Hewitt, and at least two redacted names representing the Agency.[20]

Despite mixed feelings about the success of the group, the meetings found favor with the consultants themselves. A February 1952 letter from Gordon Gray to General Smith praised the panelists, in particular C. Burton Fahs. Fahs really knew the Far East, Gray said. "He is not hopelessly confused about the Communists as 'simple agrarian reformers' or the other nonsense which men like [Owen] Lattimore spout." But Gray wanted to contest the consensus of the meeting, saying he was in "sharp disagreement" with the estimate on Soviet intentions they had discussed. He did not believe that the Communists were seeking a truce in Korea; instead the Russians and Chinese found the situation to their advantage. Nor did he agree that the military situation had improved: while the US ground forces were better, in air power things had worsened, leaving the United States vulnerable to nuclear attack. In the Near and Far East, things were in even poorer shape. The US military position would improve over time, but "until we have such strength," wrote Gray, "we are confronted by the dilemma we will lose the cold war if we allow the Soviets to expand, while we face the possibility of a general war if we effectively stop Soviet expansion."[21]

But by this time the Princeton group was becoming a bit of a backwater to the real work being done by CIA at headquarters. Discussions tended to center around the expertise that was available, and when knowledge was needed of regions outside of their fields, their value was limited. Without the security clearances that would give them up-to-date intelligence on Soviet intentions and military capabilities, their contribution in that area was even more restricted. Kent remembered it like this:

> So the Princeton sessions came to be more and more a series of meetings at which ONE staffers gave extensive briefings to the Panel members. We began to feel from the point of view of the bread-and-butter work of the ONE, we were making a mighty outlay for something less than a commensurate return. . . . The trouble was that they were not only not in residence, but also that they only had a few hours preparation to ready themselves for the consulting stint. In the beginning, this was not as severe a handicap as it became. But we ourselves, after years on the job and in daily contact with the best—and highly privileged—intelligence, found we were not getting the sort of criticism that Mr. Jackson had in mind.[22]

Actually, William Langer had probably understood this right at the very beginning. On June 29, 1951, Jackson advised Langer that [redacted name] had complained that the consultants' meetings would not take place over the summer months. Langer did not appear worried about it; he said ONE regularly talked to individual consultants when their expertise was required for certain reports.[23]

Yet Kent, in his more diplomatic way, had described the maturing of the strategic intelligence discipline as it was brought in-house at CIA and the idea of sourcing outside academic help started to wane. It was a natural evolution. CIA's analysts could digest the information and arrive at conclusions faster than an outside consultant with little access to classified information could. And, as Kent had acknowledged, the social science skills they brought to CIA had begun—through trial and error—to morph into a discipline that understood the nuances that came with success and failure and was learning to live with the latter. The consultants could provide a sounding board for assessments that

CIA analysts had already arrived at, but they could contribute little that was new and useful to these seasoned intelligence analysts.

Kent says there were successive moves made to wind the Princeton Consultants down but that DCIs Allen Dulles, John McCone, and Richard Helms all resisted. Indeed, Helms went so far as to say the consultants provided a valuable link with academia, one that was sorely needed while CIA's relationship with the universities was tense (Helms was director of central intelligence between 1966 and 1973). The panel was refreshed when Willard Matthias assumed the chair. He undertook to recruit younger members with new skills and fields, and this continued until ONE was disestablished in 1973.[24]

Max Millikan as Consultant

Of all the Princeton Consultants, Millikan's judgment and skills were probably the most in demand. This is evident by the number of times, and range of years, in which his advice was solicited. Sometimes the requests for guidance were a little unreasonable, perhaps fitting his being "one of the boys" and a senior statesman of CIA's economic intelligence unit. A letter to Millikan in April 1956 asks him to review NIE-100-36 "Sino-Soviet Policy and Its Probable Effects in Undeveloped Areas." The writer says he realizes that the NIE will arrive on Millikan's desk the same day it is due to be presented to the IAC, but Jim Graham, chief of the Far East branch, would appreciate his comments nonetheless. The CIA courier who has brought the package to CENIS, in Cambridge, Massachusetts, the writer says, will wait for Millikan and return the NIE to Washington, DC, with his notes appended.[25]

Millikan's advice was not just restricted to economics. Another sign of the high regard Washington held him in was his being asked to chair the Soviet Vulnerabilities committee, which met for the first time in Robert Cutler's office at the White House in mid-September 1954. Richard Bissell, his former economics associate at Yale, was CIA's representative in the group. Cutler, who was at the time special assistant to the president, wrote to Dulles telling him the committee would concentrate first on the problem of Soviet nationality. Cutler wanted this given urgent priority, seeing the value of exploiting the many ethnic and national divisions in the USSR for American propaganda.[26]

Millikan clearly had a good intellectual relationship with Dulles, who became DCI in 1953. An example is a conversation between the two, presumably in Dulles's office, in 1956. Millikan introduces the idea that the Soviets have replaced the now discredited Stalinism with a return to Leninism. This is somewhat problematic because Lenin's ideas about imperialism are convincing, and the neutral countries have always found them attractive. Lenin was also willing to countenance debate, up to a point, where Stalin simply shot the people who disagreed with him. Dulles switches the conversation to Marx, saying that "he was really a SOB in his personal life and his dealing with friends. . . . We should show them the deceit, trickery and betrayal, ruthlessness that ran through his whole life." Millikan warns Dulles that, for American propaganda purposes, character assassination won't get much traction. He says the Leninist ideas are what matter, and they are deeply entrenched. But he does think that, in the case of the Soviet satellite states, there is a new generation of bureaucrats who don't like being told what to think: "Nobody likes to be shut up. And nobody particularly likes to be shut up by somebody else whom he's certain didn't like him very much."[27]

George Kennan

It is interesting the degree of influence George Kennan appears to have had on ONE's thinking. A May 1951 memorandum Comments on a Preliminary Draft of NIE-32, presumably by either Langer or Kent, details an explanation for Chinese involvement in the Korean War. The Russians, it argues, chose to support the North Koreans as part of a deliberate exclusion of Chinese interests. This was a miscalculation, and when the United States intervened, Moscow was in the difficult position of not being able to make its support obvious without being dragged into a general war. It needed, then, to bring in the Chinese, and Beijing drove a hard bargain for its commitment.

> To a rather considerable extent the above ideas are borrowed from Mr. Kennan, who expressed them in a less formidable fashion at Princeton last Saturday. I appreciate the difficulties of writing and coordinating a paper with reference to the kind of reasoning I have followed. However, it is also essential not to become a slave to evidence, or the lack of it, but to develop our analysis on the basis of logical, ideological and historical factors which, we must not forget, have the greatest influence upon the Soviet and Chinese action.[28]

In fact, there was a love/hate relationship between Kennan and CIA, with Kennan's role as head of the Policy Planning Staff and interest in covert operations, his membership of the Princeton Consultants, and his "Mr. X" article and subsequent ambassadorships all influencing CIA thinking. Kennan's name appears repeatedly in CIA minutes and memoranda of the period. In 1946, having recently come from a role as chargé d'affaires at the Moscow embassy, Vandenberg appointed Kennan as a special consultant to CIG on Russian matters. "Mr. Kennan has agreed to spend as much time as possible with the Central

Intelligence Group," the memo stated. "It is hoped that as time goes on his services will be available at increasingly frequent and extended periods."[29] Yet the Agency had every reason to be on their guard as well: In 1948 Admiral Souers told Gen. Edwin Wright, deputy director under Hillenkoetter, that there appeared to be an effort to discredit CIA, mostly coming from Kennan at State.[30]

General Smith valued the relationship with Kennan. In 1952 we see him writing to Frank Nash at the Department of Defense about a paper, *Political Advisors in a Military Theatre of Operations*: "I cannot help but think that if a man like George Kennan, for instance, had been sitting inconspicuously behind the principal negotiators at Panmunjom, our playmates there would not have scored their political and psychological successes which have been the only products so far of their negotiations."[31]

In July of 1950 Kennan met with CIA's chief of maps for four hours, asking him about the terrain on the border of Greece and Bulgaria, in the event of a Bulgarian attack. Kennan told him he had already asked the Army for the information but had received feedback that was "overgeneralized and equivocal."[32] In July 1951 we see Kennan recommending a book on Russian émigré politics to General Smith, which included a chapter he had written.[33] In a May 1952 cable from Moscow, his first since his appointment as ambassador, Kennan describes the Soviets approach to religion as "cynical and sadistic," where religions of all denominations were made to work for the regime despite their mutual distrust of each other.[34] The following month, General Smith wrote to him thanking him for his feedback on NIE-56/1 and asking for his comments on SE-30, a special estimate on Berlin. He also thanked Kennan for his contributions to a psychological campaign.[35]

Later the same year Ambassador Kennan suggested the Soviets were trying to foment a civil war in Japan, a prediction CIA analysts seem to have considered unlikely.[36] In August 1953 an Agency deputies meeting noted that Kennan had become disgusted with the critical press and public reception of a presentation he had given at Johns Hopkins University and had decided to withdraw from "the Russian question" and instead devote his time to his foreign policy studies.[37] By 1955 Kennan was still being used to provide comments to CIA reports, but by now with some reservations: Dulles asked Ray Cline to approach him but to do it "quietly."[38]

Kennan's relationship with CIA seems to have been well known to Moscow. On his appointment to US ambassador to the USSR in 1952, a Warsaw radio station said, "his whole career has been devoted to preparing for a new war and dealing with spies and diversionists." The station exhorted good communists to keep an eye on "so-called American diplomats who exploit diplomatic privileges to disguise their espionage activities."[39]

William Langer

As an indication of how Langer felt about the early days of the Princeton Consultants, a letter to Kent in February 1952 is illustrative. He wrote that he was sorry Kent had not made it to the meeting, but he had been glad to catch up with Raymond Sontag and "the rest of the boys." He missed "the old crowd," although he was happy being back at Harvard. Langer noted there would be some "ruction" caused by him pulling out of CIA but felt Kent, the Board of National Estimates, and ONE could manage very well without him.

The relationship between Langer and Kent had been a hierarchical one. Langer could be sarcastic and even scornful in his dealings with his deputy, and Kent notes that even as early as January 1951 their working relationship was tense. Yet Langer could be that way with everyone, and Kent acknowledges there had been bumpy times during the war when he had been put in purgatory by his boss. However, we see a cozier relationship in the personal letters between the two.[40] Langer writes to "Sherm" or "Shermo," and Kent addresses his boss as "Bill" or "dear maestro" in later letters.

For Langer, the Princeton Consultants was a fading association with an earlier time, and it was not obvious that he needed it. Yet it held a certain nostalgia for him. In January 1963 he wrote to Kent at his home at 2824 Chain Bridge Road, telling him of his retirement from the group. He would soon write to John McCone, resigning formally. He told Kent that it had been increasingly difficult to fit meetings into his schedule, and that as a member of the President's Foreign Intelligence Advisory Board, the link to CIA had not helped him maintain independence. "I need hardly tell you how reluctant I am to make this decision. I have a very real affection for all the people in this shop and have thoroughly enjoyed the Princeton meetings. I will miss you all very much and must console myself with the thought that for fully a dozen years it has been my privilege to work with so splendid and devoted a group of men and women."

Kent's reply is similarly emotional:

Dear Bill,

You were terribly kind to give me advance notice of your impending withdrawal from the Princeton group. Having written this I am overwhelmed with great melancholy. Your knowledge, wisdom, and resounding good sense have been a sort of keystone in the institution and one which we will not soon replace. I can't tell you how warming it has been to me to reflect that our association in the business has endured these 20 odd years and that one of your many important roles was propping our confidence that we were doing the right thing.

You know better than anyone that the sentiments above are those of your other devoted admirers at the Office of National Estimates, many of whom have been here from the beginning. All of us, old boys and new, are greatly saddened by your decision.[41]

Conclusion

The Princeton Consultants had started out as a checks-and-balances approach to the BNE and ONE: it showed William Harding Jackson's desire to keep an eye on the professors. Instead, it very quickly became a group dominated by the academics. George Kennan spoke of his fear that those who were capable of "cool and rational analysis in the unfirm substance of the imponderables" might be becoming irrelevant. The Consultants showed—at least initially—that an alternative view to ONE's analysis was indeed needed.

However, it was still adding another layer of cross-referencing, one that should already have been established by the watchfulness of the IAC and the BNE. It was as if CIA remained fearful that any estimate might miss something and therefore set up many checkpoints before it finally made its way out of the Agency doors.

Kennan's concern also points to another factor: that the "cool and rational" heads were all of a generation that had gone through the war together. They had a heightened concept of "the Enemy" and an acute sense of the work that winning a war took. They had a network of contacts, people they trusted and could call on in time of need. Some of those relationships were informal, some formal enough to lead to job offers. They also had a wartime understanding of how to get the job done. It might require long hours of overtime and rule-breaking that might otherwise not be tolerated in peacetime. In war, getting the job done was more important than meeting the budget, and half measures were better than missing the deadline. In other words, they were successful amateurs. But CIA was going through a period where professionalism was necessary, and it was understandable that the amateurs were going to be left behind.

Yet Kent's view was that "guidance becomes rare as intelligence mounts in augustness." He seems to be warning here about self-importance getting in the way of common sense, and he appears to be talking specifically about CIA's sense of self-importance. It is a valuable takeaway about organizational change and about keeping a sense of humility in the work of a national security practitioner.

Notes

Epigraph: Robert Amory (citing Kent, *Strategic Intelligence for American World Policy*, 182), The Intelligence Community, n.d., CIA-RDP79-01048A000100070010-0, CIA, CREST Archive.

1. Kent, "The Law and Custom," 106.
2. Mosely, *Dulles*, 246.
3. "Establishment of the Office of General Services, 29 December 1952 [*sic*]," CIA-RDP81-00728r000100110006-6 (1950), 92, CIA, CREST Archive.
4. Mosely, *Dulles*, 246.
5. Director's Diaries, September 1, 1950–October 6, 1950, 1950-09-01-2 (1950), 30, CIA, CREST Archive.
6. "Establishment of the Office of General Servies," 92.
7. Letter to William Jackson from Allen Dulles (1956), CIA-RDP80R01731R000500 470001-9, CIA, CREST Archive.
8. DCI Lt. Gen. Walter Bedell Smith, October 7, 1950–March 31, 1951 (1951), 44, 1950-10-07-2, CIA, CREST Archive.
9. Tex McCrary and Jinx Falkenburg, "New York Close Up," *New York Herald Tribune*, September 15, 1950, 19.
10. Kennan, *Memoirs*, 499.
11. DCI Lt. Gen. Walter Bedell Smith, 7 October 1950–31 March 1951, 58.
12. Kent, "The Law and Custom," 107.
13. Charles B. (Charles Burton) Fahs, Rockefeller Archive Center, https://dimes.rock arch.org/agents/8fgdhQozzVZpzKucKCQP9W.
14. DCI Lt. Gen. Walter Bedell Smith, October 7, 1950–March 31, 1951, 59.
15. Kent, "The Law and Custom," 106.
16. Advisory Committees, February 26, 1959, CIA-RDP80B01676R004300020010-4, CIA, CREST Archive.
17. Letter from William Jackson to unknown, December 26, 1950, CIA-RDP80R017-31R003100080026-26, CIA, CREST Archive.
18. Kent, "The Law and Custom," 108.
19. Staff Memorandum 76-54, Report on O/NE Consultants Meeting at Princeton, NJ, 7–8 October 1954, https://www.cia.gov/readingroom/document/02924300, CIA, CREST Archive.
20. Staff Memorandum 19-56, Princeton Consultant's Meetings February 8–9, 1956, https://www.cia.gov/readingroom/document/03436549, CIA, CREST Archive.
21. Letter to General Smith (sanitized), February 25, 1952, CIA-RDP80R0173R00050 04100008-8, CIA, CREST Archive.
22. Kent, "The Law and Custom," 109.
23. Friday April 6, 1951, 74, CIA-RDP80R01731R002600530001-9, CIA, CREST Archive.
24. Kent, "The Law and Custom," 109.
25. Letter to Max Millikan, April 20, 1956, CIA-RDP79R01012A008400030020-6, CIA, CREST Archive.
26. Letter to Honorable Robert Cutler from Allen Dulles (1954), CIA-RDP80R01731-R000900110043-8, CIA, CREST Archive.
27. The transcript of this conversation is sanitized, with "D" standing for Dulles and "M" for Millikan. The evidence points toward it being Millikan: He talks about

Cambridge (MIT), "Walt" (Rostrow), and Dulles at one point says "you people up there in science," probably a typo for "CENIS." Stenographic Notes of Conversation between DCI and (sanitized) on 21 July 1956 at 1600 hours (1956), CIA-RDP 80R01731R000800210007-8, CIA, CREST Archive.

28. Comment on Preliminary Draft NIE-32, May 23, 1951, CIA-RDP79R01012A0008 00050053-9, CIA, CREST Archive.

29. Mr. George Frost Kennan, Special Consultant to the Director of Central Intelligence (1946), CIA-RDP80B0167R004000040012-3, CIA, CREST Archive.

30. Memorandum for the Record from E. K. Wright, May 6, 1948 (1948), CIA-RDP80 R01731R002700030028-4, CIA, CREST Archive.

31. Letter to Frank (C. Nash) from Bedell (1952), CIA-RDP80R01731R0013002000-11-8, CIA, CREST Archive.

32. Work Undertaken in D/MA, ORE, July 24, 1950, CIA-RDP79-01096A000400050 013-3, CIA, CREST Archive.

33. Russian Emigre Politics, July 17, 1951, CIA-RDP57-00384R001100050063-8, CIA, CREST Archive. See also George Fisher, *Russian Emigre Politics* (Free Russia Fund Incorporated, 1951), CIA-RDP80R0173R000500560009-1, CIA, CREST Archive.

34. Current Intelligence Digest, May 15, 1952, CIA, CREST Archive.

35. To Ambassador George Kennan from Bedell Smith, June 7, 1952, CIA-RDP80R0 173R000500560006-4, CIA, CREST Archive.

36. Current Intelligence Digest, August 11, 1952, CIA-RDP79T01146A0012000200 01-7, CIA, CREST Archive.

37. Deputies Meeting, August 19, 1953, CIA-RDP80B01676R002300130020-3, CIA, CREST Archive.

38. Deputies Meeting, Wednesday June 8, 1955, CIA-RDP80B01676R0023001700-05-6, CIA, CREST Archive.

39. Kennan's Appointment, February 13, 1952, CIA-RDP80R01731R003100050028-7, CIA, CREST Archive.

40. Series 1, Box 12, Folder 253, MS854, Sherman Kent Papers.

41. Folder 253, Sherman Kent Papers.

CHAPTER 9

Kent's "Theory of the Fuck Up of the Imponderables"

R. Jack Smith: *Sherm, I don't like what I see in our recent papers. A 2-to-1 chance of this; 50-50 odds on that. You are turning us into the biggest bookie shop in town.*

Kent: *R. J., I'd rather be a bookie than a [blank-blank] poet.*

Uncertainty plays the greatest part in any assessment of the world situation or any event critical to national security. Sherman Kent recognized this in one particularly colorful letter to Bernard Brodie where he discussed what he called "Kent's Theory of the Fuck Up of the Imponderables."[1] The *Cambridge Dictionary* defines "imponderable" as "something that cannot be guessed or calculated because it is completely unknown."[2] *Merriam-Webster* gives "incapable of being weighed or evaluated with exactness" as its meaning.[3] Both definitions give us some understanding of what Kent meant by his theory. His view was that the more unpredictable variables that the analyst had to grapple with in answering the what, when, why, where, who, and how of a problem, the greater the risk of failure. (Brodie found Kent's characteristic foul language amusing: "Chaucerian," he called it.) What makes this theory so interesting is that it was expressed in 1947—three years before Kent was seconded to CIA. He was writing to Brodie to sound him out on an idea he was working on for *Strategic Intelligence for American Foreign Policy*: how an intelligence analyst might think about the potential capabilities of a state faced with the likelihood of war. Kent was not just struggling to put the concept into words; by naming the theory "Kent's Theory of the Fuck Up of the Imponderables," he seems to be describing uncertainty as a personal fault.

Kent did in fact take personally his problems with uncertainty. One example we have already seen is the case of NIE-29/1 "Probability of an Invasion of Yugoslavia in 1951." Paul Nitze confronted Kent over ONE's ambiguity over whether the Soviets would invade. Here the problem was of weighing or evaluating a problem with exactness. Kent's first reaction was to say that assessing

FIGURE 9.1. Sherman Kent in Tokyo, October 1959. *SKP*

probability was not the task of the intelligence analyst. Then he thought about it more and came up with a solution: words of estimative probability. Nitze tells the story like it is a victory over the scholarly narrow-mindedness of the Office of National Estimates. It is really a victory of Kent's integrity—and his fear of getting analysis wrong.

Uncertainty is a constant theme in Kent's work, as we see him trying to impose a framework on the chaos of information that CIA's analysts had to deal with. In particular, his pyramid analogy, which takes the analytical problem from the inductive to the deductive, demonstrates Kent's desire to find an ordering principle for dealing with chaos. Here Kent's imponderable problem is about calculating something that is unknown: how much research is needed to refine a question down to a conclusion. It is also interesting to see George Kennan raise the question of imponderables in his comment about "cool and rational analysis in the unfirm substance of the imponderables."[4] This suggests that the concept of imponderability was well and truly embraced at the time.

Uncertainty, therefore, was something the intel intellectuals were acutely aware of, particularly failure or the futility of the analyst's fight against uncertainty. And again, it is expressed each time as a personal battle either in the search for truth or in the credibility that was needed to succeed in one's job. In this chapter we look at four human attributes an intelligence analyst might need to cope with uncertainty: self-criticism, humor, the ability to collaborate, and self-awareness.

Self-Criticism

In a characteristically frank admission over an assessment of whether the Soviets would put nuclear missiles into Cuba (SNIE-85-3-62, September 19, 1962), Kent wrote: "there is no blinking the fact we came down on the wrong side."[5] The conclusion of the special estimate had been thorough and, in Kent's view, in accordance with the scientific method, developing hypotheses "as to the proper meaning" of information that had been the work of thousands of people. Each hypothesis had been checked against the facts, weighed up against other possibilities, and judged by analysts with experience of assessing the world situation. And yet the estimate had been proven wrong.

"How could we have misjudged?," Kent asked himself. "The short answer is that, lacking the direct evidence, we went to the next best thing, namely, information which might indicate the true course of developments. In brooding over an imponderable, like the probable intentions of the Soviets in Cuba—there is a strong temptation to make no estimate at all." Worse, in his opinion, was to yield and offer up every possible contingency. It might be a relief to the analyst to know he had covered every base, but the consumer would either dismiss his worst-case scenarios as crying wolf or would act on them and risk a foreign policy disaster.[6]

The process of estimating, then, was one of choosing what seemed right even though the act of selection itself was flawed. This is what separated the university academic from the civilian intelligence analyst. Writing in 1978, the veteran Bureau of Intelligence and Research analyst Roger Hilsman put it plainly:

> While the academic researcher is relatively free to define a problem in his own terms, our research problems are generally defined by the requirements of US foreign policy. The academic researcher chooses a topic for which data are available, whereas it is often new problems (or old problems defined in new ways) for which the policymaker requires intelligence analysis. For these kinds of problems there is usually a serious lack of good and current data. The quantitatively oriented scholar can easily limit his work to those variables that can be operationalized, but the government analyst seldom enjoys that luxury. The issues he deals with are generally characterized by a large number of variables in complex and poorly understood relationships. Further, the government analyst is far more concerned with matters of presentation. He is writing for an audience that, by and large, does not understand the procedures or tolerate the jargon of social science methodology, and he must keep his presentation brief if he wants it read by persons in authority.[7]

Kent was circumspect about whether the analyst could achieve any kind of "certainty" in an assessment. Similarly, an analyst would be wary of assuming the position of objectivity: "No matter how hard intelligence people try," believed Kent, "no matter with what skill and insight they work, they cannot objectively and factually describe everything the way they might choose."[8] In his 1991 autobiography Kent states:

> In my heart, I do not believe that anyone is capable of such perfect objectivity, but I think as far as ONE was concerned, the best that we can say is that if we were advocating a particular policy for one issue or another, it was a matter of inadvertence on our part. Nor do I recall our ever having set out to pitch an estimate so that it might sustain a policy position in which we happened to believe. . . . Whatever point of view I was presenting in the various estimates was the one that had developed from a purely objective consideration of the data.[9]

Looking back on Kent's pithy summaries, it is hard not to imagine some sort of catharsis might set in. After all, the ONE analysts were carefully walking on eggshells for every estimate. Without surety over their ability to stand at a distance from the facts and survey them coldly, or without any likelihood of arriving at a judgment they could feel certain about, estimating appeared to be a thankless task.

As a result, Kent could be pessimistic about the reception ONE's reports would receive. If a policymaker did not get the answer he was looking for, he would be tempted to look closely at the report and "find some loose masonry which can be jimmied apart."[10] If he had reason to believe the answer was fabricated, then the analyst and CIA would bear the brunt of some "very weighty weaponry."[11] If the conclusion was the same as his preconception, the policymaker was just as likely to wonder aloud why the estimate was needed in the first place. If unhappy, he would be quick to accuse it of being "misleading." If the conclusion had political significance—for example, if it went against something domestic the policymaker was fighting for—then the intelligence analyst would be branded as "irrelevant," or even "naive."

This created a situation where the analyst's credibility would be called into question:

> They [the analysts] have been caught out in their stupidity, and their credibility, at least for this estimate, is dead. It is dead not merely for the reader who found the conclusions abhorrent, but for all the others who found out for themselves or were told. If the same group of estimators are caught out for a second or third time, their credibility will probably be dead for good.

Thereafter almost any intelligence pronouncement they or their associates make will be slightingly referred to as propaganda, and perhaps not even read. They have not only lost all hope of directly influencing policy, they have lost what is even more important because [it is] more attainable than direct influence. This is the indirect influence which they might have exercised through an honest contribution to the debate which ought to precede every substantial policy decision.[12]

We can see now why Kent so brazenly called his theory the "Theory of the Fuck Up of the Imponderables." In doing so, he both took responsibility for his faults and failures and also marked out the impossible terrain the analyst was meant to cover.

Humor

Predicting future Pearl Harbors in the Cold War environment might be likened to a game of whack-a-mole. While this is at heart a game of frustration, it is also one where frustration plays out as comedy.

On his departure from the Board of National Estimates in 1951, Calvin Hoover sent a letter to Kent with a parody of a national intelligence estimate titled NIE-1001 "A Farewell Message to My Colleagues at O/NE." The source is a fictional Mati Scheherazade, a close associate of the Emir of Afghanistan. A report was purchased from him for $100,000 in grants by the US ambassador to Iran but unfortunately transmitted to British Prime Minister Clement Attlee by mistake, instead of Truman. Brought to America by Sir Percy Sillitoe, head of MI5, it was then handed to J. Edgar Hoover of FBI. From there it comes into the possession of ONE. (A copy, says Hoover, also went to Lavrentiy Beria at MVD, via Guy Burgess and Donald Maclean.)

NIE-1001 "A Farewell Message to My Colleagues at O/NE."[13]
Problem:
To estimate the likelihood of general war breaking out in the next twelve months.
Discussion:
1. There once lived in the city of Baghdad a devout servant of Allah named Mahmud Ali Beg.
2. Mahmud had nine cats. The largest cat was a huge Persian, called Genwar. The others, Koreawar, Chinawar, Indo-Chinawar, Jugwar, Germwar, Japwar, Turkwar, and Iranwar were graduated in size down to Burmawar, who was of the tiny bantam-like breed commonly known in Baghdad as Alicats.

3. Mahmud realized that any of the cats might decide to leave the house in a hurry. Consequently he cut nine holes in his door, appropriate in size for each of his cats.

4. It was only after his door came to look like a Swiss cheese that Mahmud realized he had labored unnecessarily. "Allah be merciful," he cried, "if I had but realized it, even the great Genwar could have got through the hole I cut in the door for tiny Burmawar!"

Conclusion:

5. The likelihood of war breaking out some place is much greater than war breaking out at one particular place.

Here we see the uncertainty of determining future wars, including general war, packaged by Hoover as parody. Hoover's letters to Kent were often irreverent, demonstrating not only the warm relationship with his wartime friend but also Kent's candid behavior that Hoover expressed as "your sense of humor, inimitably clothed in the inimitable pungency of your language."[14] It is this use of humor that Jack Davis said Kent used to "put people at ease, after that to soften a substantive disagreement or other tension."[15] Particularly under the intense scrutiny—and often acid disapproval—of bosses like William Langer, or under the high-stakes pressure from stakeholders like Paul Nitze, humor was a necessary instrument to keep a sense of balance and humanity at ONE.

Collaboration

Max Millikan's ORR had drawn heavily on the work of other scholars in the economics field: so, too, did ONE work with academics studying Soviet leadership and military doctrine. A 1953 CIA inventory listed research being undertaken by RAND, the Human Resources Research Institute, the Operations Research Office, the Office of Naval Research, and MIT's Center for International Studies.[16] The Joint Chiefs of Staff had commissioned RAND to work on Soviet economic and military capabilities from 1948.[17]

RAND's early work included Nathan Leites, together with Raymond Garthoff and Elsa Burnaut's P-171 "The Politburo Images of Stalin" (July 31, 1950); Leites's solo studies R-206 "The Operational Code of the Politburo" (August 1, 1950) and P-242 "The Politburo Through Western Eyes" (October 12, 1951); and Margaret Mead's R-199 "Soviet Attitudes to Authority" (January 1951). Garthoff (who joined CIA as an analyst in December 1957) says that, while there were no specialists in Russian military doctrine at that time (Army intelligence being only interested in operational doctrine), the civilian work was funded by Harvard's Russian Research Center, other government-sponsored programs, and covertly by CIA. He remembers that, despite working for RAND at the time, the walls were pretty porous: at one point in 1950 he was researching an article in CIA's Foreign Documents Division when a stack of books arrived that had been captured in Pyongyang. They were on Russian literature, with not a secret in them, but he avidly read them.[18] Garthoff, who wrote *Soviet Military Doctrine* in 1953, remembers the field as being a network of relationships. "Personal friendships with other budding Sovietologists of the early postwar generation, as well as a few more senior government experts on the Soviet Union, brought me into contact with colleagues in the Department of State and some other agencies. Incidentally, all of these early centers of Sovietology, including RAND, were heavily salted with veterans of the USSR Division of the Research and Analysis Branch of the wartime Office of Strategic Services (OSS)."[19]

Andrew Marshall was a near contemporary of the intel intellectuals at RAND in the early 1950s and later at the Office of Net Assessment within the Department of Defense. As a result, he worked alongside CIA during and after the reform period. He knew Kent well enough to call him "Sherm" in his letters.[20] Marshall remembered frequent visits by CIA people out to RAND's headquarters. He found that CIA analysts in the 1950s were intellectually curious and interested in RAND's methods as well as their analyses. They "were very activist, sought outside help, worked long hours," Marshall recollected.[21]

This all changed in the 1970s, and it is interesting that he partially blames the career system set up by Langer and Kent.

> Well, as you know, I think the CIA of the '50s and early '60s was very, very different from the '70s, much to the discredit of the '70s. And I think I mentioned that [John] Bross himself was very concerned about that. I remember him talking to me, talking on the people he already saw in the late '60s. His view was these people didn't know anybody else but people in this agency, and that the people who formed it or who were recruited in the '50s, throughout the '50s, had a lot of other associations, they knew other people in the United States or elsewhere. By the late '60s you had the effect of this career design choice that the Agency made of trying, for security reasons, to take people out of the universities and have a one-career lifetime. There were people who spent their whole time in there. The result is that they don't know anybody else, I mean in the truly professional way, lack breadth of experience and so on, contacts."[22]

Marshall's point is very clear: the friendships and collegial relationships established during the 1940s allowed for cross-fertilization of ideas and skills during the early Cold War. The Central Intelligence Agency was open to this combination of know-how and know-who partly because of its urgent mission but also because the paths between these buildings of knowledge were already well worn. Willmoore Kendall had talked of an intelligence analyst who could simply pick up the phone and dial anywhere in the world for information, and this network existed and worked well. In many ways, as Marshall claims, the more professional CIA became, the less this healthy collaboration was exercised. Indeed, breaches of security had taken place: James Jesus Angleton's faith in his friendship with the Soviet spy Kim Philby exposed many of CIA's secrets and was at least partially responsible for many deaths. But despite the amateur levels of security clearance, these networks worked well.

It is ironic that Marshall considers the CIA people of the 1970s to be less professional than their predecessors. For Marshall, professionalism is denoted in breadth of experience and valuable contacts. Yet the urgency and importance of wartime collaboration amounted to not only this range of understandings about how things worked; it also grew understandings about people. According to Marshall, over time CIA's attitude became "We're the real experts, we don't need to talk to other people." Interestingly, according to one CIA historical report (of 1973), the high point of national intelligence estimate writing was considered to be reached in the early 1960s. After that, the NIEs "declined in prestige and drew increasingly sharp criticism."[23] There is every reason to surmise that the breakdown of collaboration may have led to this decline.

Social Science as Self-Awareness

Metacognition "is the process by which learners use knowledge of the task at hand, knowledge of learning strategies, and knowledge of themselves to plan their learning, monitor their progress towards a learning goal, and then evaluate the outcome."[24]

The process of "making social science" is bound up in the conditions of metacognition—of considering the use of information; considering strategies not only for the use of it but also for how it will be disseminated and received—and of testing, of working toward conclusions and the monitoring of those conclusions over time. To employ metacognition is to be aware, critical, and to regulate, and it's not possible to "make social science" without attendant self-awareness, self-criticism, and self-regulation. To that extent, the intel intellectuals' fear of not being objective was partially overcome: they were at least objective about themselves. The impossibility of the task of predicting disaster, the daily games of whack-a-mole against the adversary, were met by embracing uncertainty. High-pressure stakes were met with crude language and humor. Failure was to be expected, and no one understood how easily and quickly judgments could go wrong than ONE's analysts.

Writing to his brother William in 1951, Kent described the ups and downs of working at ONE: "The job here is absorbing, disturbing, & sometimes exhausting. The day by day confronting of the absolute awfulness of the world, or the possibilities of another war with the implements the boys have contrived to take life & destroy the works of man is something I think I have got used to in the daytime. At night I find out that my subconscious, at least, hasn't got used to it."[25]

It was both an introspective and deeply careworn intellectual journey. The university academic could abandon a research question for a lack of relevant data, but the intel intellectual had to make do with what he had. It resulted in, as Kent had predicted, not pure social science but something that made the best of it. It was, after all, the work of intellect.

Notes

Epigraph: Davis, *Sherman Kent and the Profession of Intelligence Analysis*, 6.
1. "Letter Kent to Brodie War Pot/Caps Formulation to BB 13 Feb 1947," Folder 51, Series 1, Box 2, MS854, Sherman Kent Papers (hereafter, SKP).
2. *Cambridge Dictionary* website, https://dictionary.cambridge.org/dictionary/english/imponderable.
3. *Merriam-Webster website*, https://www.merriam-webster.com/dictionary/imponderable.
4. Kennan, *Memoirs: 1925–1950*, 499.
5. Kent, "A Crucial Estimate Relived," 174.
6. Kent, 174.
7. Heuer, *Quantitative Approaches to Political Intelligence*, 4.
8. Kent, *Strategic Intelligence for American World Policy*, 45.
9. Kent and Thacher, *Reminiscences of a Varied Life*, 261.
10. Kent, "Estimates and Influence," 38.
11. Kent, 39.
12. Kent, 41.
13. Folder 158, SKP.
14. Folder 158, SKP.
15. Davis, *Sherman Kent and the Profession of Intelligence Analysis*, 5.
16. *RAND Reports* (1953), CIA-RDP80 01065A000300060002-7, CIA, CREST Archive.
17. Garthoff, *A Journey Through the Cold War*, 17.
18. Garthoff, 6, 11–12, 39.
19. Garthoff, 17.
20. Marshall, A. W., 1967, Correspondence, 1920–1980, Folder 268, Box 12, Series 1, MS 854, SKP.
21. Marshall, *Reflections on Net Assessment*, 125.
22. Marshall, 112–13.
23. *National Estimates: An Assessment of the Product and the Process*, April 1977, CIA-RDP80-00630A000300040001-3, CIA, CREST Archive.
24. "Metacognition," MIT Teaching + Learning Lab website, https://tll.mit.edu/teaching-resources/how-people-learn/metacognition.
25. Kent, William Jr. 1950–52, Correspondence, 1920–1980, Folder 235, Box 4, Series 1, MS 854, SKP.

Conclusion

The Intel Intellectuals as Agents of Change

> *It is true that a well selected expert comes to intelligence work like an old soldier, knowing his weapons. But he is in a new battle, and must learn new tactics, new responsibilities, a new place in a new team. . . . The people who devote their best work to the profession of intelligence must not only be engaged in the work, but must be concerned with the development of method and of the body of knowledge through a constant lively interchange of thought.*
>
> —George S. Pettee

It is inconceivable today to think of power—particularly US military, economic, and political power—without thinking of the accompanying intellectual and informational power that is embodied in the state's intelligence institutions. Yet in the world's most powerful state, that intelligence strength is a relatively new phenomenon when compared with the older institutions of military and trade power. The idea that intelligence serves a peacetime strategic function—one that accepts the corollary of total war is total peace, which in turn requires an encyclopedic understanding of the world, its peoples, their resources, and their psychologies—can be attributed to the work of the intel intellectuals in the early stages of the Cold War. They not only wrote of a future dependent on peacetime strategic intelligence but also shaped the processes by which a civilian strategic intelligence institution was built, and they helped create an organization that was partially instrumental to winning that war.

It is perfectly conceivable, however, to imagine a great power that has been failed by its intelligence institutions. How much that weakens the state is the subject of many history books. How much the institutions themselves are weakened by failure is the subject of only a few books. This book focuses on CIA's crisis between 1946 and 1950: the Executive, Congress, and intelligence community generally began to doubt the Agency's ability to arm and protect them informationally. With a mission as critical to US interests as the CIA's, however, that failure could not be tolerated for long. There was an itchy trigger finger when it came to intelligence organizations: the Coordinator of Information, the Office of Strategic Services, and the Central Intelligence Group were all examples of the bodies that piled up along the way.

By the end of his two years as CIA's director, General Smith had established the Agency's core functions: overt and clandestine collection, covert operations, intelligence analysis, and coordination of departmental activities. "Smith," said the Church Committee twenty-two years later, "supervised sweeping administrative changes which created the basic structure that remains in effect to this day."[1] Jackson's 1957 *Organizational History of the Central Intelligence Agency* says Smith's changes were to "clarify and improve the Agency's organizational position, its functional jurisdiction, and its working relationships among the other departments, agencies and echelons that made up the Government's national security structure."[2] Samuel Halpern, a Far Eastern specialist at CIA in the early years, believes Smith's tenure gave CIA the legitimacy it was looking for: "He put CIA on the map. If it hadn't been for Bedell, I don't think there would be a CIA today. He made it what it is: he firmly established it as an important element of government, both on the hill with Congress and in the Executive Branch, particularly in the Defense Department."[3]

As he prepared to leave the presidency in January of 1953, and a month before Smith himself left CIA, Truman wrote Smith a thank-you note:

> As you know, I consider the establishment of the Central Intelligence Agency one of the most important steps which I have taken, as President, in the interests of our national security. An effective intelligence service, which this country now possesses, is a vital element in our efforts for a just and lasting peace. As Director of Central Intelligence since 1950, following your superior service as Ambassador to Moscow, you have successfully and faithfully accomplished your mission of developing the Central Intelligence Agency into an efficient and permanent arm of the Government's national security structure. During this critical period the far-reaching improvements and strengthening which you have introduced in the intelligence field have been of immeasurable value to me and the other members of the National Security Council in dealing with the difficult problems facing us. I am firmly convinced that no President ever had such a wealth of vital information made available to him in such a useful manner as I have received through CIA.[4]

Truman quite clearly states that Smith's mission was to develop the CIA into "an efficient and permanent arm," suggesting there was doubt in the president's mind whether CIA would continue in its pre-1950 form. The evidence that CIA was going to suffer either the fate of OSS, and be disestablished, or the fate of CIG, and be reborn as a new organization, is not strong. The evidence across the national security community, throughout Congress, and by the public at large that CIA was thought of as failing is overwhelming and has been dealt with at length in this book. Truman continued his letter to Smith by saying the improvements during Smith's tenure at CIA were "far-reaching" and "of immeasurable value . . . in dealing with the difficult problems" facing the United States. The president closed by emphasizing his view that the information he had been provided was "vital," "useful," and abundant.

Smith's role as leader of CIA over the reform period is clear. He considered his primary responsibilities to be to improve CIA's external relationships and its intelligence performance. He worked hard at establishing good relations with the president and made sure he was a weekly visitor to the White House. Together with Jackson, he established a good working partnership with State, Defense, and the FBI. The Intelligence Advisory Committee, which had been like a squeaky hinge, the embodiment of CIA's failure to coordinate intelligence, was now working well with CIA. This, Smith believed, was one of his first accomplishments.[5] Similarly, Smith had overcome objections made before his arrival to CIA's DCI chairing the US Communications Intelligence Board. The Department of Defense and State Department had both objected in 1949 but by 1952 were happy to let CIA lead. These examples, says Jackson, illustrate "the growth of CIA's position of intelligence leadership in the Government's national security structure during General Smith's time."[6]

Kent says, "Without a doubt it was General Smith with his majestic presence and high-level contacts which made the whole new institution of the NIE possible."[7] But he also says that Smith's successor, Allen Dulles, was much more involved in the NIEs and that Dulles "made himself more available than General Smith ever had to discuss the various estimates we were working on or the dissents that had come up [from the other intelligence agencies]."[8] Indeed, Smith did get involved directly with some of the conclusions made by ONE. Montague recounts Smith interceding in the case of SE-11 'Probability of a Communist Assault on Japan in 1951." This was an example of CIA making judgments on military matters, specifically how the US might respond to an invasion. SE-11 concluded—and this was agreed to by State, G-2, and A-2—that the Communists would only attempt to invade Japan in the event of war. Smith and the DNI representative both dissented with this call. Instead, they believed the Soviets would not invade Japan, even in the event of war. The DCI and DNI both took into account that the US commitment to Japan would deter the Soviets from invasion, and that Moscow would accept superior US military capability and not take action. What was unusual here was that the dissent was included in the body of the estimate and not as a separate footnote, which was the usual procedure. This may have simply been a case of a military man being unable to resist having input into a conclusion he felt his experience told him was wrong. Montague appeared somewhat shocked that the director of central intelligence was dissenting in an estimate his own people had prepared.[9]

Otherwise, Smith seems to have been hands-off when it came to the Board of National Estimates and ONE. Montague tells another story of a fight that erupted after Langer left and a new role of director of intelligence was created to oversee all of the analytical departments, including ONE. Loftus Becker was appointed to the role, a lawyer who had served in intelligence for the 9th Army and appeared at the Nuremberg Trials as an expert witness on German military organization.[10] There was no love lost between Becker and ONE. In his memoirs, Kent talks about his concerns over losing direct access to the DCI with Becker (and, later, Ray Cline) as middlemen.[11] Becker immediately attempted to wrest control over ONE, by complaining that neither BNE nor ONE were being responsive to NSC requests. In February 1952 Becker started turning the screws on the estimates staff, demanding faster turnarounds on NIEs and more systematic planning of updates to expiring estimates. Kent seems to have used this to take the initiative and institute twelve-month programs, but Becker also managed to get NSC to insist on more evidence of the sources and facts used for NIE conclusions. Things came to a head with NIE-69 Developments in North Africa, when the BNE pushed for the inclusion of a sizable addendum to show their research. This was the start of a heated debate as to whether NIEs should contain addenda (called "tabs"). At BNE's request, General Smith ruled in favor of producing a separate supplement, argued that they should contain the background research of the other agencies and not ONE, and said he would decide whether supplements would be appropriate in future estimates. According to Montague, the BNE was not happy with this "judgement of Solomon," and from then on, NIEs got fatter and fatter.[12] The inference from this is that Kent and the other scholars largely got their way.

Yet, as befitting an ex–chief of staff, Smith knew how the organizational hierarchy worked and called the shots only where necessary to getting the job done. We can see that, even though Smith took personal responsibility for getting the national intelligence estimates right, Langer assumed that responsibility, too, as assistant director of ONE. Smith made each one of his staff accountable for their own projects. Although Langer stayed only one year at CIA, he personally led the reform of its national intelligence estimate project.

Kent's influence on that project may have been slow to manifest itself, but it was a lasting one. As a historian, Kent saw his task as concentrating on source selection and evaluation. He was acutely aware that CIA's remit took on a role of literally global proportions: there was no part of the world now where US interests weren't invested. While the Library of Congress, the largest library on the planet, had been OSS's Research and Analysis's starting point, the technologies of information-gathering that grew after World War II opened up an almost limitless amount of new data. This placed even greater responsibility on the analyst to sort the good from the bad. Kent recognized this very early on in his *Strategic Intelligence for American World Policy*. He saw the research process as moving from an inductive sense of what was needed to a deductive process of refinement and elimination. Kent saw such social science methods as hypothesis making and testing as being the only solution to the analyst's ever-present fear that he might leave that one stone unturned. He also worked hard to voice the probability of threats in a way that clearly communicated urgency to national intelligence estimate readers. Despite seeing the producer–customer relationship as a volatile one, Kent had an existential commitment to providing relevant and justifiable information to policymakers.

In May of 1951 Telford Taylor wrote an update on CIA's progress in *The New York Times*. Titled "To Improve Our Intelligence System," Taylor provided a balanced critique of the Agency. In order to foster a less "impulsive and more enlightened" public perception of intelligence, the mission needed to be better understood. The Agency was making progress, but it would not happen overnight. Before Pearl Harbor, intelligence was "in a state of woeful neglect": to this day, military intelligence still had room for improvement, and diplomatic intelligence was limited; State needed to adopt an "intelligence-mindedness" across all levels of the organization. General Smith's appointment had brought many capable men back to Washington, including "prominent academicians such as William Langer, Raymond Sontag, Sherman Kent, Neal [*sic*] Millikan, Calvin B. Hoover and numerous other highly competent men with intelligence experience."[13]

CIA historian John Ranelagh says, "The achievement of Langer and Smith in reorganizing the CIA's analytical and estimating procedures was one of the most important in the agency's history."[14] Bruce Berkowitz and Allen Goodman credit Langer and Kent, with the institutionalization of a legitimatizing analytical process. "The organization of the analysis components of the intelligence community reflect many of the beliefs of individuals such as William Langer and Sherman Kent, who were largely responsible for their development."[15] This included the embedding of the new social science processes into training programs and "institutional memory" initiatives like the in-house journal *Studies in Intelligence*, and through theory-and-practice committees like the Intelligence Research Program. Their achievement became the standard for the next thirty or more years. Harold P. Ford, who himself contributed to the discipline with his 1993 book *Estimative Intelligence*, claimed in its introduction that "our present national estimating system was basically formed at that time, the autumn of 1950. It has since been altered and improved in detail, but remained substantially unchanged to this day."[16]

The legacy of Max Millikan and his one year at CIA setting up ORR is even more keenly demonstrated. New analytical processes like the building-block model developed at ORR became a staple formula for CIA, either as the preferred tool or, much later, as a point of comparison with more up-to-date methods. Lyman Kirkpatrick says ORR's methodology proved correct in 1964 when Khrushchev was boasting about the success of the Soviet economy and how it would soon overtake US production. In response CIA made its research public. "There was initial reluctance," says Kirkpatrick, "to accept the report as accurate. Partly goaded by the press seeking stories, economists in England and the United States attacked various parts of the report as erroneous. The Russians, of course, denounced all of it. Yet within a year it had been accepted by Western economists as being authoritative and many of those who had originally denounced it, had acknowledged their error."[17] CIA's skill at assessing Soviet economic power grew in the years after the 1950–53 reforms. Kudrov believes "it is clear that the most reliable and realistic rates of Soviet economic growth calculations were made in 1970–1980s by CIA. . . . [It] became the principal source for western estimates of Soviet GNP for all post-war period till 1990."[18] Writing in 1986, one of the originators of economic Sovietology, Abram Bergson, believed the US government, and particularly CIA, had done the job of collecting and calculating Soviet statistics so well that "there is little need for academics to trouble themselves with it any longer."[19]

By the 1980s there were four complementary models of assessing the Soviet economy's strength.[20] CIA was still focusing on Soviet capabilities: how its economy was in a stronger or weaker position vis-à-vis its Western counterparts. At a conference organized by RAND in late 1984 to compare the four models, Millikan's building-block theory was indirectly criticized. Soviet accounting methods were following Marxian economic concepts, it was argued, and the idea that the two systems were "mirror images" of each other might be the wrong way to see things. James Steiner of CIA admitted that "if we are trying to predict what the Soviets are going to do, it does make sense to look at the type of data they might be looking at."[21] Yet Steiner admitted CIA was still using the concept of the building-block method for defense expenditure, primarily to keep an eye on the more sophisticated models.[22]

Kent oversaw the transition of academic recruits into peacetime strategic intelligence analysts. He became more than just a founding father of strategic intelligence; he was a guardian of its principles. A 2009 article in *Studies in Intelligence* said Kent's intellectual genetics ran deep within CIA: "The Kent legacy has survived because his approach to intelligence analysis served the United States extremely well for a long time."[23] Perhaps no one understood the limitations of social science methods better than he, but no one had thought more deeply about how social science could be adapted into a strategic intelligence methodology either. His writings gave CIA analysts a warts-and-all-but-indispensable guide to the essential elements of their craft. In a 1982 letter to economist George Grossman at Berkeley, then-DCI Robert Gates wrote, "We

FIGURE C.1. Kent (center) at a CIA-Republic of Korea briefing, 1959. *SKP*

seek (and have) intelligence professionals who consider themselves analysts first rather than econometricians, political scientists or academicians."[24] It was a tribute to Kent that CIA analysts had made the leap into a new, less cocksure frame of mind.

While it is inarguable that, as director of central intelligence, Smith railroaded through the necessary organizational changes at CIA, it is not so easy to see him as instrumental in the improved analytical processes that dramatically reduced the criticisms made of CIA's strategic intelligence product. He did hire Langer and perhaps took on board John Magruder's view that social science was a necessary instrument of peacetime strategic intelligence. Smith's prestige and clout were integral factors in creating the environment that could let Langer, Kent, and Millikan do their work, and without his leadership their efforts may have failed. Yet just six months before Smith arrived, CIA's national estimates product was in a crisis. As we see from the dissents against ORE-91 50 "Estimate of the Effects of the Soviet Possession of the Atomic Bomb upon the Security of the US," CIA's reports were creating major outrage from State, G-2, A-2, and DNI—to the extent that ORE-91 was accused of being "dangerous as an intelligence basis for national policy."[25] Could Smith then have steered the product away from such opprobrium without the skills of the intel intellectuals? That seems unlikely. Smith represented the kind of leader that the Executive and Congress felt they needed to push the reforms through: a very senior military man who could exercise command over the warring factions of the Intelligence Advisory Committee. Yet, if that is what was needed, then to some extent any senior military man could have performed that function. It was his hiring of Langer and Kent (and, indirectly, of Millikan) and the NIEs that they in turn created processes for that made the most difference, and that brought CIA out of its long struggle for a place in the national security hierarchy.

Notes

Epigraph: Pettee, *The Future of American Secret Intelligence*, 96, 98.

1. US Congress, "Ninety-Fourth Congress, Second Session," 11.
2. Jackson and Claussen, *Organizational History of the Central Intelligence Agency*, 2:2.
3. Quoted in Weber, *Spymasters*, 117.
4. "The White House Washington, Dear Bedell, January 16, 1953," CIA-RDP80B016 76R003200180002-8, CIA, CREST Archive.
5. Jackson and Claussen, *Organizational History of the Central Intelligence Agency*, 2:65.
6. Jackson and Claussen, 2:67.
7. Kent and Thacher, *Reminiscences of a Varied Life*, 261.
8. Kent and Thacher, 273.
9. Montague, *General Walter Bedell Smith*, 147.
10. Montague, 82.
11. Kent and Thacher, *Reminiscences of a Varied Life*, 261.
12. Montague, *General Walter Bedell Smith*, 145–48.
13. Telford Taylor, "To Improve Our Intelligence System; The 'Silent Service' Needs Continued Support and a Chance to Grow Without Undue Scrutiny. To Improve Our Intelligence," *New York Times*, May 27, 1951.
14. Ranelagh, *The Agency*, 192.
15. Berkowitz and Goodman, *Strategic Intelligence*, 111.
16. Ford, *Estimative Intelligence*, 8.
17. Kirkpatrick, *The Real CIA*, 115–16.
18. Kudrov, "American Sovietology and the Soviet Economy."
19. Bergson, "Recollections and Reflections of a Comparativist," 65.
20. Hildebrandt, *RAND Conference on Models of the Soviet Economy*, 17.
21. Quoted in Hildebrandt, 17.
22. Hildebrandt, 50.
23. Olcott, *Revisiting the Legacy*, 2009.
24. Letter to Dr. Gregory Grossman from Robert M. Gates, February 16, 1982, CIA-RDP83M00914R001800040001-2, CIA, CREST Archive.
25. ORE 91-50 "Estimate of the Effects of the Soviet Possession of the Atomic Bomb upon the Security of the US," April 6, 1950, pp. 28–36, 263-a1-22-ORE-58-48, NARA.

Appendix

National Intelligence Estimate: Probable Soviet Courses of Action to Mid-1952

DISSEMINATION NOTICE

1. This copy of this publication is for the information and use of the recipient designated on the front cover and of individuals under the jurisdiction of the recipient's office who require the information for the performance of their official duties. Further dissemination elsewhere in the department to other offices which require the information for the performance of official duties may be authorized by the following:

  a. Special Assistant to the Secretary of State for Intelligence, for the Department of State

  b. Assistant Chief of Staff, G-2, for the Department of the Army

  c. Director of Naval Intelligence, for the Department of the Navy

  d. Director of Intelligence, USAF, for the Department of the Air Force

  e. Director of Intelligence, AEC, for the Atomic Energy Commission

  f. Deputy Director for Intelligence, Joint Staff, for the Joint Staff

  g. Assistant Director for Collection and Dissemination, CIA, for any other Department or Agency

2. This copy may be either retained or destroyed by burning in accordance with applicable security regulations, or returned to the Central Intelligence Agency by arrangement with the Office of Collection and Dissemination, CIA.

DISTRIBUTION (NIE Series):
Office of the President
National Security Council
National Security Resources Board
Department of State
Office of Secretary of Defense
Department of the Army
Department of the Navy
Department of the Air Force
Atomic Energy Commission
Joint Chiefs of Staff
Federal Bureau of Investigation
Research and Development Board
Munitions Board

NATIONAL INTELLIGENCE ESTIMATE

PROBABLE SOVIET COURSES OF ACTION TO MID-1952

NIE-25

This document has been
approved for release through
the HISTORICAL REVIEW PROGRAM of
the Central Intelligence Agency.

Date 6/24/93

HRP 93-1

The intelligence organizations of the Department of State,
the Army, the Navy, the Air Force, and the Joint Staff
participated in the preparation of this estimate. All members of the Intelligence Advisory Committee concurred in
this estimate, except for the reservation of the Director of
Naval Intelligence noted on page 5.

TOP SECRET

CONTENTS

TOP SECRET

PROBABLE SOVIET COURSES OF ACTION TO MID-1952

THE PROBLEM

To estimate probable Soviet courses of action to mid-1952 with particular reference to the probability of direct hostilities between the US and the USSR.

ESTIMATE

I. Soviet Objectives

1. We believe that the ultimate Soviet objective is a Communist world dominated by the USSR and that the Kremlin believes its vital interests can be assured over the long run only by the elimination of all governments it cannot control. This objective probably reflects a Kremlin conviction that peaceful coexistence of the USSR and its empire on the one hand, and the US and its allies on the other, is impossible and that an armed conflict between them is eventually inevitable.

2. The principal immediate Soviet objectives evidently are:

a. To divide the West;

b. To prevent Western, West German, and Japanese rearmament;

c. To prevent implementation of the US overseas-bases policy.

3. We believe the USSR, in the pursuit of its objectives, will during the period of this estimate:

a. Seek to maintain an advanced state of war-readiness and offset any increase in the capabilities of the US and its allies;

b. Seek to prevent the development of any threat to the vital interests of the USSR or to Soviet control of the Satellites;

c. Seek to expand the territorial limits of the Soviet orbit;

d. Seek to undermine and secure control of governments not yet under Soviet domination;

e. Seek to force countries of the free world to adopt a policy of neutrality in the East-West struggle and to deny their resources, including strategic sites, to the US and its allies.

II. Military Considerations Underlying Soviet Action

4. We estimate that the armed forces of the USSR have the capability of overrunning continental Europe and the Near and Middle East (except India and Pakistan) within a relatively short period.

5. The USSR does not now have and would be unlikely to secure adequate naval forces or sufficient shipping to permit it to mount a successful invasion of the Western Hemisphere, even if it should seize the Eurasian continent and the UK.

6. The Soviet Air Force is capable of providing adequate tactical support of all ground campaigns which the USSR might launch against continental Europe and the Near and Middle East (except India and Pakistan), and simultaneously of attempting a strategic air offensive against the United Kingdom and the North American continent.

7. It is impossible to estimate with any accuracy the Kremlin's conclusion with regard to the relative effectiveness of Soviet and US atomic warfare capabilities or with regard to the relative importance of atomic and conventional weapons in determining the issue of a future general war. We believe it probable,

however, that uncertainty concerning relative atomic warfare capabilities and concerning the effectiveness of atomic weapons in determining the issue of a general war will be a major, though not necessarily a decisive, deterrent to the Kremlin in making a decision to initiate or deliberately provoke a general war with the US during the period of this estimate.

8. The USSR is capable of employing sabotage against a variety of targets and of employing clandestine methods to attack the US and its allies with atomic, biological, and chemical weapons. We believe, however, that those capabilities would be exercised on an appreciable scale only in conjunction with or immediately preceding general military operations and that they would not be a decisive factor in any Soviet decision to initiate a general war.

III. Possible Soviet Courses of Action Without Intent to Precipitate or Incur Serious Risk of General War

9. While in Soviet theory and practice war is an acceptable, and on occasion necessary, instrument for attaining Communist objectives, the Kremlin presumably prefers if possible to attain its objectives by courses of 'action short of resort to general war. The Kremlin probably estimates that opportunities exist for making limited progress toward both its immediate and long-run objectives, at least during the period of this estimate, without provoking general war, because of:

a. The deterrent effect of the estimated Communist capability to overrun most of Eurasia at will;

b. The deterrent effect of Soviet capabilities for atomic warfare;

c. The divergent interests of the Western Powers; and

d. The general reluctance of the Western Powers to become involved in general war.

10. In discussing courses of action short of general war, it is necessary for clarity to examine each separately. Soviety policy envisages various courses of action—political warfare, limited Satellite or Soviet armed aggression, and even general war. While, therefore,

separation for purposes of exposition is essential, the inseparable connection of all possible courses of action must be kept in mind.

A. Political Warfare

11. The Kremlin may consider the prospects of success by political warfare* sufficiently favorable to make other courses of action unnecessary. For example, with the immediate objective of dividing the Western Powers, undermining US mobilization, obstructing the NATO program and frustrating prospective German and Japanse rearmament and with the ultimate objective of paralyzing opposition to Communism, the Kremlin may fraudulently propose peaceful coexistence of the two systems and may encourage the West to hope for a settlement of outstanding issues by mutual agreement. In the vital area of Western Europe the Kremlin will almost certainly continue to press its "peace" campaign, to exploit the fear of war, to intimidate by display of force, to raise hopes of German unification, and to use the Communist Parties of France and Italy in an attempt to confound the political situation and obstruct effective government. Wherever elsewhere in the world non-Communist governments are weak, as in Iran, Indochina, and Burma, the Kremlin will almost certainly seek to strengthen the Communist position and, if favorable situations develop, will support Communist coups.

B. Employment of Chinese Communist Forces

12. The Kremlin might, during the period of this estimate, attempt to achieve some of its objectives by inducing the Chinese Communists to engage in additional military operations. Such operations would involve risk of general war between the US and the USSR, but the Kremlin might estimate that such operations could be so conducted that general war would not be precipitated.

---

* Political warfare, as here used, includes all manner of political and economic pressure, diplomatic action in the UN and elsewhere, propaganda and front activities, Communist Party and Communist-controlled trade union activities, support of all kinds of revolutionary movements, and psychological warfare.

13. *Indochina and Burma.* In particular, the Kremlin may estimate that a Chinese Communist invasion of Indochina or Burma would not involve a serious risk of general war and that such an invasion would facilitate a Communist advance throughout Southeast Asia and the consequent denial of the resources of that area to the free world. The Chinese Communists almost certainly have the capability for conquering Burma. We consider an invasion of Burma possible, but we do not believe it probable during the period of this estimate. The Chinese Communists are now capable of overrunning virtually all of northern Indochina, and we consider an invasion of Indochina possible at any time.

14. *Taiwan.* The Kremlin probably estimates that the Chinese Communists alone do not have the capabilities for a successful invasion of Taiwan so long as the US policy of employing US fleet units for the defense of Taiwan remains unchanged. Under existing circumstances, the Kremlin must realize that active Soviet participation in an attack on Taiwan would substantially increase the risk of general war without necessarily ensuring the success of the operation. We therefore believe it unlikely that the USSR, in prevailing circumstances, would either encourage or participate in a Chinese Communist attack on Taiwan.

15. *Hong Kong and Macao.* Chinese Communist seizure of Hong Kong and Macao probably would be militarily easy, but would presently entail political and economic disadvantages for the Communists. If present conditions continue, we believe it unlikely that forceful seizure of these ports will take place during the period of this estimate.

C. Employment of European Satellite Forces

16. The Kremlin might, during the period here considered, attempt to achieve some of its objectives through local military operations by European Satellite forces. However, the Kremlin probably estimates that, because of the more direct impact on NATO interests, such operations would involve greater risk of general war between the US and the USSR than similar local operations by Chinese Communist forces.

17. *Yugoslavia.* The Kremlin undoubtedly attaches great importance to regaining control of Yugoslavia. Yugoslavia is strategically important and is gradually developing close ties with the NATO powers. Titoism continues to be a potential menace to Soviet domination over the Satellites and over the world Communist movement. Satellite capabilities for launching an attack on Yugoslavia are steadily increasing. It is possible that the Kremlin regards the Yugoslav issue as of such importance as to warrant acceptance of the risks involved in a Satellite attack. However, in view of the increasing Western support of Yugoslavia, it is more probable that the Kremlin estimates that a Satellite attack would involve not only serious risk of war between the US or UN and the Satellites, but also the danger that such a conflict would develop into a general war between the US and the USSR. On balance, we believe a Satellite attack on Yugoslavia during the period of this estimate is possible, but not probable.

18. *Greece and Turkey.* Satellite capabilities for attack on Greece and particularly on Turkey are too limited for conquest of those countries. Furthermore, the Kremlin almost certainly realizes that an operation against either of these countries would probably entail US or UN intervention with the possibility of general war developing. We believe, therefore, that the USSR is unlikely to launch a Satellite attack on either Greece or Turkey during the period of this estimate.

19. *Berlin, West Germany, and Austria.* Satellite capabilities for military action against Allied forces in Berlin, West Germany, or Austria will probably remain so limited during the period here considered and the risk of general war involved in such action would be so great that the USSR is unlikely to launch a Satellite attack during this period.

D. Employment of Soviet Forces

20. The Kremlin must realize that commitment of major Soviet forces in any European Satellite or Chinese Communist operation would greatly increase the risk of general war between the US and the USSR. Wherever possible, therefore, the USSR would rely upon European Satellite or Chinese Communist

forces for carrying out military operations against non-Communist areas. It undoubtedly would provide such forces with technical and logistical aid and might participate in rear area operations; if it considered the risk acceptable, it might even provide "volunteer" Soviet forces in the forward areas. Open Soviet military intervention, however, would be unlikely excepting in areas considered of great importance to the USSR and where Satellite forces are either unavailable or incapable of successful action.

21. *Greece and Turkey.* The Kremlin probably aims to secure control of Greece and Turkey in order to eliminate bases that could be used for attack on the Soviet orbit and at the same time to secure bases from which the position of the free world in the Near East might be threatened. However, the available Satellite forces alone are probably not capable of conquering Greece and certainly not capable of conquering Turkey. Therefore, such operations could be accomplished only with the active participation of Soviet forces. The Kremlin probably estimates that the US and UN almost certainly would come to the support of Greece and Turkey and that in those circumstances a general war between the US and the USSR would probably result. An attack on Greece or Turkey is therefore unlikely during the period of this estimate.

22. *Iran.* Of the areas where only Soviet forces are available for immediate employment, Iran is unstable and important. Soviet control of Iran would eliminate a potential base for hostile action against the USSR, would deprive the West of a vast oil supply, and would facilitate the subversion or conquest of the Near and Middle East. However, the Kremlin probably estimates that the political and economic instability and the widespread anti-British feeling offer good prospects of increasing Communist influence and eventually of establishing Communist control without direct Soviet intervention. Under these circumstances we believe it unlikely that the Kremlin would consider it necessary to incur the risk of war with the Western Powers involved in Soviet military intervention. But if the British should use military force in their dispute with Iran, the Kremlin might then invoke the 1921 treaty and occupy at least northern Iran, estimating that it could do so with relatively little risk of general war.

E. Employment of Soviet Forces Against US Forces

23. The Kremlin almost certainly estimates that overt and recognized commitment of Soviet forces against US forces in any area would involve not only a local war with the US, in which the US might well use atomic weapons, but also the strong probability of general war with the US, including a US strategic atomic attack on the USSR. Unless, therefore, the Kremlin had decided to accept general war with the US, we believe a Soviet attack on West Germany, Berlin, Austria, or Japan would be most unlikely during the period of this estimate.

24. If the Korean conflict continues or is renewed after a cease fire, the Kremlin will probably continue to aid the Communists in ways which the Kremlin estimates would not involve serious danger of a break between the USSR and US/UN. If, however, the Communist forces in Korea were threatened with decisive defeat, the Kremlin would probably intensify its aid. This aid might well include the introduction of "volunteer" forces. It might even include the employment of Soviet forces to such an extent that a *de facto* local war between the US/UN and the USSR would exist. At every stage the Kremlin will probably endeavor to keep open the possibility of ending the Korean conflict by political negotiation if the global interests of the USSR would be served by disengagement in Korea.

IV. Possibility of General War

25 Consideration of the degree of probability of Soviet military action in specific areas must be related to over-all Soviet strategy and policy. If the Kremlin should decide to precipitate or to accept general war, it might launch an attack in any area at any time and in any form as a prelude to such general war. Soviet forces are in an advanced state of war-readiness and could initiate general war at any time with little or no warning. The danger of general war exists now and will continue to

exist so long as the USSR is in a position to take action which threatens, wholly or in part, the vital interests of the Western Powers.

26. We believe that the most important immediate objectives of the Kremlin are to divide the West and to halt Western, West German, and Japanese rearmament. If the Kremlin should fail to make sufficient progress toward that end by methods short of general war and if in addition it should become convinced that its superiority in conventional forces were about to be offset (whether through NATO and West German or Japanese rearmament or through Western advances in unconventional armaments), we believe the Kremlin would consider the advisability of precipitating general war. We believe it unlikely that the Kremlin would adopt this course of action so long as Western rearmament appeared to it only as a transitory impediment to further Soviet and Satellite expansion. On the other hand, if the Kremlin were to conclude that this rearmament threatened the vital interests of the USSR, we believe: (a) if it estimated that the USSR had sufficient means to wage war successfully and that the delay would tip the scales of power irretrievably against the USSR, the Kremlin would precipitate general war; but (b) if it estimated it did not have sufficient means to wage war successfully, the Kremlin would modify its policy and attempt to relax international tension until such time as the Western Powers relaxed their vigilance or other factors favorable to the USSR supervened. It is possible, however, that the USSR might precipitate war even under adverse circumstances if it considered the threat to its vital interests sufficiently real and immediate.

27. We do not believe that during the period of this estimate the Kremlin is likely to conclude that US, NATO, West German, and Japanese rearmament constitutes an immediate threat to the vital interests of the USSR. It is possible, however, that the Kremlin may at any time conclude that the Western rearmament program constitutes an eventual but already unacceptable threat to its vital interests,

or that the Kremlin may at any time misinterpret Western defensive measures as indicating an imminent attack on the USSR.

28. There is, moreover, a serious possibility of general war developing within the period of this estimate from an action or series of actions not intended to produce that result. The Kremlin might, for example, miscalculate the degree of risk involved in a particular action or underestimate the cumulative effect of several actions. Or, it might regard a particular action as so necessary or so advantageous as to warrant assuming even a serious risk of general war.

29. We recognize the desirability and the importance of concluding this estimate with a simple and direct statement of the likelihood or unlikelihood that the Kremlin will deliberately precipitate or provoke general war between the US and the USSR during the period here covered. Existing intelligence does not enable us to make such a precise forecast. The USSR has the capability to launch general war and may decide to precipitate general war. Moreover, the international situation is so tense that at any time some issue might develop to a point beyond control.*

---

* It is the view of the Director of Naval Intelligence, with respect to Section IV above, that the final paragraph of this estimate should read as follows:

"It is recognized that precise information on enemy intentions is rarely available and that enemy counteraction cannot be accurately predicted. However, all aspects of the Soviet problem considered, we believe it unlikely that the USSR will deliberately choose to precipitate or undergo hazards of general war during the period covered by this estimate. Although the possibility of war by miscalculation cannot be discounted during periods of high international tension, we believe that in pursuing various courses of action short of war with the US, the USSR will seek to increase its power and damage the interests of the US whenever and wherever feasible, but will at every turn attempt to exploit each course of action with such caution as to avoid direct military aggression against the vital interests of the United States."

Bibliography

Archival Collections

Chapman University Library, Leatherby Libraries, Orange California
Theodore Babbitt Second World War Correspondence
CIA, CREST Archive, Washington, DC
Dwight D. Eisenhower Library, Abilene, Kansas
Harry S. Truman Library and Museum, Independence, Missouri
John F. Kennedy Presidential Library & Museum, Boston, Massachusetts
Max Millikan Personal Papers
Massachusetts Institute of Technology, Cambridge, Massachusetts
Max F. Millikan Papers
National Archives, Kew, United Kingdom
National Archives and Records Administration (NARA), College Park, Maryland
Williams College Archives, Williamstown, Massachusetts
Yale University, Beinecke Rare Book and Manuscript Library, New Haven, Connecticut
Sherman Kent Papers (MS 854), Manuscripts and Archives
Walter L. Pforzheimer Papers, General Collection.

Primary Sources

Best, Richard A., and Herbert Andrew Boerstling. *Staff Study Permanent Select Committee on Intelligence House of Representatives One Hundred Fourth Congress. IC21: The Intelligence Community in the 21st Century. Appendix C. CRS Report: Proposals for Intelligence Reorganization 1949–1996*. Permanent Select Committee on Intelligence Staff Study, House of Representatives, 104th Congress, February 28, 1996.
CIA. *USSR: Measures of Economic Growth and Development, 1950–80*. For the Joint Economic Committee, 97th Congress, 2nd session. US Government Printing Office, December 8, 1982.
Dulles, Allen, William Jackson, and Mathias Correa. *The Central Intelligence Agency and National Organization for Intelligence: A Report to the National Security Council*. Central Intelligence Agency, 1949.
Kent, Sherman. "A Crucial Estimate Relived." *Studies in Intelligence* 8, no. 4 (1964).
Memorandum from Theodore Babbitt, Ludwell Montague, and Forrest Van Slyck of the Office of Research and Evaluation of the Central Intelligence Agency to the Deputy Director of Central Intelligence (Jackson) Washington, October 10, 1950. In *The Intelligence Community: 1950–55; Foreign Relations of the United States, 1950–1955*, ed.

Douglas Keene, Mark Warner, and Edward C. Keefer, 41–44. Washington, DC: Government Printing Office, 1992. https://2001-2009.state.gov/documents/organization/96785.pdf.

National Security Council. National Security Council Intelligence Directive No. 3. "Coordination of Intelligence Production," January 13, 1948. https://irp.fas.org/offdocs/nscid03.htm.

US Congress. "Hearings on Science Legislation (S.1297 and Related Bills): Hearings Before a Subcommittee of the Committee on Military Affairs." United States Senate, Seventy-Ninth Congress, First Session, Pursuant to S. Res. 107 (78th Congress) and S. Res. 146 (79th Congress) Authorizing a Study of the Possibilities of Better Mobilizing the National Resources of the United States, Vols. 1–4. US Government Printing Office, 1945.

US Congress. "National Defense Establishment (Unification of the Armed Services): Hearings of the Committee of the Senate Armed Forces Services." Eightieth Congress, First Session, on S.758. Part 3. April 30, May 2, 6, 7, 9, 1947. US Government Printing Office, 1947.

US Congress. "Ninety-Fourth Congress. Second Session. Senate: Elect Committee to Discover Government Operations with Respect to Intelligence Activities. Final Report: Book IV: Detailed Staff Reports on Foreign and Military Intelligence." US Government Printing Office, 1976.

US Congress. "Supplementary Detailed Staff Reports on Foreign and Military Intelligence." Book IV: "Final Report of the Select Committee to Study Government Operations with Respect to Intelligence Activities." United States Senate. Report No. 94-755. US Government Printing Office, 1976.

US Congress. "Third Supplemental Appropriation Bill for 1951: Hearings." 82d Congress, 1st Session, Part 2. US Government Printing Office, 1951.

US Congress, House Select Committee on Intelligence. "US Intelligence Agencies and Activities: Hearings Before the Select Committee on Intelligence, US House of Representatives, Ninety-Fourth Congress, First Session. Statement of James C. Graham, Former CIA Employee." US Government Printing Office, 1976.

US Naval History and Heritage Command. "Overview of The Pearl Harbor Attack, 7 December 1941," n.d. Accessed July 24, 2024. https://www.history.navy.mil/content/history/nhhc/research/library/online-reading-room/title-list-alphabetically/p/the-pearl-harbor-attack-7-december-1941.html.

US State Department, Office of the Historian. Enclosure. Memorandum by Stephen Penrose. Washington, January 2, 1948. https://history.state.gov/historicaldocuments/frus1945-50Intel/d338.

US State Department, Office of the Historian. *Foreign Relations of the United States: 1952–1954.* Vol. 8, *Eastern Europe, Soviet Union, Eastern Mediterranean* (US Government Printing Office, 1988). https://history.state.gov/historicaldocuments/frus1952-54v08.

US State Department, Office of the Historian. Letter from the Director of Central Intelligence (Hillenkoetter) to the Chairman of the Senate Armed Services Committee (Gurney), June 3, 1947, in *Foreign Relations of the United States: 1945–1950: Emergence of the Intelligence Establishment.* Central Intelligence Agency, Historical Files, HS/HC-805, Item 10. Secret. https://history.state.gov/historicaldocuments/frus1945-50Intel/d217.

US State Department, Office of the Historian. Letter from the Secretary of Defense's Special Assistant (McNeil) to Mathias F. Correa. February 2, 1948. https://history .state.gov/historicaldocuments/frus1945-50Intel/d338.

US State Department, Office of the Historian. Letter from Sherman Kent to Director of Central Intelligence Hillenkoetter, February 9, 1948. In *Foreign Relations of the United States, 1945–1950: Emergence of the Intelligence Establishment*. Central Intelligence Agency Historical Files, HS/HC–808, Item 4. Secret. https://history .state.gov/historicaldocuments/frus1945-50Intel/d339.

US State Department, Office of the Historian. Memorandum from Secretary of Defense Marshall to Director of Central Intelligence Smith, Washington, November 27, 1950. In *Foreign Relations of the United States: The Intelligence Community, 1950–1985*, ed. Douglas Keene and Michael Warner, 56. https://history.state.gov /historicaldocuments/frus1950-55Intel.

US State Department, Office of the Historian. Note from the Executive Secretary of the National Security Council (Lay) to the National Security Council: Scope and Pace of Covert Operations, NSC-10/5, October 23, 1951. https://history.state.gov /historicaldocuments/frus1950-55Intel/d90.

Secondary Sources

Adair, Bianca. "The Quiet Warrior: Rear Admiral Sidney Souers and the Emergence of CIA's Covert Action Authority." *Studies in Intelligence* 65, no. 2 (Extracts, June 2021).

Alacevich, Michele. *Paul Rosenstein-Rodan and the Birth of Development Economics*. CHOPE Working Paper, No. 2020-04. Duke University, Center for the History of Political Economy, 2020.

Aldous, Richard. *Schlesinger: The Imperial Historian*. Norton, 2017.

Andrew, Christopher. *For the President's Eyes Only. Secret Intelligence and American Presidents from Washington to Bush*. Harper Perennial, 1995.

Baber, Bernard. "Theory and Fact in the Work of Talcott Parsons." In *The Nationalization of the Social Sciences*, ed. Samuel Z. Klausner and Victor M. Lidz. University of Pennsylvania Press, 1986.

Barrett, David M. *The CIA and Congress: The Untold Story from Truman to Kennedy*. University of Kansas, 2005.

Barrett, David M. "Glimpses of a Hidden History: Sen. Richard Russell, Congress, and Oversight of the CIA." *International Journal of Intelligence and CounterIntelligence* 11, no. 3 (1998): 271–98.

Becker, Abraham. *CIA Estimates of Soviet Military Expenditure*. RAND, 1980.

Berghahn, Volker R. *America and the Intellectual Cold Wars in Europe*. Princeton University Press, 2002.

Bergson, Abram. "Recollections and Reflections of a Comparativist." In *Eminent Economists: Their Life Philosophies*, ed. Michael Szenberg. Cambridge University Press, 1992.

Bergson, Abram, ed. *Soviet Economic Growth: Conditions and Perspectives*. Row, Peterson, 1953.

Bergson, Abram. "Soviet National Income in 1937. Part 1. National Economic Accounts in Current Rubles." *Quarterly Journal of Economics* 64, no. 2 (1950): 208–41.

Bergson, Abram. "Soviet National Income in 1937. Part 2. Ruble Prices and the Valuation Problem." *Quarterly Journal of Economics* 64, no. 3 (August 1950): 408–41.

Bergson, Abram. *Soviet National Income in 1937.* Columbia University Press, 1950.

Bergson, Abram. "Wassily Leontief, 5 August 1906–5 February 1999." *Proceedings of the American Philosophical Society* 144, no. 4 (December 2000): 465–68.

Bergson, Abram, and Hans Heymann Jr. *Soviet National Income and Product, 1940–1948.* Columbia University Press, 1954.

Bergson, Abram, Alexander Erlich, Herbert S. Levine, G. Warren Nutter, Stanislaw Wellisz, and Henry L. Roberts. "Soviet Economic Performance and Reform: Some Problems of Analysis and Prognosis." *Slavic Review* 25, no. 2 (1966): 222–46.

Berkowitz, Bruce D., and Allen E. Goodman. *Strategic Intelligence for American National Security.* Princeton University Press, 1989.

Bessner, Daniel. *Democracy in Exile: Hans Speier and the Rise of the Defense Intellectual.* Cornell University Press. 2018.

Bissell, Richard. *Reflections of a Cold War Warrior: From Yalta to the Bay of Pigs.* Yale University Press, 1996.

Blake, Robert Wallace. *From Belleau Wood to Bougainville: The Oral History of Major General Robert Blake USMC and the Travel Journal of Rosselet Wallace Blake.* AuthorHouse, 2004.

Bohlen, Charles. *Witness to History, 1929–1969.* Norton, 1973.

Brodie, Janet Farrell. "Learning Secrecy in the Early Cold War: The RAND Corporation." *Diplomatic History* 35, no. 4 (2011): 643–70.

Brzeski, Andrzej, and Gregory Grossman. "Jerzy Feliks Karcz 1921–1970." *Slavic Review* 30, no. 1 (1971).

Byrnes, Robert F. "Harvard, Columbia and the CIA: My Training in Russian Studies." *Russian History / Histoire Russo* 15, no. 1 (1988): 93–114.

Carr, Edward Hallett. *What Is History?* Penguin, 1964.

Central Intelligence Agency, James S. Lay Jr., and Robert H. Johnson. *Organizational History of the National Security Council During Truman and Eisenhower Administrations.* Central Intelligence Agency, 1960.

Chamberlain, Lawrence. "Review: [Untitled] Reviewed Work: *Strategic Intelligence for American World Policy* by Sherman Kent. Review by: Lawrence H. Chamberlain." *Political Science Quarterly* 64, no. 3 (1949): 431–32.

Clifford, Clark. *Counsel to the President: A Memoir,* with Richard Holbrooke. Random House, 1991.

Cline, Ray S. *The CIA Under Reagan, Bush and Casey: The Evolution of the Agency from Roosevelt to Reagan.* Acropolis Books, 1981.

Cline, Ray S. *Secrets, Spies and Scholars: Blueprint of the Essential CIA.* Acropolis Books, 1976.

Coogan, T. P. Review of *America's Strategic Blunders: Intelligence Analysis and National Security Policy, 1936–1991,* by Willard C. Matthias. *Journal of Military History* 66, no. 1 (2002): 275–76.

Crosswell, D.K.R. *Beetle: The Life of General Walter Bedell Smith.* University of Kentucky Press, 2010.

Darling, Arthur B. *The Central Intelligence Agency: An Instrument of Government to 1950,* with introductions by Bruce D. Berkowitz and Allen E. Goodman. University of Pennsylvania Press, 1990.

Davis, Jack. "The Kent-Kendall Debate of 1949." *Studies in Intelligence* 36, no. 5 (1992): 91–103.

Davis, Jack. *Sherman Kent and the Profession of Intelligence Analysis.* The Sherman Kent Center for Intelligence Analysis, Occasional Papers, vol. 1, no. 5. Central Intelligence Agency, 2002. https://www.cia.gov/resources/csi/static/Kent-Profession-Intel-Analysis.pdf.

de Silva, Peer. *Sub Rosa: The CIA and Uses of Intelligence.* New York Times Books, 1978.

Deane, Phyllis. "Measuring Soviet Economic Growth." *Europe-Asia Studies* 14, no. 2 (1962): 132–37.

Desch, Michael. *Cult of the Irrelevant: The Waning Influence of Social Science on National Security.* Princeton University Press. 2019.

Diamond, Sigmund. *Compromised Campus: The Collaboration of Universities with the Intelligence Community.* Oxford University Press, 1992.

Dietzenbacher, Erik, and Michael L. Lahr. *Wassily Leontief and Input–Output Economics.* Cambridge University Press, 2004.

Doob, Leonard. "The Utilization of Social Scientists in the Overseas Branch of the Office of War Information." *American Political Science Review* 41, no. 4 (1947): 649–67.

Douglas, Mary. *How Institutions Think.* Routledge and Kegan Paul, 1987.

Dujmovic, Nicholas. "Fifty Years of Studies in Intelligence." *Studies in Intelligence* 49, no. 4: 1–13.

Durbin, Brent. *The CIA and the Politics of Intelligence Reform.* Cambridge University Press, 2017.

Eisenhower, Dwight D. *The White House Years*, vol. 2: *Waging Peace, 1956–1961*. Doubleday, 1965.

Engerman, David C. *Know Your Enemy: The Rise and Fall of America's Soviet Experts.* Oxford University Press, 2011.

Engerman, David C. "The Price of Success: Economic Sovietology, Development, and the Costs of Interdisciplinarity." *History of Political Economy* 42, Suppl. 1 (December 2010).

Engerman, David C. Review of "*Soviet Defense Spending: A History of CIA Estimates, 1950–1990*, by Noel E. Firth and James H. Noren." *H-Diplo*, April 1999. https://www.h-net.org/reviews/showrev.php?id=2967.

Firth, Noel, and James Noren. *Soviet Defense Spending: A History of CIA Estimates, 1950–1990.* Texas A&M University Press, 1988.

Ford, Harold P. *Estimative Intelligence: The Purposes and Problems of National Intelligence Estimating* (University Press of America and Defense Intelligence College, 1993).

Ford, Harold P. "The US Government's Experience with Intelligence Analysis: Pluses and Minuses." *Intelligence and National Security* 10, no. 4 (1995).

Freedman, Lawrence. *US Intelligence and the Soviet Strategic Threat.* Westview, 1977.

Friedberg, Aaron. *In the Shadow of the Garrison State: America's Anti-Statism and Its Cold War Grand Strategy.* Princeton University Press, 2000.

Gaddis, John Lewis. *Landscape of History: How Historians Map the Past.* Oxford University Press, 2002.

Garraghan, Gilbert J. *A Guide to the Historical Method.* Fordham University Press, 1946.

Garthoff, Raymond L. *Analyzing Soviet Politics and Foreign Policy.* Central Intelligence Agency, 2003.

Garthoff, Raymond L. "Estimating Soviet Military Force Levels: Some Light from the Past." *International Security* 14, no. 4 (1990).

Garthoff, Raymond L. *A Journey Through the Cold War: A Memoir of Containment and Coexistence.* Brookings Institution Press, 2001.

Garthoff, Raymond L. "Soviet Leaders, Soviet Intelligence, and Changing Views of the United States, 1965–91." In *The Image of the Enemy: Intelligence Analysis of Adversaries Since 1945*, ed. Paul Maddrell, 28–67. Georgetown University Press, 2015.

Gerhardt, Uta. *Talcott Parsons: An Intellectual Biography.* Cambridge University Press, 2002.

Gilman, Nils. *Mandarins of the Future: Modernization Theory in Cold War America.* Johns Hopkins Press, 2003.

Gilpin, Robert, and Christopher Wright, eds. *Scientists and National Policy-Making.* Columbia University Press, 1964.

Greenslade, Rush V. "The Many Burdens of Defense in the Soviet Union." Center for the Study of Intelligence. *Studies Archive Indexes* 14, no. 2 (1970). https://www.cia.gov /resources/csi/static/Many-Burdens-of-Defense.pdf.

Greenslade, Rush V. "Rubles vs. Dollars." *Studies in Intelligence* 6, no. 1 (1962): 1–11. https://www.cia.gov/readingroom/docs/CIA-RDP78T03194A000100060001-8.pdf

Gregory, Paul R. "Economic Growth and Structural Change in Czarist Russia and the Soviet Union: A Long-Term Comparison." In *Economic Welfare and the Economics of Soviet Socialism*, ed. Steven Rosefielde, 25–52. Cambridge University Press, 1981.

Grose, Peter. *Continuing the Inquiry: The Council on Foreign Relations from 1921 to 1996.* Council on Foreign Relations, 1996.

Grose, Peter. *Gentleman Spy: The Life of Allen Dulles.* Andre Deutsch, 1995.

Guglielmo, Mark. "The Contribution of Economists to Military Intelligence During World War II." *Journal of Economic History* 68, no. 1 (2008): 109–50.

Haines, Gerald K., and Robert E. Leggett, eds. *Watching the Bear: Essays on CIA's Analysis of the Soviet Union.* Center for the Study of Intelligence, Central Intelligence Agency, 2003.

Hammond, Thomas H. "Intelligence Organizations and the Organization of Intelligence." *International Journal of Intelligence and CounterIntelligence* 23, no. 4 (2010).

Hardt, John. "Abram Bergson and the Development of Soviet Economic Studies." *Problems of Post-Communism* 51, no. 4 (2004).

Hardt, John. "Abram Bergson's Legacy—1914–2003." University of Warwick, n.d. https:// warwick.ac.uk/fac/soc/economics/staff/mharrison/archive/noticeboard/bergson /hardt.pdf.

Haskell, Thomas L. *The Emergence of Professional Social Science: The American Social Science Association and the Nineteenth-Century Crisis of Authority.* University of Illinois Press, 1977.

Helgerson, John. "Truman and Eisenhower: Launching the Process." *Studies in Intelligence* 38, no. 5: 65–77. https://www.cia.gov/resources/csi/static/Truman-and -Eisenhower.pdf.

Helms, Richard, with William Hood. *A Look Over My Shoulder: A Life in the Central Intelligence Agency.* Random House, 2003.

Heuer, Richards J. *Quantitative Approaches to Political Intelligence: The CIA Experience.* Routledge, 2019.

Hildebrandt, Gregory G., ed. *RAND Conference on Models of the Soviet Economy, October 11–12, 1984.* RAND, 1985.

Hilsman, Roger. "Review Essay: On Intelligence." *Armed Forces and Society* 8, no. 1 (1981): 129–43.

Hogan, Michael J. *Cross of Iron: Harry S. Truman and the Foundations of the National Security State.* Cambridge University Press, 2010.

Hoover, Calvin B. *The Economic Life of Soviet Russia.* Macmillan, 1936.

Houghton, Vince. *The Nuclear Spies: America's Atomic Intelligence Operation Against Hitler and Stalin.* Cornell University Press, 2020.

Hughes, H. Stuart. "The Historian and the Social Scientist." *American Historical Review* 66, no. 1 (1960): 20–46.

International Organization Board of Editors. "Millikan, Max Franklin, 1913–1969." *International Organization* 24, no. 1 (1970): iii.

Jackson, George S. *The DCI Miscellaneous Studies: HS MS-3; Office of Reports and Estimates 1946–1951.* Vol. 1 and 2. Central Intelligence Agency, 1954.

Jackson, George S., and Martin P. Claussen. *Organizational History of the Central Intelligence Agency.* 5 Vols. Central Intelligence Agency, 1957.

Johnson, Chalmers. "The CIA and Me." *Bulletin of Concerned Asian Scholars* 29, no. 1 (1997): 34–37.

Jervis, Robert. "Review: America's Strategic Blunders: Intelligence Analysis and National Security Policy, 1936–1991." *Political Science Quarterly* 116, no. 4 (2001): 637–38.

Jervis, Robert. *Why Intelligence Fails: Lessons from the Iranian Revolution and Iraq War.* Cornell University Press, 2010.

Johnson, Loch K. "The Contemporary Presidency: Presidents, Lawmakers, and Spies: Intelligence Accountability in the United States." *Presidential Studies Quarterly* 34, no. 4 (2004): 828–37.

Jones, Frank Leith. *Blowtorch: Robert Komer, Vietnam and American Cold War Strategy.* Naval Institute Press, 2013.

Kaplan, Fred M. *The Wizards of Armageddon.* Stanford University Press, 1991.

Katz, Barry M. *Foreign Intelligence: Research and Analysis in the Office of Strategic Services 1942–45.* Harvard University Press, 1989.

Keane, Douglas, and Michael Warner. *Foreign Relations of the United States: The Intelligence Community, 1950–1955.* US Government Printing Office, 2007.

Kendall, Willmoore. "The Function of Intelligence." *World Politics* 1, no. 4 (1947): 542–52.

Kennan, George. *Memoirs: 1925–1950.* Atlantic Monthly Press / Little, Brown, 1967.

Kent, Sherman. "A Crucial Estimate Relived." In *Sherman Kent and the Board of National Estimates: Collected Essays,* ed. Donald P. Steury, 173–88. Center for the Study of Intelligence, Central Intelligence Agency, 1994.

Kent, Sherman. "Estimates and Influence" (1968). In *Sherman Kent and the Board of National Estimates: Collected Essays,* ed. Donald P. Steury, 33–42. Center for the Study of Intelligence, Central Intelligence Agency, 1994.

Kent, Sherman. "The First Year of the Office of National Estimates: The Directorship of William Langer" (1970). In *Sherman Kent and the Board of National Estimates: Collected Essays,* ed. Donald P. Steury, 143–56. Center for the Study of Intelligence, Central Intelligence Agency, 1994.

Kent, Sherman. "The Law and Custom of the National Intelligence Estimate." In *Sherman Kent and the Board of National Estimates: Collected Essays,* ed. Donald P. Steury, 43–126. Center for the Study of Intelligence, Central Intelligence Agency, 1994.

Kent, Sherman. "Words of Estimative Probability." In *Sherman Kent and the Board of National Estimates: Collected Essays*, ed. Donald P. Steury, 127–42. Center for the Study of Intelligence, Central Intelligence Agency, 1994.

Kent, Sherman. Review of *A Guide to the Historical Method*, by Gilbert J. Garraghan, edited by Jean Delanglez." *Journal of American History* 34, no. 1 (1947): 112–13.

Kent, Sherman. *Strategic Intelligence for American World Policy*. Princeton University Press, 1966.

Kent, Sherman, and Sally Newell Thacher. *Reminiscences of a Varied Life: An Autobiography of Sherman Kent*. Elizabeth G. Kent, 1991.

Kick, Ross, and National Security Counselors. *CIA's Studies in Intelligence: Tables of Contents, 1955–2012*. National Security Counselors, 2018.

Kirkpatrick, Lyman B. *The Real CIA*. Macmillian, 1968.

Kirschner, Don S. *Cold War Exile: The Unclosed Case of Maurice Halperin*. University of Missouri Press, 1995.

Klausner, Samuel Z., and Victor M. Lidz. *The Nationalization of the Social Sciences*. University of Pennsylvania Press, 1986.

Knutson, Lawrence Lauder. "Truman Beach: The 33rd President at Key West." White House Historical Association, n.d. Accessed April 23, 2020. https://www.whitehouse history.org/truman-beach-the-33rd-president-at-key-west. Originally published in *White House History Journal*, no. 18 (2006): 50–65.

Koch, Scott A., ed. *CIA Cold War Records: Selected Estimates on the Soviet Union, 1950–1959*. History Staff, Center for the Study of Intelligence, Central Intelligence Agency, 1993.

Kontorovich, Vladimir. *Reluctant Cold Warriors: Economists and National Security*. Oxford University Press, 2019.

Kreps, Sarah E. "Shifting Currents: Changes in National Intelligence Estimates on the Iran Nuclear Threat." *Intelligence and National Security* 23, no. 5 (2008): 608–28.

Kudrov, Valentin. "American Sovietology and the Soviet Economy." Paper delivered at the Abraham Bergson Memorial Conference, November 23 and 24, 2003. University of Warwick / Institute of Europe/RAS, 2003. Accessed November 19, 2025. https:// warwick.ac.uk/fac/soc/economics/staff/mharrison/archive/noticeboard/bergson /kudrov.pdf.

Kuehn, Daniel. *Before NBER: Warren Nutter's Soviet Research at the CIA* (2020). Accessed October 5, 2024. https://dx.doi.org/10.2139/ssrn.3649652.

Kuhns, Woodrow J. "The Office of Reports and Estimates." In *Central Intelligence: 50 Years of the CIA*, ed. Michael Warner and Scott A. Koch, 45–74. Central Intelligence Agency, 1998. https://www.cia.gov/readingroom/docs/fiftyyearsofthecia [15465283].pdf.

Kuklick, Bruce. *Blind Oracles: Intellectuals and War from Kennan to Kissinger*. Princeton University Press, 2006.

Langer, William L. *In and Out of the Ivory Tower: The Autobiography of William L. Langer*. Neale Watson Academic, 1977.

Langer, William L. "Scholarship and the Intelligence Problem." *Proceedings of the American Philosophical Society* 72, no. 1 (1948). https://doi.org/10.4159/HARVARD .9780674493308.C20.

Lasswell, Harold D. "Policy and the Intelligence Function" (1942). In *Propaganda in War and Crisis: Materials for American Policy*, ed. Daniel Lerner, 55–68. George W. Stewart, 1951.

Lee, Steven Hugh. *The Korean War*. Longman, 2001.

Leffler, Melvyn P. *A Preponderance of Power: National Security, the Truman Administration, and the Cold War*. Stanford University Press, 1992.

Leontief, Wassily, and Harvard Economic Research Project. *Studies in the Structure of the American Economy*. Oxford University Press, 1953.

Liebert, Herman W. "Wilmarth Sheldon Lewis (1895–1979)." *Yale University Library Gazette* 54, no. 4 (1980): 198–200.

Lowenthal, Mark M. *Intelligence from Secrets to Policy*. 3rd ed. CQ Press, 2006.

McCullough, David G. *Truman*. Simon & Schuster, 1992.

Maddrell, Paul. "The Stasi's Reporting on the Federal Republic of Germany." In *The Image of the Enemy: Intelligence Analysis of Adversaries Since 1945*, ed. Paul Maddrell, 68–92. Georgetown University Press, 2015.

Manne, Robert. *The Petrov Affair: Politics and Espionage*. Pergamon, 1987.

Marrin, Stephen. *Improving Intelligence Analysis: Bridging the Gap between Scholarship and Practice*. Routledge / Taylor & Francis Group, 2011.

Marshall, Andrew W. *Reflections on Net Assessment: Interviews with Andrew W. Marshall*, with Jeffrey S. McKitrick and Robert G. Angevine. Andrew W. Marshall Foundation / Institute for Defense Analysis, 2022.

Matthais, Willard C. *America's Strategic Blunders: Intelligence Analysis and National Security Policy: 1936–1991*. Pennsylvania State University, 2001.

"Max Franklin Millikan: 1913–1969." *International Organization* 24, no. 1 (1970): iii. https://www.jstor.org/stable/2706104.

Millar, James R. "Rethinking Soviet Economic Studies." In *Beyond Soviet Studies*, ed. Daniel Orlovsky. Woodrow Wilson Center Press, 1994.

Merton, Robert King. *Social Theory and Social Structure*. Free Press, 1949.

Millikan, Max. "Pareto's Sociology." *Econometrica* 4, no. 4 (1936): 324–47.

Montague, Ludwell Lee. *General Walter Bedell Smith as Director of Central Intelligence. October 1950–February 1953*. Pennsylvania State University, 1992.

Morawski, J. G. "Organizing Knowledge and Behavior at Yale's Institute of Human Relations." *Isis* 77, no. 2 (1986): 219–42.

Morgenthau, Hans. Review of "Strategic Intelligence for American World Policy, by Sherman Kent." *American Political Science Review* 43, no. 5 (1949): 1046–47.

Morrison, David E. *The Search for a Method: Focus Groups and the Development of Mass Communication Research*. Luton University Press, 1998.

Mosely, Leonard. *Dulles: A Biography of Eleanor, Allen, and John Foster Dulles and Their Family Network*. Dial Press / James Wade, 1978.

Myers, Robert, "Hans Morgenthau's Realism and American Foreign Policy." *Ethics and International Affairs* 11 (March 1997): 253–70.

National Intelligence Production Board. *Strategic Investment Plan for Intelligence Community Analysis*, chap. 7, "External Analysis" (2001). https://irp.fas.org/cia/product/UnclasSIP.pdf.

Neu, Charles E. "The Rise of the National Security Bureaucracy." In *The New American State: Bureaucracies and Policies Since World War II*, ed. Louis Galambos, 85–108. Johns Hopkins University Press, 1987.

Olcott, Anthony. "Revisiting the Legacy: Sherman Kent, Willmoore Kendall, and George Pettee: Strategic Intelligence in the Digital Age." *Studies in Intelligence* 53, no. 2 (Extracts, 2009): 21–32.

Owen, Christopher H. *Heaven Can Indeed Fall: The Life of Willmoore Kendall*. Lexington, 2021.

Packard, Wyman H. *A Century of US Naval Intelligence: Office of Naval Intelligence and the Naval Historical Center*. Department of the Navy, 1996.

Parsons, Talcott. "National Science Legislation. Part 2. The Case for the Social Sciences." *Bulletin of the Atomic Scientists* 3, no. 1 (1947): 3–5.

Parsons, Talcott. "Social Science: A Basic National Resource" (1948). In *The Nationalization of the Social Sciences*, ed. Samuel Z. Klausner and Victor M. Lidz, 41–112. University of Pennsylvania Press, 1986.

Parsons, Talcott. *The Structure of Social Action: A Study in Social Theory with Special Reference to a Group of Recent European Writers*. Vol. 1. Free Press, 1968.

Parsons, Talcott, and Gerald M. Platt. "Considerations on the American Academic System." *Minerva* 6, no. 4 (1968): 497–523.

Patman, Robert. *The Soviet Union in the Horn of Africa: The Diplomacy of Intervention and Disengagement*. Cambridge University Press, 1990.

Pettee, George S. *The Future of American Secret Intelligence*. Infantry General Press, 1946.

Pisani, Sallie. *The CIA and the Marshall Plan*. Edinburgh University Press, 1991.

Prados, John. *Safe for Democracy: The Secret Wars of the CIA* (Chicago: Ivan R Dee, 2006).

Prados, John. *The Soviet Estimate: US Intelligence and Soviet Strategic Forces*. Princeton University Press, 1986.

Price, David H. "Gregory Bateson and the OSS: World War II and Bateson's Assessment of Applied Anthropology." *Human Organization* 57, no. 4 (1998): 379–84.

Pringle, Robert W. "Guide to Soviet and Russian Intelligence Services." *Intelligencer Journal of US Intelligence Studies*, 18, no. 2 (2011): 51–54. https://www.afio.com/publications/Pringle_SovRus_Intel_in_AFIO_INTEL_WinterSpring2011.pdf.

Prunckun, Hank. *Handbook of Scientific Methods for Intelligence Analysis*. Scarecrow, 2010.

Ranelagh, John. *The Agency: The Rise and Decline of the CIA*. Simon & Schuster, 1987.

[Redacted]. "Analyzing Soviet Defense Program, 1951–1990." *Studies in Intelligence* 42, no. 3 (1998). https://nsarchive2.gwu.edu/NSAEBB/NSAEBB431/docs/intell_ebb_009.PDF.

Rice, Daniel F. *Reinhold Niebuhr and His Circle of Influence*. Cambridge University Press, 2012.

Rios-Bordes, Alexandre. "When Military Intelligence Reconsiders the Nature of War Elements for an Archeology of 'National Security' (United States, 1919–1941)." *Politix*, no. 104 (2013/14): 105–32.

Ross, Dorothy. "The Development of the Social Sciences." In *The Organization of Knowledge in Modern America. 1860–1920*, ed. Alexandra Oleson and John Voss. Johns Hopkins University Press, 1979.

Rostow, W. W. *Concept and Controversy: Sixty Years of Taking Ideas to Market*. University of Texas Press, 2003.

Rostow, W. W. *The Dynamics of Soviet Society*. Secker & Warburg, 1953.

Rothschild, Joseph. "Henry L. Roberts and the Study of the History and Politics of East Central Europe." In *Historians as Nation-Builders: Central and Southeast Europe*, ed. Dennis Deletant, Harry Hanak, Hugh Seton-Watson, and the University of London School of Slavonic and East European Studies, 206–215. Macmillan with University of London, 1988.

Salstonall, Leverett, and Edward Weeks. *Salty: Recollections of a Yankee in Politics*. Boston Globe, 1976.

Schlesinger, Arthur M., Jr. *A Life in the Twentieth Century. Innocent Beginnings 1917–1950*. Houghton Mifflin, 2000.

Schlegel, John Henry. "American Legal Realism and Empirical Social Science: From the Yale Experience." *Buffalo Law Review* 28, no. 3 (1979): 459–588.

Scoblik, J. Peter. "Beacon and Warning: Sherman Kent, Scientific Hubris, and the CIA's Office of National Estimates." *Texas National Security Review* 1, no. 4 (2018): 98–117.

Shambaugh, David. "Obituary: Harold Hinton Remembered, 1924–1993." *China Quarterly* 137 (1994): 212–17.

Simpson, Christopher. "US Mass Communication Research, Counterinsurgency, and Scientific 'Reality.'" In *Communication Researchers and Policy-Making*, ed. Sandra Braman, 253–92. MIT Press, 2003.

Smith, Bradley F. *Shadow Warriors: OSS and the Origins of the CIA*. Basic Books, 1983.

Smith, Bruce Lannes. Review of "Kent, Sherman. *Strategic Intelligence for American World Policy.*" *Public Opinion Quarterly* 13, no. 3 (1949): 524–26.

Smith, Bruce Lannes, and Harold D. Lasswell. *Propaganda, Communication and Public Opinion: A Comprehensive Reference Guide*. Princeton University Press, 2015.

Smith, Russell Jack, *The Unknown CIA: My Three Decades with the Agency*. Pergamon-Brassey's, 1989.

Snider, L. Britt. *The Agency and the Hill: CIA's Relationship with Congress, 1946–2004*. Center for the Study of Intelligence, Central Intelligence Agency, 2015.

Stegner, Wallace. *The Uneasy Chair: A Biography of Bernard Devoto*. Doubleday, 1974.

Steury, Donald P. "Origins of CIA's Analysis of the Soviet Union." In *Watching the Bear: Essays on CIA's Analysis of the Soviet Union*, ed. Gerald K. Haines and Robert E. Leggett, 1–16. Centre for the Study of Intelligence, Central Intelligence Agency, 2003.

Steury, Donald P., ed. *Sherman Kent and the Board of National Estimates: Collected Essays*. Center for the Study of Intelligence, Central Intelligence Agency, 1994.

Stout, Herald F. *Stout and Allied Families*. Eagle Press, 1951.

Stout, Mark. "World War I and the Birth of American Intelligence Culture." *Intelligence and National Security* 32, no. 3 (2017): 378–94.

Stout, Mark. *World War I and the Foundations of American Intelligence*. University of Kansas Press, 2023.

Thomas, Evan. *The Very Best Men. Four Who Dared: The Early Years of the CIA*. Touchstone / Simon & Schuster, 1995.

Thomas, Stafford T. "A Political Theory of the CIA." *International Journal of Intelligence and CounterIntelligence* 11, no. 1 (1998): 57–72.

Trahair, Richard. *Encyclopedia of Cold War Espionage, Spies, and Secret Operations*. Enigma, 2012.

Troy, Thomas F. *Donovan and the CIA: A History of the Establishment of the Central Intelligence Agency*. Central Intelligence Agency, Center for the Study of Intelligence, 1991.

Truman, Harry S. *Memoirs by Harry S. Truman*. Volume 2: *Years of Trial and Hope*. Doubleday, 1956.

Trumpbour, John, ed. *How Harvard Rules: Reason in the Service of Empire*. South End Press, 1989.

Turner, Stansfield. *Burn Before Reading: Presidents, CIA Directors and Secret Intelligence*. Hyperion, 2005.

van der Linden, Marcel. "Gerschenkron's Secret: A Research Note." *Critique* 40, no. 4 (2012): 553–62.

Verdery, Katherine. "The Cold War Is Not a Trope." *Journal of Ethnographic Theory* 6, no. 2 (2016): 447–51.

Vickers, Robert, and CIA History Staff. *The History of CIA's Office of Strategic Research, 1967–81.* Center for the Study of Intelligence, 2019. https://fas.org/irp/cia/product /osr.pdf.

Walton, Timothy R. "Lessons Learned from the CIA's Assessment of the Soviet Economy." *International Journal of Intelligence and CounterIntelligence* 28, no. 3 (2015): 468–79.

Warner, Michael. *The CIA Under Truman.* Center for Intelligence Studies / Central Intelligence Agency, 1994.

Warner, Michael. *The Office of Strategic Services. America's First Intelligence Agency.* Central Intelligence Agency, 2000. https://www.cia.gov/resources/csi/static/Office -of-Strategic-Services.pdf.

Warner, Michael. "Sources and Methods for the Study of Intelligence." In *Handbook of Intelligence Studies,* ed. Loch Johnson, 17–27. Routledge, 2007.

Warner, Michael, and Scott A. Koch, eds. *Central Intelligence: 50 Years of the CIA.* Central Intelligence Agency, 1998. https://www.cia.gov/readingroom/docs/fifty years of the cia[15465283].pdf.

Weber, Ralph E. *Spymasters: Ten CIA Officers in Their Own Words.* Scholarly Resources, 1999.

Westerfield, H. Bradford, ed. *Inside the CIA's Private World: Declassified Articles from the Agency's Internal Journal, 1955–1992.* Yale University Press, 1995.

White, A. B. Review of "Writing History, by Kent, Sherman." *American Historical Review* 47, no. 4 (1942): 823–24.

Winks, Robin. *Cloak and Gown: Scholars in America's Secret War.* Collins Harvill, 1987.

Wohlstetter, Roberta. *Pearl Harbor: Warning and Decision.* Stanford University Press, 1962.

Wolfers, Arnold. *Discord and Collaboration: Essays on International Politics.* Johns Hopkins Press, 1962.

Wolff, Robert Lee. "William Leonard Langer." In *Proceedings of the Massachusetts Historical Society* 89 (1977): 187–95.

Yarhi-Milo, Keren. *Knowing the Adversary: Leaders, Intelligence and Assessment of Intentions on International Relations.* Princeton University Press, 2014.

Zegart, Amy B. *Flawed by Design: The Evolution of the CIA, JCS and NSC.* Stanford University Press, 1999.

Zelikow, Philip. "American Economic Intelligence: Past Practice and Future Principles." *Intelligence and National Security* 12, no. 1 (1997): 164–77.

Zlotnik, Jack. "Bayes Theorem for Intelligence Analysis." In *Inside the CIA's Private World: Declassified Articles from the Agency's Internal Journal, 1955–1992,* ed. H. Bradford Westerfield, 255–63. Yale University Press, 1995.

Zucker, Lynne. *Institutional Patterns and Organizations: Culture and Environment.* Ballinger, 1988.

Zucker, Lynne G. "Organizations as Institutions." In *Research in the Sociology of Organizations: A Research Annual.* Vol. 2, ed. Samuel B. Bacharach. Jai Press, 1983.

Index

About the Author

PETER C. GRACE teaches intelligence history, international security, and foreign policy at the University of Otago. He is the co-director of the Otago National Security School. Peter lives with his partner, Beth, in an 1860s synagogue, which was subsequently converted to a Freemasons' hall, in Dunedin, New Zealand.